THE ADOLESCENT
THROUGH FICTION

The Adolescent Through Fiction

A PSYCHOLOGICAL APPROACH

Norman Kiell

INTERNATIONAL UNIVERSITIES PRESS, INC.
New York

Contents

Acknowledgments

One of the pleasurable tasks attendant on the writing of this book is to acknowledge the several institutions and individuals who were moving factors in getting the volume done. My grateful thanks go to the Ford Foundation's Committee for the Study of Liberal Education for Adults for their initial subvention and encouragement. I am equally indebted to President Harry D. Gideonse of Brooklyn College for financial assistance in the preparation of the manuscript through funds administered by the Dean of Faculty, William R. Gaede. To my graduate and undergraduate students at Brooklyn College and the Great Neck (L.I.) Adult Education Program, I acknowledge my gratefulness for their cooperation in carrying on my experimental work in attempting to bridge the two disciplines of the novel and the psychology of adolescence.

The author is beholden to Professor Ray Margaret Lawrence of the Department of Personnel Service at Brooklyn College for her interest, her valuable suggestions, and her generous allowance of time and patience for innumerable discussions. Special thanks are due her for the chapter On Family Relations.

Finally, I must express my appreciation to Professor Herbert A. Bloch of the Department of Sociology and to Professor Sidney Lind of the English Department for their unfailing support and encouragement and stimulation. What is contained in this book, however, is, of course, my responsibility.

Introduction

"Learning to read novels, we slowly learn to read ourselves."
MARK SCHORER, "An Interpretation," in Ford Madox Ford,

The Good Soldier, p. v.

"Every man is a volume if you know how to read him."
MARGARET FULLER

I have taken the point of view, in this book, that fiction can be examined as a fruitful field for exploration in the study of adolescent personality. There is historical evidence to support this thesis. Freud admired artists, especially writers, for their intuitive access to the unconscious. "Storytellers are valuable allies," he wrote in his analysis of Wilhelm Jensen's novel *Gradiva*, "and their testimony is to be rated high, for they usually know many things between heaven and earth that our academic wisdom does not even dream of. In psychological insights, indeed, they are far ahead of us ordinary people, because they draw from sources that have not yet been made accessible to science" (10).* Freud pointed out, too, that the first steps in the discovery of the unconscious were taken long before his time by poets and philosophers.

Instead of in any way detracting from the scientific study of psychology, as some scholars fear, an appreciation of great literature enhances and increases the psychological approach. Shakespeare's intuitive understanding of human personality and his incomparable ability to reproduce the many facets of human experience seem even more remarkable in the light of present-day psychology. Browning's appreciation of the

* The numbers in parentheses correspond to the numbered references at the end of each chapter.

9

complexity of human personality and his ability to re-create character only reinforce Freud's statement that the literary men and philosophers through intuition have arrived at much in human personality that man is now groping with scientifically. But Freud went on to say that while the thinkers and students of mankind have said similar things as he, psychoanalysis has worked them out in detail and employed them to unravel many psychological riddles (11).

In the very first conclave of the International Psycho-Analytic Congress held in Salzburg on April 26, 1908, Otto Rank presented a passage from a letter sent by Schiller to a friend, in which he advised the latter "to release his imagination from the restraint of critical reason by employing a flow of free association" (21). The creative novelist, the analyst of human personality, has always been a psychologist in an untechnical sense. Emile Zola once defined his novels as a fragment of the world "seen through a temperament." Samuel Butler, in *The Way of All Flesh,* said "that it is our less conscious thoughts and our less conscious actions, which mainly mould our lives and the lives of those who spring from us." Oliver Wendell Holmes, in a work published when Freud was only a fifteen-year-old adolescent, revealed how sharply the concept of the unconscious was recognized even in pre-Freudian days: "There are thoughts that never emerge into consciousness, which yet make their influence felt among the perceptible mental currents, just as the unseen planets sway the movements of those which are watched and mapped by the astronomer. Old prejudices, that are ashamed to confess themselves, nudge our talking thought to utter their magisterial veto. . . . The more we examine the mechanism of thought, the more we shall see that the automatic, unconscious action of the mind enters largely into all its processes" (15).

George Eliot, in 1872, one year after the publication of the Holmes book, was trying to show that "mental acts were like the subtle muscular movements which are not taken account of in the consciousness, though they bring about the end that we fix our mind on and desire." And in 1850, six years before Freud was born, Hawthorne's *The Scarlet Letter,* from which the following paragraph is taken, appeared. Nearly everything in psychoanalytic theory but the furniture is present!

Roger Chillingworth scrutinized his patient carefully, both as he saw him in his ordinary life, keeping an accustomed pathway in the range of thoughts familiar to him, and as he appeared when thrown amidst other moral scenery, the novelty of which might call out something new to the surface of his character. He deemed it essential, it would seem, to know the man, before attempting to do him good. Wherever there is a heart and an intellect, the diseases of the physical frame are tinged with the peculiarities of these. In Arthur Dimmesdale, thought and imagination were so active, and sensibility so intense, that the bodily infirmity would be likely to have its groundwork there. So Roger Chillingworth —the man of skill, the kind and friendly physician—strove to go deep into his patient's bosom, delving among his principles, prying into his recollections, and probing everything with a cautious touch, like a treasure-seeker in a dark cavern. Few secrets can escape an investigator, who has opportunity and license to undertake such a quest, and skill to follow it up. A man burdened with a secret should especially avoid the intimacy of his physician. If the latter possess native sagacity, and a nameless something more,—let us call it intuition; if he show no intrusive egotism, nor disagreeably prominent characteristics of his own; if he have the power, which must be born with him, to bring his mind into such affinity with his patient's, that this last shall unawares have spoken what he imagines himself only to have thought; if such revelations be received without tumult, and acknowledged not so often by an uttered sympathy as by silence, an inarticulate breath, and here and there a word, to indicate that all is understood; if to these qualifications of a confidant be joined the advantages afforded by his recognized character as a physician,—then, at some inevitable moment, will the soul of the sufferer be dissolved, and flow forth in a dark, but transparent stream, bringing all its mysteries into the daylight [14].

The influence of the unconscious on people's lives and its occasional bitter consequences when they are not discovered is described so beautifully by Dostoevsky in *The Idiot* "that it has been the marvel of psychologists ever since" (2). The naturalistic characterology found in Plutarch's *Lives* is a challenge to those who believe sensitivity and profundity in the analysis of character began only with modern psychology. But Freud's great contribution in this respect was to give writers the confidence to attempt to portray the unconscious in rich detail.

Fiction has made us perhaps overfamiliar with the agonies and absurdities of adolescence. Probing the souls of adolescents has become one of the vices of tired writers all over the world, as perhaps can be seen from the nearly five hundred novels of adolescence since 1900 listed in the bibliography at the end of the text. Among the earliest of the modern men of genius who dealt with the adolescent in fiction is Romain Rolland with *Jean-Christophe* (1904). That same year saw the appearance of G. Stanley Hall's two-volume work, *Adolescence*. Thus, at a time when psychologists were not yet generally involved in the problem of adolescent development and psychology, Rolland's treatment of Jean-Christophe exhibits a systematic and comprehensive exposition of this period. Of course there were novelists prior to Rolland, "writers of perception and insight whose accounts of this period mirror so accurately a time we have all shared" (19). There were Goethe, Tolstoy, Dostoevsky, Dickens, Meredith, and Twain. There were Hardy, Fontane, Thackeray, Stendhal, Fielding and Freytag. And there were Alcott, Kipling, James, Crane, Balzac and Zola—all of them keen observers of the adolescent.

But it was not until the turn of the twentieth century that the great spate of novels dealing with adolescence began to appear. By the 1930's, the psychologists were working on depth studies of adolescents, and novelists were trying to illuminate the womb. The psychologist said adolescence is a period of storm and stress; the writer described it as "a kind of emotional seasickness. Both are funny, but only in retrospect" (18). The cultural anthropologists and the sociologists, along with the psychologists, were demonstrating how we furnish adolescents an elaborate culture all their own, with brassy, respected institutions and rich, distinct patterns of behavior to carry them through what the writers describe as the awful springtime of beauty.

Adolescence is a season of shames. It is the most recent such season, but the least clearly remembered one and hence the most sensitive subject for the adult reader. The current popularity of novels of adolescence is a reflection, in some measure, of the adult reader's need to recapture memories of a lost past, memories which he has repressed of his—largely— unhappy adolescent years. Herman Wouk, the author of *City Boy* and *Marjorie Morningstar,* expresses his feelings about his own adolescence for nearly all adults: "I do not think I am wrong in remembering the teens as an uncomfortable, on the whole, a wretched, time. To the staggering colt, the world around him must seem a drunkenly reeling nightmare of sights and sounds. I understood very little of what was happening around me. It was like living in a foreign country, vainly pretending to be a native and getting mocked at and fleeced from all sides. And there was this brutal joke that nature had played, springing the feverish puzzle of sex at a time when I was barely learning to read and write and to navigate among the common dangers of existence. Girls were half marvels and half horrors. Adults were unfriendly, nagging nuisances. Education was an old man of the sea, and the social code existed to make a lout of me. I felt I would be a lumpy, pimply fifteen forever. Maybe I had a high old time and was a glamorous, enviable figure. I do not remember it that way" (26).

Nor do most adults. Most adults are so removed from their own adolescence and have so repressed from conscious memory their painful experiences of this period, that they can neither identify with nor understand the adolescent who comes into their purview. Byron wrote that of all the barbarous Middle Ages, that which is most barbarous is the Middle Age of Man. Today's culture, and American society particularly, would more likely put this label on the prepuberty child suddenly crossing the bridge into adolescence. Many adults feel adolescence is a mistake to be corrected or a sorrow to be alleviated rather than a wonderfully direct apprehension of the truth too soon poisoned, perhaps, by doubt and dulled by experience. Butler describes it this way: "To me it seems that youth is like spring, an overpraised season—delightful if it happen to be a favoured one, but in practise very rarely favoured and more remarkable, as a general rule, for biting east winds than genial breezes" (5).

The work of the novelist can help tremendously toward understanding the adolescent of today. For the first-rate writers get their sense of life from life, not from psychology books. But since a novel is a work of art, since it is organic, it must, of necessity, be psychological because it deals with people who are alive. While literature and psychology are fellow disciplines, literature is not watered-down psychology nor is psychology methodized literature (1). Freud agreed with the French writer Leonormand that writers who made use of psychology and psychoanalysis by simply taking over its data were to be condemned as "dangerous and undignified" (17). With too much systematic equipment the novel becomes a psychological tract.

Literature is one way of projecting life. In it we look for trends, problems, attempts at solutions and struggles with which we are familiar or want to become more familiar. Psychology can illuminate the work of the artist, but the textbook writer must usually adhere to strict, and sometimes vague, terminology. The novelist is not limited. While literature provides an enormous store of observations on man, the work of art is economical: it contains what it intends to and what it means. The relation of truth to fiction was expressed by the novelist, Elizabeth Bowen, in this fashion: ". . . the novel is not confining itself to what happened. The novel does not simply recount experience, it adds to experience . . . And here comes in what is the actual living spark of the novel: the novelist's imagination has a power of its own. It does not merely *invent,* it *perceives.* It intensifies, therefore it gives power, extra importance, greater truth and greater inner reality to what well may be ordinary and everyday things" (4). It is the acute perceptual faculties of the creative writer which give us the overpowering sense impressions he conveys.

There is, of course, no adequate substitute for the full and direct living of life. But art of whatever kind, sensitively experienced, can give breadth and depth to our vision of life. The textbook writer's intimate experience of reality, whatever its nature, is not enough. There remains the distillation that is arrived at only by the transforming power of imagination. It is this that the creative novelist achieves and which the textbook writer rarely atempts. Aldous Huxley has one of his characters say, "The trouble with fiction is that it makes too much sense . . . Fiction has unity, fiction has style. Facts possess neither . . . " (16).

This book is an attempt to bridge the two great regions of psychology and literature, where the study of human personality dwells. I have attempted to set down some of the dynamic principles of adolescent development and psychology and illuminate these concepts by illustrations from good contemporary fiction. For the student, as Allport hopes, it would humanize the study of psychology and demonstrate to him that the scientific account of human nature has its parallels in the insights of great authors.

Half a dozen and more authors of current textbooks have testified to the value of such methodology. Stone and Church say, "We should like to suggest that the perceptiveness of fictional studies often surpasses anything child study proper has to offer. As a means of becoming oriented to the nature of children, the student could not do better than to look into the literature of childhood" (23). Gesell, in introducing the bibliography in his book on adolescence, writes: "The techniques of the artist can often serve far better than those of the scientist to convey the feelings and sensations that accompany the process of growing up" (12). Coleman states almost categorically that literature and psychology "can and should complement the other" (7). Shrodes writes that the purpose of her anthology "is to lead the student of human motivation and behavior to a better understanding of himself and his world through the vicarious experience that literature affords . . . Implicit in literature are all the facts of psychology. The facts constitute the center of the experience which is literature. But the facts alone are not truth. They become true to the scientist as his imagination plays upon them and weaves them together into a consistent and organic whole. They become true to the poet or dramatist when his imagination has ordered them into a living organism" (22). Cole feels that because fiction gives "a more detailed and more lifelike interpretation than the impersonal presentation of a text, novels are useful in connection with the study of adolescence" (6). And Wertham sums up the relationship of literature and psychoanalysis in this paragraph: "What brings the science of psychiatry in the psychoanalytic era into such close and fruitful relationship with the art of literature is that psychoanalysis is analysis of a special kind. It does not delve into the mind to isolate disparate elements. Psycho-analysis always aims to relate the detail, the symbol, to the living organism as a whole. It is here that the research of the scientist and the search of the artists find a common ground. Great writers know how to give a unified picture of a whole personality through minute observation of a meaningful expression, a characteristic mannerism, or an unconscious habit" (25).

The novel of adolescence can be a direct revelation of reality. It can, to paraphrase Camus' Nobel Prize address,

stir man by providing him with a privileged image of common joys and woes. In the fictional adolescent, we can see,
as Gide points out, the rivalry between the real world and
the representation of it which we make to ourselves (13). But
the genius of the writer creates images so realistic that we see
before our mind's eye a true character. The manifold facets
of the adolescent's development are caught in imaginative
writing by the author's psychological astuteness and intuition
and profound knowledge of his character's mind and unconscious impulses.

The adolescent's conflicts, insecurities and uncertainties
stem from the conflicts between generations in a changing
society, sexual frustrations arising out of physical maturation
and societal restrictions, difficulties in emancipation from
parents, inconsistencies in authority relationships, and dis-
continuities in socialization patterns. The adolescent's behavior is the outcome not of physical causes nor psychological
causes nor sociological causes, in and of themselves, but
rather the result of "psycho-*and* somatic, psycho-*and* social,
and interpersonal factors" (8). All too often, as Bettelheim
suggests, adolescence is a period during which almost too
much is happening. He is constantly preoccupied with the
question, "Who am I?" He is bedeviled by the need to make
preparations for an occupational choice. He feels the aliena-
tion of parts of his psychic structure. He must learn to ac-
commodate himself to his changing body image, and to make
a healthy heterosexual adjustment. He has to wean himself
psychologically from his family. In analytic terms, the abandonment of the incestuous aim and the replacement of the
infantile objects are the decisive objectives in adolescent
development.

The psychological study of adolescence, when coupled
with fictional illustrations, provides primary sources for re-
creating the conditions independent of explicit hypotheses.
The classroom student is rather discouraged, and rightly so,
when presented with case histories, for there is little chal-

lenge in them and little opportunity for him to hypothesize, evaluate and interpret. What can the student do with a finished case history? Further, most case histories are pedantic, pedestrian and boring. Experimental techniques remove persons from meaningful life situations and develop either artificial or confining pictures of the individual. The artist, on the other hand, has the gift of portrayal in recognizable, realistic fashion and has the capacity to marshall words to depict real people.

Through fiction, the student can come closer to the dynamics of adolescent development. Thus, as Wood* suggests, if we take the novel and for pedagogical purposes assume the characters are or could have been real youngsters, we can set up hypotheses, test and establish them, and come to conclusions—on the same basis as the scientific psychologist. The validity of the use of fiction for this kind of study has been attested to by Allport (3) and others.

Of course, there are limitations to the use of novels of adolescence. All fiction, to some extent, is dressed-up autobiography. As such, the writing is limited to the more or less conscious recorded memories of the author. Thus it is necessary to take into account the novelist's omissions, his idealizations or his intensifications of a conflict. Feminine authors, depicting the female adolescent, for instance, seem to be gentler in their treatment than their male author counterpart. In the delineation of the male adolescent, the male author usually depicts a youngster in open rebellion, rejecting of adult standards of judgment, who acts out his conflicts. The female author, seemingly more sensitive, tends to idealize the girl adolescent. Perhaps it is the authors' way of telling *their* mothers what they would have liked to have happened to them!

Two other limitations come to mind. Because of the com-

* I am grateful to Professor Austin Wood of the Department of Psychology of Brooklyn College for the talks we had on this subject. Much of the material in this passage is derived from these conversations.

parative sex reticence prevalent in our culture, few details of sexual action are shown in the novel of adolescence. And as Foster points out, "in the peculiarly discredited field of sex variance authors often avoid even implying action. For this reason scientists tend to disparage studies based on literature . . ." (9). There are, of course, any number of examples of the blundering, sweet, and painful first awakenings of sexual impulses to be found in adolescent fiction. But most novelists tend to shy away from closer scrutiny of this phase of development.

The other limitation deals with the intellectual awakening of the adolescent. The difficulty the author faces in delineating such ferment is probably insuperable. As far back as 1912, Thibaudet pointed this out (24). A quarter of a century later, O'Brien noted little change in literary output on this subject. In attempting to represent in literature the intellectual growth of the adolescent, an author "runs the risk of either aging [him] or making the intellect childish. Moreover, the intellectual evolution, impossible by its nature to observe minutely in others, is the most difficult phase of one's early experience to remember faithfully in maturity. At any rate, when a novelist sets out to evoke his early years, he soon discovers that his memory recalls most readily, even almost exclusively, events, facts, and sensory impressions" (20). And in 1958, the literary situation in this respect has not radically changed. Brief and casual passages are to be found, but even these are the exception rather than the rule.

However, these limitations, such as they are, that the novel of adolescence places on the scientific study of this period, are not crucial enough to dismiss the work of the creative writer out of hand. This is precisely where the complementary features of the two disciplines of psychology and literature can produce understandings and insights into human behavior and permit the serious student to follow the Aristotelian injunction of enjoying while learning.

The fifty-four selections from novels of adolescence contained in this book to illustrate principles of adolescent be-havior represent the selective bias of the author. Others would undoubtedly have chosen their favorite passages for one reason or another. I combed the literature for what I felt was the most appropriate excerpt. The selections may delight some, displease others. But there is so much to choose from that substitutions can readily be made without distortion to the text proper. My aim was to choose fictional examples that seemed to illuminate psychological principles universally seen in the adolescent period. Too many people feel adolescents are not of the stuff that are born; rather, that Hemingway and Salinger wrote them. Perhaps the examples contained herein will give the lie to this.

May 11, 1958
Freeport, New York

REFERENCES

(1) Adams, Robert M. "Literature and Psychology: A Question of Significant Form," *Lit. & Psychol.*, 5:67-72, 1955.

(2) Adler, Alfred. *Understanding Human Nature.* NY: Permabooks, 1949, p. 85.

(3) Allport, Gordon W. "The Use of Personal Documents in Psychological Science," *Soc. Sci. Res. Coun. Bull.* No. 49, 1942.

(4) Bowen, Elizabeth. British Broadcasting Corporation program, 1956.

(5) Butler, Samuel. *The Way of All Flesh.* NY: Black, 1902, p. 28.

(6) Cole, Luella. *Psychology of Adolescence.* NY: Rinehart, 1948, p. 619.

(7) Coleman, James C. *Abnormal Psychology and Modern Life,* 2nd Ed. Chicago: Scott, Foresman, 1956, pp. 6-7.

(8) Erikson, Erik H. *Childhood and Society.* NY: Norton, 1950, p. 19.

(9) Foster, Jeannette H. *Sex Variant Women in Literature.* NY: Vantage, 1956, p. 12.

(10) Freud, Sigmund. *Delusion and Dream.* Boston: Beacon, 1956, p. 27.

(11) Freud, Sigmund, in a letter to Dr. van Eeden. In Jones, Ernest, *The Life and Works of Sigmund Freud,* Vol. II. NY: Basic Books, 1955, p. 369.

(12) Gesell, Arnold, et al. *Youth: the Years from 10 to 16.* NY: Harper, 1956, p. 521.

(13) Gide, André. *The Counterfeiters.* NY: Knopf, 1952, p. 189

(14) Hawthorne, Nathaniel. *The Scarlet Letter,* 1850. From Chapter 9.

(15) Holmes, Oliver W. *Mechanism in Thought and Morals.* Boston, 1871, pp. 44, 48.

(16) Huxley, Aldous. *The Genius and the Goddess.* NY: Harper, 1955, p. 9.

(17) Jones, Ernest. *The Life and Works of Sigmund Freud*. Vol. III. NY: Basic Books, 1957, p. 114.
(18) Koestler, Arthur. *Arrow in the Blue*. NY: Macmillan, 1952, p. 82.
(19) Lindner, Robert. *Must You Conform?* NY: Rinehart, 1956, p. 9.
(20) O'Brien, Justin. *The Novel of Adolescence in France*. NY: Columbia University Press, 1937, p. 145.
(21) *Schiller's Briefwechsel mit Körner*, Vol. I, 1847, pp. 381-385.
(22) Shrodes, Carolyn, et al. *Psychology Through Literature*. NY: Oxford University Press, 1943, p. ix.
(23) Stone, L. Joseph & Church, Joseph. *Childhood and Adolescence*. NY: Random House, 1957, p. 400.
(24) Thibaudet, Albert. "Réflexions sur le roman," *La Nouvelle Revue Française*, 8:213-220, 1912.
(25) Wertham, Frederic. In Aswell, Mary L. (Ed.), *The World Within*. NY: McGraw-Hill, 1947, p. xvi.
(26) Wouk, Herman. "The Terrible Teens," *Good Housekeeping*, 146:60, 1958.

CHAPTER ONE

On Physical Development

"For young hot colts being raged, do rage the more."

SHAKESPEARE, *Richard II*, Act 2, Sc. 1

The onset of puberty is perhaps the most dramatic aspect of adolescent development because for adolescents and adults alike it is the most obviously observable manifestation of change. For characteristic of puberty is the rather rapid series of physical changes which occur. The body shoots up, the body adds on weight; hips widen, breasts emerge; sexual maturity is arrived at; physiological processes complicate the growth spurt.

It is only natural, therefore, that the adolescent should become aware of his body as he never was before (21). This awareness involves more than physical growth, for along with the growth, complex emotional, mental, and social forces are evolving as well. The body becomes for the adolescent a "symbol of self" (25) and he must learn to consolidate this new self. He feels different, has disconcerting new impulses, an overflow of energies, new and exciting interests in the other sex, and a need to achieve status.

He is moved to wonderment and bewilderment at the changes taking place within him. He may be amazed that this is his body and bewildered that these changes are happening to him. The adolescent almost overnight finds himself in a body which is no longer familiar, which is entirely new to him (14). This is the feeling that Emily experiences in *A High Wind in Jamaica.** There are so many bodily changes,

* From *A High Wind in Jamaica* by Richard Hughes. Copyright 1929, 1957 by Richard Hughes. Reprinted by permission of Harper & Brothers. Pp. 188-191.

internal, glandular, and outward, and of such a nature as to produce a set of almost entirely new sensations (22). The sudden realization that her arms and legs are part of herself brings a warm and good feeling to Emily.

And then an event did occur, to Emily, of considerable importance. She suddenly realized who she was.

There is little reason that one can see why it should not have happened to her five years earlier, or even five later; and none, why it should have come that particular afternoon.

She had been playing houses in a nook right in the bows, behind the windlass (on which she had hung a devil's-claw as a doorknocker); and tiring of it was walking rather aimlessly aft, thinking vaguely about some bees and a fairy queen, when it suddenly flashed into her mind that she was *she*.

She stopped dead, and began looking over all of her person which came within the range of her eyes. She could not see much, except a fore-shortened view of the front of her frock, and her hands when she lifted them for inspection; but it was enough for her to form a rough idea of the little body she suddenly realized to be hers.

She began to laugh, rather mockingly. "Well!" she thought, in effect: "Fancy *you*, of all people, going and geting caught like this!—You can't get out of it now, not for a very long time: you'll have to go through with being a child, and growing up, and getting old, before you'll be quit of this mad prank!"

Determined to avoid any interruption of this highly. important occasion, she began to climb the ratlines, on her way to her favourite perch at the masthead. Each time she moved an arm or a leg in this simple action, however, it struck her with fresh amazement to find them obeying her so readily. Memory told her, of course, that they had always done so before: but before, she had never realised how surprising this was.

Once settled on her perch, she began examining the skin of her hands with the utmost care: for it was *hers*. She slipped a shoulder out of the top of her frock; and having peeped in to make sure she really was continuous under her clothes, she shrugged it up to touch her cheek. The contact of her face and the warm bare hollow of her shoulder gave her a comfortable thrill, as if it was the caress of some kind friend. But whether the feeling came to her through her cheek or her shoulder, which was caresser and which the caressed, that no analysis could tell her.

Hughes has described Emily just at the point where she achieves her first insight into and acceptance of her physical being. The need for the adolescent to accept his bodily appearance is vital for the acceptance of self, because a person's physique represents, in large measure, his image of himself.

As the rapidity and intensity of bodily changes take place, the adolescent may become tremendously preoccupied with them. He may no longer feel the same person he once was; he becomes lonely for his old self. "In even the mildest cases, where the change does not penetrate the center of awareness, it constitutes a security threat. This is undoubtedly a factor in the 'negative phase' of puberty, the loneliness, moodiness, and intractability . . ." (18). Changes in the appearance of the adolescent are so noticeable that people are always passing comment on them, tactlessly, humorously or surprisedly. It is no wonder that many adolescents show an increased motor awkwardness. Ungainly coordination is not due so much to lack of skill but the result of embarrassment and self-consciousness. The following brief passage* demonstrates this clearly.

She loved her mother and father but she didn't love the things they lived by—professorial dignity, scholarship, old books, old furniture, old china, and brand new amusing gossip. She liked storms, lightening and thunder, excitement; and the climate of her home was unfortunately a temperate one.

When there were too many arguments in too short a time, she took a few clothes and moved into the sorority house where she ran into similar difficulties. She was expected to be careful of her appearance and of her friends, and to re-

---

* From *The Folded Leaf* by William Maxwell. Copyright 1945 by William Maxwell. Reprinted by permission of the author. Harper & Brothers. Pp. 126-127.

member at all times that she belonged to the best sorority on the campus. She didn't try to do any of these things and so there were more arguments, especially in chapter meetings. She moved around the house in a cloud of disapproval, which had the curious effect of making her clumsy. She tripped over rugs, her feet slid out from under her on the stairs. The girls that she wanted to have like her did, actually, but they also laughed at her, because she was so enthusiastic and so like an overgrown puppy; and this hurt her pride.

The girls who were not amused by her behavior were appalled by it. No room that she walked into was ever quite large enough, nothing was safe in her apologetic hands. She didn't mean to drop Emily Noyes' bottle of Chanel No. 5 or split open the seams of Joyce Brenner's white evening dress which she had asked to try on, but the result in each case was disastrous. The girls snatched fragile things from her if she showed any sign of picking them up, and the girl she bumped into hurrying around a corner of the upstairs hall took to her bed, with cold compresses on her head. It seemed to her that all girls were made of glass and she alone was of flesh and blood and constantly cutting herself on them. She gave up trying to please them.

It was social awkwardness rather than lack of skill in managing the body that prompted Sally's "dropsy." When the adolescent's already accentuated awareness becomes even more acute with attention focused on him (19), the effect can be extremely disconcerting. Self-consciousness becomes heightened when the adolescent finds himself the topic of conversation, the butt of jokes or the isolate in a social group. It is important to stress that the onset of activity of the reproductive glands not only results in a heightening of the sexual responsiveness of the individual and an increased body sensitiveness but also in a general increase in sensitivity (15). During the entire period of adolescence, the individual is more responsive to all stimuli.

Much emphasis is placed on appearance and beauty in the American culture. The adolescent is bombarded by television commercials, beauty magazines and newspaper advertisements to be freckle-free, pimple-free, blackhead-free, and body odor-free. He is advised to have his teeth straightened and his vision corrected, to gain weight or to lose weight, to wear elevated shoes to increase height or loafers to give the appearance of reduced height. In a society as conscious of physical beauty as ours, even slight physical deviations or impairments may pose difficult adjustment problems (7). The importance of defects and blemishes is well displayed in a case reported by Blos. Betty's self-esteem was held down because of a mole on her cheek which made her feel ugly and repulsive (3). However, lowered self-esteem, while focused on such minor things, may be due to other causes, such as guilt or hostility. The mole or the acne is the symptom, rather than the cause, of the anguish.

The adolescent's sensitivity to his appearance and his need for peer acceptance may precipitate personality difficulties, even if there are only very slight or transient physical defects. Adolescence is a physical phenomenon. Yet the emotional problems and the emotional growth of this period are closely related to the rapid physical and glandular development. Any marked deviation from the norm is likely to create an emotional problem. More than three hundred years ago, Robert Burton wrote, "Deformities and imperfections of our bodies, as lameness, crookedness, deafness, blindness, be they innate or accidental, torture many men . . ." (4). Philip, the young protagonist in *Of Human Bondage,** has been bedeviled, humiliated and isolated by his schoolmates because of his clubfoot. The emotional impact of this on Philip is almost devastating.

As time went on Philip's deformity ceased to interest. It was accepted like one boy's red hair and another's unreasonable corpulence. But meanwhile he had grown horribly sensitive. He never ran if he could help it, because he knew

* From *Of Human Bondage* by W. Somerset Maugham. Copyright 1915, 1936 by Doubleday & Company, Inc. Reprinted by permission of the publishers. Pp. 44, 48.

it made his limp more conspicuous, and he adopted a peculiar walk. He stood still as much as he could, with his club-foot behind the other, so that it should not attract notice, and he was constantly on the lookout for any reference to it. Because he could not join in the games which other boys played, their life remained strange to him; he only interested himself from the outside in their doings; and it seemed to him that there was a barrier between them and him. Sometimes they seemed to think that it was his fault if he could not play football, and he was unable to make them understand. He was left a good deal to himself. He had been inclined to talkativeness, but gradually he became silent. He began to think of the difference between himself and others.

*   *   *   *   *

Philip passed from the innocence of childhood to the bitter consciousness of himself by the ridicule which his club-foot had excited. The circumstances of his case were so peculiar that he could not apply to them the ready-made rules which acted well enough in ordinary affairs, and he was forced to think for himself. The many books he had read filled his mind with ideas which, because he only half understood them, gave more scope to his imagination. Beneath his painful shyness something was growing up within him, and obscurely he realised his personality. But at times it gave him odd surprises; he did things, he knew not why, and afterwards when he thought of them found himself all at sea.

Philip, like most people, naïvely assumed that his external world possessed the meaning of life, and consequently he believed that his happiness depended upon his success in extracting and adjusting himself to this meaning. As the novel progresses, it is seen that each time Philip feels he has perceived the meaning of life, and attempts to adjust to that meaning, his organism revolts because of emotional conflict, the meaning vanishes, and he begins his futile search all over again. He repeatedly attempts to wring happiness from his life by pitifully trying to reconcile certain diametrically opposed drives of his organism. It is only when Philip finally learns that the meaning of life must emerge from his own integrated personality, instead of from his external world, that he achieves a permanent happiness (17).

It is obvious that overt physical defects are apt to be highly stressful for the individual. More subtle, however, is the role physique plays in personality development of the more normally endowed adolescent. Physique, particularly as it pertains to athletic ability in boys and beauty in girls, plays a twofold part: it is the basis of the adolescent's feelings of competency in physical prowess and it is the basis for social judgments and acceptability.

H. E. Jones, commenting on the relationship between strength and social status of adolescents, says, "The positive relation of strength to 'prestige traits'. . . may be regarded as evidence of the role of physical prowess in the adolescent value system. Superior strength is a part of a complex of physical characteristics valued highly in preadult culture; the absence of these characteristics is a handicap which can be overcome only by strongly compensating traits in other areas which are also highly valued" (16). Boys with good physique and physical fitness were found by Jones to be high in social prestige and in general level of adjustment. Boys in poor health or with poor physique, on the other hand, tended to be unpopular, to have feelings of inferiority, and to show other personal maladjustments.

Tom, in *Through the First Gate,** has to prove both to himself and his friends that he can dive off the high tower. The challenge is almost too great for him. He is torn by self-doubts and excruciating fears. If only it would suffice to show them he was a fast swimmer or if only some one would get cramps and he could rescue him, that would be enough! But Tom triumphs and the immeasurable happiness he achieves through the quiet acceptance of his friends is a very

* From *Through the First Gate* by John Craig Stewart. Reprinted by permission of Dodd Mead & Co. Copyright © 1949, 1950 by John Craig Stewart. Pp. 180-191.

measurable indication of the feelings of esteem and belonging which are now rightfully his.

They took their swimming suits even though it was a secluded pond far from town, because, as Douglas said, "sometimes girls come out there—the time they caught us naked and we had to take off into the woods and everybody got poison oak—"

"Suits me," Tom said with a grin which belied his anxiety. Out in the yard waiting, there were five boys, including George, Andrew, and Spunky. Each one of them had dived from the tower. Tim, who said he never would, was not there; neither were the others who had neither dived from it nor made any commitments concerning it.

Tom had never seen the tower except in his mind but he had heard reports of this or that boy who had lost his nerve, another who had knocked the wind out of himself and of the few who had braved it and succeeded. He himself had never dived from a height of more than fifteen feet; that was off a section of the dam at Dansby. No one ever went off from the high floodgate tower. Legend had it that a boy had dived from there many years ago—when the power company still used the dam—and had never come up, never been found. Some said he was sucked into the turbines under the power house.

They all dived, Tom knew, but no one of them but Douglas had done the gainer, the back dive or the one and a half —not from the tower. That was something, he told himself; he would only have to do a plain dive to hold his own with the majority. Douglas, of course, was beyond challenge.

They joined the others waiting in the yard. "Let's take off," Douglas said and Tom felt a thrill of pride come over him as the group moved out as one. It was almost as if a casual command had been given which no one of them ever could or would ignore. I wish Rufus was here, Tom thought, just to see him and Douglas meet. And then a lightning thought struck through him suddenly. He felt himself wince at the idea and he was ashamed. That would not be fair— but if *I* could dive from there—if it is as high as the floodgate tower—maybe—if I can, then Rufus—if I have the nerve— I wonder if they know I am afraid now?

They moved briskly out of town onto the sandy road

leading through the simmering hot cotton fields, through the occasional shaded woods where the yellow sand was cool and damp. The movement seemed to dispel the heat. Their spirits rose as they approached the spot, four miles from town. The talk became louder, more braggadocio, their voices more shrill—all but Douglas'. He said little and walked at a steady pace. No one of them knew his plan for the day, but the thrill and certainty of it pervaded them all. It was an occasion and what went into it was the best from each of them which something in Douglas called forth. And Tom kept remembering on the trip out how Uncle Thomas' face had changed when Douglas asked to stay home with him. He wondered if Douglas' father had felt the same thing these boys felt.

"You going to dive from the tower, Tom?" George asked quickly in an excited voice.

Tom grinned. "I don't know," he said, "I never tried it before." No one replied but he felt their eyes on him and knew their doubts and their curiosity. And the old doubt of himself, the old terror of an unknown trial took hold of him again. They could see the tower standing up against the sky above the tree tops even before the lake was in sight. It's higher than the floodgate tower, Tom thought, way higher.

"There it is, there it is," George yelled. And they began to move out in a run. Tom could feel his heart beating hard and fast inside him.

"I don't see any gals," Robert Phillips yelled, snatching at his clothes as they came up to the sandy bank of the lake. "Let's go in raw."

They were dropping their clothes behind them as they came up to the edge. Their naked bodies pitched into the cold water like rapid fire. The seven of them struck out across the pond toward the opposite bank and the sky searching tower. The water was icy.

He thought, now I will swim fast. (He was a fast swimmer.) If I show them my speed in swimming it'll give me something to back me up if I can't go off the tower. Maybe they won't all try diving from the top this time. Maybe the thing won't be brought up at all. (Now he noticed that the ferocity of his strokes had carried him several yards out in front of the others. He was swimming the crawl and hardly looking where he was going, only lifting his mouth above the water's edge to breathe.) There's a diving board on the pier—we can dive from there—we can play alligator—if I can only ignore this thing and if they only won't care—

He did not know that the hardest challenge on earth to ignore is the silent implacable challenge from some dread inanimate thing which calls to a doubt inside and sucks you toward itself, the thing you fear and despise.

If somebody got the cramps and I could pull them out of the water—that would be enough. He looked up and saw the bank looming above him. The wooden, slime-mossy ladder to the pier rose ahead of them. He grasped it and pulled up. Before he was out of the water the others were fighting to get first hold on the ladder. Douglas dived beneath the surface, came up on the other side of the pier and pulled himself up on the cross braces. The seven naked bodies gleamed in the sunlight and the chests, some with a few dark hairs showing proudly, heaved with a pulsating rhythm.

"You—ought—to enter—the meets at—the—the—Y, Tom," George gasped. "You really got -a-a-fast crawl."

"Aw—it's nothing," Tom answered with a shrug. "I can't hold out, anyway, got no wind."

"The hell you couldn't," Robert said. "With a little training, you'd win."

They were all looking at him now, their eyes admiring, their heads rocking slightly to the heavy breathing. He sat down modestly and grinned again. The sensation was pleasant, even more so than when he hit the home run in that first game. He glanced at Douglas. He was leaning against the tower, an expression of alert interest in his eyes.

"You ever clock yourself, Tom?" he asked.

"What?"

"You ever have anybody time you on fifty or hundred yards free style?"

"Oh, no," Tom said. "Up in Dansby we just swim. Nobody's got a watch."

Douglas grinned and nodded toward the opposite bank. "From here to that tree where the grass rope is hanging is exactly fifty yards. I'll go get my watch and time you when you get your breath—if you want to try it."

"O.K.," Tom said. Now I have the chance. If I can break the record swimming I won't have to go off that tower at all.

"I'll get your watch, Doug," George said. "Why don't

you swim with Tom? You got the Y record for the hundred yards, if he beats you—he must be good."

Tom had not realized he was so good a swimmer. And it was as though he had discovered inside himself an unknown source of power, a defense, a short way to glory and esteem —not the way of the tower.

"All right." He heard Douglas' casual voice.

George hurtled his long bony body back into the water and swam toward the sand bar where the clothes were scattered. Tom and Douglas looked at each other and Tom felt self-conscious and somewhat doubtful now. He breathed hard and fast. He had not yet gotten his wind. Leaning against the tower Douglas hardly seemed to breathe at all. He probably didn't even try coming over. Why do I have to get into these fixes all the time? Why can't I be the one to stand back and see somebody else get challenged and have to win or lose? If I lose, the tower's next, sure as fire. Quickly he glanced up at it out of squinted eyes. The top of it seemed to sway against the white hot summer clouds. George came back across the catwalk, the watch on his wrist. As he walked his body swung back and forth with the swaying of the catwalk, and that private part of him, which seemed already fully grown to manhood as if it had sapped the meat and strength from his long-boned thin body, swayed like a length of heavy rope.

Robert pointed at him. "Lordy, ain't George hung though? No wonder he's so skinny carrying that thing around all the time."

"Hell, he ain't but fifteen. I'd hate to see him when he's twenty," Andrew said.

"If any of these gals see him on that catwalk, he won't live that long," Spunky Davis said. Spunky was the freckle faced, cotton headed one, the one who for some strange reason had become noted as a sheik. They grinned knowingly.

"You tell em Spunky," Robert said.

Douglas said nothing; he looked on indifferently and smiled occasionally. George, sensing that he was the center of attraction, whooped and did a caper on the catwalk. He probably thought they were praising him as a good and generous soul for going to get the watch. At any rate, they were amused. As he danced, that better part of him performed various gyrations which threw them all into up-

roarious laughter. Then he lost his footing and slipped. He
came off beneath the rope with a loud groan, loyally holding
high the hand with the watch. As he swam to the pier, he
held his arm up, swimming with one hand and grinning and
yelling.

"I didn't get it wet—I didn't get it wet." He's a silly clown,
Tom thought, but he dives off the tower.

He and Douglas leaned over, their hands on their knees,
chins stuck out toward the distance of water they were to
travel. George's long hand was pointed up. "Get ready, get
set—go," he shrilled and the hand came down. The two
bodies knifed into the water simultaneously. Tom came up
with his arms working in full powerful strokes, his feet, fluttering elongations of his legs from his hips down, churning
the water savagely. He could feel the wave of water banking
up against his head as he drove himself on, not looking back
nor forward as he twisted his head around and cupped his
mouth above the surface for air. He knew he was swimming
faster than he had ever swum before. He felt confident that
no one, not even Douglas, could pass him in this one supreme
burst of speed. He remembered strangely and suddenly that
taut strained body of Skipper when he raced Charlie on
Mary Lee last winter, and again he got that same sensation
of being apart from the earth driven by a separate power,
not subject to the drag of weight and time and the dreary
stillness of the earth. He knew the effort could not last, he
only hoped he could hold out to the tree; he knew that if it
did last, the sensation would carry over into death. He
stopped breathing, feeling there was not even time for that.
He kept his head down, and the air was a hot ball in his
chest. But the feeling of speed and victory was strong in him,
forcing every muscle to its utmost. He could hear nothing
but the steady churning splash of his own strokes blended
with Douglas' somewhere to the side of him.

Now, he thought, I'll look up and gauge my strokes to the
bank. I ought to be there in a second. He raised his head
and brought his eyes slightly over water level. The bank
loomed close. Against it Douglas' arms and shoulders
gleamed. He was clinging to some bushes and knocking his
head against his hand as though he had forgotten the race
already and the important thing was the water in his ear.
Tom came up beside him like a motor boat coming into the

bank under full speed. He grasped the roots of the tree, pulled to a stop and took a deep breath.

"Da-mn," he gasped, "where did you come from? How did you get here?"

Douglas grinned. "A straight line is the shortest path between two points," he said. "You zig-zagged off your course like a plane without a stabilizer. You had me beat in speed but you went crooked."

"Lordy," Tom said, "I'm winded." He pulled himself up on the bank and lay back on the grass. He felt the beating of his heart and wondered if the painful suction of his lungs would ever catch up with that strength lost in the fifty yards of pond water. He could hardly think, but as the blood ebbed back into his brain and he was able to feel the sweat pouring out on his body, like a quinine sweat, he thought, the tower.

He heard the voices of the boys jeering good humoredly from across the pond. George squeaked, "Douglas twenty-eight seconds, Tom thirty. Tom swam over the dam and back and never knew it." They all laughed loudly.

"Come on," one of them yelled, "let's go off the tower, Doug." Tom opened his eyes and the breakfast he had eaten churned in his stomach. He could hear their voices as from a great distance now calling impatiently. Douglas was standing up.

"How you feel, Tom?" he asked.

"All right, just winded, that's all—"

"When you're ready we'll go."

"O.K." And still lying on his back he looked up at the thick green leaves rustling lightly in an otherwise unknown summer breeze, he looked at the blue sky beyond rippled by the shimmering colorless waves of heat. Slowly his strength came back.

Now, he said to himself, now I must follow Douglas. I must watch him and move as he moves, speak as he speaks, think as he thinks, and follow until I can go no farther. I do not know where it will lead but it must lead somewhere. (I will not think, I will not even know, I will walk like Douglas to whatever I must and I must—) A banning of consciousness deep inside him, a denial of instinct, a reversal of the natural dictate from his own knowledge of himself was accomplished with the drawing of a deep breath and a sitting up and turning of his head toward Douglas.

"I'm ready, I got my wind now, let's go."

With his stomach muscles he controlled the nausea he felt and forced it back into the deeper cavities of his body, denying it as he denied his fear. They dove in and swam leisurely across to the pier. Spunky Davis was already on top of the tower shouting and cavorting. He was noted for his courage and he was not letting that glory die today. Robert was climbing up the ladder; the others lolled about on the pier waiting.

"What you going to do, Doug?" George asked. "Show us something good."

"How about you, Tom?" Robert asked. "You going to try it today?"

Tom grinned, "I don't know, I'll go up and see what it looks like from the top." Again that strange terrible silence which fell over the group when he spoke of his doubts. Then he thought, I am Douglas' cousin, I am Douglas' cousin.

"Want to go on up and take a look, Tom?" Douglas asked.
"Sure."

Voice tight, lips drawn, nerves which could cause trembling, all held in the bare hands of his spirit. If any fear could be read in him it was by more astute observers than were on the pier. Douglas was going up the ladder in his squirrel-like style, a sort of easy run which gently shook the whole tower frame. His leisurely and offhanded grace defied the growing distance beneath him. Tom followed slowly and carefully behind him. When they reached the top he could see over the trees to fields beyond, green with cotton and corn. A Negro was plowing in a field south of them, a wisp of white dust rose behind him. Faintly his song floated up, no song Tom had ever heard; it was probably the man's improvisation, a weary laden chant which followed the slow rhythm of his mule and plow. The Negroes at home sing like that, he thought, but Charlie could sing real songs. Charlie left his guitar—

Beyond the tree tops the broad muddy river curled through the green land in the sunsparkle. The tops of the tall buildings of Rutledge wavered in the heat. Tom thought, I came from there, my father and my mother, my grandpa and grandma, and they had courage. They hate cowardice above all things. Am I a coward? Miss Lenoir kissed me but she would not have kissed me if she knew me now. He gripped the rail as the tower creaked and swayed in the stirring air. Spunky Davis moved about, grinning foolishly and shaking the railing.

"Go on, Spunky," Douglas said, "hit it."

Tom watched the freckled shoulder tighten as Spunky poised on the edge, looking down. Suddenly everything seemed still and then Spunky was gone, as though he had been swept off by a soft wind. They watched him falling and he entered the water easily, like the point of a knife.

"Want to go next, Doug?" Robert asked.

"Go on, I'll wait," Douglas said.

Robert went down in a jackknife which was timed beautifully; his body straightened out just in time to enter the water. Tom turned to look at Douglas and saw the look of appraisal, the admiring flicker in the great eyes. They were alone now and Douglas looked at him with a grin. Tom's knuckles hurt with the pressure of his grip on the railing.

"You a little bit afraid, Tom?" he asked casually. Tom's throat was dry and sealed with terror and shame. He jerked his head up and down. Douglas looked away. "That's natural," he said, "we all were scared our first time. And anyway, you don't have to dive off. Nobody will think anything of it. Some people don't like high diving."

And Tom knew that had Douglas been afraid or had he not wanted to dive from the tower for any reason, he would simply have said, "I don't want to dive off the tower," and that would have been the end of it. Douglas could have done it. But could he? He thought of Tim. Nobody disliked him or thought him cowardly. But Tim was anonymous, lost like a grain of sand in the myriad usual clods. He looked back at Douglas and saw his proud head against the sky.

"I want to," he said.

"O.K., it's easy," Douglas said. "Just grip your toes over the edge and go off easy. Keep your head down and open your palms before you hit the water. It's not high as it looks from here."

Tom stepped to the edge and squared his shoulders. He looked down and then out across the heat-misted fields, then back again at the water. It was impossible. He stepped back. "You-go-first-Douglas."

Douglas was leaning loosely against the front corner post, his expression unchanged. "Tell you what," he said, "go down and start on the twenty foot platform. Get the feel of it and then come up a few steps on the ladder each time. In a few tries you'll be going off up here like a bird. That is, if you want to—there's no sense in it if you don't want to."

"I want to," Tom said. He grasped the railing and he could feel his heart again, pounding with an impotent rage.

"I'll go off now," Douglas said. "You go on and try it like I said." He moved up to the edge and with his arms at his sides he raised his chin slightly then lowered it. He came up on his toes and with a quick spring left the platform, seeming to move upward instead of downward. As his body gave in to the pull of gravity, he arched it into a living curve, head up, eyes on the sky, arms spread like a bird, and he glided toward the earth. A few feet from the water he broke the curve and knifed in with a neat splash.

"Oh Lord," Tom said.

He did not look down at the others as he lowered himself on the ladder to the twenty foot platform. From there he immediately felt the difference in altitude. He stepped up quickly and went off in a jackknife, his best dive. He did not say anything to the others when he swam out and mounted the ladder again. He knew that they were watching and waiting. Suddenly he realized that probably nowhere else would he have been allowed this margin among boys who had already faced and conquered the thing he feared. He went back up and dove from three rungs higher. It was easy. This is twenty-six feet, he said to himself as he pushed off.

He repeated it three more rungs up; he mounted steadily. The others were diving from the board or from the high tower. Occasionally he saw Douglas watching him. He reached the top of the tower sooner than he expected. He did not look away but down steadily at the water. It was the same, like going off lower. His toes tightened over the edge and he poised himself and shoved off. He could feel himself smiling as he fell with control and grace and immeasurable happiness toward the cool green depths below.

Tom came back in triumph through the fading day. He felt sure now that he was afraid of nothing. He thought of Rufus, of the whole gang, and grinned. It was very doubtful if any boy in Hopper County would dive from the floodgate tower, and Tom knew now that he could.

All of the boys were tired and hungry—the sardines and cheese and crackers at the country store did not last long, and they talked little on the road home. But when any of them spoke to him, Tom recognized that tone of acceptance, of respect. No one mentioned his accomplishment, but that was the way it was when you did something right, he mused. He realized with a silent thanksgiving that the swimming alone would never have done for him what the dive had done. If he never dived again it did not matter.

Swinging down the gravel road toward home and supper they sang the Artillery Song, rolling the caissons along in discord and in tune. Tom's voice was loudest among them.

Thus, the importance of physical strength and ability is very great, and especially for boys. They have significant effects on his social acceptance and status as well as on his emotional adjustment. In a setting very similar to *Through the First Gate,* but with antithetical results, Lymie Peters, in *The Folded Leaf,* is made to feel isolated and unaccepted. His lack of competency in swimming affects him adversely not only in this way but also in his attitude toward himself.

Complicating the adolescent's problem of physical growth further are the bewilderingly unequal rates of growth in different parts and organs of the body. Adolescents grow unevenly, not at a smooth, consistant pace; at the same age, some grow faster than others. Two basic principles in adolescent physical growth are apparent: first is the fact of individual variation; and secondly, the range of the normal is wide. Adolescents differ in regard to physical traits, body form, and capacities. They differ in respect to the rates at which the whole body grows, to the growth of the various parts of the body, and to the various systems of organs—just as adolescents differ in regard to the development of their mental and emotional characteristics.

Joan and Peter, in the novel of the same name,* have been brought up as brother and sister and have not seen each other for some time. The obvious physical change in Joan

* From *Joan and Peter* by H. G. Wells. Copyright by the author. Reprinted by permission of the Executors of the Estate of H. G. Wells. Macmillan Co. Pp. 303-304.

has its decided psychological effect on Peter; and Joan, too, is aware of her new powers.

They grew irregularly, and that made some quaint variations of relationship. Peter, soon after he went to Caxton, fell to expanding enormously. He developed a chest, his limbs became great things. There was a summer bitten into Joan's memory when he regarded her as nothing more than a "little teeny female tick," and descanted on the minuteness of her soul and body. But he had lost some of his lightness, if none of his dexterity and balance, as a climber, and Joan got her consolations among the lighter branches of various trees they explored. Next Christmas Joan herself had done some serious growing, and the gap was not so wide. But it was only after her first term at Newnham that Joan passed from the subservience of a junior to the confidence of a senior. She did it at a bound. She met him one day in the narrow way between Sidney Street and Petty Cury. Her hair was up and her eyes were steady; most of her legs had vanished, and she had clothes like a real woman. We do not foregather even with foster brothers in the streets of Cambridge, but a passing hail is beyond the reach of discipline. "Hullo, Petah!" she said, "what a gawky great thing you're getting!"

Peter, a man in his second year, was so taken aback he had no adequate reply.

"You've grown too," he said "if it comes to that";—a flavourless reply. And there was admiration in his eyes.

An encounter for subsequent regrets. He thought it over afterwards. The cheek of her! It made his blood boil.

"So long, Petah," said Joan, carrying it off to the end.

There is a difference in timing in physical growth between the sexes. Girls grow taller sooner and weigh more than boys, but usually by the time the boy is fourteen or fifteen, he has overtaken the girl and frequently surpassed her in both height and weight. This is the "average" picture; there are exceptions; and there are considerable differences in the ages at which adolescents have their growth spurts or attain their maximum growth. The early maturing child tends to differ from the late maturer in the following ways: the maximum growth increment is greater in amount; the whole growth cycle is completed in a shorter time; the children are larger before maximum growth but are likely to be more alike or even shorter at the end because growth is completed more quickly; and maximal growth occurs rather typically in broad-hipped persons and those with relatively short legs (23). The differences between early and late maturing boys and early and late maturing girls are not large or overly important; what is important is the situation at the extremes. The tallest girl or the shortest boy have equal difficulties: the tallest and biggest girl has in magnified form the usual troubles of malcoordination plus distress over being much too big and the shortest boy is usually even shorter than the shortest girl (5).

Puberty brings with it the development of the primary and secondary sex characteristics. There is a natural sequence to this manifestation and it is followed with great consistency. But just as there are marked differences in the ages at which the various physical and physiological milestones are passed, so there are marked variations as to when sexual development occurs. Also, the extent of the change of size and appearance of the sex characters is widely variable between boys of the same age and girls of the same age.

These changes involve, for the boy, the nearly doubling in size of the penis, the enlargement of the testes, and the development of the secondary sex characteristics, which include the deepening of the voice and the appearance of body and facial hair. For the girl, the hips begin to round, the breasts develop, down appears on the upper lip and hair on the body, and there is rapid growth of the sex organs.

Some time between the ages of eleven and fifteen (24), and most usually at thirteen (20), girls begin to menstruate. In the beginning, menstrual periods are usually irregular, with wide intervals between each. Once the menses are established, some girls menstruate a little oftener than every twenty-eight days, others a little less often. Few have an ab-

solutely regular cycle. Irregularity may be brought about by
emotional tension, prolonged physical strain, illness, or even
a change of climate (12).

The attitude the girl has to her monthly period is of great
importance. The headaches, backaches, cramps, general irritability, nervousness, fatigue, and depression which are so
frequently attributed to menstruation often have some psychological rather than physical basis (1). Ignorance and fear
are handmaidens to the precipitation of difficult menses. In
*Prince Bart,** Valerie's mother tries to prevent this by telling
her daughter that she herself welcomes the period and that
when she does, she experiences no pain; it is only when she
does not that she has cramps.

"Mummy, wake up, I'm bleeding."
The coffin snapped. She sat up at once, switching on the
light. This was no dream. It was two hours since she had
received Bart's wire.
"Bleeding—why—what happened?"
"I got the curse."
"Curse?"
"My period."
"Oh," Mollie almost wept with relief. She took Valerie to
the bathroom, initiated her into the procedures. Valerie
listened and learned with a sort of curiosity Mollie would
have expected about impersonal school studies.
"This is an important event for you."
Valerie nodded. "It's an awfully sticky feeling."
Mollie wanted to say that when a man makes love to you
sometimes that's a sticky feeling too. So was eating candy
when you were a baby, or sweating it out when you gave
birth to one. Sticky wasn't bad. Being immaculate, no matter what Winnie may have taught you out of her own barren-
ness using daddy and me as a grim object lesson, isn't the
key to a clean and happy life. Sticky with living can be
something good.
She wanted to say all this. But she didn't.

* From *Prince Bart* by Jay Richard Kennedy. Copyright 1953 by Jay
Richard Kennedy. Used by permission of the publishers, Farrar, Straus &
Cudahy, Inc. Pp. 287-291.

When they were finished in the bathroom Mollie asked, "Why do you call it the curse?"

"That's what Winnie calls it."

So did lots of girls. Women, too. As a child she had called it falling off the roof. Same principle. Even 'unwell' was in that troubled, time-worn family of defeated definitions ending on the downbeat with the sad symbol—'period'.

"It isn't the curse, dear. It can be a fine and happy thing."

"Will I have cramps?"

"Not if you welcome it, no."

"Winnie has cramps. Don't you?"

"When I don't welcome it, yes. But only when I don't welcome it."

"None of the other girls have it yet. I'm the first."

Mollie smiled. It hurt. "That's right. It's something to be proud of. It will make you even prettier and allow you to feel wonderful things you never felt before."

Valerie stared, disbelieving.

Mollie had a need to prove that, a pressing need.

Proof!

If only her own life were proof one's daughter could believe. It was too early to wake Katey, who lived by her love of Andy, nourished it through their child, kept the faith in little ways. Katey could prove it.

"Let's wake grandma and tell her."

Mollie peered at the clock. "It's only four-thirty A.M."

Mollie wanted to wake Ma. Someone. Anyone! Especially Ma. But this was the one time she would do her own labor of love by and for herself. She led Valerie past Ma's door and down the stairs.

Below in the living room they found Ma starting a fire. Her huge coffee mug rested empty on the flat, broad, raw wood arm of her chair.

"You're up early," Ma said.

How little a daughter knows of her mother. How much one forgets. Ma was always up at four. And how little a mother knows of her daughter.

"Valerie has started to menstruate. We wanted to share the good news."

Ma said, "Ah," the sound coming to her lips from a deep involuntary breath as she continued to place the logs in position. Then she lit the match with her nail and set flame to the kindling and rose from the kneeling position. Her old face, firm under the wrinkles, energetic but no longer eager, exhausted but not decayed, was very thoughtful as her eyes, still bright blue, rested in a solemn gaze on Valerie's flushed face. It reminded Mollie of the past sunset when Ma had come out of the barn and stood in the radiance of the dying sun wearing her patchwork skirt and the unfeminine khaki shirt, her arthritic hand living a separate life of its own and trembling slightly as she explained that the cow was three weeks late in calfing because the old woman who worked for her had lacked the strength to lead the beast in heat over the hill to the bull in sufficient time. A sigh escaped Ma's lips as she nodded.

"That means you will be a woman soon."

"I'm not afraid," Valerie answered combatively, then blushed and turned to Mollie asking with a nervous laugh, "Now what did I say that for?"

Ma's network of wrinkles remained unmoved. She nodded her head again and bent forward, kissing Valerie on the forehead. "Bless you, granddaughter, bless you. Amen."

"What's going on?"

It was Katey, wakened again.

"Valerie just got un—she started to menstruate."

Katey smiled from the head of the stairs, sleep and vague dreams still in her eyes. "What a night," she said. "It certainly came early. From excitement over your daddy's success, I guess. Well, that wonderful, darling." She yawned.

It *is* wonderful. But Katey didn't make it sound wonderful. In the feeble light she suddenly looked, because that's how she sounded, like a widow no matter how many regrets she did not have. A young, stopped-dead-in-her-tracks-by-death widow of twenty-five, saying that's wonderful, you may look forward to great and delightful experiences like widowhood, at the top of the stairs, small and wasting in the dream-trapped morning light. And in the presence of Valerie now she looked no longer young or on the verge. A double chin was forming, the arms had grown too thick for the want of a man to embrace. Even if one day raw animal needs would send her body reaching for other men or man, each time it happened it would be Andy in her fattened embrace, quickening her powerless pulse, making the half hunger's gratification right with her, unfair to future lovers

and to herself because her man had died before she was
ready to lose him. Mollie had a swift, insistent sense of time
and space for the future was here! Four-thirty in the small
hours of a fast fleeting day. A tiny dot of a farm in the bulls-
eye sprawling middle of America. Four women. Three faced
by one.

Confronted.

I got the curse.

One looked to three.

She looked *at* three.

Proof!

Dear God, what sort of life have we built that when this
child faces us, we must turn away.

I got the curse which makes you fall off the roof from
even higher than the top of the stairs into the bottomless
unwell. No! Other words must be found.

But proof.

Three women, three wives, three thousand, three million,
their numbers legion, starting with high hopes laid low and
for those to come it could, it must be different.

But proof!

Reaching for other proof she recalled earlier today. No,
that day was already spent, so fast do they come and go. It
was yesterday, before Ma had joined them near the barn.
She and Valerie had stood quietly, almost holding their
breaths as they watched the cow, swollen-bellied, big with
life, lowing gently as she grazed on the almost cleared slope.
Either side of her were the wispy twigs, brown, not yet even
green, with shoots faintly visible, as yet more like silky hairs
on the head of a newborn child and glistening in the late
sun with the transparence of jeweled icicles. A blessed study
in the immediate and the eternal; processes that kept the
ledger of regeneration ahead of decay by however small a
margin since the beginning of time.

"Doesn't she look pleased with herself, though," Valerie
had finally said, smiling and squeezing Mollie's hand.
Neither had dared walk closer to pet the cow for fear of
disrupting the perfection of the moment. On tiptoe they
had backed away.

"Remember the cow late yesterday?" Mollie said.

"Oh, mummy, don't be silly!"

"Just you remember her all the same." Valerie put her

head on her mother's shoulder. "Where is the wine?" Mollie asked.

"In the kitchen."

Ma brushed down her apron. "I'm going to the barn."

"Wine," Katey groaned. "At this hour. Yipes."

She walked, still half asleep, back into her bedroom where Petey was shouting, "I have to tinkle," and Katey switched on the bedroom light demanding, "Then who's stopping you?"

Mollie took Valerie's arm and led her toward the kitchen. Valerie kept adjusting her bathrobe and glancing back over her shoulder.

"Don't worry," Mollie assured, "It doesn't show."

"It sure *feels* funny."

Mollie squeezed her arm. In the kitchen she poured two glasses of wine. She handed one to Valerie. "To your womanhood."

Valerie stared at the wine for a moment. "It's red," she said. So many things are red. I never realized. Sunset, the color of healthy cheeks, strawberries, one third of my country's flag. The body of a newborn baby. Mollie's glass clinked against hers. They both took tiny sips. "Grandma would call it the curse," Valerie said, "and so would Aunt Katey."

"They judge by their lives. You judge by yours. Ask yourself whether it should be bad to become what you have been preparing to be since you were born."

"No," Valerie said with sudden force. "How could it be?"

"It shouldn't, so welcome it," Mollie answered. "Welcome it and it will welcome you. Do you understand?"

"Yes, mummy, I really think I do."

Valerie suddenly felt that her own eyes were as blue as Mollie's but with added lights in them. A wider lens that needed only things worth seeing and reporting to every growing part of her. She had a chance to do and be something. How? By *not* doing the things mummy had done. It hurt her to think that. But this was a serious occasion, one on which she could not afford to lie to herself.

"I'm sorry, mummy," she said aloud. She was suddenly shaken by sobs, and when Mollie reached for her she pulled away.

"That it's come?" Mollie whispered.

Valerie shook her head. Abruptly the sobbing stopped. "No." She took another sip of wine less tentative, less for the ritual. A tasting sip. "I'm glad it's come." She raised her glass to the light. "You can see through it," she said. And then with an abruptness in keeping with a not quite twelve-year-old child in the midst of her first experience as a woman, she asked, "Is it wrong for me to toast myself?"

"No, darling, it's wrong not to."

Valerie nodded solemnly. *Yes. Be like her. And do the opposite.* "To me!" She lifted her head high, brought the glass to her lips and drank.

"To me," Mollie repeated softly. *Or at least as I try to shape a new life—for me with Bart. And when I tell Valerie later today why she and Doris must stay here while I go alone to New York to face Bart and what facing him means for all of us she will be able to hear as I shall be able to find the right words.*

So cling tight to the beginning of Valerie's life and follow hers to the reshaping of your own.

"To us."

Mollie drank.

Outside the big red rooster was noisily crowing.

Perhaps it would have helped more if Valerie had been prepared for her menses some time before they actually occurred, rather than at the precise moment. For many reasons of their own, mothers are reluctant to anticipate the event. The girl who is happy about becoming a woman will accept menstruation as a natural part of growing into womanhood. But for the girl who resents her femininity, and whose relations with her mother have been unhappy to the point where she can not identify with her, menstruation may be troublesome, both emotionally and physically (9).

The adolescent is often disquieted by certain aspects of his growth to which he has not yet become accustomed or which he does not like. When a change occurs which makes radical revisions necessary in his physical self-concept, it may be difficult for the adolescent to adjust to the new physical actuality and to the new physical self-concept which that actuality involves (10). He may be neither prepared for the new changes nor understand their meaning.

Why he consumes such great quantities of food is as much a needless mystery to him as it is to his mother who must prepare it and to his father who may supply the wherewithal to purchase the chili, the banana split, and the milkshake with which to wash them down. Because of the rapid growth of the body, the adolescent needs more nourishment. An enlarged stomach capacity and glandular changes brought on by puberty result in a ravenous appetite. Snacks before and after regular meal times, snacks before retiring and snacks in between snacks are almost inevitable because of his almost endless expenditure of energy. The human "garbage can" described in the following paragraph from *The City of Trembling Leaves*,* is fairly typical of the "tape-worm" adolescent.

[Timmy] began to grow as if he had been transplanted into more fertile earth or set out nearer water. By the end of his sophomore year in high school, this sprouting had transformed him from a nimble-footed, scurrying creature five feet tall and ninety pounds in weight, to a drifting, incomprehensible being six feet tall and weighing one hundred and fifty. . . . From the first of it, so much of his energy went to lengthening his bones and enlarging his hands and feet that he could never eat or sleep enough. His own plate would be filled two and three times at a meal, and after he had devoured all that, he would clean up anything left by the rest of the family. Often he drank a quart of milk at breakfast or supper, and worked another in some time between. His mother cheerfully called him the family garbage can, and left odds and ends out on the kitchen table for him to pick up after school.

Not all adolescents' appetites are as large as Tim's, nor as hearty. And even for Tim, there were times when it was finicky and poor. Rapid shifts from overeating to undereating are common. "Because emotional disturbances interfere with appetite, adolescents who are subject to emotional ups and downs, and this is more common than unusual, find that their appetites vary as their emotional states vary. There is a hereditary difference in digestive capacity, and eating habits acquired during childhood days play their role also. The type of child-training methods used, whether strict or lenient, affects the food habits of the adolescent. Good food habits are definitely related to the adolescent's general adjustment" (13). There is, as well, a revival of oral interests, as indicated in Tim's milk-drinking bouts, which reflect the adolescent's struggle to remain an infant and at the same time grow up.

Dennis has suggested that the central interest of the psychology of adolescence is to portray the effects of biological adolescence upon the behavior of the individual (8). In terms of the preceding discussion, the physical development of the adolescent may serve to explain some of the deeper sources of his behavior. During adolescence, the organism is in a state of disequilibrium due to unevenly developing organs and functions, and therefore can be thrown into a state of emotional disturbance very readily (6). Hence the adolescent tends to respond emotionally to comparatively slight stimuli (2). Much of his behavior becomes, characteristically, negative, leading to difficult social adjustments for him and the people with whom he comes in contact. Growing older is not necessarily disturbing to the adolescent; rather it is the sudden growth spurts and the unforeseen changes which depart from his expectations that provide the disturbing element (11).

REFERENCES

(1) Beverly, Bert I. *A Psychology of Growth*. NY: Whittlesey, 1947, p. 168.
(2) Blanchard, Phyllis. "Adolescent Experiences in Relation to Personality and Behavior," in Hunt, J. McV. (Ed.), *Personality and the Behavior Disorders*, Vol. II. NY: Ronald, 1944, p. 692.
(3) Blos, Peter. *The Adolescent Personality*. NY: Appleton-Century-Crofts, 1941, p. 40.

(4) Burton, Robert. *Anatomy of Melancholy.* NY: Farrar, c. 1927, p. 251.

(5) Cole, Luella. *Psychology of Adolescence.* NY: Rinehart, 1948, p. 22.

(6) Cole, Luella. *Ibid.,* p. 17.

(7) Coleman, James C. *Abnormal Psychology and Modern Life.* Chicago: Scott, Foresman, 1950, p. 109.

(8) Dennis, Wayne. "The Adolescent," in Carmichael, Leonard (Ed.), *Manual of Child Psychology.* NY: Wiley, 1946, p. 637.

(9) Faegre, Marion L. *The Adolescent in Your Home.* Washington, DC: Children's Bureau of Publications, 1954, p. 21.

(10) Horrocks, John E. *The Psychology of Adolescence.* Boston: Houghton Mifflin, 1951, p. 259.

(11) Horrocks, John E. *Ibid.,* p. 261.

(12) Hurlock, Elizabeth. *Adolescent Development.* (2nd Ed.) NY: McGraw-Hill, Inc., 1955, p. 41.

(13) Hurlock, Elizabeth. *Ibid.,* p. 70.

(14) Josselyn, Irene. "The Ego in Adolescence," *Amer. J. Orthopsychiatry,* April 1954.

(15) Josselyn, Irene. *The Happy Child: a Psychoanalytic Guide to Emotional and Social Growth.* NY: Random House, 1955, p. 122.

(16) Jones, H. E. *Motor Performance and Growth.* Berkeley, Calif: University of California Press, 1949, p. 167.

(17) Maier, Norman R. F. & Reninger, H. Willard. *A Psychological Approach to Literary Criticism.* NY: Appleton, 1933, pp. 82-83.

(18) Murphy, Gardner. *Personality: a Biosocial Approach to Origins and Structure.* NY: Harper, 1947, p. 508.

(19) Sherif, Musafer & Cantril, Hadley. *The Psychology of Ego-Involvements: Social Attitudes and Identifications.* NY: Wiley, 1947.

(20) Shuttleworth, Frank K. *The Adolescent Period: a Graphic Atlas.* Monographs of the Society for Research in Child Development, 1949, 14, Ser. No. 49, 1 & 2. Evanston, Ill: Child Development Publ., 1951.

(21) Spiegel, Leo A. "A Review of Contributions to a Psychoanalytic Theory of Adolescence: Individual Aspects," in Eissler, Ruth S., et al. (Eds.), *The Psychoanalytic Study of the Child,* Vol. VI. NY: International Universities Press, 1951, p. 387.

(22) Stewart, Robert S. & Workman, Arthur D. *Children and Other People.* NY: Dryden, 1956, p. 114.

(23) Stuart, Harold C. "Physical Growth and Development," in Seidman, Jerome M. (Ed.), *The Adolescent, a Book of Readings.* NY: Dryden, 1953, p. 95.

(24) Stuart, Harold C. *Ibid.,* p. 104.

(25) Zachry, Caroline B. *Emotion and Conduct in Adolescence.* NY: Appleton-Century, 1940, p. 34.

CHAPTER TWO

On Developing Equilibrium

> "Every life in many ways, day after day. We walk through our-
> selves, meeting robbers, ghosts, giants, old men, young men,
> wives, widows, brothers-in-love. But always meeting ourselves."
>
> JAMES JOYCE, *Ulysses*

Mental health at any age is based on respect for one's self,
out of which emerges a realistic and healthy regard for the
needs and demands of social living. The child who gets a
good start will continue to develop well and the one who
starts off poorly will continue to be handicapped. It is probably within the first half dozen years of life that the child
will have begun to clarify what is himself and what are the
others in his environment. From this time until adolescence,
the child is relatively stable in his definition of himself.

At adolescence, however, a host of changes occur which
subject the individual's concept of his self and of others to
marked strain. Adolescents characteristically exhibit a number of contradictory traits, says Fenichel, such as generosity
and selfishness, modesty and exhibitionism, gregariousness
and solitariness, indulgence and asceticism; these contradictory attitudes are due to newly strengthened drives and
the defenses against them (7). It is at this time that another
period of personality development begins. It is frequently
called a period of storm and stress, for there are so many
changes going on simultaneously that not only does the
adolescent find life difficult but so do the adults who have
to live and work with him.

These changes involve physical growth and physiological
growth; the need to be independent from yet dependent
upon the family; the feeling of belonging; the development

of heterosexual relationships; choice of and preparation for a vocational goal; and the organization of the self. There are no regulatory bases for these changes as they come about; they are erratic and so irregular from individual to individual, and from one organic system to another within the same individual, that the complications are compounded.

Some children begin the changes of adolescence by ten, and by twelve have undergone most of the structural changes that will occur. Others may begin at the same time, but the development will take longer. Still others begin much later and develop at varied paces just as those who began earlier. In addition, some children show a rapid and complete growth of muscular development, and a retarded development of sex characteristics. Because of the variability in this growth curve, it is easy to see that even a healthy character structure undergoes strain.

The central problem of adolescence is what Erikson (6) calls establishing a "sense of identity." In the serious business of organizing his ideas about himself, the adolescent has to make clear just who he is and what his relations with others are. Does he become an adult three years before his parents think he does—or two years after he thinks he does? In the American culture, the adult does not look on the adolescent as a child nor does he give him adult status, roles or functions. How, then, and with whom, does the adolescent identify? How look upon himself as future husband, worker, wage-earner? And how look upon himself presently as a buddy or a date, son or sibling, student or athlete?

The adolescent is concerned with these questions. He wonders how he appears to others compared with his own conception of himself. How does he assess himself accurately and attain selfhood in relation to the world about him? The adolescent takes himself very seriously and because he does, he may express himself dogmatically, violently, sadly, extravagantly, eruditely, opinionatedly, discursively. According to Bernfeld (3) and Anna Freud (8), the defensive role of the intellect during adolescence manifests itself in endless discussions on abstract, political and philosophical themes. "The level of thinking may be high and the viewpoint astonishingly broad, but a close connection between this intellectual activity and its application to life is characteristically absent. Discussions exist for their own sake" (16). In a remarkable passage from James Joyce's *A Portrait of the Artist As a Young Man*,* a conversation illustrating all of the adjectives used above takes place among Stephen Dedalus and some of his college friends.

Stephen shook his head.—You're a terrible man, Stevie— said Davin, taking the short pipe from his mouth—always alone.—

—Now that you have signed the petition for universal peace—said Stephen—I suppose you will burn that little copybook I saw in your room.—

As Davin did not answer Stephen began to quote:

—Long, pace, fianna! Right incline, fianna! Fianna, by numbers, salute, one two!—

—That's a different question—said Davin.—I'm an Irish nationalist first and foremost. But that's you all out. You're a born sneerer, Stevie.—

—When you make the next rebellion with hurley-sticks— said Stephen—and want the indispensable informer, tell me. I can find you a few in this college.—

—I can't understand you—said Davin.—One time I hear you talk against English literature. Now you talk against the Irish informers. What with your name and your ideas . . . are you Irish at all?—

—Come with me now to the office of arms and I will show you the tree of my family—said Stephen.

—Then be one of us—said Davin.—Why don't you learn Irish? Why did you drop out of the league class after the first lesson?—

—You know one reason why—answered Stephen.

Davin tossed his head and laughed.

—Oh, come now—he said.—Is it on account of that cer-

* From *A Portrait of the Artist as a Young Man* by James Joyce. Copyright 1916 by B. W. Huebsch, 1944 by Nora Joyce. Reprinted by permission of The Viking Press, Inc., N.Y. Pp. 236-240.

tain young lady and Father Moran? But that's all in your own mind, Stevie. They were only talking and laughing.—

Stephen paused and laid a friendly hand upon Davin's shoulder.

—Do you remember—he said—when we knew each other first? The first morning we met you asked me to show you the way to the matriculation class, putting a very strong stress on the first syllable. You remember? Then you used to address the jesuits as father, you remember? I ask myself about you: *Is he as innocent as his speech?*—

—I'm a simple person—said Davin.—You know that. When you told me that night in Harcourt Street those things about your private life, honest to God, Stevie, I was not able to eat my dinner. I was quite bad. I was awake a long time that night. Why did you tell me those things?—

—Thanks—said Stephen.—You mean I am a monster.—

—No—said Davin.—but I wish you had not told me.—

A tide began to surge beneath the calm surface of Stephen's friendliness.

—This race and this country and this life produced me— he said.—I shall express myself as I am.

—Try to be one of us—repeated Davin.—In your heart you are an Irishman but your pride is too powerful.—

—My ancestors threw off their language and took another —Stephen said.—They allowed a handful of foreigners to subject them. Do you fancy I am going to pay in my own life and person debts they made? What for?—

—For our freedom—said Davin.

—No honourable and sincere man—said Stephen—has given up to you his life and his youth and his affections from the days of Tone to those of Parnell but you sold him to the enemy or failed him in need or reviled him and left him for another. And you invite me to be one of you. I'd see you damned first.—

—They died for their ideals, Stevie—said Davin.—Our day will come yet, believe me.—

Stephen, following his own thought, was silent for an instant.

—The soul is born—he said vaguely—first in those moments I told you of. It has a slow and dark birth, more mysterious than the birth of the body. When the soul of a man is born in this country there are nets flung at it to hold it back from flight. You talk to me of nationality, language, religion. I shall try to fly by those nets.—

Davin knocked the ashes from his pipe.

—Too deep for me, Stevie—he said.—But a man's country comes first. Ireland first, Stevie. You can be a poet or mystic after.—

—Do you know what Ireland is?—asked Stephen with cold violence.—Ireland is the old sow that eats her farrow.—

Davin rose from his box and went towards the players, shaking his head sadly. But in a moment his sadness left him and he was hotly disputing with Cranly and the two players who had finished their game. A match of four was arranged, Cranly insisting, however, that his ball should be used. He let it rebound twice or thrice to his hand and struck it strongly and swiftly towards the base of the alley, exclaiming in answer to its thud:

—Your soul!—

Stephen stood with Lynch till the score began to rise. Then he plucked him by the sleeve to come away. Lynch obeyed, saying:

—Let us eke go, as Cranly has it.—

Stephen smiled at this sidethrust.

They passed back through the garden and out through the hall where the doddering porter was pinning up a notice in the frame. At the foot of the steps they halted and Stephen took a packet of cigarettes from his pocket and offered it to his companion.

—I know you are poor—he said.

—Damn your yellow insolence—answered Lynch.

This second proof of Lynch's culture made Stephen smile again.

—It was a great day for European culture—he said—when you made up your mind to swear in yellow.—

They lit their cigarettes and turned to the right. After a pause Stephen began:

—Aristotle has not defined pity and terror. I have. I say . . .—

Lynch halted and said bluntly:

—Stop! I won't listen! I am sick. I was out last night on a yellow drunk with Horan and Goggins.—

Stephen went on:

—Pity is the feeling which arrests the mind in the presence

of whatsoever is grave and constant in human sufferings and unites it with the human sufferer. Terror is the feeling which arrests the mind in the presence of whatsoever is grave and constant in human sufferings and unites it with the secret cause.—

—Repeat—said Lynch.

Stephen repeated the definitions slowly.

—A girl got into a hansom a few days ago—he went on—in London. She was on her way to meet her mother whom she had not seen for many years. At the corner of a street the shaft of a lorry shivered the window of the hansom in the shape of a star. A long fine needle of the shivered glass pierced her heart. She died on the instant. The reporter called it a tragic death. It is not. It is remote from terror and pity according to the terms of my definitions.

—The tragic emotion, in fact, is a face looking two ways, towards terror and towards pity, both of which are phases of it. You see I use the word *arrest*. I mean that the tragic emotion is static. Or rather the dramatic emotion is. The feelings excited by improper art are kinetic, desire or loathing. Desire urges us to possess, to go to something; loathing urges us to abandon, to go from something. The arts which excite them, pornographical or didactic, are therefore improper arts. The esthetic emotion (I used the general term) is therefore static. The mind is arrested and raised above desire and loathing.—

—You say that art must not excite desire—said Lynch—I told you that one day I wrote my name in pencil on the backside of the Venus of Praxiteles in the Museum. Was that not desire?—

—I speak of normal natures—said Stephen.—You also told me that when you were a boy in that charming carmelite school you ate pieces of dried cowdung.—

Lynch broke again into a whinny of laughter and again rubbed both his hands over his groins but without taking them from his pockets.

—O, I did! I did!—he cried.

Stephen turned towards his companion and looked at him for a moment boldly in the eyes. Lynch, recovering from his laughter, answered his look from his humbled eyes. . . .

The characters in this selection are saying, as most adolescents say, that their problems lie in the environment, not within themselves; that the solution to their problems lies in changing the environment, not themselves; that their feelings of omniscience give them the answers to all their problems. But despite such feelings, or perhaps partly because of them, the adolescent is terribly unsure of himself, very uneasy because of his insecurities, and easily tormented by his doubts. The adolescent is unknown even to himself, at times, fearful of what is going on within him physically and emotionally, and anxious about the external world which he must inhabit. Jean-Christophe,* in Romain Rolland's novel of the same name, is experiencing just such torments in trying to crystallize his feelings about himself.

Christophe was conscious of extreme weariness and great uneasiness. He was for no reason worn out; his head was heavy, his eyes, his ears, all his senses were dumb and throbbing. He could not give his attention to anything. His mind leaped from one subject to another, and was in a fever that sucked him dry. The perpetual fluttering of images in his mind made him giddy. At first he attributed it to fatigue and the enervation of the first days of spring. But spring passed and his sickness grew only worse.

It was what the poets who only touch lightly on things call the unease of adolescence, the trouble of the cherubim, the waking of the desire of love in the young body and soul. As if the fearful crisis of all a man's being, breaking up, dying, and coming to full rebirth, as if the cataclysm in which everything, faith, thought, action, all life, seems like to be blotted out, and then to be new-forged in the convulsions of sorrow and joy, can be reduced to terms of a child's folly!

All his body and soul were in a ferment. He watched them, having no strength to struggle, with a mixture of curiosity and disgust. He did not understand what was happening in himself. His whole being was disintegrated. He spent days together in absolute torpor. Work was torture to him. At night he slept heavily and in snatches, dreaming mon-

* From *Jean-Christophe* by Romain Rolland. Copyright, 1910, 1911, 1913, by Henry Holt & Co., Inc. Copyright, 1938, 1939, 1941, by Gilbert Cannan. By permission of the publishers. Pp. 249-251.

strously, with gusts of desire; the soul of a beast was racing
madly in him. Burning, bathed in sweat, he watched himself
in horror; he tried to break free of the crazy and unclean
thoughts that possessed him, and he wondered if he were
going mad.

The day gave him no shelter from his brutish thoughts.
In the depths of his soul he felt that he was slipping down
and down; there was no stay to clutch at; no barrier to keep
back chaos. All his defenses, all his citadels, with the quad-
ruple rampart that hemmed him in so proudly—his God, his
art, his pride, his moral faith, all was crumbling away, falling
piece by piece from him. He saw himself naked, bound,
lying unable to move, like a corpse on which vermin swarm.
He had spasms of revolt: where was his will, of which he
was so proud? He called to it in vain: it was like the efforts
that one makes in sleep, knowing that one is dreaming, and
trying to awake. Then one succeeds only in falling from one
dream to another like a lump of lead, and in being more
and more choked by the suffocation of the soul in bondage.
At least he found that it was less painful not to struggle. He
decided not to do so, with fatalistic apathy and despair.

The even tenor of his life seemed to be broken up. Now
he slipped down a subterranean crevasse and was like to
disappear; now he bounded up again with a violent jerk.
The chain of his days was snapped. In the midst of the
even plain of the hours great gaping holes would open to
engulf his soul. Christophe looked on at the spectacle as
though it did not concern him. Everybody, everybody,—
and himself—were strange to him. He went about his business, did his work, automatically: it seemed to him that the
machinery of his life might stop at any moment: the wheels
were out of gear. At dinner with his mother and the others,
in the orchestra with the musicians and the audience, suddenly there would be a void and an emptiness in his brain:
he would look stupidly at the grinning faces about him: and
he could not understand. He would ask himself:

"What is there between these creatures and . . .?"

He dared not even say:

". . . and me."

For he knew not whether he existed. He would speak
and his voice would seem to issue from another body. He
would move, and he saw his movements from afar, from

above—from the top of a tower. He would pass his hand over his face, and his eyes would wander. He was often near doing crazy things.

It was especially when he was most in public that he had to keep guard on himself. For example, on the evenings when he went to the Palace or was playing in public. Then he would suddenly be seized by a terrific desire to make a face, or say something outrageous, to pull the Grand Duke's nose, or to make a running kick at one of the ladies. One whole evening while he was conducting the orchestra, he struggled against an insensate desire to undress himself in public: and he was haunted by the idea from the moment when he tried to check it: he had to exert all his strength not to give way to it. When he issued from the brute struggle he was dripping with sweat and his mind was blank. He was really mad. It was enough for him to think that he must not do a thing for it to fasten on him with the maddening tenacity of a fixed idea.

So his life was spent in a series of unbridled outbreaks and of endless falls into emptiness. A furious wind in the desert. Whence came this wind? From what abyss came these desires that wrenched his body and mind? He was like a bow stretched to breaking point by a strong hand,—to what end unknown?—which then springs back like a piece of dead wood. Of what force was he the prey? He dared not probe for it. He felt that he was beaten, humiliated, and he would not face his defeat. He was weary and broken in spirit. He understood now the people whom formerly he had despised: those who will not seek awkward truth. In the empty hours, when he remembered that time was passing, his work neglected, the future lost, he was frozen with terror. But there was no reaction: and his cowardice found excuses in desperate affirmation of the void in which he lived: he took a bitter delight in abandoning himself to it like a wreck on the waters. What was the good of fighting? There was nothing beautiful, nor good: neither God, nor life, nor being of any sort. In the street as he walked, suddenly the earth would sink away from him: there was neither ground, nor air, nor light, nor himself: there was nothing. He would fall, his head would drag him down, face forwards: he could hardly hold himself up; he was on the point of collapse. He thought he was going to die, suddenly, struck down. He thought he was dead. . . .

Christophe was growing a new skin. Christophe was growing a new soul. And seeing the worn out and rotten soul of his childhood falling away he never dreamed that he was taking on a new one, young and stronger. As through life we change our bodies, so also do we change our souls: and the metamorphosis does not always take place slowly over many days; there are times of crisis when the whole is suddenly renewed. The adult changes his soul. The old soul that is cast off dies. In those hours of anguish we think that all is at an end. And the whole thing begins again. A life dies. Another life has already come into being.

"Everybody, everybody,—and himself—were strange to him." Jean-Christophe understood no one and no one understood him, least of all himself. So it is with many adolescents. The adult tends to judge the teenager mainly by his actions, forgetting that adolescence is a period of flux and that which he does and that which he feels do not necessarily coincide. In his attempt to identify with the adult, some confusion may result, for in adolescence the youngster has the need to experience the self as a separate entity (17) and the need to wean himself away, psychologically, from the adults in his world, particularly those in his family. The Captain in Humphrey's *Home from the Hill,* while watching his son, thinks to himself that "a boy had two births to go through: he was delivered from his mother, and then (for convenience the world had fixed that date at age 21) he had to deliver himself from his father. It was not easy to become your own man." Freud has stated that the effects of the first identification in early childhood will be profound and lasting (10). In this process, the child observes, imitates, and incorporates into himself the attributes of his parents to the best of his ability. It is more than mere imitation, however; it is, rather, that the child behaves like his parents because he wants to be identical with them. According to Stoke, "Not only is identification the source of our 'higher natures'; it is the persistent core of them. As adults, our relations with the opposite sex, our attitudes toward our children, our persistence in traditional ways, all these stem from the identifications which we made as young children" (18). Identification is the basis of all learning which is not acquired independently by trial and error (1).

By adolescence, the far-reaching identifications have been established and integrated. But there are also transitory identifications. One week, the girl in her search for identity may imitate a favored actress, the next her teacher. In this search, it may be difficult for the adolescent to identify with her parents, to the latters' chagrin and feelings of rejection. Parents do not know how to strike the right note of "chumminess" with those whom they have always enjoyed as children, and children are literally helpless to accept their parents in a new role as big brothers or sisters (13). In the ego-involved Gant family portrayed in *Look Homeward, Angel,** Eugene can identify with no one. There is no one with whom he can get close, no one to whom he can look up. He acts out his need for identification extravagantly and flagrantly, roaming the dark corners of strange towns and his own mind in order to express this need to identify with someone, even the great dead of bygone days.

During these years Eugene would go away from Pulpit Hill, by night and by day, when April was a young green blur, or when the Spring was deep and ripe. But he liked best to go away by night, rushing across a cool Spring countryside full of dew and starlight, under a great beach of the moon ribbed with clouds.

He would go to Exeter or Sydney; sometimes he would go to little towns he had never before visited. He would register at hotels as "Robert Herrick," "John Donne," "George Peele," "William Blake," and "John Milton." No one ever said anything to him about it. The people in those towns had such names. Once he registered at a hotel, in a small Piedmont town, as "Ben Jonson."

* Reprinted from *Look Homeward, Angel* by Thomas Wolfe (Copyright 1929, Charles Scribner's Sons. © 1957, Edward C. Aswell, as Administrator, C.T.A. of the Estate of Thomas Wolfe, and/or Fred W. Wolfe) with permission of the publisher. Pp. 596-598.

The clerk spun the book critically.

"Isn't there an *h* in that name?" he said.

"No," said Eugene. "That's another branch of the family. I have an uncle, Samuel, who spells his name that way."

Sometimes, at hotels of ill-repute he would register, with dark buried glee, as "Robert Browning," "Alfred Tennyson," and "William Wordsworth."

Once he registered as "Henry W. Longfellow."

"You can't fool me," said the clerk, with a hard grin of disbelief. "That's the name of a writer."

He was devoured by a vast strange hunger for life. At night, he listened to the million-noted ululation of little night things, the great brooding symphony of dark, the ringing of remote churchbells across the country. And his vision widened out in circles over moon-drenched meadows, dreaming woods, mighty rivers going along in darkness, and ten thousand sleeping towns. He believed in the infinite rich variety of all the towns and faces: behind any of a million shabby houses he believed there was strange buried life, subtle and shattered romance, something dark and unknown. At the moment of passing any house, he thought, someone therein might be at the gate of death, lovers might lie twisted in hot embrace, murder might be doing.

He felt a desperate frustration, as if he were being shut out from the rich banquet of life. And against all caution, he determined to break the pattern of custom, and look within. Driven on by this hunger, he would suddenly rush away from Pulpit Hill and, as dusk came on, prowl up and down the quiet streets of towns. Finally, lifted beyond all restraint, he would mount swiftly to a door and ring the bell. Then, to whoever came, reeling against the wall and clutching at his throat, he would say:

"Water! In God's name, water! I am ill!"

Sometimes there were women, seductive and smiling, aware of his trick, but loath to let him go; sometimes women touched with compassion and tenderness. Then, having drunk, he would smile with brave apology into startled and sympathetic faces, murmuring:

"Pardon me. It came on suddenly—one of my attacks. I had no time to go for help. I saw your light."

Then they would ask him where his friends were.

"Friends!" he glanced about wildly and darkly. Then,

with a bitter laugh, he said, "Friends! I have none! I am a stranger here."

Then they would ask him what he did.

"I am a Carpenter," he would answer, smiling strangely.

Then they would ask him where he came from.

"Far away. Very far," he would say deeply. "You would not know if I told you."

Then he would rise, looking about him with grandeur and compassion.

"And now I must go!" he would say mysteriously. "I have a long way to go before my journey is done. God bless you all! I was a stranger and you gave me shelter. The Son of Man was treated not so well."

Sometimes, he would ring bells with an air of timid inquiry, saying:

"Is this number 26? My name is Thomas Chatterton. I am looking for a gentleman by the name of Coleridge—Mr. Samuel T. Coleridge. Does he live here? . . . No? I'm sorry . . . Yes, 26 is the number I have, I'm sure . . . Thank you . . . I've made a mistake . . . I'll look it up in the telephone directory."

But what, thought Eugene, if one day, in the million streets of life, I should really find him?

These were the golden years.

The adolescent does identify with his parents to some extent but essentially he is trying to identify his own self, to be himself rather than any one else, to be free from the opinions of adults. The youngster is more apt to identify transitionally with a grownup other than parents, such as his teacher, or a sports or movie star because the latter do not control him to the same extent as parents. Not all of the struggle for identity is conscious. The adolescent's need to find and be himself is often a real defense against the revival of incestuous ties, a warding off of the recapitulation of infantile love objects and dependency needs. The tremendous impulse most adolescents have to belong to a gang, sorority, fraternity or some organized social group expresses a real need, which may or may not be conscious, to be part of an ongoing, successful group.

When he is not accepted or when he has not learned to act many different roles, the adolescent—like all age levels—learns to adjust by various means at his disposal. He learns to establish and maintain emotional equilibrium by his unconscious drives, by the dictates of social behavior, and by what he himself wants (9). He may repress uncomfortable feelings and keep them out of his consciousness. He may displace his angry feelings onto a substitute rather than the actual cause of the anger. John's father, in *Go Tell It on the Mountain,** has rejected him in favor of his younger brother Roy, who has just been involved in a serious scrape. Unable to vent his anger on Roy, the father takes it out on John.

There were some boys standing on the stoop. They watched him as he approached, and he tried not to look at them and to approximate the swagger with which they walked. One of them said as he mounted the short stone steps and started into the hall: "Boy, your brother was hurt real bad today."

He looked at them in a kind of dread, not daring to ask for details; and he observed that they, too, looked as though they had been in a battle; something hangdog in their looks suggested that they had been put to flight. Then he looked down, and saw that there was blood at the threshold, and blood spattered on the tile floor of the vestibule. He looked again at the boys, who had not ceased to watch him, and hurried up the stairs.

The door was half open—for Sarah's return, no doubt—and he walked in, making no sound, feeling a confused impulse to flee. There was no one in the kitchen, though the light was burning—the lights were on all through the house. On the kitchen table stood a shopping-bag filled with groceries, and he knew that his Aunt Florence had arrived. The washtub, where his mother had been washing earlier, was open still, and filled the kitchen with a sour smell.

There were drops of blood on the floor here too, and there

---

* From *Go Tell It on the Mountain* by James Baldwin. Reprinted by permission of the publishers, Alfred A. Knopf, Inc. Copyright, 1953. Pp. 46-50.

had been small, smudged coins of blood on the stairs as he walked up.

All this frightened him terribly. He stood in the middle of the kitchen, trying to imagine what had happened, and preparing himself to walk into the living-room, where all the family seemed to be. Roy had been in trouble before, but this new trouble seemed to be the beginning of the fulfillment of a prophecy. He took off his coat, dropping it on a chair, and was about to start into the living-room when he heard Sarah running up the steps.

He waited, and she burst through the door, carrying a clumsy parcel.

"What happened?" he whispered. She stared at him in astonishment, and a certain wild joy. He thought again that he really did not like his sister. Catching her breath, she blurted out, triumphantly: "Roy got stabbed with a knife!" and rushed into the living-room.

Roy got stabbed with a knife. Whatever this meant, it was sure that his father would be at his worst tonight. John walked slowly into the living-room.

His father and mother, a small basin of water between them, knelt by the sofa where Roy lay, and his father was washing the blood from Roy's forehead. It seemed that his mother, whose touch was so much more gentle, had been thrust aside by his father, who could not bear to have anyone else touch his wounded son. And now she watched, one hand in the water, the other, in a kind of anguish, at her waist, which was circled still by the improvised apron of the morning. Her face, as she watched, was full of pain and fear, of tension barely supported, and of pity that could scarcely have been expressed had she filled all the world with her weeping. His father muttered sweet, delirious things to Roy, and his hands, when he dipped them again in the basin and wrung out the cloth, were trembling. Aunt Florence, still wearing her hat and carrying her handbag, stood a little removed, looking down at them with a troubled, terrible face.

Then Sarah bounded into the room before him, and his mother looked up, reached out for the package, and saw him. She said nothing, but she looked at him with a strange, quick intentness, almost as though there were a warning on her tongue which at the moment she did not dare to utter.

His Aunt Florence looked up, and said: "We been wondering where you was, boy. This bad brother of yours done gone out and got hisself hurt."

But John understood from her tone that the fuss was, possibly, a little greater than the danger—Roy was not, after all, going to die. And his heart lifted a little. Then his father turned and looked at him.

"Where you been boy," he shouted, "all this time? Don't you know you's needed here at home?"

More than his words, his face caused John to stiffen instantly with malice and fear. His father's face was terrible in anger, but now there was more than anger in it. John saw now what he had never seen there before, except in his own vindicative fantasies: a kind of wild, weeping terror that made the face seem younger, and yet at the same time unutterably older and more cruel. And John knew, in the moment his father's eyes swept over him, that he hated John because John was not lying on the sofa where Roy lay. John could scarcely meet his father's eyes, and yet, briefly, he did, saying nothing, feeling in his heart an odd sensation of triumph, and hoping in his heart that Roy, to bring his father low, would die.

His mother had unwrapped the package and was opening a bottle of peroxide. "Here," she said, "you better wash it with this now." Her voice was calm and dry; she looked at his father briefly, her face unreadable, as she handed him the bottle and the cotton.

"This going to hurt," his father said—in such a different voice, so sad and tender!—turning again to the sofa. "But you just be a little man and hold still; it ain't going to take long."

John watched and listened, hating him. Roy began to moan. Aunt Florence moved to the mantelpiece and put her handbag down near the metal serpent. From the room behind him, John heard the baby begin to whimper.

"John," said his mother, "go and pick her up like a good boy." Her hands, which were not trembling, were still busy: she had opened the bottle of iodine and was cutting up strips of bandage.

John walked into his parents' bedroom and picked up the squalling baby, who was wet. The moment Ruth felt him lift her up she stopped crying and stared at him with a wide-eyed, pathetic stare, as though she knew that there was trouble in the house. John laughed at her so ancient-seeming distress—he was very fond of his baby sister—and whispered in her ear as he started back to the living-room: "Now, you let your big brother tell you something, baby. Just as soon as you's able to stand on your feet, you run away from *this* house, run far away." He did not quite know why he said this, or where he wanted her to run, but it made him feel instantly better.

While the father displaces his anger onto John, the latter, frustrated because he fears to show his resentment toward his father, displaces his rage in turn by telling his infant sister what *she* should do when she grows up! There are many other ways by which people learn to adjust to troublesome situations. There is the very sweet girl who can refuse a favor to no one because she may have learned, quite unconsciously, that this is the best way for her to make peace in her world. In the chapter "On Choosing a Career," it will be seen how the mechanism of projection is used by many parents in the selection of an occupation for their children. Such parents, and many teachers as well, attempt to influence and control another person so that they may live out their own needs. Many adolescents, as well as their parents and teachers, use projection to ascribe to others those characteristics of their own personalities which they do not particularly admire. The high school or college student who has been found cheating on a quiz may subsequently become a paragon of honesty, suspicious of every other student, projecting onto them his own feelings of inadequacy, self-contempt or whatever it is he may be feeling.

Lying and stealing are still other forms of adjustment. Almost all children lie to escape punishment, to cover attitudes of inferiority or guilt and to enhance their prestige (14). Stealing has its basis in a multiplicity of adjustive causes. Sometimes the youngster feels a real sense of deprivation and in order to compensate for this feeling, steals. It may be he has been deprived of candy or of parental love;

his emotional hunger for either, or for what they represent, may prompt such symbolic behavior. George, the young adolescent protagonist in *The Fool Killer,** has in a very real sense been deprived of the food of life and love, and in his search for both, he lies and steals. George has run away from home because he has found no sustenance there. In the home of the Galts, he has had his first real taste of love; but his past deprivations egg him on for more and, at the age of twelve, he engages in a very brief career of pilfering.

Galts done like they promised and give me my nickel ever week, along with a receipt for the twenty cents they banked for me. I kept them nickels under the paper of my dresser drawer, with the quarter I found in the road, and sometimes I'd get em all out to hold and count and chink against one another. For the life of me I couldn't decide whether when I'd saved up five I'd trade them in for a quarter so's I'd have two, or take the first quarter and the five nickels to trade for a fifty-cent piece. One time I'd decide one way, another time, another.

Then one day Miz Galt says to me, "George, don't forget you get your candy wholesale price at the store. I never saw a boy before didn't want to spend his money on candy!"

And I hemmed and hawed and says finally, "Yes, mam— no, mam—I been saving up—I ain't got much of a sweet tooth."

Which meant that besides having become a thief, I'd gone back to being a liar, too.

Because I'd been stealing candy right along.

They ain't no use to say I ain't ashamed to tell it, because I am. And you can believe me or not, I was ashamed when I done it, too, only it didn't stop me. I often wisht I'd had the chance to tell Milo about it and have him explain to me how a person could act so. But I never did.

The best I can say is something like this: I always did love candy, long as I can remember—jawbreakers and licorish and pepmint sticks and butterscotch and taffy—anything you can name. And I'd never before et my fill of it—never in

---

* From *The Fool Killer* by Helen Eustis. Copyright 1954 by Helen Eustis. Reprinted by permission of Doubleday & Co., Inc. Pp. 169-179.

my life. The Old Crab and the Old Man never bought none, that was sure, and it was only once in a blue moon back there when I was with them that I'd run a errand for some other folks and earn a cent, or once I found a whole nickel under the church steps.

When I went to work in the store, Mr. Galt says I was to wait on the children wanted candy; he told me how much was each kind, and showed me the kegs down underneath the counter which I was to fill the jars from when they got empty. All the time he was explaining it, my mouth was watering so bad he must of noticed it, for he says, "Have a piece, George," and I says, "Thank you, sir," and taken a jaw-breaker-green.

He never said nothing about not to take any without saying so, so, thinks I: *If I sell it to them others, why shouldn't I to myself?* Right off, I begun taking a piece ever now and then, but making a mark on a piece of paper ever time, so's at the end of the week I'd know how much I owed, and pay up.

But then, it must of been I took one more often than you'd think was likely, because when the end of the week come and I got my nickel, I added up the marker, meaning to pay for sure, and it was twenty cents. I mean twenty cents wholesale.

I put the marker in my pocket, and I thought: *I'll tell em tomorrow.* 'Twas my first week working for them and already I had run up a debt I couldn't pay. Course, they had the twenty cents belonged to me, but I'd agreed I wasn't to touch that until I left for good. And then, they was the quarter I picked up in the road. But some way I couldn't get myself to part with that until I couldn't think of nothing else at all. Like I said, I'd never had a whole quarter at once before.

I guess 'twas the night after that I begun to dream of the Fool Killer again, and woken in the night, tossing and turning. *Even if I give my quarter,* I'd think, *I can just see her thinking how much candy I ate, and laughing at me! It was a lot, I reckon, but, well, I ate it, and I can't see nothing funny in it . . . But worsen that, supposen they reckon they can't trust me no more if I buy on credit like that without telling no one, and they say, "We're sorry, but we think we'll look for another boy"? Then I'd lose my quarter and the job and not have nobody to travel with me no more and—it ain't fair! Other boys has folks buys them candy and clothes and keeps them till they're growed, and don't nobody say they got unusual luck! I never asked to be no orphan! I run away on my own hook, to be sure, but . . .*

Well, the upshot of it was, I got up then and there, in the middle of the night; taken the marker out of my pants pocket, tore it up in little pieces, chewed the pieces, and spit the wad out the window in the top of the maple tree, went back to bed and had bad dreams. And I never said nothing about the candy—just went on taking it—stealing it—with nobody noticing or saying nothing until she asked me why wasn't I buying none that day.

After that, I figgered I ought to be careful and not take none for a while . . . But that was the whole thing of it. I'd never of taken any at all if it hadn't been for having such a terrible hankering I couldn't stop myself . . . Oh, haven't you ever felt so—known you was doing wrong, but kept on doing it? And not only wrong. Wrong or wicked or sinful I could of stood easier. What about drove me crazy was knowing all the time what a blamed fool I was. Because I known the Galts was good to me; they fed me fine, and give me time off and never worked me to death; first she borryed them clothes for me, then she made some of my own out of his old ones cut down; this week they was talking of driving me over to town with him to buy me some brand-new shoes so's I could go to church with them—not that that'd be any treat. Another thing, sometimes of a afternoon, Miz Galt'd make doughnuts. Then she'd tell me to go get a good straight stick and clean it off. When I brought it in, she'd say take it in my fist and hold it up, and she'd drop warm doughnuts on it, right to the top . . . Why, I even took to saying my prayers at night without nobody telling me I should so's I could put Galts in the God-blesses along with Milo and my ma and pa which I'd never knowed . . . Yet there I was, robbing them all the while—and why? Because I had a sweet tooth. Wasn't no better answer. Well, if the Fool Killer wouldn't come for a person acting so, who'd he bother with at all?

But it didn't last long after that day she passed the remark about me buying candy . . . The time I usually done it was right after dinner, when Mr. Galt'd lay down on the parlor sofa for a snooze, and she'd be in the kitchen, washing up.

After I'd got the hang of things, that was the time they'd send me up front to tend store by myself. Not many folks would come in that time of day; the store'd be shady and cool; I'd set in the rocker, dreaming about Milo, mostly, and ever now and then I'd sneak down by the candy kegs and take a piece. I might as well of took a handful in the first place. But each time I'd fool myself that this time would be the last.

Well, she caught me at it. I guess they was a wagon going by on the road, making a rattle so's I didn't hear her footsteps in the hall. The first I heard was her voice saying, "George." I had my hand right in the keg and my mouth full. I just froze.

"Are you buying that candy or taking it?" she says.

I dropped what was in my hand and straightened up, but I couldn't look at her, nor say nothing at all.

"I think you're taking it," she says. "I think maybe you been taking it quite a time."

"I—" I started out, but then they wasn't nothing more to say.

"Answer me, George. Is that true?"

I looked at her, then, and she was looking at me like that first time she caught me in the lie, with her eyes like rifle shots going right through. I couldn't say nothing, only nod and look at the floor.

"Go to your room and stay there," she says. "I won't say more until I thought what to do."

So I come towards her to go through the door, and when I passed her, I noticed the way she stepped back like she didn't want to have nothing more to do with me, which made me feel worse than anything.

I went up to my room and closed the door. Nobody come near me all the afternoon. I could hear folks' voices in the road, and footsteps and talking I couldn't make out down below me in the store; I wondered did she mean for me to do my evening chores, or stay there until I was told; I got out my nickels and my quarter and turned them over a little, like I was kind of saying goodbye, because I figgered I'd pay my debts before I left, anyways. Then I lain on the bed, looking at the shipwreck picture, and feeling miserable. I thought of that first time I run away, and I known that running away and being turned out is surely two different things.

Finally I heard footsteps coming up the stairs and acrost the upstairs hall. They was too heavy to be hers.

It's him, is it? thinks I, and all to once I was mad, for a lot of things, all mixed up in my mind. *He never gives a person the time of day; can't tell you if you done right or wrong; don't know if you're a human being or a ghost and don't care! Let him tell me to go! 'Twas her took me in and was good to me mostly anyways!* Then I jumped off the bed and taken the money in my hand.

"Here's your money!" I says, the minute he opened the door. "Don't need to tell me to go—I'm going! But I ain't no thief! I'm going to pay! I may be a orphan and rag, tag, and bobtail, but I ain't no thief! And you can keep the rest of what I earned, too! I got along before and I'll get along again! I don't need to be beholden to nobody!"

He just stood there, looking biggern usual, and it got awful quiet. Then he says:

"Put the money on the dresser."

I didn't want to, yet I didn't know what else to do, so I put it there.

Then he set down on the bed. "Lay over my knees," he says, and I known he was going to lick me, and he was a awful big feller, and I was scared.

"You ain't my pa!" I yells.

"Never said I was," says he. "Lay over my knees!"

"I won't!" I hollers.

"Oh yes, you will!" says he, and he taken hold of the back of my neck and bent me over as easy as a green twig. Then he held me down with the one hand while with the other, he walloped the daylights out of me. 'Tweren't but a hand licking, and I don't think it went on so terrible long, but I can't think of nothing to compare with it but getting kicked by a mule. I cussed and swore all the bad words I known while he was starting out, but at last I come to bawl. Finally he quit and let go my neck. I stood up. He taken a bandana handkerchief outen his pocket and handed it to me, saying, "Blow your nose." I blown, but I couldn't stop bawling yet.

He kept on setting. "Why did you do it?" says he.

That set me off blubbering worse. 'Twas enough to get a licking without a jawing, too.

"Quit carrying on," he says. "Why did you do it?"

I couldn't stop crying, but finally I says, "I—I never had enough candy before!"

"Why didn't you pay for it?" he says.

"I *said* I'd pay for it! I'll give you the money—you—you—"

"You wouldn't of if you hadn't been caught," he says. "Now you listen to me, George, and listen hard. Ever hot spell, candy melts and I lose moren you could of et in twice the time. I ain't worrying about the candy nor the money neither, because I just ain't that hard up. What I want to know is this. How did you feel when you was taking it?"

I didn't say nothing, nor look at him, just blown my nose once more.

"Maybe they's men can go on stealing and feeling right with thesselves at the same time, but from what I've seed of you so far, you ain't going to be that kind of a man. So you might's well give up the habit right now, because they ain't nothing in the world you're going to want enough to make up for how stealing it will make you feel."

"It ain't a habit," I says, choking some. "I never done it before."

"Well," he says, and got up from the bed, "don't do it again. I'll say no more." And he went out the door and shut it behind.

Then I lain down on the bed (on my stomach) and reglar bellered. I couldn't even think of Milo, because I known even he'd be ashamed of me. I tried to think about the Fool Killer, and how maybe he'd come for me this time at last, but it seemed like that was when I finally known for sure that only a baby could believe in that tale. Because I'd almost of felt better if he *had* come after me, then and there.

I was bawling still when, after a long time more, footsteps come—hers, this time—and I heard her open the door. I just lain with my face in the piller and went on sobbing there.

"All right, George," she says. "You had the pleasure of feeling like a miserable sinner long enough. Set up and eat your supper."

I lain still, but the bawling stopped.

"Come on," she says. "You done wrong, you got licked, and that's that."

But I still couldn't move.

"Now listen, George," she says, "I see you're feeling sorry for yourself, but I hope you don't by no chance think I'm going to feel sorry for you, too. I'll tell you who I'm sorry for, which may come to you as something of a surprise. I'm sorry for Mr. Galt, because it ain't easy to give somebody a licking when you ain't angry and you ain't naturally mean, but because you think it's right. I seen him before he come up here, and I seen him after he come down, and he didn't look like he'd enjoyed himself no moren you. Now get up off that bed right now, *and I mean it!*"

I could tell she did, so I got up, handling myself kind of ginger, because, to tell the truth, I was sore.

Then she set down on the bed and says, "Turn round and take down your pants."

She still didn't sound like it was time for arguing, so I done what she said.

"Hmm!" she says, and laid her hand on the place, real gentle and cool. "I'm going to get some witch hazel and rub you off. That'll feel good." And then—there she was, off again. She begun to laugh. "Oh, George," she says, "you really got a humdinger, now didn't you? That was a licking a boy could be proud of, it really was—I can see!"

Now here was the thing about the way she'd laugh at me. 'Twas always some kind of teasing so it would start off making me mad, yet there was always something in it—maybe just the catchy laugh she had—would get me going, too. What's there to laugh at in having your own tail warmed so's you can't set down easy for several days? Not a dad-burned thing! Yet she got me doing it, too—still half mad, but not able to stop it—till there was the two of us, laughing over nothing so awful funny *I* could see, until the tears run down.

"There!" she says finally. "Get your nightshirt on and I'll bathe your battle scars. Your supper's on the tray."

So I undressed while she went off for the witch hazel; she put it on and set with me while I et, telling me different stories of mischief she got into when she was a youngun; then she made me go to bed though it weren't but dusk-dark, and before she taken out the tray and the lamp, she leaned over to tuck me in, and kissed me on the cheek like a baby or a girl.

I didn't mind much at all.

George had not established effective controls to prevent his thefts. Typically with such children, love itself has no particular value; it has proved to be an ephemeral experience at best (11). But with George's acceptance by his foster parents, who were insightful and understanding and handled the situation ably and with dispatch, his stealing becomes meaningful when he, as a total personality, and the home of which he is a part, become discernable. Sometimes, however, the adolescent may experience a single, traumatic situation which teaches him, rightly or wrongly, that he must behave one way in order to maintain his emotional integrity. Such an experience is recounted in André Gide's *The Counterfeiters.** The speaker has learned that in order to prevent herself from being hurt, she will have to hurt others before they can get at her.

She settled down on the rug beside the bed, crouching between Vincent's legs like an Egyptian statue, with her chin resting on her knees. When she had eaten and drunk, she began:
"I was on the *Bourgogne,* you know, on the day of the wreck. I was seventeen, so now you know how old I am. I was a very good swimmer, and to show you that I'm not hard-hearted, I'll tell you that if my first thought was to save myself, my second was to save someone else. I'm not quite sure even if it wasn't my first. Or rather, I don't think I thought of anything; but nothing disgusts me so much in such moments as the people who only think of themselves —oh, yes—the women who scream. There was a first boatload, chiefly of women and children, and some of them yelled to such an extent that it was enough to make anyone lose his head. The boat was so badly handled that instead of dropping down on the sea straight, it dived nose foremost and everyone in it was flung out before it even had time to fill with water. The whole scene took place by the light of torches and lanterns and search-lights. You can't imagine how ghastly it was. The waves were very big and everything

* From *The Counterfeiters*, by André Gide. Reprinted by permission of Alfred A. Knopf, Inc. Copyright 1952. Pp. 56-58.

that was not in the light was lost in darkness on the other side of the hill of water.

"I have never lived more intensely; but I was as incapable of reflection as a Newfoundland dog, I suppose, when he jumps into the water. I can't even understand now what happened; I only know that I had noticed a little girl in the boat—a darling thing of about five or six; and when I saw the boat overturn, I immediately made up my mind that it was her I would save. She was with her mother, but the poor woman was a bad swimmer; and as usual in such cases, her skirts hampered her. As for me, I expect I undressed mechanically; I was called to take my place in the second boatload. I must have got in; and then I no doubt jumped straight into the sea out of the boat; all I can remember is swimming about for a long time with the child clinging to my neck. It was terrified and clutched me so tight that I couldn't breathe. Luckily the people in the boat saw us and either waited for us or rowed towards us. But that's not why I'm telling you this story. The recollection which remains most vividly with me and which nothing will ever efface from my mind and my heart is this—There were about forty or so of us in the boat, all crowded together, for a number of swimmers had been picked up at the last gasp like me. The water was almost on a level with the edge of the boat. I was in the stern and I was holding the little girl I had just saved tightly pressed against me to warm her—and to prevent her from seeing what I couldn't help seeing myself—two sailors, one armed with a hatchet and the other with a kitchen chopper. And what do you think they were doing? . . . They were hacking off the fingers and hands of the swimmers who were trying to get into our boat. One of these sailors (the other was a Negro) turned to me, as I set there, my teeth chattering with cold and fright and horror, and said, 'If another single one gets in we shall be bloody well done for. The boat's full.' And he added it was a thing that had to be done in all shipwrecks, but that naturally one didn't mention it.

"I think I fainted then; at any rate, I can't remember anything more, just as one remains deaf for a long time after a noise that has been too tremendous.

"And when I came to myself on board the X., which picked us up, I realized I was no longer the same, that I never could again be the same sentimental young girl I had been before; I realized that a part of myself had gone down with the *Bourgogne*; that henceforth there would be a whole heap of delicate feelings whose fingers and hands I should hack away to prevent them from climbing into my heart and wrecking it."

She looked at Vincent out of the corner of her eye and, with a backward twist of her body, went on: "It's a habit one must get into."

This may seem a ruthless way to adjust to life and fortunately comparatively few adolescents learn this method. The adolescent characteristically is secretive about himself and his feelings. Most of the time it is extremely difficult for him to express how he does feel. Furthermore, even if he can put his feelings into words, he is reluctant to expose himself to others (12). A more common adjustive mechanism is daydreaming. Every one daydreams. The child's dream of being Buck Rogers or Superman is a science-age youngster's view of the old fairy tales and magic. His older brother sees himself making the winning touchdown or modestly accepting a Nobel Prize for his world-shaking discoveries. His fifteen-year-old sister buys a new sweater and works up a little scene, as she tries it on, in which all the boys are devastated and all the girls envious. Dad and Mother are giving their imagination free play, too. Dad sees himself owning the business, buying that new car. Mom may see herself ringing the dinner bell for the maid to bring in the next course.

Fantasies like Superman help the child to develop a feeling of strength and power and serve to drain off some of his irrepressible energy. His teen-age brother sees himself, whether in his dreams of football glory or in some fantastic scientific achievement, as temporarily accepting responsibility and achieving self-esteem and prestige among the fellows. His adolescent sister begins to anticipate her role as a woman in her view of herself as desirable and popular. Dad and Mother are able to forget some of their anxieties in daydreams that give them some of the comforts real life may lack.

A certain amount of daydreaming is therefore normal, necessary, and good for all of us. For some, it makes a bleak world more habitable. Others begin to anticipate, in a fantasy world where one is powerful, the responsibilities and satisfactions which solid work in a real world may help to achieve. "When we cannot act, don't we all retire to our imaginations for solace?" asks Allan Seager's *Amos Berry*. "Would not the history of anyone's imagination present a series of little dramas, sumptuously produced, violent, gloomy, or ecstatic as the occasion required but enacted indoors for an audience of one with nothing at all showing on the billboards outside?"

For adolescents, however, daydreaming may present a real hazard. The adolescent must leave the world of the child. He must make friends, be popular, find love and fall in love, prepare for the right job, and he does not yet feel entirely ready. In daydreams, the world remains static, manageable. It may seem like a more attractive world than the one in which rebuffs, disappointments, insensitive adults, and uninteresting tasks are part of the daily portion. He needs kindness and understanding on the part of adults and stimulating and enjoyable experiences to help him find real life more exciting than imagination.

In H. G. Wells's *tour de force, The Bulpington of Blup,** Theodore Bulpington uses daydreams to satisfy his unfulfilled wants and to compensate for some very real inferiorities. Theodore, who has bestowed upon himself the imaginative title of "The Bulpington of Blup," has been rejected by his sweetheart, Margaret, in favor of another chap, Laverock.

His reverie took to itself scenery. A wild tumult of rocks mounted to the snows above, and below, on a gigantic cliff, lonely and cold now in the light of eve, was a large bare building. It was the Alpine retreat of the Trappists. A

* From *The Bulpington of Blup* by H. G. Wells. Reprinted by permission of the Executors of the Estate of H. G. Wells. Copyright 1933. Macmillan Co. Pp. 334-335.

solitary figure halted upon a craggy crest, a knapsacked figure, a dark lean man still young, but with a face worn by suffering, seared by pain. He stood for a time looking up at the sky and sea and mountain crests, then turned as if for a last farewell to where, far down the valley, the cities and the villages of the great plains of life spread blue and dim. At last he sighed deeply and began to descend the steep path towards the monastery. They were awaiting him. The grave old janitor answered the jangling bell. He was led through the cool clean corridors to the little chapel and there, dropping his knapsack, as Christian once had dropped his burthen, he sank to his knees before the altar. He became as still as a stone. The stormy heart of the Bulpington of Blup had found peace at last.

The scene changed to a snowstorm so terrible that none had ventured forth albeit the dogs—(Do the Trappists keep St. Bernard dogs? Never mind; *these* Trappists did)—although the dogs had shown by their baying that there were travellers lost upon the mountains. None—save the most intrepid of all, the indefatigable Father Theodore.

A struggle with the whirling elements; stumbling; blinded, near frozen; and at last the faithful creatures guide him to where, cowering under a ledge, are two lost and terrified mountaineers, a woman and a man.

"Take me!" cries the man. "Save *me*! I can't endure it."

The woman, crouched on the inner recess, says not a word.

"We have met before, Laverock," says the priest. "Spite of my vows, I take the woman first."

He lifts her in his arms. A faint stir of response shows that she is not insensible.

Does she whisper, "Theodore"?

But the struggle home is too terrible. They stumble and fall. The very dogs lose their sense of direction. In the morning they are found—reunited in death.

Theodore sighed in his seat and stirred. The reveries faded as a dream fades, but he was aware of an immense consolation.

Theodore's daydreams were not unhealthy in themselves; they became unhealthy because of their excessive frequency. All through life, "The Bulpington" thought he achieved the satisfactions of his motives but he never realized real accomplishment. He found the rewards of reality pale by comparison with his daydreams and the last we see of "The Bulpington" is his resort to pathological lying as an extension of his excessive and profound use of fantasy.

In a very comparable situation but in a healthier vein, a more normal adolescent's daydreams about unrequited love is described in *Seventeen*.*

It is to be supposed that William considered his condition a lonely one, but if all the seventeen-year-olds who have known such half-hours could have shown themselves to him then, he would have fled from the mere horror of billions. Alas! he considered his sufferings a new invention in the world, and there was now inspired in his breast a monologue so eloquently bitter that it might deserve some such title as A Passion Beside the Smoke-house. During the little time that William spent in this sequestration he passed through phases of emotion which would have kept an older man busy for weeks and left him wrecked at the end of them.

William's final mood was one of beautiful resignation with a kick in it; that is, he nobly gave her up to George and added irresistibly that George was a big, fat lummox! Painting pictures, such as the billions of other young sufferers before him have painted, William saw himself a sad, gentle old bachelor at the family fireside, sometimes making the sacrifice of his reputation so that *she* and the children might never know the truth about George; and he gave himself the solace of a fierce scene or two with George: "Remember, it is for them, not you—you *thing*!"

After this human little reaction he passed to a higher field of romance. He would die for George—and then she would bring the little boy she had named William to the lonely headstone—Suddenly William saw himself in his true and fitting character—Sydney Carton! He had lately read *A Tale of Two Cities,* immediately rereading until, as he would have said, he "knew it by heart"; and even at the time he had seen resemblances between himself and the appealing

* From *Seventeen* by Booth Tarkington. Reprinted by permission of Harper and Brothers. Copyright 1915, 1916 by the Metropolitan Magazine Co.; copyright 1943, 1944 by Booth Tarkington. Pp. 186-188.

figure of Carton. Now that the sympathy between them was perfected by Miss Pratt's preference for another, William decided to mount the scaffold in place of George Crooper. The scene became actual to him, and, setting one foot upon a tin milk-pail which some one had carelessly left beside the smoke-house, he lifted his eyes to the pitiless blue sky and unconsciously assumed the familiar attitude of Carton on the steps of the guillotine. He spoke aloud those great last words:

"It is a far, far better thing that I do, than I have ever done; it is a far, far better rest that I go to—"

A whiskered head on the end of a long, corrugated red neck protruded from the smoke-house door.

"What say?" it inquired, huskily.

"Nun-nothing!" stammered William.

Eyes above whiskers became fierce. "You take your feet off that milk-bucket. Say! This here's a sanitary farm. 'Ain't you got any more sense 'n to go an'—"

But William had abruptly removed his foot and departed.

Willie, it can be predicted, will survive Miss Pratt's preference for another. Theodore Bulpington, on the other hand, will use nearly every defense mechanism available to him in order to get along but in a maladaptive way. He will rationalize and say that Margaret "isn't good or intelligent enough" for him. This is the "sour grapes" mechanism. He will say that "no one understands" him, just as his father said before him. This is introjection, an unconscious form of identification, where unbeknownst to himself, the individual takes on the ideals, values and attitudes of another person. The Bulpington will say that "marriage is not for him" and return to an earlier point in his development where he feels safe and secure. This is regression.

It is normal to use these mechanisms; everyone does at one time or another. When the adolescent rationalizes, he is finding a "good" excuse which satisfies him when he wants to follow his own wishes. It is an attempt to make his conduct appear suitable. The tennis player, after missing a lob, looks at his racket; the poor workman blames his tools; the awkward adolescent, knocking his shin against a chair, kicks the chair. When the adolescent is not accepted by a group, he will say, "Who wants to be friends with them, anyhow?" Natalie and Rosalind, two college freshmen living in a girls' dormitory, console themselves in this fashion in Shirley Jackson's *Hangsaman*.*

A knock on her door was as strange a thing to her as the fact of the door itself; at first she thought, It is across the hall, how clearly it sounds; then she thought, It is a mistake; she wasted a minute thinking of someone looking at the outside of the door steadfastly, as she looked at the inside, and meant to mark the next day whether the panels outside were the same as those inside; odd, she thought, that someone standing outside could look at the door, straight ahead, seeing the white paint and the wood, and I inside looking at the door and the white paint and the wood should look straight also, and we two looking should not see each other because there is something in the way. Are two people regarding the same thing not looking at each other?

The knock came again. "Come in," occurred to Natalie then as a reasonable thing to say, but the door was locked, so she stumbled, hastily and spilling her book, off the bed and across the room and finally remembered how to turn the key and open the door.

"Yes?" she said blindly, now that the door was removed.

"Hello," said the girl outside; Natalie remembered, as though once the door was opened the world outside it slowly established itself, small section after small section—as though, in fact, it had not been prepared tonight for Natalie to open her door again, and had been caught completely unaware, and was putting a bold face on things and getting everything back together as quickly as possible, so that Natalie should not perceive it, looking through her door, and say, "Just as I thought; this confirms everything I have always suspected"—she remembered, slowly, seeing the girl's face before and then, that her name was Rosalind.

"Hello," Natalie said.

* From *Hangsaman* by Shirley Jackson. Copyright 1951 by Shirley Jackson. Used by permission of the publishers, Farrar, Straus and Cudahy, Inc. Pp. 84-91.

"Are you busy?" Rosalind said, leaning slightly to look over Natalie's shoulder and into her room. "I mean, I just thought I'd come over and say hello, but if you're busy . . ."

"No," said Natalie, surprised. "I'm not at all busy." She stood away from the door, and Rosalind came into the room, looking around curiously, as though she had not left one just like it immediately before, although perhaps Rosalind's bedspread was blue instead of patterned, and she had perhaps been reading different books, and the clothes in the closet would of course be different.

"I wanted to talk to someone," Rosalind offered; once in, she sat quickly on the bed and tucked her feet under her. "I saw your light on and thought that since we didn't know each other very well it might be a good time to come and make friends with you."

"I'm glad," Natalie said. She was happy at having been disturbed; her books would still be there after Rosalind left, and who knew what odd thoughts and notions Rosalind might have brought with her? Natalie sat uneasily on the desk chair, knowing it was her duty to speak, and able to think of nothing but the list of irregular French verbs she would not be able to remember half so clearly tomorrow. "I was just trying to do my French," she said, with an embarrassed laugh that she deplored.

"French," Rosalind said, and shuddered. "I'm glad I took Spanish."

"Is Spanish terribly hard?" Natalie asked politely.

"Listen," Rosalind said, obviously feeling that the amenities were over and it was time to get down to business, "do *you* know any of the girls around here?"

"No," said Natalie, "not very many." Not that I *want* to know them, she longed to add, I'm *very* careful about my friends, I dislike knowing lots of people, I don't make friends easily because I keep them for a long time, I make friends slowly and with discrimination, I devote myself to my studies . . . "Not any of them, really," Natalie said.

"That's what I thought," Rosalind said! "Did you *ever* see anything like them? I mean, they certainly aren't very *friendly.*"

"I haven't really tried—" Natalie said.

"Peggy Spencer and *her* friends," Rosalind said disdainfully. "Helen Burton and *her* friends . . . and such a noise going on all night. I can't even *sleep.*"

"I've never had any trouble getting to sleep," Natalie said eagerly.

"We ought to show them they're not so very special," Rosalind said. She lifted her chin and shrugged. "You go into one of their rooms and they're all there and they stop talking and say, 'Yes?' as though you were a beggar until you turn around and go and then you can hear them laughing after you shut the door. I don't think they're *that* important, I *must* say."

"I've never gone into any of their rooms," Natalie said, feeling that she had an end of this conversation to keep up.

"Well, you know what they say about *you*," Rosalind said. She looked at Natalie as though for the first time aware of the particular person she was addressing, calling to mind this person's special liabilities. "*They* say you're crazy. You sit here in your room all day and all night and never go out and *they* say *you're* crazy."

"I go out to class," Natalie said quickly.

"They say you're spooky," Rosalind said. "That's what they call you, Spooky, I heard them."

"Who?" Natalie said. "*Who* knows what I do?"

"Well, *I* think it's your own business," said Rosalind critically. "I mean, everyone has the right to live the way they want, and naturally none of *them* has any right to call a person names just because a person wants to live their own way."

Feeling a sudden quick warmth toward Rosalind for not having watched her, Natalie said, "All I want them to do is leave me alone."

"Well, *that's* what *I* say," Rosalind said, "but if you really don't belong to their little crowd, *naturally* they think you're crazy, and they never even stop to think that maybe you and I don't *want* to run around with people like *that,* and what I'd like to know is how does anyone get to belong with them if they look at you like you were a beggar and then laugh when you go out? Does it really seem *fair?*"

"What they think is actually not at all important," Natalie said with dignity.

Even as she spoke she knew her position, and her mind, racing ahead of her, was counting over its special private blessings: there was her father, of course, although he seemed, right now, far away and helpless against laughing girls, there was Arthur Langdon and the fact that she seemed, more than any other, to be comprehending and alert in his class, and had received a sort of recognition, as though they were kindred, from him—but then perhaps, she thought, frightened, perhaps not everyone thought of Arthur Langdon's regard as special. Perhaps he was not so valuable to these watching, laughing girls as other things. Natalie had never heard of. But then, of course, there was always and beyond all laughter and beyond all scrutiny her own sweet dear home of a mind, where she was safe, protected, priceless . . . "They're trivial people, really. Mediocre."

"Try and get anywhere *without* them," Rosalind said cynically. "They're *every*thing."

Not everything, Natalie thought hastily, not quite everything. Not the place ten, fifteen, twenty years from now, the place of pure honor and glory, from which one perhaps looked down and said, "*Who?* What was the name, please? Did I ever meet you before? In *college?* Dear heaven, so *long* ago . . ."

"They get away with murder," Rosalind said. "Think any of *them* has to do what *we* do?" She put out her lip sullenly and began to swing one foot back and forth. Looking at her, Natalie saw clearly what had not seemed important before now: that Rosalind was squat and ugly, and had a drab dull face and a faint growth of hair on her upper lip. "Listen," Rosalind said, "you know that girl, the skinny one who's such a good friend of Peggy Burton's? The one they call Max, because her name's Maxine? Well, the reason *she* went away last weekend was because she had an *abortion.*"

"Oh," said Natalie.

"Heard them talking about it through the door," Rosalind said. "And Peggy Burton—*she's* only been lucky. You know that guy of hers, the football player?" She nodded emphatically, and glanced slyly at Natalie. "I mean," she said, "not that I want to repeat scandal, but they're *all* like that. We ought to be thankful we don't have more to do with them. I mean, I'm *sure* the college people know all about them, and if you hang around with them, first thing you know they think the same about *you.*"

"About me?" said Natalie. Far off, in the untouched, lonely places of her mind, an echo came: It isn't true, it didn't happen . . .

"Not that either of *us,*" Rosalind said, and laughed lightly.

"I mean," she said, looking again at Natalie, "I know about *me,* and I guess about *you.*"

Pride caught at Natalie; here was this hideous girl attempting an alliance on the grounds that Natalie was—what? was there a word? (Innocent? Who was innocent—this girl with her nasty eyes? Chaste? Chaste meant no impure thoughts; virginal meant clear and clean and could not include this Rosalind with her low coarse face; untouched? Spotless? Pure?) Could I, Natalie thought, in the second when her eyes met Rosalind's, could I possibly associate on any grounds with this girl? Whichever way I speak, she will follow me. "It isn't true," she said.

"Of *course* it's true," Rosalind said indignantly. "Don't I hear them talking every night through the wall? Some nights they're in there giggling until I think I'll go crazy, things you and I don't even think about, much less talk about, and then when I pound on the wall you'd think *I* was the one, the way they yell back."

"I mean," Natalie said apologetically, "if *we* don't meddle with *them* . . ."

Rosalind shrugged. "I just think it's terrible," she said, "them thinking they're so good, and the things they do. What they don't realize is that no one *wants* to be in their crowd, for fear of having people think things about them."

Suddenly (and it gave a sudden clear picture of her decision to come here in the first place: suddenly, on a phrase, perhaps not even considered, so that she knocked on Natalie's door at random, because it was the third from the end of the hall, or because the door somehow resembled, in some mystic, impossible way, the door to her own room, far away at home) she rose, pushed her hair back with an unattractive gesture, and said wearily, "Anyway, I wouldn't want anyone knowing *I* had anything to do with them."

"Of course not," said Natalie helplessly; she answered the girl's leaving as she had answered her coming, without volition, without desire, without conviction.

"Listen," said Rosalind, as though it were a sudden idea, "let's go to breakfast together tomorrow. OK?"

"I have an early class," said Natalie hastily.

"So do *I*," said Rosalind. "I'll come and knock on your door about seven-thirty. You be ready."

"I don't know if I'll have breakfast before class," Natalie said. "I always wake up so late—"

"I'll see that you're up," Rosalind said. "We'll show them they're not the *only* people in the world. OK?"

To belong, to feel wanted, to be part of a group are emotional feelings which are part of the agony and joy of adolescence. The particular adjustive response that occurs will vary widely depending on the total personality organization of the adolescent and his specific life situation. He learns to develop and maintain emotional equilibrium as he attempts to cope with actual or perceived stress and as he tries to satisfy his basic needs. Every person uses defensive activities such as daydreaming or overcompensation and defense mechanisms to some extent at one time or another, whether it be projection, introjection, rationalization, denial, identification, repression, sublimation, regression, displacement or some other category of ego defense mechanism. They are essential for softening failures, minimizing guilt, preserving inner peace, and maintaining good feelings of self-esteem. At the same time, they protect the individual from intolerable anxieties aroused by threats to his ideas about himself. The protection of the self from overwhelming devaluation and thus from anxiety is the very essence of the defensive functions of those mechanisms (4).

Thus, unless the mechanisms are used to such excess as to interfere with the maintenance of self-integrity instead of aiding it, they are well within the range of normal adjustment devices. Much of the difficulty that exists between adolescent and adult stems from the latter's calling attention, unwittingly, to whatever use the adolescent does make of the defense mechanisms. It leaves the adolescent, as it would the adult, vulnerable because most of the mechanisms which he employs are used unconsciously. To call attention to them usually brings resentment, for once the mechanism becomes a conscious instrument for maintaining equilibrium, it does not serve as well; the defenses are somewhat broken down and the individual feels exposed and therefore uncomfortable and vulnerable.

No matter how they are used, their purpose is to maintain and enhance the individual's concept of self (15). It is only as the individual sees himself and his self that the mechanisms make sense. Only in this framework are we able to understand our ability to change "facts" to fit our needs and evaluations and utilize these mechanisms to protect ourselves from anxiety (5). They are essential for the maintenance of a good concept of self; they operate on relatively habitual and unconscious levels; they are learned behavior patterns by which the individual adjusts and copes with life situations which otherwise might be overly destructive for him. Within good limits, the use of the defense mechanisms is normal and inevitable. The basic function of the ego is to maintain constant conditions in the organism (2). It is the agent of the stability principle. Freud formulated this by saying that the ego's function is to keep the amount of excitation in the organism at a constant level (10).

Thus, the four major adjustments the adolescent must make—the organization of the self, the psychological weaning away from the family, the satisfactory establishment of heterosexuality, and the determination of a vocation and preparation for it—revolve around and depend upon the establishment of good emotional equilibrium. If personality development up until the time of adolescence has progressed fairly well, these four aims can be achieved without too great stress. With their accomplishment, the adolescent will achieve great satisfaction; and the members of his family, if they have exercised reasonable tact and forbearance and given evidence of sympathy and affection, will derive considerable pleasure from having helped him.

REFERENCES

(1) Alexander, Franz. *Fundamentals of Psychoanalysis.* NY: Norton, 1948, p. 92.
(2) Alexander, Franz. *Ibid.,* p. 89.
(3) Bernfeld, S. "Über eine typische Form der männlichen Pubertät," *Imago,* IX, 1923.

(4) Coleman, James C. *Abnormal Psychology and Modern Life*. Chicago: Scott, Foresman, 1956, p. 86.

(5) Coleman, James C. *Ibid.*, p. 87.

(6) Erikson, Erik H. *Childhood and Society*. NY: Norton, 1950, p. 228.

(7) Fenichel, Otto. *The Psychoanalytic Theory of Neurosis*. NY: Norton, 1945.

(8) Freud, Anna. *The Ego and the Mechanisms of Defense*. NY: International Universities Press, 1946.

(9) Freud, Sigmund. *The Basic Writings of Sigmund Freud*. NY: Modern Library, 1938.

(10) Freud, Sigmund. *The Ego and the Id*. London: Hogarth, 1927.

(11) Josselyn, Irene. *The Happy Child*. NY: Random House, 1955, p. 314.

(12) Josselyn, Irene. *Ibid.*, p. 127.

(13) Murphy, Gardner. *Personality: A Biosocial Approach to Origins and Structure*. NY: Harper, 1947, p. 515.

(14) Shaffer, Laurance F. *The Psychology of Adjustment*. Boston: Houghton Mifflin, 1936, p. 166.

(15) Snygg, Donald & Combs, Arthur. *Individual Behavior*. NY: Harper, 1949.

(16) Spiegel, Leo A. "A Review of Contributions to a Psychoanalytic Theory of Adolescence: Individual Aspects," in Eissler, Ruth S., et al. (Eds.), *The Psychoanalytic Study of the Child*, Vol. VI. NY: International Universities Press, 1951, p. 384.

(17) Spiegel, Leo A. *Ibid.*, p. 388.

(18) Stoke, Stuart M. "An Inquiry into the Concept of Identification," *J. Genet. Psychol.*, 76:163-189, 1950.

CHAPTER THREE

On Getting Along Socially

"If I talk, everyone thinks I'm showing off; when I'm silent they think I'm ridiculous; rude if I answer back, sly if I get a good idea, lazy if I'm tired, selfish if I eat a mouthful more than I should, stupid, cowardly, crafty, etc."

ANNE FRANK, *The Diary of a Young Girl*, p. 57.

So Little Time*

During all of his four years at Harvard Jeffrey went home for Saturday and Sunday because it was cheaper than stoping at the rooming house near Central Square where he stayed during the week. Besides his tuition, his grandfather gave him four hundred dollars annually for room and board, a limitation which practically prohibited any social activities, even if he had understood that they existed at college. When they asked him at home how he liked it there, he always said, of course, that he had a fine time, but even then he did not entirely believe it. He only realized later that he was one of those boys to whom others referred as grease balls, or other less printable names. He was a part of that grim and underprivileged group that appeared in the Yard each morning with small leather bags containing books and papers. He was one of the boys who wore celluloid collars which you could wash off in your room, and who used the reading room in the Library as a resting place because there was no other place to go, and who ate a sandwich there for lunch, and to whom no one spoke unless it was absolutely necessary. He was one of those grease balls who used to swallow and stammer and mispronounce long words, but he was more sorry for himself later than he had been then. It was hard for him even to understand his former attitude of patient unawareness, for later, he could only be appalled by his utter immaturity, and his ignorance of other modes of living.

* From *So Little Time* by John P. Marquand. Copyright 1943, by John P. Marquand. By permission of Little, Brown & Co. Pp. 175-189.

A professor might occasionally reveal a disturbing vista, might allude to student days at Heidelberg, or pass on to Jeffrey his contagious enthusiasm for a line of poetry or a historical personage, but Jeffrey never felt that he could fully share this knowledge. He thought humbly that this was due to his natural stupidity and only realized later that those men and those books seldom used his terms of expression or resorted to any illustrations with which he was familiar. It was the same with the students who would not speak to him after class was over. It was only later that he knew any of them and that was during discussions in advanced courses, when he had developed a certain ability in prose composition. He could only recall a few occasions when glimpses of this difference had been revealed to him, for he was too absorbed in his own struggles then to understand their meaning.

One morning, for instance, at a section meeting of a large elementary course, which he learned years later was known as a "necktie course," there were a hundred or so students waiting when the section man came in and laid his books and papers on the desk. The section man, young and handsome, dressed in tweeds, spoke in a weary voice.

"I suppose," he said, "that most of you, like me, were at the dance last night at the Plaza."

The Plaza and the dances were unknown to Jeffrey then.

"It may be," the section man went on, "although I hope for your sakes it is not the case, that a great many of you feel the way I do this morning. Anyone who was at the ball last night may leave now, and take a walk in the fresh air, or do anything else he may think proper—anyone who was at the ball."

The room was filled with applause and merry stamping and two thirds of the students left the room while the section man watched them, smiling. Those who were left were the plain boys, the last pieces of candy in the box, and Jeffrey was among them. He still could remember their anxious serious features, their hunched shoulders and their shining elbows. The section man's glance passed slowly over them, and then he smiled.

"So you weren't at the ball last night," he said. "Well, we'll go on. We'll talk about something that does not require too much effort."

When you were young, of course you accepted the environment in which you lived and which was beyond your power to change. It sometimes seemed to Jeffrey that his father must have always accepted it, living incuriously just where he was, not successfully, but placidly. Occasionally in the evenings, when Jeffrey was back from college, his father would talk to him about getting ahead. It was only later that Jeffrey realized that the Old Man knew nothing much about this except in theory. When he was Jeffrey's age, he got a job in Mr. Wilkin's Real Estate and Insurance office, and when Mr. Wilkins died, he had gone right on with it from there. That was virtually all he ever told Jeffrey about himself, but sometimes he spoke of Jeffrey's mother. "She was a mighty pretty girl," he said once. "You can tell it from her picture." But that was about all he said. Perhaps he did not want to talk about her, or perhaps he thought that Jeffrey knew of her already.

"Everybody has a chance in this country," he said once. "If you work hard and are honest, you'll get where you want to get."

The town and home meant much more to Jeffrey than anything he learned at college. Later when he heard people talk of the democracy of the small town, he knew it was a half truth, because a small town was actually a complicated place, with social gradations which one accepted without being entirely aware of them. There were people who lived on Center Street whom his father spoke to with a special tone, such as the Thompsons and the Nestleroades and the Barneses. And then there were people like themselves and Dr. Adams and Mr. Pratt who ran the clothing store. And then there were people whom his father referred to as "scrubs," the workers in the carpet mills and the employees in the shoeshop and the people who did odd jobs.

When Jeffrey walked up Center Street, he always had an uneasy feeling. The houses there had striped awnings in the summertime and there were round flower beds on the lawns. They kept watering the lawns on Center Street with sprinklers that whirled around, and the Thompsons and the Nestleroades had automobiles. That was where Louella lived —on Center Street. Sometimes on Saturdays he would meet her downtown and he would always take off his hat quickly and smile. Sometimes he would see her at church on Sundays but he never thought of talking to her, and he never called on Louella until the spring of his last year at college.

He was taking a course on the English Novel that year and it was a hard course for him because it was necessary to read and read. First there was Samuel Richardson's *Clarissa,* and then *The Castle of Otranto* and *Roderick Random* and *Joseph Andrews,* dealing with phases of English life which were completely beyond the scope of his imagination. When they reached the Victorians, it was not much simpler for him. The people in *Middlemarch* or *David Copperfield* or *Vanity Fair* never could fit into his surroundings. It was grim work for him, always, acquiring an education against the narrow background of his own experience.

One Saturday close to the time for the final examination he went to the Bragg Public Library to borrow Meredith's *Diana of the Crossways.* Years later when he heard someone say that Meredith was a young man's writer, his mind went back to his efforts with *Diana of the Crossways* up in the hall bedroom where he lived in Cambridge during the week. When he tried to read *Diana* again he seemed to be back sitting on that iron bed of his that smelled faintly of kerosene, listening to the trolley cars on Massachusetts Avenue. He had that old feeling that he must finish it and remember it, that he must make notes on the physical appearance of all the characters because that was the sort of question which would be on the examination.

The public library was a brick building, like the Town Hall, only smaller. To the left was the reading and periodical room, to the right Miss Jacobs sat behind her desk with the catalogues in their golden-oak cases and with three lilacs in a vase in front of her. The room smelled of floor oil and of books arranged along the wall and in alcoves. *Diana of the Crossways* was there in the catalogue, and Miss Jacobs told him that he could find it himself over by the window.

"Well," Miss Jacobs said, "you're quite a stranger."

"Yes," Jeffrey said, "I'm just home Saturdays and Sundays."

"I see your father and your aunt," Miss Jacobs said. "They say they haven't heard from Alf."

"No," Jeffrey said, "Alf doesn't write much."

"Dear me," Miss Jacobs said, "how everybody flies away."

Then there was a footstep behind him and the light glinted on Miss Jacob's glasses.

"Why, hello," Miss Jacobs said, "here's someone else who's quite a stranger."

Jeffrey stepped away from the desk, holding *Diana of the Crossways*. It was Louella Barnes.

Jeffrey sometimes wondered later what he would have been like if there had been anything in his youth to promote self-confidence or self-assurance—if he had ever owned a suit of clothes that had cost more than fifteen dollars, if he had gone to one of the preparatory schools or had played football, or if his father had owned a car which he had been allowed to drive. It was always a difficult and thankless game to stack the decks of the cards which had been dealt in the past, for there was no way of telling whether he would have been better or worse for it. But he was sure of one thing, he would not have felt that Louella Barnes was an unapproachable vision that afternoon. He would have possessed some standard for comparison. He would have placed her in a gallery of other girls whom he had met. It did not mean, of course, that he was entirely without experience. He had been on picnics with Alf and with girls Alf knew, but they were noisy and provocative and they smelled of musk and perfume. They were not nice girls like Louella Barnes. If he had known more, if he had "loosened up" as Alf often advised him, that vision of Louella in the library might not have been quite so compelling. As it was, no one living was ever like the Louella Barnes that he saw that afternoon.

She was standing by Miss Jacob's desk, and the light of the window in the alcove just behind her put her face in the shadow, but it made a glow on her yellow hair, which was done up in a tight, uncompromising knot just below her little hat. She wore a gray tailored suit with the frills of a shirtwaist in front. Her lisle stockings looked almost like silk, and she wore low tan shoes with high heels. She was like Beatrix Castlewood walking down the stairs. All sorts of thoughts like that passed through Jeffrey's mind. It was the first time in his life that his academic studies had assumed any practical significance. She was like Botticelli's Spring, she was like Milton's pagan nymphs. . . .

He did not want to look at her for more than a brief instant. Instead he backed slowly away from Miss Jacob's desk and gazed intently at two posters on the wall behind her. One was a British Tommy, saying that England expected every man to do his duty, and the other was of a French poilu saying *"On les aura."*

"Oh, Miss Jacobs," Louella said, "doesn't the library look nice?"

"That's sweet of you to say it," Miss Jacobs said. "We try to keep it nice."

Jeffrey was still staring at the posters, trying to detach himself from the group, wondering whether he should speak to her first, or whether she would speak to him.

"Why," Louella said, "if it isn't Jeffrey Wilson. Hello, Jeffrey."

She was holding out her hand to him. He forgot that he was holding *Diana of the Crossways* and when he tried to shift it over, it fell with a flop on the brown linoleum floor.

"Oh," he said, "hello, Louella." And then he stooped to pick it up. He felt the blood rushing to his face as he stooped and he knew that his coat was too tight behind and his trousers were binding. But Louella was still speaking.

"Father wants to know," Louella was saying, "if it's time for him yet to have *Letters from America*."

Miss Jacobs opened a drawer in her desk and consulted a white sheet of paper.

"If Mr. Barnes wants it," Miss Jacobs answered, "we'll just forget that anyone's ahead of him if he brings it back on Monday."

"That's dear of you," Louella said, "thank you, Miss Jacobs."

"Besides," Miss Jacobs said, "there's no one else ahead on Center Street." She tapped a little bell on her desk.

"Walter," she called, "Walter!" Miss Jacobs' voice dropped to a kind and gentle murmur: "We have Walter Newcombe now. He's a West Ender who dusts books and tidies, when he's back from Dartmouth."

Miss Jacobs meant that the three of them standing at the desk, although they might not all come from Center Street, were certainly not West Enders.

"Oh." Louella also lowered her voice.

There was no time for an answer because the door at the end of the main room opened. Walter Newcombe was a gangly boy of seventeen, who obviously knew he was a West Ender. His hair was not brushed, and his nose was shining.

"Walter," Miss Jacobs said, "get *Letters from America*, please."

"Who wrote it, ma'am?" Walter asked.

"Rupert Brooke," Miss Jacobs told him, very gently indicating that West Enders never knew things like that. Jeffrey knew that he should be going, but if he left he would not hear Louella speak again.

"How does it feel to be a college girl?" Miss Jacobs asked. Louella gave a deprecating laugh.

"College girls are just the same as other girls," she said. "At least, I feel the same, and this is my last year." And she looked at Jeffrey and smiled.

"A college boy and a college girl," Miss Jacobs said, "right together in the library at once. My, it's quite a day."

She did not seem to think of Walter as a college boy. Jeffrey knew that they were both expecting him to say something and he cleared his throat, but he was spared the effort, because Walter Newcombe was back.

"Give it to Miss Barnes, Walter," Miss Jacobs said. "I won't bother to stamp it, because I *know* you'll bring it back on Monday."

Anyone would have known who saw Louella smile.

"Thank you, Miss Jacobs, it's sweet of you," she said. "Well, good-by."

Jeffrey did not know exactly what to do, but there was no reason for him to stay because he also had his book.

"Well," he said, "it's time I was going. Good-by and thank you, Miss Jacobs."

He thought Louella would walk out first, but she waited for him, and they walked down the hall together. He lunged forward and opened the door for her.

"What's the book you're reading?" Louella asked.

"Just a tough old book," he said. "*Diana of the Crossways* by George Meredith."

"Oh," Louella said, and she nodded with knowing sympathy. "It must be the English Novel course. We have it too, at Smith."

"It's sort of hard to understand," Jeffrey said. "Well—"

He stopped, and Louella stopped, too. They had come to the end of the library path.

"It's just the right afternoon for iced tea, isn't it?" Louella said.

"What?" Jeffrey asked her.

"Iced tea," Louella said. "I've got some made. Wouldn't you like to have some on the porch?"

It took a moment to grasp that she was asking him to accompany her to her home to have iced tea, asking him to walk with her up Center Street and right to her front porch. His common sense told him that he ought to take it casually and so he framed his words carefully in his head before he spoke them.

"I wouldn't mind some iced tea at all," he said.

The new leaves of the maple trees on Center Street were all yellowish green, but he was not thinking of the leaves. He was thinking that his trousers were baggy. He was wondering what the people on Center Street would be saying when they saw him walking with Louella Barnes without a hat.

"May I carry your book for you?" he said.

"Oh, no," she answered, "it's very light." He did not want to snatch for it, but he knew that it would not look right unless he carried the book.

Her heels tapped sharply on the brick walk beneath the maple trees. She was almost as tall as he was, but not quite, and he wished that his trousers were pressed. He wanted her to see that she had made no mistake in asking him to walk home with her.

"It's funny," Louella said, "we haven't seen each other for a long while, have we? That is, not to talk to."

"It's because we've been away at college," Jeffrey said.

"Some men in your class," Louella said, "were at the Senior Prom this winter. I had a blind date with one of them."

He did not know what a blind date was, but he certainly did not want her to know that he did not know it.

"Did you?" he said. "Who was it?" He did not know whether you should have said "it" or "he" but it must have been all right.

"Dick Elwell," she said. "He comes from New York. Do you know him?"

"Elwell?" Jeffrey said, and he pretended to be groping through the endless list of his acquaintances. "Maybe I've met him, but I don't know him."

"Then there's Tommy Rogers," she said, "the one who plays hockey. He's in your class, isn't he?"

"Rogers," Jeffrey said. "It's a pretty big class at college. Rogers—maybe I've met him, but I don't know him."

"Then there was a boy named Ames," Louella said. "A red-headed boy with freckles who had a new way of dancing the Boston. I think his first name was Tom. He's in your class, too; do you know him?"

"Ames," Jeffrey said. "Let's see, Ames—It's a pretty big class. Did anybody come up there whose name begins with 'W'?"

"Why with 'W'?" Louella said.

"Well, you see, it's a pretty big class," Jeffrey said, "but all the 'W's' sit together. I know a good many men whose names begin with 'W'."

"Williams," Louella said, "why then you must know Bert Williams."

"Williams," Jeffrey said, "there was a man named Williams in Phil I, but we didn't talk much."

Louella was right. It was just the day for iced tea. It had not struck him as being particularly hot, until he walked with Louella up Center Street, but after all, though he hardly knew anyone to speak to after four years in college, he was a college man. The iron fence of the Barnes lawn was in front of him. They were turning in the gate. They were walking up the tarred walk and the white lilacs by the yellow porch were all in bloom. The awnings were out above the downstairs windows. Jeffrey drew his shoulders back. After all, he was a college man.

"In English 12," Jeffrey said, "there's a man named Winterstein. He's quite a writer. That's English 12, under Professor C. T. Copeland. We call him 'Copey.' Did you ever meet a man named Winterstein?"

"Winterstein," Louella said, "let me see. I seem to know the name, but I don't think I ever met him."

The porch was cool and shaded from the afternoon sun, with a slate-gray floor and a bilious yellow railing. There was not much effort at beauty on porches in those days—no colored rugs, no tables with plate glass tops—but Louella's porch remained in his mind ever afterward as a sort of metric standard. Ever afterward, he found himself supporting a fixed belief that no porch was in proper taste unless it had heavy dull-green rocking chairs, and a round wicker table painted black, and unless it had one of those Cape Cod hammocks made of khaki canvas with a purple denim cushion in each corner, suspended from the ceiling by galvanized iron chains. For years the Barnes porch was clear and solid in his mind. He dreamed of it once in the war—he saw the green rocking chairs and the white lilacs that half-concealed the street. He was standing there again with that same sensation of happiness and there was that same sound, the faint squeak of the Cape Cod hammock, swinging on its chains.

"I'll get the tea," Louella said.

"May I help you?" Jeffrey asked. It must have been the right thing to say, because she smiled, although she shook her head.

"Oh, no," Louella said. "I'll be only a minute. Just sit down and make yourself at home."

Jeffrey smoothed his coat and mopped his forehead and then folded his handkerchief carefully and put it in his breast pocket. A Cadillac car went by and then a Ford with a brass radiator and brass lamps, and then an ice wagon. He was trying to plan what to say to Louella next, telling himself that he must not laugh or talk too loudly, and that he must not shuffle his feet. Louella was gone for such a long while that he wondered whether she might not be sorry that she had asked him and whether she might not be waiting in the house, hoping that he would go away, but just as that thought came to him the front door opened and there was Louella, carrying a tray. She had taken off her tailored coat; and her shirtwaist had more frills and pleats on it than he had expected and her hair did not look so tight. On the tray she carried was a pitcher of real cut glass, and two tall goblets and a cut-glass sugar bowl, and also a large glass plate containing some thin sandwiches cut in hearts and circles with a little ring of parsley around them. From the top of the pitcher arose a green spray of mint leaves.

"There," Louella said, "sit down and make yourself at home."

Jeffrey could not take his eyes from the tray and the cut glass and, without intending, he must have looked at it too hard.

"I think it's nice to have things nice when you have iced tea, don't you?" Louella asked.

"Yes," Jeffrey said, "that's right."

He sat down in one of the rocking chairs and Louella sat down on the one beside him and crossed her ankles carefully and smoothed her gray skirt.

"I suppose you have to work pretty hard, now," Louella said, "with final exams coming. I do."

"If you do your work every day," Jeffrey said, "there's no

reason to be afraid of examinations." He sipped his iced tea thoughtfully. "I'm not afraid of them."

He smiled when he said it, because he did not want to show off.

"I'm not either," Louella said, "but a lot of people are."

He was glad that they were both brave and not afraid of examinations, but now that they both had said so, the subject seemed to be completely exhausted. He leaned back in an effort to think of something else to say. He forgot it was a rocking chair. He had to raise his legs straight off the floor to right himself.

"They rock back pretty quickly, if you're not used to them," Louella said, and she laughed and Jeffrey laughed.

"Yes," Jeffrey said, and changed his center of gravity by hitching himself forward.

"Some men are so silly, aren't they?" Louella said, "and some girls, too."

It made him forget about the rocking chair.

"I like men who do things, and girls, too," Louella said, "I mean worth-while things."

He felt easier, even in the rocking chair, because it must have meant that she thought he was doing worth-while things.

"Have you read *The Winning of Barbara Worth?*" Louella asked.

"No," Jeffrey said, "I don't have much time. I only read what they hand me out to read."

"I'll lend it to you when you go," Louella said.

Jeffrey pulled his feet under him. The rocking chair pitched slightly forward. He put his hands on the arms to steady himself.

"Maybe I'd better be going now," he said.

"Oh, no," Louella said, "no, please."

Jeffrey leaned backward and again he forgot it was a rocking chair.

"I'll tell you what we'll do," Louella spoke quickly before he could answer. "We'll play the phonograph. We'll bring it out here, that is, if you like music, but I guess you'll have to help me."

Jeffrey wiped his feet on the jute mat by the front door and followed Louella into the hall. The phonograph was in the little sitting room, on the left. He saw the beveled mirror over the fireplace and a fan of white paper between the andirons. He had never seen white paper made into a fan like that. The phonograph was square and heavy, but even with the iced tea, there was room for it on the porch table.

"Here is 'Gems from The Pink Lady,' " Louella said. And they sat side by side in the rocking chairs.

There was no need to talk as the songs went on. He could sit relaxed, and occasionally he could look at her, as she listened. He could see her profile as she looked out toward Center Street. He could see the way her hair curled tightly over her ears, held in place by her hair net. She was the beautiful lady to whom he raised his eyes. He was the gay roué who was saying Not yet, he'd be single for six months more. The river was flowing on to the sea, and she was the girl from the Saskatchewan.

"It's lovely music," Louella said.

"Yes," he said, "it's fine."

There was a moment's silence, but he was not embarrassed by the silence. He was still by the banks of the Saskatchewan.

"Now, we'll play the 'Gems from The Quaker Girl,' " Louella said. "Here it is—"

As he sat there, he seemed to be dancing with Louella Barnes at the Senior Prom at Smith. His arm was around her waist. Her hand was resting on his shoulder. He forgot that he did not know how to dance.

"There're lots more," Louella said. "I'll play them when you come again."

Jeffrey hitched himself forward in the rocking chair.

"Maybe I'd better be going now," he said.

"No, no," Louella said, "it's early. Father isn't back yet."

It occurred to Jeffrey that it might be better if he left before Mr. Barnes appeared, but he sank back in his chair.

"We haven't talked about anything at all," Louella said. "What are you going to do when you're finished with college?"

It must have been the music, it could not have been the iced tea. It must have been some strain of romanticism within him which made him think of the impossible. He had only taken a drink once in his life, and that had been with Alf, but the music had the same effect, relaxing, blotting out all inhibition. The idea that his father wanted him to help out at the office selling real estate was repellent there on the Barnes porch. He thought of mentioning the Foreign

Legion or the Lafayette Escadrille, but he was sure that she would think that he was showing off.

"I guess I'll be a newspaper man," he said.

He had never intended to be a newspaper man, and he did not know how one went about it, but now he knew he would have to do it, or he could never speak to Louella Barnes again.

"Oh, Jeffrey," she said, "why, I think that's wonderful."

He could see himself with a horrible clarity afterwards, seated there by the cut-glass pitcher and the cut-glass goblets, trying to reach beyond himself.

"Oh, Jeffrey," she said again, "I think that's wonderful. Do you know anyone who works on a newspaper?"

"No," Jeffrey said, "that is, not exactly."

"Well, I think it's wonderful," Louella said. "Here come Mother and Father now."

Jeffrey pushed himself out of the rocking chair. "I've got to be going now," he said. "Really."

"Oh, no," Louella said, and she put her hand on his arm. He could not believe it, but there it was. "Please wait. Father and Mother would love to see you."

He could see Mr. and Mrs. Barnes walking slowly up the tarred path. Mr. Barnes wore a straw hat and carried a rolled-up newspaper which meant that he must have come from the city on the 6:01 train. Mr. Barnes waved his paper when he saw Louella.

"Hello," he called, "hello, Chick."

Jeffrey felt that he ought not to have been there to have heard that term of endearment.

"Well, of all things," said Mrs. Barnes, "if it isn't Jeffrey Wilson."

"Well," Mr. Barnes said, "I'm glad to see you, Jeffrey. Are they working you hard at college?"

"And iced tea," Mrs. Barnes said, "and the best pitcher. It's a real party."

"Oh, Mother," Louella said, "you know the pitcher makes it nicer."

"I could do with some of that myself," Mr. Barnes said.

"I'll get you some in the kitchen, Harold," Mrs. Barnes told him, and she smiled at Jeffrey. "Are you coming, Harold?"

But Mr. Barnes lingered on the porch.

"Where's that brother of yours?" he asked. "Where's Alf?"

"He's down in New York, sir," Jeffrey said, "the last we heard of him."

Mr. Barnes laughed.

"Of course he is," he said. "This town couldn't hold a boy like Alf. Alf was quite a card."

"Yes sir," Jeffrey said, "we miss him."

"The girls must miss him," Mr. Barnes said. "Alf was quite a ladies' man."

"Father," Louella said, "what do you think—Jeffrey's going to be a newspaper man."

"Well, well," Mr. Barnes said, "are you? Now that's an interesting thing to do."

"Harold," Mrs. Barnes called from the house. "Can I talk to you a minute?" And Jeffrey and Louella were on the porch alone.

"I've got to be going, really," Jeffrey said.

"Oh, no, please don't," Louella told him. "I'll get you some more iced tea. Father and Mother don't like sitting on the porch. They like to sit inside."

"It's pretty near time for supper," Jeffrey said. "I've got to be going, really."

"Wait a minute," Louella said, "I'll get you *The Winning of Barbara Worth*, and next time you come, you can tell me how you like it." She looked at the empty cut-glass pitcher. "I'm afraid I didn't make enough iced tea."

"There was plenty of it," Jeffrey said. "Thank you very much."

"Good-by," Louella said, "and come back soon, now that you've found your way."

She was smiling at him when he held her hand. "Come as soon as you can," she said, "now that you've found your way."

"Come back soon," Louella says to Jeffrey, "now that you've found your way." It is obvious that Jeffrey has a long way to go until he finds his social self, until he is comfortable in either male or female relationships, for he has not yet "found his way." At Harvard College, Jeffrey belongs and he does not belong. He goes to classes but does not participate in any social activity. He brings his lunch which he eats in solitude; he is a "grease ball," studying hard but studying alone. He sees the differences between himself and his peers but seems helpless to change himself or to bridge the gap. "When you are very young," Marquand writes, "of course you accepted the environment in which you lived and which was beyond your power to change."

Social consciousness is high at adolescence, in part because high school and college life force the adolescent into close contact with individuals from all sorts of backgrounds. He meets people his own age who are better or poorer dressed than he, who are richer or as rich or less rich, who are better mannered or more ill-behaved, who are more or less socially active. As a result, attention is focused on such differences. Sheer presence in a school culture which abounds with cliques and more formal social groups intensifies the need to belong to these groups (5). Jeffrey Wilson could not share or participate because he was, at this particular moment in his adolescent development, too absorbed in his own struggles to understand the meaning of what was going on around him.

The young and handsome instructor, well-dressed in tweeds, who tiredly assumes his class has attended the dance at the Plaza the night before, speaks of a world unknown to Jeffrey. Those left in the class after the teacher had dismissed the students who had attended the dance were the plain boys, "the last pieces of candy in the box . . ."

We sense a feeling of uneasiness in Jeffrey. Adjustment at every age is difficult and is accompanied by emotional tension. Such tension is heightened for Jeffrey because he is undergoing that period of adolescence in which many new and varied social adjustments have to be made. This causes the adolescent to be anxious, to worry, to feel insecure, to be sensitive about, and suspicious of, others (2). Many adolescents are slow in developing their social selves; this social development is a continuous and cumulative process, becoming increasingly conscious with the onset of puberty. It is accompanied by very different ideas about one's concept of self, which are reflected in changes in social behavior.

Too old to be led by the hand, too young to be left on his own recognizance, the always-changing, strenuously-living adolescent is regarded by society both as an adult and as a child. The adolescent himself wants all the advantages of childhood and all the rights of adulthood. His social behavior becomes at once sophisticated and immature, it seems to many. Never to know what to expect and to expect the unexpected is the norm.

Jeffrey has learned how to get along with one segment of his world: the adult sphere. He is much more at home, although far from completely so, in his town and with his family than he is at college. As an adolescent, he believed and accepted the introjected values of his father: "Everybody has a chance in this country. If you work hard and are honest, you'll get where you want to get." He believed in the democracy of the small town and learned only later that a small town is actually a complicated place, with social gradations which one accepted without being entirely aware of them. A clouded realization of the social pecking order evolves in the fragile relationship which develops with Louella. Problems of ego identity with intricate social and unconscious reverberations become of acute importance. Social mobility in connection with adequate instinctual gratification and defense becomes significant (8).

Social mobility allows Jeffrey to move away from the restraining environs of his neighborhood to Center Street, where people like Louella Barnes and her parents, to whom Jeffrey's father spoke with a special tone, live. But this same mobility produces strain when he does meet up with Center Street in reality. He is as uncomfortable with the wealthy Louella as he is with Walter Newcombe, the "gangly boy of seventeen, who obviously knew he was a West Ender." His social status places him somewhere in the middle, but closer to the poorer West End section of town, and Jeffrey is uncomfortable in the presence of either of his peers. The well-meaning but unintuitive librarian plagues all three with her insipid comments and attitudes. "How does it feel to be a college girl?" "A college boy and a college girl right to-gether in the library at once. My, it's quite a day." How is the adolescent supposed to react to such inanities, particu-larly when he meets up with them from adults with such frequency. Behind the good-natured banter and hearty good fellowship of the adult, the adolescent often feels himself to be in the presence of something false or patronizing. Jeffrey's lack of social poise makes him feel rather helpless under such an onslaught. Louella, on the other hand, has a good amount of self-assurance and she is able to handle the situation.

Louella, in fact, is the aggressor throughout the scene. Al-though Louella and Jeffrey are the same age, she, like most adolescent girls, has matured ahead of the male. She is so-cially more adept and knowing. It is she who keeps the con-versation going, flat and pedestrian though it is. It is she who smooths over the awkward spots and performs the gracious ritual of the social tea while the bumbling Jeffrey daydreams he is dancing with her at the Senior Prom at Smith—when, in fact, he does not know how to dance at all!

The most outstanding change that takes place in the social life of the child as he emerges into adolescence is his asso-ciation with and attitude toward the opposite sex. Up until the child is of school age, play between the two sexes is com-mon; then, from about the ages of six to eleven or twelve, the period of middle childhood, boys tend to play with boys and girls with girls, with ultimately a total rejection of one for the other. But a gradual change takes place beyond this age level. Each sex becomes markedly more interested in the other, associating together more and more frequently. Het-erosexual relationships become the norm.

As the Marquand passage reveals, the earlier emergence, or more aggressive display, of heterosexual interest on the part of girls is apparent. Girls mature socially before boys, possibly because of earlier physical maturation. Because of this and because the American culture overtly gives the prerogative of initiating relationships with the opposite sex to the male, girls tend to date boys older than themselves while boys choose younger girls (6). Girls also tend to marry earlier than boys.

The fumbling, awkward, painful first social contacts of early adolescents are skillfully drawn in Walter Van Tilburg Clark's *The City of Trembling Leaves.** In it, a variety of levels of sophistication is revealed which is typical of the wide range of adolescence.

After supper, Billy led them all into the living room. "Let's play something," he said.

"What?"

"I know," one of the girls said. "Drop the handkerchief."

There was groaning. She was reminded that she was in high school now, and was questioned about her age and mentality.

"Charades," another girl said, and there was more groaning.

There was some hope about musical chairs, but Billy said they couldn't play that because of the new floor, and anyway there was no piano and the new phonograph hadn't come yet.

There was more groaning about Teakettle.

"Oh, let's play something that's some fun," Billy said. "I'll tell you what. Let's play spin-the-bottle."

Tim didn't know what spin-the-bottle was, except that it was probably a boy-girl game and embarrassing, because several of the boys whooped and laughed, and the girl with the big mouth suddenly clutched him by the arm, as if to save herself from falling into a paroxysm of laughter, and when she got barely enough breath, squealed, "He *would* want to play that."

Tim saw that Rachel also either didn't know the game, or was afraid of it. She was standing like a soldier by herself

* From *The City of Trembling Leaves* by Walter Van Tilburg Clark. Copyright 1945 by Walter Van Tilburg Clark. Reprinted by permission of Random House, Inc. Pp. 116-124.

at the other end of the couch, trying to smile and look as if she understood. There was a row of many, small, red-and-yellow plaid buttons down the front of her velvet jacket. They bound the jacket closely over her sharp, small breasts, and he could see how quickly she was breathing.

Some of the boys were pushing the couch out of the way against the fireplace. Tim helped to roll the rug and put it against the wall. Billy stood out in the middle of the shining floor with an empty pop bottle in his hand.

"O.K., here we go," he yelled. "Everybody get in a big ring. First a boy, then a girl, all the way round like that."

He came over and dragged Rachel into the ring, and then went back out in the middle. "O.K.," he said again. "No moving. You gotta stay right where you are."

He laid the bottle down on its side, and spun it between his thumb and finger. The bottle twinkled rapidly, glittered as it slowed down, and finally lay still and gleaming, with its neck pointing at a boy. There was lamentation, as if this were a disappointment.

"Be a fish," Billy told him.

The boy lay down full length on the floor, and vaguely imitated some sort of a swimming creature. He was mildly applauded and heavily insulted.

"You spin now," Billy told him.

The game went on. The modest purpose of its first stage was to inflict upon the person chosen by the bottle a physical maneuver entailing some indignity. The transition period began when the dark boy called Sheik, who wore a college-cut suit and a red necktie, was told to go around the circle and bow to each girl and kiss her hand. There were fake protests from the girls and cheers from the boys. One boy yelled, "That ain't nothin' for you, is it, Sheik?" When Sheik went around the circle the girls giggled, and posed haughtily, like movie countesses. Rachel became red and then white, and Sheik had to reach for her hand. When he kissed it, she had a spasm of laughter.

After that all the penalties were of the same sort, and everyone watched the spinning bottle intently, and sometimes a victim would try to change his place when he saw that the bottle might pick him. Timmy had to get down on his knees before each girl, and touch his forehead to her right hand, as in token fealty. When he finished this labor he was sweating, although it wasn't hot in the room, for the door and the windows were open, so that the night breathed in, and pale moths came and quivered upon the screens or drummed against them. He believed that the only hand he could still feel on his forehead was Rachel's, which was small and cold. He felt that probably there was a sacred mark left by her fingers, their imprint shining like a light.

It was Rachel who ended spin-the-bottle before its possibilities were fully explored. When the bottle picked her, the ringmaster ordered her to go around the circle and kiss each boy on both cheeks. Rachel stood like the soldier. The fields of her soul were given over to battle. Some of the boys offered loud advice. One of them cried that he would take two in the middle instead of one on each side, and everybody laughed explosively, and then stopped laughing suddenly, and only giggled. They all felt their personal futures involved in the battle Rachel was fighting.

Rachel was very red. She made quick little gasping laughs, and looked quickly at different girls, but when she wasn't laughing her lower lip trembled. Her hands were pulling at each other in front of her. She still didn't say anything. The circle broke up, and she was besieged. She began to shake her head. She was bombarded by arguments, ridicule and doubts of her innocence. She kept shaking her head and trying hard to laugh, but getting further and further from really laughing. Tim was a prisoner watching his own destroyed. Even Billy's powers were weakened by internal dissension. His desire to remain the champion of the liberals was checked by the threat to his personal privilege.

The siege was lifted by accident. One of the boys, intending only to add his bit to the popular pressure, yelled, "I know what's the trouble with her. She wants to play post-office, so we can't see her, don't you, Rachy?" But the suggestion turned a common desire, and at once pressure groups began to form to make it a real plan. A few extremists continued the personal fight though. They agreed to post-office, but worked up a chant, "Rachy has to go first, Rachy has to go first."

Rachel dumbly opposed this action also, and finally the chant died because she could hardly keep herself from crying. The debate shifted to method. One faction insisted that the choice should be personal, and the other that the names should be drawn. Feeling the swing of opinion, Billy voiced the majority preference.

"We'll draw," he yelled. "Then it won't be just one fellow getting all our mail or something." He was cheered, and also accused of fearing to risk himself in open contest. He began to give orders.

"Everybody write his name on a slip of paper," he yelled. He went into a side room and came back with several sheets of paper and a fistful of pencils. While he was folding the sheets together and tearing them into strips, he was assailed as having had the whole thing plotted out beforehand. Tim signed like an illiterate putting his name to a contract before a lawyer he mistrusted. He didn't know how post-office was played either, except that it must be an advance over spin-the-bottle because there was secrecy connected with it. Billy collected all the boys' names in one hat, and the girls' in another.

"First one I pick is post-master," he announced.

There was silence as he drew a slip from the girls' hat.

"Pauline Chester," he announced.

There was an uproar. The bosomy girl in whom Tim's elbow had been buried at supper stepped forth.

"Where do I go?" she asked, when it was quiet.

"The study is the post-office," Billy announced. "You go on in," he said to Pauline. "Then I'll hold the hat in for you."

"No lights," somebody cried.

"No lights," everybody shouted.

"No fakes, either," somebody else shouted. "You have to really kiss. Anybody that won't really kiss has to kiss everybody." This rule was adopted by acclaim, although there were a few skeptics who wanted to know how it was going to be enforced when they couldn't see what was going on. "If they're both a-scared, how do we know what they did?"

This simple game did not grow dull. There was an outburst as each name was read. There was an intense quiet during each interval in which Billy held the hat, and the hand from the dark room reached out and chose a name. There was a fleeting expression of dread or doubt, but also the room was electrical with particular hopes. On a few faces was the blanched agony of the card players in the Suicide Club. As each post-master emerged, he was hailed, belittled and cross-examined. The girls all attempted to appear unmoved by this public prominence. The boys, assuming the license of the double standard, came out in different ways. Some looked knowing and remained silent. Some expressed glee. One skinny youth, blond and freckled, whose pants were too short, came out with his hands clasped before him, his face raised in praise of the Lord who gave such bliss, and his knees sagging and wavering. This interpretation was popular, and was played frequently, with variations. The most successful imitator was practically original. He came out on his hands and knees, rolled over, and expired in jerking agony.

Even though the game was turned over to Fortune, the spear of personal implication was felt often. There was loud booing when one girl chanced to pick the name of a boy who spent most of his time with her anyway. There was laughter and satire when a notoriously unilateral affair attained the secret climax. Loud suggestions for deliberate manipulation were made to Billy, and he pretended to act upon them. Billy himself was called, and somebody else took over the hat. If the door opened too soon, the deed was questioned. If it remained closed a long time, protest, scandalized accusation, and expressions of envy rose into a storm.

Tim kept looking back at Rachel. The davenport had been turned around, and she was sitting on one arm of it. She laughed every time everybody laughed, but never said anything. Tim understood that she was practicing the art of disappearing into the background. He was saying a good many things himself, but they all arose from that same desire to appear inconspicuous, and most of them were just poor imitations of previous successes. Each time it was a girl's hand working around the door, his breath and his pulse were suspended. He took as a sweet if brief reprieve each period during which a boy held office. It was in these moments that he made his few really witty comments which could be quoted. Only one hope, and that half dread, remained constant in him. The numerical chances of entering the study with Rachel were small. Still, he kept thinking how it would be, and each time the chance came up that it might be, suddenly the inside diplomatic preliminaries appeared insurmountable, and a desert without water would begin to expand between his chair and the door of the study.

There were several repeats, one boy being called so often that there were accusations of fixing, and still Rachel wasn't called, and neither was Tim. Tim allowed himself guardedly to begin to hope both ways. He began to look at Rachel even more often, hoping to establish a union by means of their isolation, but she would accept no ally.

The skinny boy who had first swooned was acting as panderer. The dark boy with the red necktie was in the study. The dark hand held up the slip, and the skinny boy took it. He read solemnly, "Rachel Wells."

When the skinny boy said "Rachel" Tim's breath stopped as if it had been his own name. He didn't even hear as far as Wells.

"About time," somebody shouted.

"Do a gook job on her, Sheik."

"One ain't enough, Sheik. Take one for all of us."

"Two, you mean," somebody amended.

This became a chorus. "Two for each of us, Sheik."

Finally Rachel got up and walked across to the study door quickly, smiling hard and with her arms straight down. She was cheered and hooted. At the door she stood and waited. She was speaking. Everybody became quiet. She was making a last desperate appeal to Pander.

"I don't have to pick one too, do I?"

She received a great many replies, among which Pander's was lost. It required another moment to quell her own rebellion, and then she entered. The skinny boy put his finger to his lip and his ear to the door. There was silence outside. There was also silence inside. The skinny boy straightened up, shrugging his shoulders and spreading his hands.

The boy called Sheik chose to be non-committal when he came out, and so far as the public was concerned Rachel remained a figure of mystery, as inviolate as upon her entrance. Her hand chose and the skinny boy intoned, "Tim Hazard."

This was also greeted as overdue, and Tim received a good many suggestions. The desert between his chair and the door swelled and sank under him. He entered the difficult portal, and it was closed behind him. He was standing in absolute darkness. He also felt that many-eared silence outside. He waited. Since she was already there, and had seen him come in, Rachel should make the overture. He didn't even know where she was in there. He couldn't even remember what shape the room was, or where the furniture was. He stood very still, except for the roaring in his brain, and listened. Rachel finally made the overture.

"Well," she whispered hard, "don't take all night. I don't want to be in here all night with any boy."

It was impossible to tell from the whisper how angry or tearful or merely matter-of-fact and in a hurry she was.

"Where are you?" he whispered.

This became at once, to him, a question of great significance. The dark study took on the dimensions of a dead planet in eternal night, and across its vast wastes, its tundras and glaciers and cold and whispering seas, he ran and swam and climbed frantically, in quest of a tiny, solitary, lost, perhaps dying, Rachel.

"Here," Rachel whispered.

"Where?"

"Right here," she whispered angrily, "behind the door."

It was shocking that she was so close. Even their whispering had not told him she was so close. He moved only one step, with his hand out, and touched her. He was shivering with expectation, dread and ignorance. It was the velvet jacket he had touched. He was terribly ashamed and bewildered. He didn't know what part of the velvet jacket he had touched. She didn't say anything, or move to help him.

"Is that you?" he asked. The word "you" in his mind began with a capital and from its letters arose tongues of oriflamme.

"It's my sleeve," she whispered.

He ventured to close his hand.

"Hurry up, will you?" she whispered sharply.

He felt that this was an accusation of timidity. He put his other arm around her waist. She was rigid and trembling. It was impossible to pass this barrier of fear. He was the hunter paralyzed by the eyes of the deer that has turned.

The tittering began outside. It had seemed to Tim that the laws of time were revoked. Now they returned in force, at once, and even retroactively. Probably he had been in this darkness with Rachel for a hundred years, and they would never dare to come out. The comments began in the living room.

"Hurry up, will you?" Rachel said again, almost out loud this time. He felt a paroxysm, as of a breath of wind through the aspen, pass down the little body in his arm.

He stammered when he whispered, "You don't really want me to kiss you really, do you?"

"I don't care what you do," she whispered, "only for goodness' sakes do something, will you?"

Tim was bewildered by a great tenderness. He was trembling more than she was. He had no pride and wanted only to do what she wished.

The comments outside had become a clamor.

Suddenly she was pushing him off and whispering, "Let go of me, will you? Let go of me."

She got him loose from her, and scurried past him, and he heard the door knob rattle as she found it, and then saw her in the beam of light as she opened the door quickly. She controlled herself enough to go out slowly, but her face must have given something away about which he wasn't sure himself, because she was met by a sudden outburst of laughter and cries.

Tim started to follow her out, and this brought on another burst of laughter.

"Oh, no, you don't," the skinny boy said, and pushed him back in. Tim remembered that he was supposed to pick a name also.

"What's the matter, Tim? Want more?" somebody called.

Another answered him. "Go on. I bet they didn't even kiss. I bet it was a fake. They just stayed in there to make us think it was something."

Everybody began to ask Rachel if it had been just a fake.

Tim reached into the hat in the opening of the doorway, and then the slip was taken from him.

After a moment the skinny boy announced, "Pauline Chester."

The bosomy girl, the girl like cushions or a woman, came in. The door closed. There was nothing religious about this encounter, but there was no delay either. There was nothing said. Tim reached out to let know where he was. She took his hand and worked up along his arm and closed on him. He tried to stimulate cooperation, but that probably wouldn't have mattered anyway. It was a long and suffocating kiss. For one minute he forgot Rachel, but not because of any change of heart.

Such painful first experiences continue for a while in the adolescent's social development. They are marked by long, anonymous telephone conversations, initiated by either sex, in which the teasing "Guess who this is?" plays a dominant part. They are frequently marked by terrible feelings of self-consciousness, in which both sexes are aware of their physical clumsiness and their conversational ineptitude in social situations.

"Now," writes Arnold Bennett in *The Old Wives' Tale*,* "when everybody was served with mussels, cockles, tea and toast, and Mr. Povey had been persuaded to cut the crust off his toast, and Constance had, quite unnecessarily, warned Sophia against the deadly green stuff in the mussels, and Constance had further pointed out that the evenings were getting longer, and Mr. Povey had agreed that they were, there remained nothing to say. An irksome silence fell on all of them, and no one could lift it off. Tiny clashes of shell and crockery sounded with the terrible clearness of noises heard in the night. Each person avoided the eyes of the others. And both Constance and Sophia kept straightening their bodies at intervals, and expanding their chests, and then looking at their plates; occasionally a prim cough was discharged. It was a sad example of the difference between young women's dreams of social brilliance and the reality of life. These girls got more and more girlish, until, from being women . . . they sank back to about eight years of age— perfect children—at tea-table."

While heterosexual relationships are the most outstanding characteristic of adolescent social development, it represents only a part of the total social development. At all ages people seek friendship with others of the same sex and age as well as develop attachments for individuals older or younger. Adolescents are no exception. Rather, it is particularly important and imperative for them to have a good number of friends of the same sex and not merely friends in the casual and indifferent sense in which friendship is often understood. For adolescents in our culture, according to the documenta-

* From *The Old Wives' Tale* by Arnold Bennett. Doubleday & Co., Inc. P. 24.

tion of the California Adolescence Study, it is more important to accept and imitate the norms of one's peers than those of the new, strange, or even hostile world of adults (7). The American adolescent learns to value the opinions of his peers and to care most about their opinion and move with them—what David Riesman calls "radar personality." This need for approval and acceptance colors the adolescent's outlook on life and influences almost every aspect of his behavior. As the adolescent works out his social adjustment, adult approval or disapproval means little except as it affects success with others. Good social adjustment with peers has a profound effect on his happiness and consequent emotional stability.

In one period of Eugene Gant's early adolescence, as Thomas Wolfe describes it in *Look Homeward, Angel*,* there is a wonderful feeling of camaraderie, warmth and acceptance that comes through the raw, callow speech of Eugene and his friend George.

As he leaped down the stairs into the yard he heard Dirk Barnard's lusty splashing bathtub solo. Sweet Thomas, run softly till I end my song. Tyson Leonard, having raked into every slut's corner of nature with a thin satisfied grin, emerged from the barn with a cap full of fresh eggs. A stammering cackle of protest followed him from angry hens who found too late that men betray. At the barnside, under the carriage shed, "Pap" Rheinhart tightened the bellyband of his saddled brown mare, swinging strongly into the saddle, and with a hard scramble of hoof, came up the hill, wheeled in behind the house, and drew up by Eugene.

"Jump on, 'Gene," he invited, patting the mare's broad rump. "I'll take you home."

Eugene looked up at him grinning.

"You'll take me nowhere," he said. "I couldn't sit down for a week last time."

"Pap" boomed with laughter.

* Reprinted from *Look Homeward, Angel* by Thomas Wolfe (Copyright 1929, Charles Scribner's Sons. © 1957 Edward C. Aswell, as Administrator, C.T.A. of the Estate of Thomas Wolfe, and/or Fred W. Wolfe) with permission of the publisher.

"Why, pshaw, boy!" he said. "That was nothing but a gentle little dog-trot."

"Dog-trot your granny," said Eugene. "You tried to kill me."

"Pap" Rheinhart turned his wry neck down on the boy with grave dry humor.

"Come on," he said gruffly. "I'm not going to hurt you. I'll teach you how to ride a horse."

"Much obliged, Pap," said Eugene ironically. "But I'm thinking of using my tail a good deal in my old age. I don't want to wear it out while I'm young."

Pleased with them both, "Pap" Rheinhart laughed loud and deep, spat a brown quid back over the horse's crupper, and, digging his heels in smartly, galloped away around the house, into the road. The horse bent furiously to his work, like a bounding dog. With four-hooved thunder he drummed upon the sounding earth. *Quadrupedante putrem sonitu quatit ungula campum.*

At the two-posted entry, by the bishop's boundary, the departing students turned, split quickly to the sides, and urged the horseman on with shrill cries. "Pap," bent low, with loose-reined hands above the horse-mane, went through the gate like the whiz of a cross-bow. Then, he jerked the mare back on her haunches with a dusty skid of hoofs, and waited for the boys to come up.

"Hey!" With high bounding exultancy Eugene came down the road to join them. Without turning, stolid Van Yeats threw up his hand impatiently and greeted the unseen with a cheer. The others turned, welcoming him with ironical congratulation.

" 'Highpockets,' " said "Doc" Hines, comically puckering his small tough face, "how'd you happen to git out on time?" He had an affected, high-pitched nigger drawl. When he spoke he kept one hand in his coat pocket, fingering a leather thong loaded with buckshot.

"J. D. had to do his spring plowing," said Eugene.

"Well, if it ain't ole Handsome," said Julius Arthur. He grinned squintly, revealing a mouthful of stained teeth screwed in a wire clamp. His face was covered with small yellow pustulate sores. How begot, how nourished?

"Shall we sing our little song for Handsome Hal?" said Ralph Rolls to his copesmate Julius. He wore a derby hat jammed over his pert freckled face. As he spoke he took a

ragged twist of tobacco from his pocket and bit off a large
chew with a rough air of relish.

"Want a chew, Jule?" he said.

Julius took the twist, wiped off his mouth with a loose
male grin, and crammed a large quid into his cheek.

He brought me roots of relish sweet.

"Want one, Highpockets?" he asked Eugene, grinning.

I hate him that would upon the rack of this tough world
stretch me out longer.

"Hell," said Ralph Rolls. "Handsome would curl up and
die if he ever took a chew."

In Spring like torpid snakes my enemies awaken.

At the corner of Church Street, across from the new imitation Tudor of the Episcopal church, they paused. Above
them, on the hill, rose the steeples of the Methodist and
Presbyterian churches. Ye antique spires, ye distant towers!

"Who's going my way?" said Julius Arthur. "Come on,
'Gene. The car's down here. I'll take you home."

"Thanks, but I can't," said Eugene. "I'm going up-town."
Their curious eyes on Dixieland when I get out.

"You going home, Villa?"

"No," said George Graves.

"Well, keep Hal out of trouble," said Ralph Rolls.

Julius Arthur laughed roughly and thrust his hand through
Eugene's hair. "Old Hairbreadth Hal," he said. "The cut-
throat from Saw-Tooth Gap!"

"Don't let 'em climb your frame, son," said Van Yeats,
turning his quiet pleasant face on Eugene. "If you need
help, let me know."

"So long, boys."

"So long."

They crossed the street, mixing in nimble horse-play, and
turned down past the church along a sloping street that led
to garages. George Graves and Eugene continued up the
hill.

"Julius is a good boy," said George Graves. "His father
makes more money than any other lawyer in town."

"Yes," said Eugene, still brooding on Dixieland and his
clumsy deception.

A street-sweeper walked along slowly uphill, beside his
deep wedge-bodied cart. From time to time he stopped the
big slow-footed horse and, sweeping the littered droppings
of street and gutter into a pan, with a long-handled brush,

dumped his collections into the cart. Let not Ambition mock their useful toil.

Three sparrows hopped deftly about three fresh smoking globes of horse-dung, pecking out tid-bits with dainty gourmandism. Driven away by the approaching cart, they skimmed briskly over to the bank, with bright twitters of annoyance. One too like thee, tameless, and swift, and proud.

George Graves ascended the hill with a slow ponderous rhythm, staring darkly at the ground.

"Say, 'Gene!" he said finally. "I don't believe he makes that much."

Eugene thought seriously for a moment. With George Graves, it was necessary to resume a discussion where it had been left off three days before.

"Who?" he said, "John Dorsey? Yes, I think he does," he added, grinning.

"Not over $2,500, anyway," said George Graves gloomily.

"No—three thousand, three thousand!" he said, in a choking voice.

George Graves turned to him with a sombre, puzzled smile. "What's the matter?" he asked.

"O you fool! You damn fool!" gasped Eugene. "You've been thinking about it all the time!"

George Graves laughed sheepishly, with embarrassment, richly.

From the top of the hill at the left, the swelling unction of the Methodist organ welled up remotely from the choir, accompanied by a fruity contralto voice, much in demand at funerals. Abide with me.

Most musical of mourners, weep again!

George Graves turned and examined the four large black houses, ascending on flat terraces to the church, of Paston Place.

"That's a good piece of property, 'Gene," he said. "It belongs to the Paston estate."

Fast falls the even-tide. Heaves the proud harlot her distended breast, in intricacies of laborious song.

"It will all go to Gil Paston some day," said George Graves with virtuous regret. "He's not worth a damn."

They had reached the top of the hill. Church Street ended levelly a block beyond, in the narrow gulch of the avenue.

They saw, with quickened pulse, the little pullulation of the town.

A negro dug tenderly in the round loamy flowerbeds of the Presbyterian churchyard, bending now and then to thrust his thick fingers gently in about the roots. The old church, with its sharp steeple, rotted slowly, decently, prosperously, like a good man's life, down into its wet lichened brick. Eugene looked gratefully with a second's pride, at its dark decorum, its solid Scotch breeding.

"I'm a Presbyterian," he said. "What are you?"

"An Episcopalian, when I go," said George Graves with irreverent laughter.

"To hell with these Methodists!" Eugene said with an elegant, disdainful face. "They're too damn common for us." God in three persons—blessed Trinity. "Brother Graves," he continued, in a fat well-oiled voice, "I didn't see you at prayer-meeting Wednesday night. Where in Jesus' name were you?"

With his open palm he struck George Graves violently between his meaty shoulders. George Graves staggered drunkenly with high resounding laughter.

"Why, Brother Gant," said he, "I had a little appointment with one of the Good Sisters, out in the cow-shed."

Eugene gathered a telephone pole into his wild embrace, and threw one leg erotically over its second foot-wedge. George Graves leaned his heavy shoulder against it, his great limbs drained with laughter.

There was a hot blast of steamy air from the Appalachian Laundry across the street and, as the door from the office of the washroom opened, they had a moment's glimpse of the negresses plunging their wet arms into the liquefaction of their clothes.

George Graves dried his eyes. Laughing wearily, they crossed over.

"We oughtn't to talk like that, 'Gene," said George Graves reproachfully. "Sure enough! It's not right."

He became moodily serious rapidly. "The best people in this town are church members," he said earnestly. "It's a fine thing."

"Why?" said Eugene, with an idle curiosity.

"Because," said George Graves, "you get to know all the people who are worth a damn."

Worth being damned, he thought quickly. A quaint idea.

"It helps you in a business way. They come to know you and respect you. You don't get far in this town, 'Gene, without them. It pays," he added devoutly, "to be a Christian."

"Yes," Eugene agreed seriously, "you're right." To walk together to the kirk, with a goodly company.

Making a real place for himself in his social group is not always an easy task for the adolescent. He needs props, such as gangs, cliques or fraternities, to bolster his self-assurance. In early adolescence, when rebellion seems to threaten all previously accepted standards of behavior, the modification of the conscience by the mores of the group becomes apparent. Security in the group is extremely significant at adolescence; it helps handle the panic resulting from unresolved conflicts at this age (3). This is particularly true when the adolescent is not yet fully at home with his new awareness of sex differences and wants to feel the security of friends who are very much like himself. The adolescent's own group dominates his thinking and his behavior, a group composed of individuals of approximately the same emotional level of development; the deeper cohesive force is the mutual emotional empathy that exists (4). Not all youngsters are as lucky as Eugene Gant was at that moment in his development. Henry Trotter, the young protagonist in *The Newcomer*,* tries desperately to break into the new social milieu he finds himself in when his family moves to a new town. But no matter how hard he tries to impress the fellows with what a "regular" guy he is, rebuff meets him at every turn. Fortunately, Henry has a healthy concept of himself. He feels adequate and acceptable, even though he is bedeviled at the moment; he has vital interests and developed skills; he has a lot of inner resources and a good sense of humor which will see him through this situational crisis. The desire for approval and acceptance of other adolescents transcends all

* From *The Newcomer* by Clyde Brion Davis. Copyright 1954 by Clyde Brion Davis. Published by J. B. Lippincott Company. Pp. 57-64.

his other feelings just now, because he is an outsider and wants to be in the ingroup more than anything else.

Of course I was quite jittery about going out with this whole gang, but there was nothing at all I could do about it and I tried hard to brace myself against what the history books call an "incident". By what I thought was a fairly clever maneuver I managed to get in between two groups of chattering girls who naturally paid no attention to me but acted as a sort of convoy down the stairs and through the lower hall and out on the sidewalk. I wasn't exactly congratulating myself yet, but was certainly feeling fairly hopeful when I heard somebody yell behind me, "Hey, Screwball!" and another voice call out, "Hey, Dopey!"

Now there is a good chance that in any class that size there's some unlucky kid getting the business from the gang at all times, and, as it developed, this was true in the case of Christopher Albritten, so I said to myself it's probably somebody else they're yelling at although I could not convince my stomach of that and it felt as if I had swallowed several large lumps of dry ice.

Then that first voice called again, "Hey, Screwball, wait a minute!" And the second voice called, "Hey, Dopey, do you smoke it or shoot it?"

That dry ice in my stomach swelled and, walking along the sidewalk with these chattering girls in front of me and the other girls behind me, I felt my legs grow weak because my legs know those voices *did* mean me although I was whispering to myself that they didn't. I could remember back in LaSalle helping to give the business to several swellheads, nuts and sissies, which usually mean one and the same thing, and I don't think it occurred to me that ever in the world anybody would think I was a sissy unless, of course, I should fall in with some actual bank robbers or pirates.

I kept walking along alone with the girls in front and girls behind and suddenly I heard feet running and here were the two boys that turned out to be Spengler Devereaux and Claude Shanks grinning beside me.

"What's your hurry, Screwball?" Spengler Devereaux asked.

My voice said, "If you're talking to me, I'm not in any hurry."

Spengler Devereaux was a homely boy and when he grinned

he showed that his lower teeth fit outside his upper teeth. But homely boys are quite often the best boys, such as old Harvey Ellis in LaSalle, and I could have felt friendly toward Spengler Devereaux if he hadn't been calling me an epithet, and because of this I felt worse than I would if he had struck me as a repulsive person. From the way his shoulders filled out his striped jersey I felt also that it would be a great deal better to have this boy on your side instead of against you.

He said, "Good thing you're in no hurry. Miss Burchfield said we should ought to make you feel at home and we thought we'd tip you off about a few things around here."

"Yeah," the boy who was Claude Shanks said.

I said, "Thanks."

The girls who had been behind us now pulled out around us frowning because we blocked their way on the sidewalk, but they didn't say anything.

Claude Shanks was grinning and he had adenoids, I think, because he usually stood with his mouth partly open showing his big buck rabbit teeth whether he was grinning or not and he was kind of pale in spite of his freckles and red hair and he was nowhere as muscular-looking as Spengler Devereaux, although just as tall, which was a little taller than I because they were both approximately a year older.

Claude Shanks had a high voice and he said, "Yeah, we thought maybe we could help you feel at home by telling you where you live. Look, Dopey, you been talking to Mars and places so much maybe you forgot where you are. This is the world you're on now, see?"

My voice said, "Well, thanks for telling me."

"What you say your name was?" Spengler Devereaux asked. "That is, the one you couldn't remember?"

My voice, sounding tight and queer, said, "Henry Trotter."

Claude Shanks shook his grinning head. "I think," he said, "that Dopey Screwball's a better name. Don't you, Speng?"

In spite of feeling hollow and sick I was beginning to get a little mad. I said to Claude Shanks, "You're going to be sorry if you call me anything like that."

Spengler Devereaux said, "Well, you want to make something of it?"

Of course I did want to make something of it but not the

way I was feeling and against two of them. I said, "Look, I'm no dope and I'm no screwball. You'll find that out." But I'm afraid I didn't sound very confident.

Claude Shanks said, "Look, Dopey, they tell me you ain't got all your buttons."

I said, "Look, you don't need to worry any about my buttons. You worry about your own buttons."

Spengler Devereaux laughed and reached out and took hold of the top button on my suit coat. "Do you want *that* button?" he asked, seriously.

I said, "Of course I want that button."

So he gave a quick yank and pulled it right off my coat. "All right," he said, "if you want it, here it is," and handed it to me.

Now if anybody had done that to me in LaSalle, and I don't care how his shoulders filled out his jersey, I would have socked him right on the nose. But here in Franklin because of everything that had happened before, it just made me sicker and all I could do was to say, "Now that's a fine thing to do to a guy," and my voice was practically a whimper.

I don't know what would have happened next if just then some teachers hadn't come out of the school and Spengler Devereaux and Claude Shanks saw them and went on their way laughing.

I felt so very bad and ashamed of myself and sick and humiliated and dreary that when I got home I went right up to my room and shut the door and lay down on by bed that faced the wrong way and just bawled.

* * * * *

One thing that people like parents never seem to understand is that boys can't very well tell their fathers and mothers about serious trouble of this kind and it really wouldn't do any good even if they told and might do harm.

A boy just can't stand to have his parents, and particularly his father, be ashamed of him. He will brag and even lie to make them think he is getting along fine and is a sure enough jet-powered wonder and hero when what you might call his social relations are just so downright horrible that sometimes he can't stand it any longer and goes to playing cowboy with a piece of clothesline here and there around the house until he wanders up in the attic or down in the basement and then you read in the paper about his getting his neck tangled up in a rope while playing cowboy, or if there is a gun around it can go off accidentally while he is playing with it.

I know how that is, all right. Up there in my room bawling to myself I may have wished I were dead, but I can't say I had any serious thought about getting a rope or hunting up my father's Army forty-five because, after all, I knew there was nothing permanently wrong with me personally on account in LaSalle everything had been fine and even wonderful, but just consider how it is with some kid who got off on the wrong foot early in life and has always lived in the same place and has always been pretty much a patsy with some such name as Dopey Screwball hooked onto him which he can't shed and every time he tries to do something to show himself regular it goes wrong, one way or another, just making things worse, and at home he probably has been bragging and lying to keep his parents and particularly his father from finding out and being ashamed of him.

Consider a boy like that and you can see it would be a perfectly horrible life and there is just about one thing that will keep him from really cracking up some day and start playing cowboy up in the attic or down in the basement and that is to convince himself it isn't any fun at all playing with a stupid gang with stupid baseball and football and marbles and all that, but take up fascinating hobbies very feverishly like raising guinea pigs or making millions of model airplanes or collecting stamps or being a genius by pounding the piano six or eight hours a day or painting pictures or any of those things that cause grown-up neighbors and relatives to say how wonderful and superior he is, which make his parents proud of him even if a little puzzled. That way, perhaps, he can be about as happy as if he were living a nomal life, or at least not miserable.

The trouble is, of course, that every patsy can't be a genius. . . .

In his desire to attract attention and so be accepted as one of the gang, Henry had unwittingly gone beyond the established norms of his new community. He laid himself open to ridicule and rejection; he was marked as "different," which, particularly in early adolescence, brings with it social ostracism by other peers. The need to conform to the standards, ideals, ideas and attitudes of his agemates is paramount for the adolescent. In his heart, he may not agree with every facet of such standards, but he learns to acquire, at least, a protective coloring that will enable him to move confidently among his peers. Innumerable new relationships, writes Spiegel, are formed in part with contemporaries, and in part with older people, who are obviously substitutes for the renounced parents. These relationships are stormy, exclusive, and brief, and are repeated each time in identical form. They represent identifications of so primitive a type that the adolescent may change his beliefs, his style of clothing, his writing, with each new friend (9). This aspect of friendship is a response to the fragility of the newly acquired relationships (1).

The coping mechanism that Sylvia Marshall used in *The Bent Twig*,* a novel by Dorothy Canfield Fisher, was withdrawal. Sylvia is not invited to join a sorority at the university she attends. It comes as a blow to her, at first; she is bewildered by the rejection, for she has beauty, intelligence, athletic ability and the social graces. Nonetheless, she was not given a bid to pledge. ". . . a mark was left on her character by her affronted recognition of her total lack of success in this, her first appearance outside the sheltering walls of her home; her first trial by the real standards of the actual world of real people."

When the child first attempts to make adjustments outside the home situation, he is confronted with many new conditions that cause him to feel insecure and somewhat inadequate. In the home, he is usually sheltered by older persons who accept many responsibilities for his needs and provide him with affection and sympathy, whereas in the environment outside his own home, he finds his peers judging him by factors which may never have occurred to him.

Within the community culture are definite class distinc-

* From *The Bent Twig* by Dorothy Canfield. Copyright, 1915, by Henry Holt and Company, Inc. Copyright, 1943, by Dorothy Canfield Fisher. By permission of the publishers. Pp. 145-152.

tions. Sylvia's father, a professor at the university, belongs to a particular category within this occupational and social sphere. It is a category which Sylvia's peers do not find acceptable because it differs from their values. "After all, the sororities made no claim to be anything but social organizations. Their standing in the college world depended upon their social background. . . ." And how could it run the risk of acquiring a dubious social connection by extending a bid to a girl who came from such an impossible family?

To any one who is familiar with State University life, the color of Sylvia's Freshman year will be avidly conveyed by the simple statement that she was not invited to join a fraternity. To any one who does not know State University life, no description can convey anything approaching an adequate notion of the terribly determinative significance of that fact.

The statement that she was invited to join no sorority is not literally true, for in the second semester when it was apparent that none of the three leading fraternities intended to take her in, there came a late "bid" from one of the third-rate sororities, of recent date, composed of girls like Sylvia who had not been included in the membership of the older, socially distinguished organizations. Cut to the quick by her exclusion by the others, Sylvia refused this tardy invitation with remorseless ingratitude. If she were not to form one of the "swell" set of college, at least she would not proclaim herself one of the "jays," the "grinds," the queer girls, who wore their hair straight back from their foreheads, who invariably carried off Phi Beta Kappa, whose skirts hung badly, whose shoe-heels turned over as they walked, who stood first in their classes, whose belts behind made a practice of revealing large white safety-pins; and whose hats, even disassociated from their dowdy wearers, and hanging in the cloakroom, were of an almost British eccentricity.

Nothing of this sort could be alleged against Sylvia's appearance, which she felt, as she arrayed herself every morning, to be all that the most swagger frat could ask of a member. Aunt Victoria's boxes of clothing, her own nimble fingers and passionate attention to the subject, combined to turn her out a copy, not to be distinguished from the original, of the daughter of a man with an income five times that of her father. As she consulted her mirror, it occurred to her also, as but an honest recognition of a conspicuous fact, that her suitable and harmonious toilets adorned a person as pleasing to the eye as any of her classmates.

During the last year of her life at home she had shot up very fast, and she was now a tall, slender presence, preserved from even the usual touching and delightful awkwardness of seventeen by the trained dexterity and strength with which she handled her body, as muscular, for all its rounded slimness, as a boy's. Her hair was beautiful, a bright chestnut brown with a good deal of red, its brilliant gloss broken into innumerable highlights by the ripple of its waviness; and she had one other positive beauty, the clearly penciled line of her long, dark eyebrows, which ran up a trifle at the outer ends with a little quirk, giving an indescribable air of alertness and vivacity to her expression. Otherwise she was not at that age, nor did she ever become, so explicitly handsome as her sister Judith, who had at every period of her life a head as beautiful as that on a Greek coin. But when the two were together, although the perfectly adjusted proportions of Judith's proud, dark face brought out the irregularities of Sylvia's, disclosed the tilt of her small nose, made more apparent the disproportionate width between her eyes, and showed her chin to be of no mold in particular, yet a modern eye rested with far more pleasure on the older sister's face. A bright, quivering mobility like sunshine on water, gave it a charm which was not dependent on the more obvious prettinesses of a fine-grained, white skin, extremely clear brown eyes, and a mouth quick to laugh and quiver, with pure, sharply cut outline and deeply sunk corners. Even in repose, Sylvia's face made Judith's seem unresponsive, and when it lighted up in talk and laughter, it seemed to give out a visible light. In contrast Judith's beautiful countenance seemed carved out of some very hard and indestructible stone.

And yet, in spite of this undeniably satisfactory physical outfit, and pre-eminent ability in athletics, Sylvia was not invited to join any of the best fraternities. It is not surprising that there was mingled with her bitterness on the subject a justifiable amount of bewilderment. What *did* they want? They recruited, from her very side in classes, girls without half her looks or cleverness. What *was* the matter with her? She would not for her life have given a sign to her family of her mental sufferings as, during that first autumn, day after day went by with no sign of welcome from the social leaders of her new world; but a mark was left on her character by her affronted recognition of her total lack of success in this, her first appearance outside the sheltering walls of her home; her first trial by the real standards of the actual world of real people.

The fact, which would have been balm to Sylvia's vanity, had she ever had the least knowledge of it, was that upon her appearance in the Freshman class she had been the occasion of violent discussion and almost of dissension in the councils of the two "best" fraternities. Her beauty, her charm, and the rumors of her excellence in tennis had made a flutter in the first fraternity meetings after the opening of the autumn term. The younger members of both Sigma Beta and Alpha Kappa counseled early and enthusiastic "rushing" of the new prize, but the Juniors and Seniors, wise in their day and generation, brought out a number of damning facts which would need to be taken into consideration if Sylvia wore their pin.

There were, in both fraternities, daughters of other faculty families, who were naturally called upon to furnish inside information. They had been brought up from childhood on the tradition of the Marshalls' hopeless queerness, and their collective statement of the Marshalls' position ran somewhat as follows: "The only professors who have anything to do with them are some of the jay young profs from the West, with no families; the funny old La Rues—you know what a hopeless dowd Madame La Rue is—and Professor Kennedy, and though he comes from a swell family he's an awful freak himself. They live on a farm, like farmers, at the ends of the earth from anybody that anybody knows. They are never asked to be patrons of any swell college functions. None of the faculty ladies with any social position ever call on Mrs. Marshall—and no wonder. She doesn't keep any help, and when the doorbell rings she's as apt to come running in from the chicken house with rubber boots on, and a basket of eggs—and the *queerest* clothes! Like a costume out of a book; and they never have anybody to wait on the table, just jump up and down themselves—you can imagine what kind of a frat tea or banquet Sylvia would give in such a home—and of course if we took her in, we couldn't very well *tell* her her family's so impossible we wouldn't want

their connection with the frat known—and the students who
go there are a perfect collection of all the jays and grinds
and freaks in college. It's enough to mark you one to be
seen there—you meet all the crazy guys you see in classes
and never anywhere else—and of course that wouldn't stop
if Sylvia's frat sisters began going there. And their house
wouldn't do at *all* to entertain in—it's queer—no rugs—
dingy old furniture—nothing but books everywhere, even in
their substitute for a parlor—and you're likely to meet not
only college freaks, but worse ones from goodness knows
where. There's a beer-drinking old monster who goes there
every Sunday to play the fiddle that you wouldn't have speak
to you on the street for anything in the world. And the way
they entertain! My, in such a countrified way! Some of the
company go out into the kitchen to help Mrs. Marshall serve
up the refreshments—and everything homemade—and they
play charades, and nobody knows what else—bean-bag, or
spelling-down maybe—"

This appalling picture, which in justice to the young de-
lineators must be conceded to be not in the least over-drawn,
was quite enough to give pause to those impetuous and immature young Sophomores who had lacked the philosophical
breadth of vision to see that Sylvia was not an isolated phenomenon, but (since her family had lived in La Chance) an
inseparable part of her background. After all, the sororities
made no claim to be anything but social organizations. Their
standing in the college world depended upon their social
background, and of course this could only be made up of a
composite mingling of those of their individual members.

Fraternities did not wish to number more than sixteen or
eighteen undergraduates. That meant only four or five to be
chosen from each Freshman class, and that number of "nice"
girls were not hard to find, girls who were not only well
dressed, and lively and agreeable in themselves, but who
came from large, well-kept, well-furnished houses on the
right streets of La Chance; with presentable, card-playing,
call-paying, reception-giving mothers, who hired caterers for
their entertainments; and respectably absentee fathers with
sizable pocketbooks and a habit of cash liberality. The social
standing of the co-eds in State Universities was already pre-
carious enough, without running the risk of acquiring dubious social connections.

If Sylvia had been a boy, it is almost certain that the

deficiencies of her family would have been overlooked in consideration of her potentialities in the athletic world. Success in athletics was to the men's fraternities what social standing was to the girls'. It must be remarked parenthetically that neither class of these organizations had the slightest prejudice against high scholastic standing. On the contrary it was regarded very kindly by fraternity members, as a desirable though not indispensable addition to social standing and physical prowess.

But Sylvia was not a boy, and her fine, promising game of tennis, her excellence in the swimming-pool, and her success on the gymnasium floor and on the flying rings, served no purpose but to bring to her the admiration of the duffers among the girls, whom she despised, and the unspoken envy of the fraternity girls, whose overtures at superficial friendliness she constantly rebuffed with stern, wounded pride.

The sharpest stab to her pride came from the inevitable publicity of her ordeal. For, though her family knew nothing of what that first year out in the world meant to her, she had not the consolation of hoping that her condition was not perfectly apparent to every one else in the college world. At the first of the year, all gatherings of undergraduates not in fraternities hummed and buzzed with speculations about who would or would not be "taken" by the leading fraternities. For every girl who was at all possible, each day was a long suspense, beginning in hope and ending in listlessness; and for Sylvia in an added shrinking from the eyes of her mates, which were, she knew, fixed on her with a relentless curiosity which was torture to one of her temperament. She had been considered almost sure to be early invited to join Alpha Kappa, the frat to which most of the faculty daughters belonged, and all during the autumn she was aware that when she took off her jacket in the cloakroom, a hundred glances swept her to see if she wore at last the coveted emblem of the "pledged" girl; and when an Alpha Kappa girl chanced to come near her with a casual remark, she seemed to hear a significant hush among the other girls, followed by an equally significant buzz of whispered comment when the fraternity member moved away again. This atmosphere would have made no impression on a nature either more sturdily philosophic, or more unimaginative than Sylvia's (Judith, for instance, was not in the least affected by the experience), but it came to be a morbid obsession of this strong, healthy, active-minded young creature. It tinged with bitterness and blackness what should have been the crystal-clear cup holding her youth and intelligence and health. She fancied that every one despised her. She imagined that people who were in reality quite unaware of her existence were looking at her and whispering together a wondering discussion as to why she was not "in the swim" as such a girl ought to be—all girls worth their salt were.

Above all she was stung into a sort of speechless rage by her impotence to do anything to regain the decent minimum of personal dignity which she felt was stripped from her by this constant play of bald speculation about whether she would or would not be considered "good enough" to be invited into a sorority. If only something definite would happen! If there were only an occasion on which she might in some way proudly proclaim her utter indifference to fraternities and their actions! If only the miserable business were not so endlessly drawn out! She threw herself with a passionate absorption into her studies, her music, and her gymnasium work, cut off both from the "elect" and from the multitude, a proudly self-acknowledged maverick. She never lacked admiring followers among less brilliant girls who would have been adorers if she had not held them off at arm's length, but her vanity, far from being omnivorous, required more delicate food. She wished to be able to cry aloud to her world that she thought nothing and cared nothing about fraternities, and by incessant inner absorption in this conception she did to a considerable extent impose it upon the collective mind of her contemporaries. She, the yearningly friendly, sympathetic, praise-craving Sylvia, came to be known, half respected and half disliked, as proud and clever, and "high-brow," and offish, and conceited and so "queer" that she cared nothing for the ordinary pleasures of ordinary girls.

This reputation for a high-brow indifference to commonplace mortals was naturally not a recommendation to the masculine undergraduates of the University. These young men, under the influence of reports of what was done at Cornell and other more eastern co-educational institutions, were already strongly inclined to ignore the co-eds as much as possible. The tradition was growing rapidly that the proper thing was to invite the "town-girls" to the college proms and dances, and to sit beside them in the grandstand during football games. As yet, however, this tendency had not gone so far but that those co-eds who were members of a socially recognized fraternity were automatically saved from the neglect which enveloped all other but exceptionally flirtatious and undiscriminating girls. Each girls' fraternity, like the masculine organizations, gave one big hop in the course of the season and several smaller dances, as well as lawn-parties and teas and stage-coach parties to the football games. The young men naturally wished to be invited to these functions, the increasing elaborateness of which kept pace with the increasing sophistication of life in La Chance and the increasing cost of which made the parents of the girls groan. Consequently each masculine fraternity took care that it did not incur the enmity of the organized and socially powerful sororities. But Sylvia was not protected by this aegis. She was not invited during her Freshman year to the dances given by either the sororities or fraternities; and the large scattering crowd of masculine undergraduates were frightened away from the handsome girl by her supposed haughty intellectual tastes.

Here again her isolation was partly the result of her own wish. The raw-boned, badly dressed farmers' lads, with red hands and rough hair, she quite as snobbishly ignored as she was ignored in her turn by the well-set-up, fashionably dressed young swells of the University, with their white hands, with their thin, gaudy socks tautly pulled over their ankle-bones, and their shining hair glistening like lacquer on their skulls (that being the desideratum in youthful masculine society of the place and time). Sylvia snubbed the masculine jays of college partly because it was a breath of life to her battered vanity to be able to snub some one, and partly because they seemed to her, in comparison with the smart set, seen from afar, quite and utterly undesirable. She would rather have no masculine attentions at all than such poor provender for her feminine desire to conquer.

Thus she trod the leafy walks of the beautiful campus alone, ignoring and ignored, keenly alive under her shell of indifference to the brilliant young men and their chosen few feminine companions.

The adolescent can be rocked to his emotional core when he finds himself actively rejected by his peers. Sylvia imagines

CHAPTER FOUR

On the Meaning of Sex

> "For every youth and maiden who is not strictly secluded or very stupid, adolescence is a period of distressful perplexity, of hidden hypothesis, misunderstood hints, checked urgency, and wild stampedes of the imagination."
>
> H. G. WELLS, *Joan and Peter*, p. 298.

With the achievement of puberty, the adolescent becomes sexually active and competent (15). This maturity involves the whole process of physiological development, emotional feelings and social conditioning. It may well be for the adolescent a period of turmoil and awkward adjustment, of mystery and exchange of ignorance with other adolescents. He becomes aware of the painful yet thwarted need for fulfillment in a society which frowns upon, and places innumerable taboos on, sexual play. The powerful physical drive the adolescent has for sexual pleasure is intensified because of his social environment. He has had many prohibitions and restrictions of sexual expression placed on him from his earliest years. In addition, instead of having had the characteristics and social implications of sex explained to him, it has usually been suppressed with expressions of shame or embarrassment. In all likelihood, were many of the strict prohibitions and some of the secrecy surrounding sex lifted, much of the bewilderment and anguish the adolescent experiences could be minimized. American society is confused about sex because sex is still a tabooed subject; it is only to be expected then that the adolescent's problems in this area are compounded because they are so largely rooted in ignorance, fear or stealthy experimentation.

Ideas of sin and guilt associated with masturbation, noc-

turnal emissions, pe ting and sexual intercourse have been
evolved over centures in Western civilization. Premarital
intercourse, in part cular, has been condemned by mores
which go back to Biblical days and before. Although the
child is brought into a world that is filled with physical love
and affection, as he grows up he is taught to resist his biologically normal responses. Further, the adolescent has all
the sexual appetites of the adult, but because of his ethical
values, he must pos pone the gratifications of this appetite
until marriage, and then economic conditions force him to
delay marriage into well beyond adolescence (16). The conflict between physic desire and social codes is one of the
most intense problems many adolescents have to face. The
cultural postulate demands abstinence from masturbation
and postponement of the love object choice. "The adolescent
is to be a man by renouncing his infantile sexual activity, i.e.,
masturbation; at the same time, he is not to be a man because
he is not supposed to choose a sexual object. The actual
present situation for the adolescent is such that it offers no
compensation for this renunciation. It offers only punishment for defiance of the prohibition, and strives to divert
the adolescent's desires for sexual activity into 'spiritual'
channels" (17).

The young adolescent is prey to much nonsense, inflicted
on him by adults, peers and his reading of "literature," in
the matter of sex. Oftimes, moral preachments instill in the
malleable youngster distorted ideas and attitudes leaving a
warped picture of sex which he may carry into marriage. The
impressionistic passage which follows from the novel, *Death
of a Hero*,* exemplifies the resulting confusion when sex information passed on to a youth is couched in obscure,
mysterious half-truths or untruths.

One part of the mystery was called SMUT. If you were
smutty you went mad and had to go into a lunatic asylum.

* From *Death of a Hero* by Richard Aldington. Copyright 1929 by, and
reprinted with permission of, the author. Covici-Friede, Inc. Pp. 73-75.

Or you "contracted a loathsome disease" and your nose fell off.

The pomps and vanities of this wicked world, and all the sinful lusts of the flesh. So it was wicked, like being smutty, to feel happy when you looked at things and read Keats? Perhaps you went mad that way too and your eyes fell out?

"That's what makes them lay eggs," said the little girl, swinging her long golden hair and laughing, as the cock leaped on a hen.

O dreadful, O wicked little girl, you're talking smut to me. You'll go mad, I shall go mad, our noses will drop off. O please don't talk like that, please, please.

From fornication and all other deadly sins. . . . What is fornication? Have I committed fornication? Is that the holy word for smut? Why don't they tell us what it means, why is it "the foulest thing a decent man can commit"? When that thing happened in the night it must have been fornication; I shall go mad and my nose will drop off.

Hymn Number. . . . A few more years shall roll.

How wicked I must be.

Are there two religions? A few more years shall roll, in ten years half you boys will be dead. Smut, nose dropping off, fornication and all the other deadly sins. Oh, wash me in Thy Precious Blood, and take my sins away. Blood, Smut. And then the other—a draught of vintage that has been cooled a long age in the deep-delved earth, tasting of Flora and the country green, dance and Provençal song, and sun-burned mirth? Listening to the sound of the wind as you fell asleep; watching the blue butterflies and the Small Coppers hovering and settling on the great scented lavender bush; taking off your clothes and letting your body slide into a cool deep clear rock-pool, while the grey kittiwakes clamoured round the sun-white cliffs and the scent of sea-weeds and salt water filled you; watching the sun go down and trying to write something of what it made you feel, like Keats; getting up very early in the morning and riding out along the white empty lanes on your bicycle; wanting to be alone and think about things and feeling strange and happy and ecstatic— was that another religion? Or was that all Smut and Sin? Best not speak of it, best keep it all hidden. I can't help it, if it is Smut and Sin. Is "Romeo and Juliet" smut? It's in the same book where you do parsing and analysis out of "King

John." Seize on the white wonder of dear Juliet's hand and steal immortal blessing from her lips. . . .

One of the adolescent's first sexual anxieties probably revolves around the practice of masturbation. In the hope of breaking this practice, untold number of parents have threatened their children, both male and female, with the "fact" that the perpetuation of masturbation would result in every conceivable ill, from blackheads to insanity, from impotency to feeblemindedness. "Dr." Buck Mulligan, in the bacchanalian scene in James Joyce's *Ulysses*, jocularly diagnoses "Dr." Leopold Bloom as "prematurely bald from selfabuse, perversely idealistic in consequence, a reformed rake, and has metal teeth." But no scientist, physician, or psychologist has ever proved these "facts." Rather, masturbation is a sign of healthy sexual growth, universally practiced, which serves as a substitute for normal sexual outlets, particularly at adolescence when sexual maturity has been attained.

While masturbation in itself is not an unhealthy physical act, what may be injurious is the attitude taken toward it. Severe and emotionalized condemnation, which many parents exercise when they discover the existence of masturbatory practice in their households, can be a most disturbing drawback to the adolescent's psychosexual adjustment. The adolescent's own attitude toward masturbation often creates serious mental conflict, largely brought about by the emotional aspects of the act and its attendant fantasies. Some adolescents may derive such gratification from the act that they have no impetus to enter a more mature sexual relationship. On the other hand, many boys and girls pass through a periodic succession of attempts to stop the habit, failure in these attempts, consequent periods of remorse, the making of new resolutions— and a new start of the whole cycle (2). It is difficult to imagine anything better calculated to do permanent damage to the personality of the individual (6). Conflict and guilt feeling interfere with the gratifying effect of masturbation (14). From a psychological viewpoint, the most striking factor among the effects of masturbation, etiologically as well as symptomatologically, is anxiety (19). The loss of self-esteem may have repercussions on the adolescent's work efficiency, studies and social relationships.

Like masturbation, nocturnal emissions are a common outlet for adolescents; but unlike masturbation, the wet dream is accepted by most as a usual part of the male sexual picture. Kinsey reports that such emissions are considered to be products of dreams that are forgotten by their author and that they come about because one is not so inhibited during sleep (7). The phantasmagoria evoked in the following scene from *The Bulpington of Blup** reveals the growing sexual development of young Theodore Blup and the perplexing capriciousness which sex plays in his active waking and kaleidoscopic sleeping hours.

The four years of adolescence that followed Theodore's first meeting with Margaret Broxted were years of incessant discovery and complication for the teeming grey matter which was the material substance both of Theodore and of that second self of his, the Bulpington of Blup. Strange things, affecting both of them, were being thrust upon that incessant brain by the body it directed; new ferments and stimulants came, whispers on incitement, to its stirring cells. These whispers asked: What are you doing? What are you going to do? What are your plans about life? What do you think you are? There is strange business to be done. Get on with it all. Time is short for life.

The whispers were so subtle that Theodore's mind was only plainly aware of the evasive, reluctant, perplexed answers, the confusing impulses, they evoked. He did not perceive that he was changing; he realized only that he was growing up and learning new things about the world, masses of things about this world and about himself; some of them extraordinarily distressing and unpalatable.

Sex was becoming a more powerful and perplexing influence. It was no longer simply lovely and romantic. It was

* From *The Bulpington of Blup* by H. G. Wells. Reprinted by permission of the Executors of the Estate of H. G. Wells. Macmillan Co. Pp. 53-57.

entangling itself with unclean and repellent processes in life. Bodily forms and animal movements that had once been merely mystically attractive and beautiful were now becoming infected with intimations and gestures of urgency. Some profoundly obscene business was afoot in the universe amidst its engaging patterns and appearances. The apprehension of that urgent sustaining activity became more and more pervasive. The lines and contours of life converged upon disconcerting issues.

At fifteen Theodore had a great store of bookish and romantic knowledge and a belated ignorance and innocence. Francolin and Bletts came along to hint and tell, with flushed cheeks and a furtive defiance in their manner, of remarkable discoveries. And Theodore told nobody of certain discoveries of his own body was forcing upon him. His chosen ideas of love were after the sublimated fashion of the Troubadours. There was at last an ecstasy, a physical ecstasy. He had found out something of the nature of that for himself during his bedtime reveries on the verge of dreamland. But his wilful and waking life recoiled from too exacting a scrutiny of that close and thrilling embrace. The secrets of the adults about him, he knew, were heavy stuff, and Francolin abounded in the gross particulars.

The tension on Francolin's mind relieved itself in facetiousness. Dawning adolescence had turned the world upside down for him and filled him with laughter at the trick. He saw everything as it were from the pedestal upward, all "bums" and "bubs" and bellies. He developed an unsuspected gift for drawing, seeking to adorn his environment with formidable reminders of the great secret. His vocabulary was increased by a virile sexual terminology. He would not, if he could, have anything to hide.

There was less indecent uproar about Bletts, but a more direct and personal intentness. A quiet covetousness had come into his eyes. There had been something with the "slavey" at home, and he was for accosting girls and wandering off with them to quiet places. A large part of his leisure was devoted to prowling to that end. He sought Theodore's company for his prowling, because hunter and quarry, amidst the mysteries of petting and flirting, work best in confidential couples. The couples pair off for their researches, in silence on the male side and with a disposition to giggle and say "Star pit" on the female. Bletts said things about servants and work-girls and girl visitors to the seaside, gross things, that put Theodore into a state of great uneasiness. Theodore felt such things should not be said of any girl, that they smeared a sort of nastiness across all femininity, but they haunted his imagination afterwards and he was never able and decisive enough about it to stem the flow of Blett's magnetized preoccupation.

Amidst such influences as these, in the atmosphere created by a Christian civilization that, for better or worse, had substituted rigid restriction, concealment and shame for the grotesque initiations and terror-haunted taboos of pagan peoples, Theodore grew towards sexual maturity. There was a steady resistance in him to this self-induction into sexual life. For some time, therefore, more and more of their common grey matter was diverted from the material existence of Theodore to the purposes of his partner, the Bulpington of Blup and the life of reverie. The Bulpington of Blup had no use for the squalid adventures of Bletts; and Francolin approached him only distantly as a court jester under reproof. The Bulpington of Blup was the sublimating genius. He went through the air with ease while Theodore stumbled in the mire. He vanished whenever Theodore wallowed. Blup was still a high upstanding place, but now it was coming into more rational relations with prevalent and established things. It had shifted out of past times and away from such fantasies as Varangia towards, for example, the contemporary north-west Frontier of India; it bordered upon current possibilities; it was sometimes a quasi-independent State after the fashion of Sarawak in the very very Far East of these days; sometimes remotely South American like Bogota; sometimes in Ruritanian Europe. Elaborately concealing the practice from Raymond and Clorinda, Theodore read the contemporary novel-romance and particularly the stirring inventions of Mr. Rudyard Kipling, Mr. A. E. W. Mason and Mr. Anthony Hope. There he found heroes of the very blood and mettle of the Bulpington of Blup. He knew that by the standard of the higher criticism he ought not to like these stories, just as he knew that he ought not to hum that Barcarolle so frequently. But he did.

The Delphic Sibyl, who was sometimes altogether herself and sometimes more or less Margaret Broxted, remained the ruling heroine of his adolescent reveries. He and she went about side by side, they had great adventures and she was lost

and rescued, they embraced and kissed, but everything between them was always very clean and splendid. Only once or
twice on the very borderland of dreaming did that bodily
ecstasy occur, and then it was very indistinct and confusing
because suddenly it seemed that the Sibyl was someone else
—who vanished. And the strange and forcible dreams that
were now assailing him had only the remotest connexion
or no connexion at all with his world of fantasy.

Dreams and day-dreams belong to different orders of experience. The Bulpington of Blup was never in Theodore's
dreamland, nor the Sibyl, nor Margaret. Only the queerest
caricatures of familiar faces and scenes appeared there. Very
rarely was dreamland a pleasant land to wander in, and never
was one safe in it from disagreeable surprises. Strange gales
and storms of terror and menace arising in his growing and
ripening glands and pervading his being troubled it; head-
long pursuits would break out, flights from familiar things
suddenly become terrible. He fell down precipices; he had
insane impulses to leap down the fronts of buildings and
glissade down staircases into horror. He flew—but always
precariously. It was sometimes doubtful if even Theodore
was Theodore in his dreams or only a sort of sub-Theodore, a
primitive animal out of the core of him, to which a staircase
was still terrible and for which the pursuing carnivore
lurked incessantly.

This dreamland was becoming now more and more obscured by a monstrous sexual life of its own. Dreadful old
witches, young women with absurdly opulent contours who
exaggerated every distinctly feminine trait, caressing animal
monsters, sphinxes, mermaids, strange creatures, and yet
labelled, as it were, so that they were identified with, rather
than resembled, persons he knew, chased and seduced this
sub-Theodore in a warm and weedy underworld, overwhelmed him in soft rotundities, lured him into a false intimacy and found him helplessly responsive to startling em-
braces.

A dismayed youth would sit up rubbing the cobwebs of
sleep from his eyes, and slip out of bed to sponge off a sense
of clammy uncleanness with cold water.

So slovenly old Mother Nature, presiding inexactly and
inconsiderately over this Dame-School of hers which is our
world, scribbled athwart Theodore's reluctant intelligence

her intimations of what she has ever insisted upon as the main business of her children.

The onset of physical change for Theodore, Francolin and Bletts, as for most boys, came on more or less abruptly. The change usually begins between the ages of eleven and fourteen; during this time sexual activities are suddenly increased until, within another few years, most adolescents reach the maximum intensity of their whole lives. Among most females, sexual development comes on more gradually than in the male and is spread over a longer period of time (6). There is great variation in the ages at which the male or female adolescent experiences sexual development; the range of the normal is wide. What remains persistent and demanding, however, is the need for sexual satisfaction, for attention, self-assertion and social approval. It is not possible for the adolescent to be indifferent to sex. He may be afraid of sex, or worried, or mystified but he is never apathetic or neutral.

Mid-adolescence, which Sullivan terms the patterning of genital behavior (16), frequently brings with it as the first adolescent love object someone of the same sex. There is, on the part of boy for boy or girl for girl, a need for intimacy, for collaboration with at least one other person, for sharing secrets, for exploring the erogeneous zones of the body, for hero worship and crushes. This homosexual phase is transient and fleeting, usually, but can range from the passing miserable and joyful innocence of fourteen-year-old Tonio Kröger and Hans Hansen* to the passionately consummated attachment sixteen-year-old Ursula Brangwyn has for her schoolmistress, Winifred Inger in D. H. Lawrence's *The Rainbow*. It is also seen in the passage quoted from Stewart's *Through the First Gate* in the chapter "On Physical Development," where the boys admire the size of the penis of

---

* From *Tonio Kröger* by Thomas Mann. Copyright 1936. Reprinted by permission of Alfred A. Knopf, Inc. Pp. 90-92.

one of their peers; and it is seen in Victor Margueritte's *La Garçonne,* when on a sweltering afternoon, Elizabeth and Monique slip off their blouses and compare the sizes of their breasts.

"There comes Irwin Immerthal," said Hans.

Tonio stopped talking. If only the earth would open and swallow Immerthal up! "Why does he have to come disturbing us? If he only doesn't go with us all the way and talk about the riding-lessons!" For Irwin Immerthal had riding-lessons too. He was the son of the bank president and lived close by, outside the city wall. He had already been home and left his bag, and now he walked towards them through the avenue. His legs were crooked and his eyes like slits.

"'lo, Immerthal," said Hans. "I'm taking a little walk with Kröger. . . ."

"I have to go into town on an errand," said Immerthal. "But I'll walk a little way with you. Are those fruit toffees you've got? Thanks, I'll have a couple. Tomorrow we have our next lesson, Hans." He meant the riding-lesson.

"What larks!" said Hans. "I'm going to get the leather gaiters for a present, because I was top lately in our papers."

"You don't take riding-lessons, I suppose, Kröger?" asked Immerthal, and his eyes were only two gleaming cracks.

"No . . ." answered Tonio, uncertainly.

"You ought to ask your father," Hans Hansen remarked, "so you could have lessons too, Kröger."

"Yes . . ." said Tonio. He spoke hastily and without interest; his throat had suddenly contracted, because Hans had called him by his last name. Hans seemed conscious of it too, for he said by way of explanation: "I call you Kröger because your first name is so crazy. Don't mind my saying so, I can't do with it all. Tonio—why, what sort of name is that? Though I know of course it's not your fault in the least."

"No, they probably called you that because it sounds so foreign and sort of something special," said Immerthal, obviously with intent to say just the right thing.

Tonio's mouth twitched. He pulled himself together and said:

"Yes, it's a silly name—Lord knows I'd rather be called Heinrich or Wilhelm. It's all because I'm named after my mother's brother Antonio. She comes from down there, you know. . . ."

There he stopped and let the others have their say about horses and saddles. Hans had taken Immerthal's arm; he talked with a fluency that *Don Carlos* could never have roused in him. . . . Tonio felt a mounting desire to weep pricking his nose from time to time; he had hard work to control the trembling of his lips.

Hans could not stand his name—what was to be done? He himself was called Hans, and Immerthal was called Irwin; two good, sound, familiar names, offensive to nobody. And Tonio was foreign and queer. Yes, there was always something queer about him, whether he would or no, and he was alone, the regular and usual would have none of him, although after all he was no gypsy in a green wagon, but the son of Consul Kröger, a member of the Kröger family. But why did Hans call him Tonio as long as they were alone and then feel ashamed as soon as anybody else was by? Just now he had won him over, they had been close together, he was sure. "How had he betrayed him, Tonio?" Hans asked, and took his arm. But he had breathed easier directly Immerthal came up, he had dropped him like a shot, even gratuitously taunted him with his outlandish name. How it hurt to have to see through all this! . . . Hans Hansen did like him a little, when they were alone, that he knew. But let a third person come, he was ashamed, and offered up his friend. And again he was alone. He thought of King Philip. The king had wept. . . .

"Goodness, I have to go," said Irwin Immerthal. "Goodbye, and thanks for the toffee." He jumped upon a bench that stood by the way, ran along it with his crooked legs, jumped down and trotted off.

"I like Immerthal," said Hans, with emphasis. He had a spoilt and arbitrary way of announcing his likes and dislikes, as though graciously pleased to confer them like an order on this person and that. . . . He went on talking about the riding-lessons where he had left off. Anyhow, it was not very much farther to his house; the walk over the walls was not a long one. They held their caps and bent their heads before the strong, damp wind that rattled and groaned in the leafless trees. And Hans Hansen went on talking, Tonio throwing in a forced yes or no from time to time. Hans talked eagerly, had taken his arm again; but the contact gave Tonio no pleasure. The nearness was only apparent, not real; it meant nothing. . . .

They struck away from the walls close to the station, where they saw a train pull busily past, idly counted the coaches, and waved to the man who was perched on top of the last one bundled in a leather coat. They stopped in front of the Hansen villa on the Lindenplatz, and Hans went into detail about what fun it was to stand on the bottom rail of the garden gate and let it swing on its creaking hinges. After that they said good-bye.

"I must go in now," said Hans. "Good-bye, Tonio. Next time I'll take you home, see if I don't."

They put out their hands, all wet and rusty from the garden gate. But as Hans looked into Tonio's eyes, he bethought himself, a look of remorse came over his charming face.

"And I'll read *Don Carlos* pretty soon, too," he said quickly. "That bit about the king in his cabinet must be nuts." Then he took his bag under his arm and ran off through the front garden. Before he disappeared he turned and nodded once more.

And Tonio went off as though on wings. The wind was at his back; but it was not the wind alone that bore him along so lightly.

Hans would read *Don Carlos,* and then they would have something to talk about, and neither Irwin Immerthal nor another could join in. How well they understood each other! Perhaps—who knew?—some day he might even get Hans to write poetry! . . . No, no, that he did not ask. Hans must not become like Tonio, he must stop just as he was, so strong and bright, everybody loved him as he was, and Tonio most of all. But it would do him no harm to read *Don Carlos.* . . . Tonio passed under the squat old city gate, along by the harbour, and up the steep, wet, windy, gabled street to his parents' house. His heart beat richly: longing was awake in it, and gentle envy; a faint contempt, and no little innocent bliss.

A short time later, Tonio is in the throes of first love with a girl, Ingeborg Holm, blonde little Inge, the daughter of Dr. Holm who lived on Market Square opposite the tall old Gothic fountain with its many spires. The intensity of the first experience of "I am in love" is often as fleeting as transient adolescent homosexuality. Two weeks later, the adolescent is painfully and giddily in love with someone else. The number of wretched experiences connected with adolescents' first heterosexual attempts is legion (16), as is illustrated in Peter's feelings in H. G. Wells's *Joan and Peter*.* The real achievement of development comes after puberty when the individual finally succeeds in subordinating his or her different libidinal drives to a love object of the opposite sex and externalizes the drive in the social form of marriage.

"The first effect of the young woman upon Peter was a considerable but indeterminate excitement. It was neither pleasurable nor unpleasurable, but it hung over the giddy verge of being unpleasant. It made him want to be very large, handsome and impressive. It also made him acutely ashamed of wanting to be very large, handsome and impressive. It turned him from a simple boy into a conflict of motives. He wanted to extort admiration from Adela. Also he wanted to despise her utterly. These impulses worked out no coherent system of remarks and gestures, and he became awkward and tongue-tied."

The adolescent's sexuality is a very powerful drive and his desires can be somewhat satisfied, as was seen in *The Bulpington of Blup,* by release in daydreams, masturbation or nocturnal emissions. Fenichel says that "adolescence begins with the anatomical and physiological genital changes which constitute a necessary precondition for the discharge of sexual excitement via the genital apparatus . . . [and] ends when sexuality is fully integrated into the personality" (4). As the early adolescent moves on to his middle and late adolescent years, he normally begins heterosexual relationships. The pattern usually followed is dating, petting, courting, and culmination in marriage. In the present generation,

* From *Joan and Peter* by H. G. Wells. Reprinted by permission of the Executors of the Estate of H. G. Wells. Macmillan Co. P. 307.

it is considered desirable for young people to "circulate" rather than to "go steady," for the feeling is that through many dating experiences the adolescent will eventually be able to select a mate in whom he will find compatible emotional and intellectual tastes (5). Dating helps the individual to judge personality differences, the wise evaluation of which is a prime requisite for happy marriage. For personality adjustment and sex adjustment cannot be separated; they represent social learning superimposed upon a highly complicated physical structure. "Most young people after a certain amount of normal experience in dating come to appreciate that there are many individuals of the opposite sex with whom they could live happily and that there are certain other individuals with whom they could not possibly be happy" (12). Joan, in Wells' novel, *Joan and Peter,** is discovering this. As she reviews her dating experiences with several young men, her personality evaluation of each figures prominently in her thoughts. She is perplexed by many sexual urgings the while and is troubled because of the indefinable dissatisfaction she feels.

Joan had since lost that happiness, that perfect assurance, that intense appreciation of the beauty in things which had come to her with early adolescence. She was troubled and perplexed in all her ways. She was full now of stormy, indistinct desires and fears, and a gnawing, indefinite impatience. No religion had convinced her of a purpose in her life, neither Highmorton nor Cambridge had suggested any mundane devotion to her, nor pointed her ambitions to a career. The only career these feminine schools and colleges recognized was a career of academic successes and High School teaching, intercalated with hunger strikes for the Vote, and Joan had early decided she would rather die than teach in a High School. Nor had she the quiet assurance her own beauty would have given her in an earlier generation of a discreet choice of lovers and marriage and living "hap-

* From *Joan and Peter* by H. G. Wells. Reprinted by permission of the Executors of the Estate of H. G. Wells. Macmillan Co. Pp. 340-347.

pily ever afterwards." She had a horror of marriage lurking in her composition; Mrs. Pybus and Highmorton had each contributed to that; every one around her spoke of it as an entire abandonment of freedom. Moreover there was this queerness about her birth—she was beginning to understand better now in what that queerness consisted—that seemed to put her outside the customary ceremonies of veil and orange blossoms. Why did they not tell her all about it—what her mother was and where her mother was? It must be a pretty awful business, if neither Aunt Phyllis nor Aunt Phoebe would ever allude to it. It would have to come out—perhaps some monstrous story—before she could marry. And who could one marry? She could not conceive herself marrying any of these boys she met, living somewhere cooped up in a little house with solemn old Troop, or under the pursuing eyes, the convulsive worship of Wilmington. She had no object in life, no star by which to steer, and she was full of the fever of life. She was getting awfully old. She was eighteen. She was nineteen. Soon she would be twenty.

All her being, in her destitution of any other aim that had the slightest hold upon her imagination, was crying out for a lover.

It was a lover she wanted, not a husband; her mind made the clearest distinction between the two. He would come and unrest would cease and beauty would return. Her lover haunted all her life, an invisible yet almost present person. She could not imagine his face nor his form, he was the blankest of beings, and yet she was so sure she knew him that if she were to see him away down a street or across a crowded room, instantly, she believed, she would recognize him. And until he came life was a torment of suspense. Life was all wrong and discordant, so wrong and discordant that at times she could have hated her lover for keeping her waiting so wretchedly.

And she had to go on as though this suspense was nothing. She had to disregard this vast impatience of her being. And the best way to do that, it seemed to her, was to hurry from one employment to another, never to be alone, never without some occupation, some excitement. Her break with Peter had an extraordinary effect of release in her mind. Hitherto, whatever her resentment had been she had admitted in practice his claim to exact a certain discretion from her; his opinion had been, in spite of her resentment, a standard for

her. Now she had no standard at all—unless it was a rebellious purpose to spite him. On Joan's personal conduct the
thought of Oswald, oddly enough, had scarcely any influence
at all. She adored him as one might a political or historical
hero; she wanted to stand well in his sight, but the idea
of him did not pursue her into the details of her behavior
at all. He seemed preoccupied with ideas and unobservant.
She had never had any struggle with him; he had never
made her do anything. And as for Aunts Phyllis and Phoebe
—while the latter seemed to make vague gestures towards
quite unutterable liberties, the former maintained an attitude of nervous disavowal. She was a woman far too uncer-
tainminded for plain speaking. She was a dear. Clearly she
hated cruelty and baseness; except in regard to such things
she set no bounds.

Hitherto Joan had had a very few flirtations; the extremest
thing upon her conscience was Bunny Cuspard's kiss. She
had the natural shilly-shally of a girl; she was strongly moved
to all sorts of flirtings and experimentings with love, and
very adventurous and curious in these matters; and also she
had a system of inhibitions, pride, hesitation, fastidiousness,
and something beyond these things, a sense of some ultimate
value that might easily be lost, that held her back. Rebelling
against Peter had somehow also set her rebelling against
these restraints. Why shouldn't she know this and that? Why
shouldn't she try this and that? Why, for instance, was she
always "shutting up" Adela whenever she began to discourse
in her peculiar way upon the great theme? Just a timid
prude she had been, but now—.

And all this about undesirable people and unseemly
places, all this picking and choosing as though the world
was mud; what nonsense it was! She could take care of herself surely!

She began deliberately to feel her way through all her
friendships to see whether this thing, passion, lurked in any
of them. It was an interesting exercise of her wits to try over
a youth like Troop, for example; to lure him on by a touch
of flattery, a betrayal of warmth in her interest, to reciprocal
advances. At first Troop wasn't in the least in love with her,
but she succeeded in suggesting to him that he was. But the
passion in him released an unsuspected fund of egotistical
discourse; he developed a disposition to explain himself and
his mental operations in a large, flattering way both by word

of mouth and by letter. Even when he was roused to a sense
of her as lovable, he did not become really interested in her
but only in his love for her. He arrived at one stride at the
same unanalytical acceptance of her as of his God and the
Church and the King and his parents and all the rest of the
Anglican system of things. She was his girl—"the kid." He
really wasn't interested in those other things any more than
he was in her; once he had given her her role in relation to
him his attention returned to himself. The honour, integrity,
and perfection of Troop were the consuming occupations of
his mind. This was an edifying thing to discover, but not an
entertaining thing to pursue; and after a time Joan set herself to avoid, miss, and escape from Troop on every possible
occasion. But Troop prided himself upon his persistence. He
took to writing her immense, ill-spelt, manly letters, with
sentences beginning: "You understand me very little if—."
It was clear he was hers only until some simpler, purer, more
receptive and acquisitive girl swam into his ken.

Wilmington, on the other hand, was a silent covetous
lover. Joan could make him go white, but she could not
make him talk. She was a little afraid of him and quite sure
of him. But he was not the sort of young man one can play
with, and she marvelled greatly that any one could desire
her so much and amuse her so little. Bunny Cuspard was a
more animated subject for experiment, and you could play
with him a lot. He danced impudently. He could pat Joan's
shoulder, press her hand, slip his arm round her waist and
bring his warm face almost to a kissing contact as though
it was all nothing. Did these approaches warm her blood?
Did she warm his? Anyhow it didn't matter, and it wasn't
anything.

Then there was Graham Prothero, a very good-looking
friend of Peter's, whom she had met while skating. He had a
lively eye, and jumped after a meeting or so straight into
Joan's dreams, where he was still more lively and good-looking. She wished she knew more certainly whether she had
got into his dreams.

Meanwhile Joan's curiosity had not spared Jelalludin. She
had had him discoursing on the beauties of Indian love, and
spinning for her imagination a warm moonlight vision of
still temples reflected in water tanks, of silvery water shining
between great lily leaves, of music like the throbbing of a
nerve, of brown bodies garlanded with flowers. There had

been a loan of Rabindranath Tagore's love poems. And once he had sent her some flowers.

Any of these youths she could make her definite lover she knew, by an act of self-adaptation and just a little reciprocal giving. Only she had no will to do that. She felt she must not will anything of the sort. The thing must come to her; it must take possession of her. Sometimes, indeed, she had the oddest fancy that perhaps suddenly one of these young men would become transfigured; would cease to be his clumsy, ineffective self, and change right into that wonderful, that compelling being who was to set all things right. There were moments when it seemed about to happen. And then the illusion passed, and she saw clearly that it was just old Bunny or just staccato Mir Jelulludin.

In Huntley, Joan found something more intriguing than this pursuit of the easy and the innocent. Huntley talked with a skilful impudence that made a bold choice of topics seem the most natural in the world. He presented himself as a leader in a great emancipation of women. They were to be freed from "the bondage of sex." The phrase awakened a warm response in Joan, who was finding sex a yoke about her imagination. Sex, Huntley declared, should be as incidental in a woman's life as it was in a man's. But before that could happen the world must free its mind from the "superstition of chastity," from the idea that by one single step a woman passed from the recognizable into the impossible category. We made no such distinction in the case of men; an artist or a business man was not suddenly thrust out of the social system by a sexual incident. A woman was either Mrs. or Miss; a gross publication of elemental facts that were surely her private affair. No one asked whether a man had found his lover. Why should one proclaim it in the case of a woman by a conspicuous change of her name? Here, and not in any matter of votes or economics was the real feminine grievance. His indignation was contagious. It marched with all Joan's accumulated prejudice against marriage, and all her growing resentment at the way in which emotional unrest was distracting and perplexing her will and spoiling her work at Cambridge. But when Huntley went on to suggest that the path of freedom lay in the heroic abandonment of the "fetish of chastity," Joan was sensible of a certain lagging of spirit. A complex of instincts that conspired to adumbrate that unseen, unknown, and yet tyrannous lover, who would not leave her in peace and yet would not reveal himself, stood between her and the extremities of Huntley's logic.

There were moments when he seemed to be pretending to fill that oppressive void; moments when he seemed only to be hinting at himself as a possible instrument of freedom. Joan listened to him gravely enough so long as he theorized; when he came to personal things she treated him with the same experimental and indecisive encouragement that she dealt out to her undergraduate friends. Huntley's earlier pose of an intellectual friend was attractive and flattering; then he began to betray passion, as it were, unwittingly. At a fancy dress dance at Chelsea—and he danced almost as well as Joan—he became moody. He was handsome that night in black velvet and silver that betrayed much natural grace; Joan was a nondescript in black and red, with short skirts and red beads about her pretty neck. "Joan," he said suddenly, "you're getting hold of me. You're disturbing me." He seemed to soliloquize. "I've not felt like this before." Then very flatteringly and reproachfully, "You're so damned intelligent, Joan. And you dance—as though God made you to make me happy." He got her out into an open passage that led from the big studio in which they had been dancing, to a yard dimly lit by Chinese lanterns, and at the dark turn of the passage kissed her more suddenly and violently than she had ever been kissed before. He kissed her lips and held her until she struggled out of his arms. Up to that moment Joan had been playing with him, half attracted and half shamming; then once more came the black panic that had seized her with Bunny and Adela.

She did not know whether she liked him now or hated him. She felt strange and excited. She made him go back with her into the studio. "I've got to dance with Ralph Winterbaum," she said.

"Say you're not offended," he pleaded.

She gave him no answer. She did not know the answer. She wanted to get away and think. He perceived her confused excitement and did not want to give her time to think. She found Winterbaum and danced with him, and all the time, with her nerves on fire, she was watching Huntley, and he was watching her. Then she became aware of Peter regarding her coldly, over the plump shoulder of a fashion-plate artist. She went to him as soon as the dance was over.

"Peter," she said, "I want to go home."

He surveyed her. She was flushed and ruffled, and his eyes and mouth hardened.

"It's early."

"I want to go home."

"Right. You're a bit of a responsibility, Joan."

"Don't, then," she said shortly, and turned round to greet Huntley as though nothing had happened between them.

But she kept in the light and the crowd, and there was a constraint between them. "I want to talk to you more," he said, "and when we can talk without someone standing on one's toes all the time and listening hard. I wish you'd come to my flat and have tea with me one day. It's still and cosy, and I could tell you all sorts of things—things I can't tell you here."

Joan's dread of any appearance of timid virtue was overwhelming. And she was now blind with rage at Peter—why, she would have been at a loss to say. She wanted to behave outrageously with Huntley. But in Peter's sight. This struck her as an altogether too extensive invitation.

"I've never noticed much restraint in your conversation," she said.

"It's the interruptions I don't like," he said.

"You get me no ice, you get me no lemonade," she complained abruptly.

"That's what my dear Aunt Adelaide used to call changing the subject."

"It's the cry of outraged nature."

"But I saw you having an ice—not half an hour ago."

"Not the ice I wanted," said Joan.

"Distracting Joan! I suppose I must get you that ice. But about the tea?"

"I *hate* tea," said Joan, with a force of decision that for a time disposed of his project.

Just for a moment he hovered with his eye on her, weighing just what that decision amounted to, and in that moment she decided that he wasn't handsome, that there was a something *unsound* about his profile, that he was pressing her foolishly. And anyhow, none of it really mattered. He was nothing really. She had been a fool to go into that dark passage, she ought to have known her man better; Huntley had been amusing hitherto and now the thing had got into a new phase that wouldn't, she felt, be amusing at all; after this he would pester. She hated being kissed. And Peter was a beast. Peter was a hateful beast. . . .

Joan and Peter went home in the same taxi—in a grim silence. Yet neither of them could have told what it was that kept them hostile and silent.

Joan has repelled the sexual advances of her dates for reasons which she herself cannot define too well. Her own latent sex urgings, the prudish restrictions of Victorian society, and the unrecognized fact of her love for Peter keep her from freer sexual expression.

In the instance of Sylvia, in *The Bent Twig* by Dorothy Canfield, a very specific area of concern—petting—is manifested. Petting, or necking, has been defined by Kinsey as physical contacts between the two sexes which do not involve a union of the genitalia (11). The practice of petting is common and widespread in the United States today, although it is frequently criticized particularly as it reflects on the girl participant. Petting serves as an end in itself, in order to bring about immediate satisfactions, or it may serve as a substitute for intercourse. Most young people who pet recognize frankly its significance as a source of erotic satisfaction. Kinsey goes so far as to say that the girl who does not engage in petting because she considers it morally wrong, or does not engage in it because she is not attracted by males, is the one who is most likely to remain unmarried (10). However, it is more likely that successful marriage and sexual adjustment are based more on gradually established confidence, liking, and mutual respect than on any premarital trial-and-error sexual process (1). *The Bent Twig** excerpt illuminates the sexual and mental confusion revolving around the petting problem.

Sylvia did not welcome this idea at all, feeling as overwhelming an aversion to companionship as to solitude, but

* From *The Bent Twig* by Dorothy Canfield. Copyright, 1915, by Henry Holt and Company, Inc. Copyright, 1943, by Dorothy Canfield Fisher. By permission of the publishers. Pp. 226-229.

she could think of no excuse, and in an ungracious silence
put on her wraps and joined her mother, ready on the porch,
the basket in her mittened hand.

Mrs. Marshall's pace was always swift, and on that crisp,
cold, sunny day, with the wind sweeping free over the great
open spaces of the plain about them, she walked even more
rapidly than usual. Not a word was spoken. Sylvia, quite as
tall as her mother now, and as vigorous, stepped beside her,
not noticing their pace, nor the tingling of the swift blood
in her feet and hands. Her fresh young face was set in
desolate bitterness.

The Martins' house was about six miles from the Marshalls'. It was reached, the eggs procured, and the return
begun. Still not a word had exchanged between the two
women. Mrs. Marshall would have been easily capable under
the most ordinary circumstances, of this long self-contained
silence, but it had worked upon Sylvia like a sojourn in the
dim recesses of a church. She felt moved, stirred, shaken. But
it was not until the brief winter sun was beginning to set
red across the open reaches of field and meadow that her
poisoned heart overflowed. "Oh, Mother——!" she exclaimed
in an unhappy tone, and said no more. She knew no words
to phrase what was in her mind.

"Yes, dear," said her mother gently. She looked at her
daughter anxiously, expectantly, with a passion of yearning
in her eyes, but she said no more than those two words.

There was a silence. Sylvia was struggling for expression.
They continued to walk swiftly through the cold, ruddy,
sunset air, the hard-frozen road ringing beneath their rapid
advance. Sylvia clasped her hands together hard in her muff.
She felt that something in her heart was dying, was suffocating for lack of air, and yet that it would die if she
brought it to light. She could find no words at all to ask for
help, agonizing in a shy reticence impossible for an adult to
conceive. Finally, beginning at random, very hurriedly,
looking away, she brought out, faltering, "Mother, *is* it true
that all men are—that when a girl marries, she must expect
to—aren't there *any* men who—" she stopped, burying her
burning face in her muff.

Her words, her tone, the quaver of desperate sincerity
in her accent, brought her mother up short. She stopped
abruptly and faced the girl. "Sylvia, look at me!" she said in
a commanding voice which rang loud in the frosty silences

about them. Sylvia started and looked into her mother's face.
It was moved so darkly and so deeply from its usual serene
composure that she would have recoiled in fear, had she not
been seized upon and held motionless by the other's compelling eyes.

"Sylvia," said her mother, in a strong, clear voice, acutely
contrasted to Sylvia's muffled tones, "Sylvia, it's a lie that
men are nothing but sensual! There's nothing in marriage
that a good girl honestly in love with a good man need fear."

"But—but—" began Sylvia, startled out of her shyness.

Her mother cut her short. "Anything that's felt by decent
men in love is felt just as truly, though maybe not always so
strongly, by women in love. And if a woman doesn't feel that
answer in her heart to what he feels—why, he's not mate for
her. Anything's better for her than going on. And, Sylvia,
you mustn't get the wrong idea. Sensual feeling isn't bad in
itself. It's in the world because we have bodies as well as
minds—it's like the root of a plant. But it oughtn't to be a
very big part of the plant. And it must be the root of the
woman's feeling as well as the man's or everything's all
wrong."

"But how can you *tell*!" burst out Sylvia.

"You can tell by the way you feel, if you don't lie to
yourself, or let things like money or social position count.
If an honest girl shrinks from a man instinctively, there's
something not right—sensuality is too big a part of what the
man feels for her—and look here, Sylvia, that's not always the
man's fault. Women don't realize as they ought how base it is
to try to attract men by their bodies," she made her position
clear with relentless precision, "when they wear very low-
necked dresses, for instance—" At this chance thrust, a wave
of scarlet burst up suddenly over Sylvia's face, but she could
not withdraw her eyes from her mother's searching, honest
gaze, which, even more than her words, spoke to the girl's
soul. The strong, grave voice went on unhesitatingly. For
once in her life Mrs. Marshall was speaking out. She was like
one who welcomes the opportunity to make a confession of
faith. "There's no healthy life possible without some sensual
feeling between the husband and wife, but there's nothing
in the world more awful than married life when it's the only
common ground."

Sylvia gazed with wide eyes at the older woman's face,
ardent, compelling, inspired, feeling too deeply, to realize

it wholly, the vital and momentous character of the moment. She seemed to see nothing, to be aware of nothing but her mother's heroic eyes of truth; but the whole scene was printed on her mind for all her life—the hard, brown road they stood on, the grayed old rail-fence back of Mrs. Marshall, a field of brown stubble, a distant grove of beech-trees, and beyond and around them the immense sweeping circle of the horizon. The very breath of the pure, scentless winter air was to come back to her nostrils in after years.

"Sylvia," her mother went on, "it is one of the responsibilities of men and women to help each other to meet on a high plane and not on a low one. And on the whole—health's the rule of the world—on the whole, that's the way the larger number of husbands and wives, imperfect as they are, do live together. Family life wouldn't be possible a day if they didn't."

Like a strong and beneficent magician, she built up again and illuminated Sylvia's black and shattered world. "Your father is just as pure a man as I am a woman, and I would be ashamed to look any child of mine in the face if he were not. You know no men who are not decent—except two—and those you did not meet in your parents' home."

For the first time she moved from her commanding attitude of prophetic dignity. She came closer to Sylvia, but although she looked at her with a sudden sweetness which affected Sylvia like a caress, she but made one more impersonal statement: "Sylvia dear, don't let anything make you believe that there are not as many decent men in the world as women, and they're just as decent. Life isn't worth living unless you know that—and it's true." Apparently she had said all she had to say, for she now kissed Sylvia gently and began again to walk forward.

Petting specifically and sex generally were thorny mysteries for Sylvia to penetrate. Most girls do not acquire sexual information from the homes in which they are raised nor from specific instruction given by their mothers. On the contrary, the hesitancy of the home, church, and school in coming to grips in a frank and helpful fashion with the central question of the physical relations between the sexes, is the problem. For many boys and girls, sexual inhibitions, distaste for all aspects of sex, fear of a sexual relationship, and feelings of guilt which many carry into marriage, stem from misinformation and ignorance. For most girls, the first real understanding of a heterosexual experience comes from the act of petting itself, not from information given by a parent or teacher (11).

The demand for socialization of the sexual instinct is fulfilled by the prohibition of autoerotic gratification; in this manner, the individual unconsciously becomes aware of the fact that other persons have a claim on him as regards his sexual activity, that he is responsible to others for this activity, and that he has no right to indulge in sexual pleasure for personal and selfish reasons only (19).

Adolescent girls are usually held in stricter check than boys. Society is far harsher and has a greater disciplinary attitude to "erring" girls. The girl is judged to have violated the basic canons of religious and moral law. The social attitude toward her is usually one of wholesale condemnation, while for the boy there is general acceptance of premarital coitus. This double standard of morality exists probably because of the meaningfulness for the female in undertaking a significant, rich, warm and profound association with a male, with a view toward marriage and motherhood. Therefore, the whole question of the meaning of interpersonal relationships is involved here. External controls can hardly be successful if it is put on the basis of stricture. ". . . . what everybody must know is that sexual conduct, whatever it may be, is regulated personally and not publicly in modern society. If there is restraint it is, in the last analysis, voluntary; if there is promiscuity, it can be quite secret" (13). The need for conventions which will guide conduct is increasing. The adolescent himself wants limits set up, for he has very real sexual needs which he must satisfy within the accepted framework of the society in which he moves. How to reconcile his needs with the proscribed social world is a very real problem.

Ivan Bunin has described the "deadly anguish . . . the

sense of something terrible, criminal and shameful," the confused feelings of guilt and joy which overwhelm an adolescent when he becomes involved in a premarital experience.*

I was being gradually turned—outwardly at least—into an ordinary country youth, already rather accustomed to sit in his manor, no longer estranged from its everyday existence, used to go shooting, to call on his neighbors, on rainy or stormy days to go to the village, to favourite cottages, to while away one's time in the family circle round the samovar, or else to lie whole days long with a book on the sofa, to dream aloud about something with one's sister, to chat with one's brothers. . . . And so another year passed. And then happened something which had to happen sooner or later, which comes in due time to every one, and sometimes as a great calamity.

Our neighbor, Alferov, who used to lead a lonely life, died. My brother Nicholas, who had long dreamt of living on his own, leased his vacated manor and lived there that winter instead of with us. Among his servants there was a maid called Tonka. She had just married, but immediately after the wedding had been forced by poverty and homelessness to part with her husband: he was a saddler and after marrying went off again on his ambulant work, whilst she took up work with my brother.

She was about twenty. In the village people called her "the jackdaw," "the savage," and thought her, for her quietness, quite stupid. I myself had known her, of course, since childhood, as I knew everybody in our village, and I always liked her. She had a very dark complexion, a gracefully and firmly built girl's body, small and strong limbs, black nut-brown, narrow-slitted eyes. She resembled a Red Indian: the straight but rather rough features of a dark face, the coarse jet of lank hair. But in that, too, I found some charm, though truly a somewhat savage one. As for stupidity, I never heard her say anything silly—perhaps because she said only what was quite necessary and commonplace, keeping silence as easily and naturally as if she were speechless.

I used to go nearly every day to my brother's; I admired

* From *The Well of Days* by Ivan Bunin. Copyright 1934. Reprinted by permission of Alfred A. Knopf, Inc. Pp. 227-231.

her; I even liked the firm, swift tread of her feet when she brought the samovar or soup-tureen to table, the way in which she would meaninglessly look up: that stamping and that look, the coarse blackness of her hair parted in the middle and showing beneath an orange-coloured kerchief, the somewhat flat, bluish lips of her slightly elongated mouth, the slope of the dark youthful neck passing into shoulders— all this invariably roused in me a sweet and uneasy yearning. Sometimes, meeting her in the hall, or the anteroom, I would jestingly catch at her as she went, and press her to the wall. Laughing silently, she would adroitly slip away—and with that the matter ended. There was no amorous feeling between us.

But once, walking in soft winter dusk through the village, I turned absent-mindedly to Alferov's manor, passed between the snow-heaps to the house, mounted to the porch. In the dark anteroom, especially dark at the top, a pile of red-hot embers in the freshly lighted stove showed red, gloomy and fantastic as in a black cave, and Tonka, bareheaded, straddling her bare legs, their tibias shining against the light with their smooth skin, was sitting on the floor against its mouth, illumined by its dark flames, holding a poker in her hand, its white-hot end touching the embers; slightly averting from the glowing heat her dark flaming face, she was dreamily gazing at the embers, at their crimson mounts, frail and translucent, here already dying away under the fine lilac efflorescence, and there still burning with blue-green gas. I banged the door when entering—she did not even turn round.

"Why is it dark here? Is no one at home?" I asked, approaching her.

She threw her face further back, and, without looking at me, smiled somewhat uneasily and languidly.

"As if you don't know!" she said mockingly, and pushed the poker a little further into the stove.

"Know what?"

"Come on, stop it. . . ."

"Stop what?"

"You must know where they are, as they've gone to you. . . ."

"I've been taking a walk, I haven't seen them."

"Tell me about walks . . ."

I squatted on the floor, looking at her bare legs and at her bare black head, already full of inward tremors, but laughing and pretending also to admire the embers and their hot dark-crimson glow. . . . Then suddenly I sat down beside her, embraced her, and threw her on the floor, catching her reluctant lips, hot because of the fire. The poker rattled, some sparks flew up from the stove. . . .

When afterwards I jumped out to the porch, I looked like a man who had suddenly committed murder, I held my breath and quickly turned round to see whether someone was not coming. But there was no one; everything to my surprise was ordinary and quiet; in the village, in the accustomed winter darkness, the lights burned in the cottages with an incredible calmness—as if nothing had happened. . . . I looked up, listened—and quickly walked away. I could not feel the ground beneath me, for two clashing emotions: the sense of a sudden, terrible, irremediable catastrophe in my life, and that of an exultant, victorious triumph. . . .

At night, through my anxious sleep, I was now and then seized by deadly anguish, by the sense of something terrible, criminal, and shameful that had suddenly caused my undoing. "Yes, everything is over," I would think, waking up, recovering my senses with difficulty. "Everything, everything is finished, destroyed, spoilt; obviously this must be so; it can no longer be remedied or put straight. And the terrible thing is that one cannot tell it to anyone: everybody is asleep; they know nothing; they suspect nothing; and to crown it all, I am now a stranger to everybody, alone in the wide world. . . ."

Waking up in the morning, I looked with quite new eyes around me, at that room so familiar to me, lit evenly by the fresh snow which had fallen in the night: there was no sun, but in the room it was quite light from the bright whiteness. My first thought on opening my eyes was, of course, about what had happened. But that thought no longer frightened me; of the anguish, despair, shame, feeling of guilt, there was none in my soul. On the contrary. But how can I go down to tea now?—I thought. And what should I do in general? Well, nothing, I thought; nobody knows anything, and nobody will ever know, and in the world everything is just as nice as before and even more so than before; outside is my favourite, still, white weather; the garden, its bare branches covered with shaggy snow, is all piled over with white snowheaps; in the room it is warm because of the stove lit by somebody while I slept and now roaring and cracking evenly, flutteringly drawing in the brass lid. . . . It smells bitter and fresh, through the warmth, from the frosted and thawing aspen brushwood lying next to it on the floor. . . . And what happened is only that natural, necessary thing which had to happen—after all I am already seventeen and why should I be worse than the others? I am not only no worse, but even better than they, and at least I have matched them in that too. I was once more overwhelmed with triumph, pride, happiness—here I am man, I've got a mistress! How silly were all my night-time thoughts! How wonderful and terrible was the happening of yesterday! And it will be repeated again, perhaps even to-day! With what a lovely, unexpectedly childish fear, with what obvious hopelessness did she manage to whisper something rapid and imploring! O, how I do and will love her!

The adolescent's confused feelings here arise from the fact that while he has had some temporary physical pleasure, he has violated the ethical precepts of his church and his community. Although he thinks he loves Tonka, the thought arises merely to justify his act; for the basis of mature human sexual behavior is something called "love." The healthy sex act consists of very complex psychological phenomena. It depends on the spiritual merger of one personality with another. The sex impulse in humans is tied to the deepest emotions and should result in what is called true love in the finest sense. While the adolescent is sexually mature for such an experience, he usually does not have the experiential, emotional preparedness to achieve the full realization of the act. To a considerable extent adolescent love is an attempt to arrive at a definition of one's identity by projecting one's diffused ego images on one another and by seeing them thus reflected and gradually clarified. This is why many a youth would rather converse, and settle matters of mutual identification, than embrace (3).

What is imperative in the sex education of the adolescent is not so much what is taught but how. Sex becomes an intense and troublesome problem largely because of the social and moral values of "good" and "bad" which society attaches to this area. It is a forbidden subject which needs airing and enlightenment, so that the lurid mysteries of the taboo can be lifted and the imaginative effort of the adolescent to pierce these mysteries can succeed with perceptive realism. The emotional overtones of all sexual experiences have long-range significance for the individual. His ability to respond emotionally to a sexual partner inevitably contributes to the effectiveness of his other, nonsexual, social relationships.

REFERENCES

(1) Bergler, Edmund, & Kroger, William S. *J. Amer. Med. Assn.*, 154:168, 1954.
(2) Brown, Fred, & Kempton, Rudolf T. *Sex Questions and Answers.* NY: McGraw-Hill, 1950, p. 90.
(3) Erikson, Erik H. *Childhood and Society.* NY: Norton, 1950, p. 228.
(4) Fenichel, Otto. *The Psychoanalytic Theory of Neurosis.* NY: Norton, 1945.
(5) Folsom, J. K. in Becker, Howard, & Hill, Reuben (Eds.), *Marriage and the Family.* Boston: Heath, 1942, p. 180.
(6) Kinsey, Alfred C., Pomeroy, Wardell B., & Martin, Clyde E. *Sexual Behavior in the Human Male.* Phila: Saunders, 1948, p. 514.
(7) Kinsey, et al. *Ibid.,* p. 518.
(8) Kinsey, et al. *Ibid.,* p. 183.
(9) Kinsey, Alfred C., Pomeroy, Wardell B., & Martin, Clyde E., & Gebhard, Paul H. *Sexual Behavior in the Human Female.* Phila: Saunders, 1953, p. 227.
(10) Kinsey, et al., *Ibid.,* p. 235.
(11) Kinsey, et al., *Ibid.,* p. 265.
(12) Landis, Paul H. *Adolescence and Youth, The Process of Maturing.* NY: McGraw-Hill, Inc., 1952, p. 282.
(13) Lippmann, Walter. *A Preface to Morals.* NY: Macmillan, 1929, p. 286.
(14) Reich, Annie. "The Discussion of 1912 on Masturbation and Our Present Day Views," in Eissler, Ruth S., et al. (Eds.), *The Psychoanalytic Study of the Child,* Vol. VI. NY: International Universities Press, 1951, p. 85.
(15) Spiegel, Leo A. "A Review of Contributions to a Psychoanalytic Theory of Adolescence: Individual Aspects," in Eissler, Ruth S., et al. (Eds.), *The Psychoanalytic Study of the Child,* Vol. VI. NY: International Universities Press, 1951, p. 376.
(16) Sullivan, Harry Stack, *Conceptions of Modern Psychiatry.* Washington, DC: William Alanson White Foundation, 1947.
(17) Tausk, Victor. "On Masturbation," in Eissler, Ruth S., et al. (Eds.), *The Psychoanalytic Study of the Child,* Vol. VI. NY: International Universities Press, 1951, p. 70.
(18) Tausk, Victor. *Ibid.,* p. 71.
(19) Tausk, Victor. *Ibid.,* p. 74.

CHAPTER FIVE

On Family Relations

"Your son at five is your master, at ten your slave, at fifteen your double, and after that, your friend or foe, depending on his bringing up."

HASDAI, *Ben HaMelek VeHaNazir*, c. 1230, Ch. 7

Family living, in our culture, requires its members to participate in an intricate, complicated, delicately balanced series of interrelationships.

It is not surprising, therefore, that any change, even one as natural, gradual and expected as the child's becoming an adolescent may have important repercussions on the emotional equilibrium of the family.

Up to adolescence, the respective roles of the child and the adult have been fairly well defined. Cruze (2) has emphasized the importance of this early experience as follows: "It is in the family group that the young child encounters the initial experience that will largely determine his over-all outlook on life. It is here in these early relationships that he begins to develop a sense of being loved and accepted by other people—a feeling of worth and acceptance that is indispensable to mental health and satisfactory social development."

Except in rare instances, however, the child in our society is not really considered as a person big enough, powerful enough, detached enough from the family to be looked on as a separate individual. But the child grows up, and an overt striving for independence and adult status is a natural concomitant of adolescence. This new person may appear as someone whose fears, hopes, desires, and triumphs seem to draw their sustenance from sources frequently unfathomable to parents or to himself. He has some of the features and habiliments of the past, he is still living, on the surface, through the daily family routine, he seems the familiar youngster everyone is accustomed to. But he may be unpredictable now, to himself as well as to others, although his identity is beginning to be far more sharply his own. He is responding to many more aspects of living than before, some rising from within his newer self, many associated with areas and contexts quite removed from his life with his family.

The adolescent has to come to grips with many new but fundamental needs during this crucial period of his life. Not the least of his problems is learning to establish a newer pattern of interaction with his parents and siblings. It is difficult for him to do this without anxiety and tension even with a cooperative and understanding family. He has to work out his own new formula of dependence, independence, and interdependence with many new people. The pain of some of his struggles to establish himself outside the home, the anxieties and guilt he may be experiencing about himself, may be displaced onto an aggressiveness more safely displayed to the known parents and siblings, whether or not they are patient, loving, and sympathetic.

The adolescent is ready for psychological weaning from parents and other adults. Where this is denied successful expression, the adolescent may give up the struggle for independence, with serious effects on emotional health thereafter.

Part of the difficulty may lie in parents having conscious or unconscious fears about themselves and about their current or future meaningfulness to their adolescent sons and daughters. These may interfere with their timely recognition of, and respect for, the emerging strength and need for independence of their offspring. With every laudable intention, but pushed by love, pity, anxiety, fear, and the desire to save their children pain and anguish, parents may put enormous pressure on the adolescent to accept their own view of the world and their prescriptions for the "right" sort of behavior, at a time when this pressure is most disturbing to him.

Well-intentioned parents may often confuse their own hopes and ambitions with what they consider desirable goals for their children. Parents who overemphasize the material benefits to be expected from higher education may be a trial to adolescents. They themselves may be doing very well in a trade or small business, but "work with your head instead of your back" is the burden of their refrain. These may be the parents who constantly point out that the Joneses' Ethel or the Smiths' John are brilliant, have finished college, are working at wonderful professional jobs, and are a credit to their loving parents. Adolescent children in this family are sometimes afraid to point out a truism of their own generation (one perhaps illustrated in their own family) that a skilled trade, a higher bracket white-collar job or a good small business may be more highly paid and offer greater continuity of employment than a number of the professions. These adolescents experience a good deal of panic and guilt if they do not want to or cannot meet their parents' expectations in this regard.

Older parents, and sometimes younger parents with elderly ideas, may often view their adolescent children with a mixture of impatience and despair. They appear unable to find a common ground of understanding with them. An activity which may not be understood or easily classified as useful in the parents' eyes may be put into a category of "bad" or "stupid" and forbidden. Adolescents whose sense of their own worth is especially vulnerable at this time may suffer painfully at this overtly expressed disapproval.

It may be a lack of adequate communication, as much as any specific derogatory attitude of parents to children, which the adolescent finds hard to accept. The following excerpt from *Asphalt and Desire** points up this two-way difficulty in communication and understanding.

* From *Asphalt and Desire* by Frederic Morton. Copyright 1952 by Frederic Morton. Reprinted by permission of Harcourt, Brace and Company, Inc. Pp. 68-72.

And then it started. In stages, as usual.

"How is your college?" she asked.

"Hunkydunkydory, Maw."

"What? What you mean?"

"It means fine, Maw. Wonderful. Ipsipipsi."

"You don't mind if I ask? I miss mine children. I am interested to know what they doing."

"That's very nice. We appreciate that very much, Maw."

"Why don't you relax," Paw said to him. "Join with us. Take a chair."

"I'm happy here," Mister said, twisting on the couch.

"And how is your bookwriting?" Maw asked.

"I am bookwriting terrific."

"Yeh? Well, maybe my son is going to be famous yet. Don't think I wouldn't be happy. I would be the happiest person in the world."

And then there is only the slurping of tea, the crack of herring bones, the tortured yielding of the sofa springs. A quiet on which the imminence of something gnaws.

"So you got any plans for summer?"

"This summer I'm gonna take life by the horns, Maw."

"What? What you mean?"

"You're not going to help out in the store?" Paw said.

"All I'm asking is that you get somebody else. O.K.? Fair warning? All right? If you please?"

"Listen here, mine dear young man, you can't take off a few hours a week to give a hand to your parents?"

"Aw, be big about it. Give an unemployed family father the opportunity."

"You think we're not going to pay you or something? I didn't want to say nothing, but if you think we stingy, why did you have to send a telegram for money for a plane? The train isn't good enough any more?"

"I wanted my mothahs flowahs to arrive freshly," Mister said à la Winston Churchill.

"Oh!"

Maw was flying toward the askew petals on the shelf. "Isn't that beautiful! I smelled something when I came in! Oh, that's lovely of mine son! You know how easy it is to make a mother happy!"

Mister twisted on the couch.

"Look what he brings his poor old mother, look at the

beautiful yellow ones!" She was whisking them round the
rooms, gesturing them in my face. "I feel like his best girl!
Aren't I your best girl! You see the ones with the red spots?
Oh!"

"Daaaah," Mister groaned off her attack before it came
too near. She pirouetted and skipped to Paw and kissed him
and tickled the flowers under his helpless nose. Her perennial
frantic adolescence reddened and fevered her like a rash. It
was mortifying.

But she herself threw it off.

"Ah, if you sweet enough to bring your mother flowers,
don't tell me you not going to be nice and not work a little
in the store?"

"You get yourself a more trustworthy person, Maw."

"I don't care about trustworthy. I want my son to be with
me a little. That's not asking much."

"I'll be busy this summer, Maw."

"You going to run around again with these World People,
these communists?"

"Not communists, Maw. Gangsters."

"Listen, you talking to your mother—"

"That's what you called them last time, gangsters."

"Do you hear me? I want you to talk like you're talking
to your mother, not to a street scum."

"Will you leave me alone?"

But he didn't even close the door. For it was here. It had
come. The icebox whispered rustily. With laborious embarrassment Paw screwed on the infra-red lamp that's supposed to kill off all the germs; a tiny cockroach was panicky
under the cupboard. We were all braced for the ordeal of
togetherness. The question of working in the store didn't
matter, the words were irrelevant, but the shout was important, the bawl, the howl was paramount for we were
reared in it, they had fed it to us with aching throats. It's the
only thing we truly know, we must return to it from time to
time, the ancient intimacy of its pain. Loneliness is farthest
off when we cry out against each other.

"What did God give you all that brains for? To hurt your
mother? You are home half an hour and you have to act up
like that?"

"Yeah, you'd all be so much better off without me. A
happy harmonious family you'd be, eating prayers for breakfast."

"Go on, destroy everything with your talk."

"Yeah, I destroy everything. I'm a spoiler. I'm evil. I like to make love to young tawny-haired boys who died of diphtheria. And you know my biggest trouble? I *exist!*"

"Go on, destroy. I can take it. You done it before—"

"I've been *existing* for nineteen years steady. Can't stop. It's a vice, you know. Ain't it tough, having an exister for a son—"

"Talk, go on, talk! And you know something? I wouldn't have you work in the store if you gave me a million dollars! I'm very happy you not working in that store. You destroy that too."

"Oh, yes, I'm an exister of the deepest dye, I'm the ten plagues, I'm the black angel, the canker, the nemesis of all nice mothers who do everything for their sons—"

"Since you are that little I remember you had to ruin everything. You can't come home nice? Talk with me, be like a human being? No, you've got to ruin the conversation—"

"Yes, I'm the scorpion, the adder, the scourge of the Levins—"

"For years I've been begging you. I want to talk to you like a son. I've been the best mother in the world to you, but it didn't do any good. You've got all the brains there is but it's no good. I thought maybe after you went to the university it would be different, but you still the same, you've got no manners, nothing—"

"You shouldn't bother with a boy like that," Paw said. "He'll find out himself." He was still screwing the lamp on, trying to participate in the intensity but lagging behind, as usual, sighing at the lamp socket.

"But he *is* bothering me. He's destroying me. Remember what he did with the five dollars in the store?"

"Yes, I remember," Mister said. "Do you hear, I remember, I'm sorry for it, I remember, you don't have to tell me again."

"You think that was funny? Was that so smart? He's got to give five dollars to a stranger which belong to his family—"

"Help! Listen, I'm going to the blood bank to bleed out five dollars. I'm gonna go into the coal mines to make money, I'll sell my suits. I'll go naked for the five bucks. But don't *say* it again!"

"So you got a bad conscience? You don't know for five

dollars I've got to stand in the store all day with my bad feet—"

"Shut up! I'm warning you. I'm not kidding either!"

"Pearl, don't bother," Paw said at the socket, trying to be in tune. "We got over the depression. We will get over him too."

"He's an ungrateless no-good. He doesn't care that for five dollars—"

The vase with the flowers in it shattered to the floor.

The foregoing excerpt also highlights "Maw's" basic lack of concern with any needs but her own in dealing with her children. But there are overanxious and overimaginative parents who may wish to anticipate every conceivable difficulty in the life of the adolescent. They may try to warn him of all the dangers to which he may now be exposed since he is older and is participating in a wider range of activities. The net effect of their efforts may be to make the adolescent feel that they lack confidence in his judgment and his ability to cope successfully with his problems. He may set himself to prove that he can take care of himself by being unresponsive to suggestions or requirements made by his parents or by being unruly and undisciplined. On the other hand, he may accept what he considers his parents' view of him and be unable to make even minor decisions unaided by them.

The relationship between the adolescent and his parents sometimes becomes further confused because he may remain financially dependent on them long after he matures physically and intellectually. Some parents believe, unconsciously, that the adolescent who is still economically dependent is not ready for any other kind of independence. These may be parents who continue to choose food, clothing, schooling, activities and friends for their children. If the adolescent begins to feel that a little independence is worth working for and gets a job, the parents are hurt to the quick, living evidence of what it means to be a rejected parent.

There are, of course, parents who are too disturbed emo-

tionally to be able to provide any real warmth for understanding of their children. The adolescent may find this
helpful in some ways during a period when he needs a lot of
privacy in which to do his own growing. A consistent lack of
contact with his family, however, may add to a feeling of
isolation, detachment, and loneliness which some adolescents
experience in overwhelming measure.

A consistent and smoothly functioning relationship between parents and adolescents appears to be difficult to
achieve. The very nature of the changes taking place in the
adolescent, the conflicting emotional needs and ambivalent
attitudes of parents and adolescents may encourage an erratic,
fluctuating pattern of interaction. Finding a new way to communicate and to take account of each others' needs may be
difficult and painful at this time, but not necessarily destructive.

The adolescent is sensitive about his person, his appearance, his clothes, his feelings, but especially about his family.
For one thing, he is very eager to impress his friends. Leo, the
young protagonist in *The Go-Between*,* is preparing for a
month's visit to a friend's country house and he is afraid his
mother will accompany him. "I shouldn't have wanted that.
I was haunted by the schoolboy's fear that my mother
wouldn't look right, do right, be right in the eyes of the other
boys and their parents. She would be socially unacceptable;
she would make a bloomer. I could bear humiliation for myself, I thought, more easily than I could for her." Or family
peculiarities which the adolescent more or less disregarded
up to this point suddenly assume great importance for him.
He may embark on a single-handed campaign to remake his
entire family. No one is more astonished than he at the angry
resistance he may encounter at what seems to him to be a
reasonable demand that his family become perfect.

Although the adolescent may appear to flout his parents

---

* From *The Go-Between* by L. P. Hartley. Reprinted by permission of
Alfred A. Knopf, Inc. Copyright, 1955. P. 30.

and seem indifferent about their affection, he keeps a weather eye on them and may be quick to notice and resent any favor shown to siblings. He may really be more anxious about his parents' love now, because he is doing more to strain relations than before.

Where relationships with siblings are concerned, it is true, in general, that when parents accept and love each other and show warmth and understanding to their children, less friction may be experienced. But the adolescent is a bit of a lone wolf, except with his friends. He doesn't really want his brothers and sisters to know him just now. He tries to hide his own feelings because he is afraid his siblings may see what is going on and use it in reprisal in personal or family quarrels.

His relationships with siblings of varying ages may show differing degrees of complexity. If there are much younger siblings he may sometimes show the aggressiveness he dare not display too openly toward the parents by criticizing their treatment of the younger children. He may resent what he considers better treatment or more indulgence than he himself experienced. Or he may tell his parents that they are too harsh and that that was what made him miserable as a youngster. Indirectly, he is also telling his parents to be kinder and more understanding to him now.

At times the adolescent resents the much younger child because he feels that no pressure is being applied to him to change quickly and to be successful, as it is to himself. He may also unconsciously consider the younger child as a natural recipient of the anger, the frustration, and the drive for power which he may be afraid of showing elsewhere.

But the opposite may also be true. The unquestioning acceptance of himself which he experiences from a younger sibling may enable the adolescent to express the love and tenderness he is unable to share with anyone else. Chapters 21 and 22 in Salinger's *The Catcher in the Rye* subtly, humorously, and rather poignantly describe an adolescent whose relationship with his younger sister provides stability and meaning in a world which has become confused, "phoney," even overwhelming to him (7).

His parents' attitudes toward his siblings, coupled with a considerable degree of difference in their acceptance of himself, may very much influence the adolescent's relationships at home. Even if there are no open unfavorable comparisons, the knowledge that a parent prefers a sibling to himself may give many painful moments to an adolescent. He may resolve the situation in a way which makes it more acceptable to him as Francie, in *A Tree Grows in Brooklyn,** was able to do.

All of a sudden, she was frightened and lonely. She wanted her father, she wanted her father. He couldn't be dead, he just couldn't be. In a little while, he'd come running up the stairs singing, *"Molly Malone."* She'd open the door and he'd say, "Hello, Prima Donna." And she'd say, "Papa, I had a terrible dream. I dreamed you were dead." Then she'd tell him what Miss Garnder had said and he'd find the words to convince her that everything was all right. She waited, listening. Maybe it *was* a dream. But no, no dream lasted that long. It was real. Papa was gone forever.

She put her head down on the table and sobbed. "Mama doesn't love me the way she loves Neeley," she wept. "I tried and tried to make her love me. I sit close to her and go wherever she goes and do whatever she asks me to do. But I can't make her love me the way papa loved me."

Then she saw her mother's face in the trolley car when mama sat with her head back and her eyes closed. She remembered how white and tired mama had looked. Mama *did* love her. Of course she did. Only she couldn't show it in the ways that papa could. And mama *was* good. Here, she expected the baby any minute and she was still out working. Supposing mama died when she had the baby? Francie's blood turned icy at the thought. What would Neeley and she do without mama? Where could they go? Evy and Sissy were too poor to take them. They'd have no place to live. They had no one in all the world but mama.

* From *A Tree Grows in Brooklyn* by Betty Smith. Copyright 1943 by Betty Smith. Reprinted by permission of Harper & Brothers. Pp. 282-285.

"Dear God," Francie prayed, "don't let mama die. I know that I told Neeley that I didn't believe in You. But I do! I do! I just *said* that. Don't punish mama. She didn't do anything bad. Don't take her away because I said I didn't believe in You. If You let her live, I'll give You my writing. I'll never write another story again if You'll only let her live. Holy Mary, ask your son, Jesus, to ask God not to let my mother die."

But she felt that her prayer was of no use. God remembered that she had said that she didn't believe in Him and He'd punish her by taking mama as He had taken papa. She became hysterical with terror and thought of her mother as already dead. She rushed out of the flat to look for her. Katie wasn't cleaning in their house. She went into the second house and ran up the three flights of stairs, calling "Mama!" She wasn't in that house. Francie went into the third and last house. Mama wasn't on the first floor. Mama wasn't on the second floor. There was one floor left. If mama wasn't there, then she was dead. She screamed:

"Mama! Mama!"

"I'm up here," came Katie's quiet voice from the third floor. "Don't holler so."

Francie was so relieved that she all but collapsed. She didn't want her mother to know she had been crying. She searched for her handkerchief. Not having it, she dried her eyes on her petticoat and walked up the last flight slowly.

"Hello, Mama."

"Has something happened to Neeley?"

"No, Mama." (She always thinks of Neeley first.)

"Well, hello then," said Katie smiling. Katie surmised that something had gone wrong in school to upset Francie. Well, if she wanted to tell her. . . .

"Do you like me, Mama?"

"I'd be a funny person, wouldn't I, if I didn't like my children."

"Do you think I'm as good-looking as Neeley?" She waited anxiously for mama's answer because she knew that mama never lied. Mama's answer was a long time in coming.

"You have very pretty hands and nice long thick hair."

"But do you think I'm as good-looking as Neeley?" persisted Francie, *wanting* her mother to lie.

"Look, Francie, I know that you're getting at something in a roundabout way and I'm too tired to figure it out. Have a little patience until after the baby gets here. I like you and Neeley and I think you're both nice enough looking children. Now please try not to worry me."

Francie was instantly contrite. Pity twisted her heart as she saw her mother, so soon to bear a child, sprawled awkwardly on her hands and knees. She knelt beside her mother.

"Get up, Mama, and let me finish this hall. I have time." She plunged her hand into the pail of water.

"No!" exclaimed Katie sharply. She took Francie's hand out of the water and dried it on her apron. "Don't put your hands in that water. It has soda and lye in it. Look what it's done to my hands." She held out her shapely but work-scarred hands. "I don't want your hands to get like that. I want you to have nice hands always. Besides, I'm almost finished."

"If I can't help, can I sit on the stairs and watch?"

"If you've nothing better to do."

Francie sat watching her mother. It was so good to be there and know that mama was alive and close by. Even the scrubbing made a safe, pleasant sound. Swish-a-swish-a swish-a-swish-a went the brush. Slup-a slup-a slup-slup went the rag wiping up. Klunk, flump went the brush and rag as mama dropped them into the pail. Skrunk, skrunk went the pail as mama pushed it to the next area.

"Haven't you any girl friends to talk to, Francie?"

"No. I hate women."

"That's not natural. It would do you good to talk things over with girls your own age."

"Have you any women friends, Mama?"

"No, I hate women," said Katie.

"See? You're just like me."

"But I had a girl friend once and I got your father through her. So you see, a girl friend comes in handy sometimes." She spoke jokingly, but her scrub brush seemed to swish out, you-go-your-way, I'll-go-my-way. She fought back her tears. "Yes," she continued, "you need friends. You never talk to anybody but Neeley and me, and read your books and write your stories."

"I've given up writing."

Katie knew then that whatever was on Francie's mind had to do with her compositions. "Did you get a bad mark on a composition today?"

"No," lied Francie, amazed as always by her mother's

guesswork. She got up. "I guess it's time for me to go to McGarrity's now."

"Wait!" Katie put her brush and scrub rag in the pail. "I'm finished for the day." She held out her hands. "Help me to get up."

Francie grasped her mother's hands. Katie pulled heavily on them as she got to her feet clumsily. "Walk back home with me, Francie."

Francie carried the pail. Katie put one hand on the banister and put her other arm around Francie's shoulder. She leaned heavily on the girl as she walked downstairs slowly, Francie keeping time with her mother's uncertain steps.

"Francie, I expect the baby any day now and I'd feel better if you were never very far away from me. Stay close to me. And when I'm working come looking for me from time to time to see that I'm all right. I can't tell you how much I'm counting on you. I can't count on Neeley because a boy's no use at a time like this. I need you badly now and I feel safer when I know you're nearby. So stay close to me for awhile."

A great tenderness for her mother came into Francie's heart. "I won't ever go away from you, Mama," she said.

"That's my good girl." Katie pressed her shoulder.

"Maybe," thought Francie, "she doesn't love me as much as she loves Neeley. But she needs me more than she needs him and I guess being needed is almost as good as being loved. Maybe better."

But jealousy and resentment engendered by his own or other peoples' unfavorable comparisons may be explosive forces within the adolescent. Because of his needs and his experiences, the adolescent may be unable to maintain a consistent attitude toward his brothers and sisters. Since he may blow hot or cold at any given time, for reasons as mysterious to him as to others, there may be wide swings in his acceptance or rejection of siblings. Under such conditions equilibrium of outlook and behavior is particularly difficult to maintain.

The adolescent is both uncertain and unrealistic about many of his desires and expectations. He may want his family to appear and disappear as the mood strikes him. He may dislike his brother because the latter is better-looking and brighter, or stupid, or unattractive. He may like a popular brother because of reflected glory, but he might also prefer an unpopular one because no one would then make invidious (to him) comparisons. He would like to be an only child because of the advantages that might bring, but he might also want brothers and sisters to secure greater anonymity and privacy in the family. He may wish that his sister were suddenly divested of her sex so that some of his painful curiosities and anxieties were not so clearly presented to him daily. The following passage from *Young Lonigan** illustrates the peculiar sensitivity with which the adolescent boy may regard his sister.

Frances came in. She wore a thin nightgown. He could almost see right through it. He tried to keep looking away, but he had to turn his head back to look at her. She stood before him, and didn't seem to know that he was looking at her. She seemed kind of queer; he thought maybe she was sick.

"Do you like Lucy?"

"Oh, a little," he said.

He was excited, and couldn't talk much, because he didn't want her to notice it.

"Do you like to kiss girls?"

"Not so much," he said.

"You did tonight."

"It was all in the game."

"Helen must like Weary."

"I hate her."

"I don't like her either, but . . . . do you think they did anything in the post office?"

"What do you mean?" he asked.

She wasn't going to pump him and get anything out of him.

She seemed to be looking at him, awful queer, all right.

"You know. Do you think they did anything that was

* From *Young Lonigan* by James T. Farrell. Reprinted by permission of The Vanguard Press. Copyright, 1932. Pp. 61-63.

fun . . . or that the sisters wouldn't want them to do . . . or that's bad?"

"I don't know."

Dirty thoughts rushed to his head like hot blood. He told himself he was a bastard because . . . she was his sister.

"I don't know," he said, confused.

"You think maybe they did something bad, and it was fun?"

He shrugged his shoulders and looked out the window so she couldn't see his face.

"I feel funny," she said.

He hadn't better say anything to her, because she'd snitch and give him away.

"I want to do something . . . They're all in bed. Let's us play leap frog, you know that game that boys play where one bends down, and the others jump over him?" she said.

"We'll make too much noise."

"Do you really think that Weary and Helen did anything that might be fun?" she asked.

She got up, and walked nervously around the room. She plunked down on the piano stool, and part of her leg showed.

He looked out the window. He looked back. They sat. She fidgeted and couldn't sit still. She got up and ran out of the room. He sat there. He must be a bastard . . . she was his sister.

He looked out the window. He wondered what it was like; he was getting old enough to find out.

He got up. He looked at himself in the mirror. He shadow-boxed, and thought of Lucy. He thought of Fran. He squinted at himself in the mirror.

He turned the light out and started down the hallway. Fran called him. She was lying in bed without the sheets over her.

"It's hot here. Awful hot. Please put the window up higher."

"It's as high as it'll go."

"I thought it wasn't."

He looked at Fran. He couldn't help it.

"And please get some real cold water."

He got the water. It wasn't cold enough. She asked him to let the water run more. He did. He handed the water to her. As she rose to drink, she bumped her small breast against him.

She drank the water. He started out of the room. She called him to get her handkerchief.

"I'm not at all tired," she said.

He left, thinking what a bastard he must be.

He went to the bathroom.

Kneeling down at his bedside, he tried to make a perfect act of contrition to wash his soul from sin.

He heard the wind, and was afraid that God might punish him, make him die in the night. He had found out he was old enough, but . . . his soul was black with sin. He lay in bed worried, suffering, and he tossed into a slow, troubled sleep.

As illustrated here, the adolescent girl may be as troubled, confused and fumbling as her brother in their relationship. Or she may be afraid of a prettier or brighter sister. She may resent going to work because an older brother may have to be maintained at college. She may feel guilty at being told to stay in school instead of her brother, because he has to help support the family.

The problems of the adolescent and his siblings multiply rapidly where serious poverty exists, or if a parent has died, or if the home is broken. An additional burden in adjustment plagues him if there are relatives, in addition to parents, in an authoritative relationship with him living in, or in very close contact with, the household.

But even in the more normal home where these conditions are not present, it is nevertheless clear that adolescent adjustment and personality organization depend, in great part, on the attitudes of parents and on the psychological and social atmosphere of the household.

Parental attitudes cannot be neatly pigeon-holed. But some general characteristics may be summarized (1, 3, 9, 11, 12). In some homes, either or both parents, subtly or openly, show that they fundamentally dislike their children. In its more casual form, this dislike may take on the characteristic of ignoring the children, unless they interfere with the comforts or needs of the parents. In this eventuality it is the children who are forced to give way. Such parents are relieved at any excuse which keeps the children away from home—boarding school, or camp, or lengthy visits with relatives or friends. They take no interest in the associates, activities or plans of their children.

In its more destructive form, this unconscious dislike shows itself in irritability, hostility, resentment, and criticism of the child. Unreasonable and rigid rules of behavior are laid down with punishment meted out to the child for infringements, real or imagined.

The adolescent is usually anxious to get away from both sorts of homes at the earliest opportunity. Although some of these adolescents do find security and affection elsewhere, it is more than likely that psychological disturbance of a fairly serious and long-lasting nature will result from these destructive emotional experiences.

In other homes, parents adopt the attitude that there can be no question about parental authority. They find it easier all around, however, to be fairly lenient and indulgent with their children. These parents are somewhat inconsistent in discipline, since they administer it more in accordance with their temporary mood than with any real understanding of the situation involved. They are not ordinarily harsh in discipline, however. They do not supply adequate guidance to their children, nor do they show an enlightened, intelligent interest in their needs. These parents operate more as though a benevolent autocracy were involved, than a home.

The most constructive home atmosphere appears to provide the adolescent with appreciation as an individual, as well as love and warmth. Objective understanding, reasonable and consistent discipline, lack of possessiveness, guidance where needed, and above all, freedom for the adolescent to operate on his own and to take increasingly greater responsibility for making his own decisions, are equally important. Flexibility of outlook and spontaneity of behavior in dealing with their children are also desirable characteristics for parents to develop.

White (14) has an interesting word of caution about intimidating parents: "They are afraid of doing the wrong thing, creating the wrong atmosphere, not being themselves mature, and thus permanently blighting their child's development. The task of producing healthy, happy, confident children often rests in the hands of people rendered tense and anxious by their huge responsibility and awesome power."

Fear of showing their true feelings will make freedom of intercourse between parents and children very difficult. Parents are also afraid that any failure in guiding their children wisely will make them neurotic. They therefore may become easily disturbed over variations from a rather narrow pattern of prescribed "healthy" traits.

Nevertheless, a calm and happy home, with an even, stable atmosphere of acceptance will go far toward encouraging intelligent, cooperative, adult behavior on the part of adolescents. Parents who accept adolescents as mature equals, when that attitude is appropriate, are unlikely to lose the love, respect and trust of their children.

A number of investigations (4, 6, 8, 9, 10) have been reported on how a great many adolescents view their parents. A large percentage feel that their parents lack understanding and are unreasonable about school achievement, friends, timing and number of dates, curfew hours, and allowance. They also consider their parents overly strict, critical, quarrelsome and too "bossy." The behavior and temperament of the mother is more often criticized than that of the father.

An excellent fictional example of parents' respect for and understanding of an adolescent's special needs and peculiarities is offered by Jessamyn West's *Cress Delahanty* (13). The security and good feeling existing between an adolescent and her parents in an atmosphere of mutual love and acceptance is described with humor and warmth.

Raising children successfully might best be compared with raising plants, according to White (14). "This should be encouraging," he says, "because raising plants is one of mankind's most successful activities. Perhaps the success comes from the fact that the husband man does not try to thrust impossible patterns on his plants. He respects their peculiarities, tries to provide suitable conditions, protects them from the more serious kinds of injury—but he lets the plants do the growing. He does not poke at the seed in order to make it sprout more quickly, nor does he seize the shoot when it breaks ground and try to pull open the first leaves by hand. Neither does he trim the leaves of different kinds of plants in order to have them all look alike."

REFERENCES

(1) Baldwin, A. L., Kalhorn, J., & Breeze, F. H. "Patterns of Parental Control," *Psychological Monographs*, No. 58. 1945.
(2) Cruze, W. W. *Adolescent Psychology and Development*. NY: Ronald, 1953, p. 278.
(3) Martin, A. R. "A Study of Parental Attitudes and Their Influence on Personality Development," *Education*, 53:596-608, 1943.
(4) Meltzer, H. "Children's Attitudes to Parents," *Amer. J. Orthopsychiatry*, 5, 1945.
(5) Meyers, C. E. "Emancipation of Adolescents from Parental Control," *Nervous Child*, 5:251-262, 1946.
(6) Punke, H. H. "High School Youth and Family Quarrels," *School and Society*, 58:507-511, 1943.
(7) Salinger, J. D. *The Catcher in the Rye*. Boston: Little, Brown, 1951. 277 p.
(8) Shimmon, W. J. *Adolescent Problems and Attitudes to Parents*. Unpublished study. Gorton H.S., Yonkers, N.Y.
(9) Stott, L. H. "Adolescents' Dislikes Regarding Parental Behavior and Their Significance." *Ped. Sem. & J. Genet. Psychol.*, 57:393-414, 1940.
(10) Stott, L. H. "Home Punishment of Adolescents," *Ped. Sem. & J. Genet. Psychol.*, 57:415-428, 1940.
(11) Stott, L. H. "Some Family Patterns and Their Relation to Personality Development in Children." *J. Experimental Education*, 8:148-160, 1939.
(12) Symonds, Percival. *The Psychology of Parent-Child Relationships*. NY: Teachers College, 1949, p. 228.
(13) West, Jessamyn. *Cress Delahanty*. NY: Harcourt, Brace, 1953. 311 p.
(14) White, R. W. *Lives in Progress*. NY: Dryden, 1952, pp. 361, 363.

CHAPTER SIX

On Cultural Conflicts

> "Society is a masked ball, where every one hides his real character, and reveals it by hiding."
>
> RALPH WALDO EMERSON

The worship of false gods has always been a popular pursuit. Since the Children of Israel fell down before the Golden Calf, men and women have been diligent in their prostrations before idols. The most popular have always been Power, Wealth and Fame. But in our American culture, Success, which William James called "The Bitch Goddess," has had a tremendous vogue for a century now.

More recently, a new one has appeared, inspiring the most servile devotion. Her name is "Adjustment to One's Environment." Some people have equated this god with one called "Conformity," although this is far removed from actuality.

One of the great problems in our American culture is that of facing up to the inexorable demands of conformity and, at the same time, retaining our identity. We feel we have to conform in so many ways in order to be accepted. And this affects the adolescent particularly—and peculiarly. One of his great needs is to belong, to be part of a group, to be accepted. But he still needs to feel he is an individual. For the most part, he conforms to his peer group, and individualizes, to his parents' frequent bewilderment, in the home.

In a study made by Stendler (12) of contrasts between goals and child-care practices prevalent in many American homes and those of a group of middle-class Parisian families, American parents most frequently set forth aims for their offspring emphasizing independence and sociability. During the French child's early years, the qualities most desired were gentleness and obedience; it is only when the child becomes an adult that the Parisian parents want a self-disciplined person with intellectual integrity.

How do the American traditional ideals of wanting children "to stand on their own feet," to be friendly, popular, and "adjusted to the group" affect these children? Stendler believes there is some evidence to show that in building up a drive for sociability we also build up a desire to conform. The child learns that in order to be adjusted to the group he must go along with the mores of the group.

Conformity to the adolescent becomes supportive for the feelings of loneliness, for conflicted and vacillating feelings regarding needs for autonomy and independence (13). "In a moneyed and driven economy, one in which the yardsticks for success are façades of one kind or another (appearances, clothes, income, bigger and newer automobiles, etc.) the goals of education [and cultural progress] become clouded but children continue to become adolescents" (11). According to Fromm, the most beautiful as well as the most ugly inclinations of man are not a part of a fixed and biologically given human nature but result from the social process which creates man (5).

Thus, the adolescent will dress alike, if his clique calls for it, in blue jeans or Ivy League suit, saddle shoes or Capezios. He will live on hot dogs and cheeseburgers, down a "coke" chug-a-lug, subscribe to nostrums and chew benzedrine, if this is what his group does. If all the members of her group use Mum, the adolescent girl will feel she must too, or else she will not be even "half safe."

This is what Fromm calls automaton or compulsive conformity. We Americans, and particularly the adolescent, submit gladly and willingly to this pressure toward conformity. We tend to adopt blindly the pattern of the culture, bowing submissively to indoctrination, and accepting the way to live, to feel, to think, implicitly or explicitly as recommended by the group (15). The adolescent seldom asks the questions, Why should I do this? Who says so?—unless, perhaps, it happens to be mother or dad!

The adolescent who rejects the cult of conformity can do so for noble reasons, but some who defy it do so only because their egos are sensitive and prickly and they are driven to their protest, sometimes without understanding why. Idiosyncrasy in the American culture is tolerated, it is not approved. Erratic behavior may be found in the very wealthy, the intelligentsia, or the mentally disturbed. It attracts attention but certainly not emulation.

When the adolescent behaves "erratically," he is subject to the gibes of his peers, perhaps, and the censure of adults. Ostracism is swiftly meted out as his punishment. He becomes socialized quickly, if he wants to be accepted; and because of his need to be wanted, to belong, to share, he learns what is acceptable and what is not acceptable behavior for his particular group. He learns to keep his real feelings pretty well guarded if they are not generally accepted, as we see in this paragraph from *Death of a Hero*.*

Long before he was fifteen George was living a double life —one life for school and home, another for himself. Consummate dissimulation of youth, fighting for the inner vitality and the mystery. Now amusingly, but rather tragically he fooled them. How innocent-seemingly he played the fine healthy barbarian schoolboy, even to the slang and the hateful games. Be ye soft as doves and cunning as serpents. He's such a *real* boy, you know—viz., not an idea in his head, no suspicion of the mystery. "Rippin' game of rugger today, Mother. I scored two tries." Upstairs was that volume of Keats, artfully abstracted from the shelves.

But the adolescent is haunted by another need: to be admired by his peers. When the adolescent looks for group

* From *Death of a Hero* by Richard Aldington. Copyright 1929 by, and reprinted with permission of, the author. Covici-Friede, Inc. P. 72.

admiration, he may indulge in exhibitionism of some sort. This is usually short-lived, because he knows while parents will disapprove immediately, so will his peers in the long run. There are not too many adolescents hardy enough to suffer the appellation, "That crazy Delahanty girl," overlong (16).

Thus the need to conform, and at the same time to be a unique individual, overlarded by the general American cultural pattern, comes to predominate the adolescent's behavior. What the culture of the group is will determine the most important conditions which influence what the adolescent will learn and how he will learn it.

In the social learning process, most adolescents learn socially acceptable and desirable forms of behavior. When the situation is fraught with punishment of some sort, he learns how to cope with it and anticipate future social situations. Davis (2) refers to this anticipation as "socialized anxiety." He suggests that successful socialization is dependent upon the degree of socialized anxiety which has been inculcated in the adolescent. The price for successful socialization based on internalization of anxiety may be the experiencing of personal tension and lack of spontaneity or pleasure in dealing with others, and a fluctuating rather than a stable self-esteem.

The poet, Auden, has referred to the period we live in as "The Age of Anxiety." He might also have characterized the years of adolescence in this way. Thus, when you combine the anxious adolescent with the anxious world, the two organisms may very well prove to be rather combustible and even explosive, at times.

For it is quite true that the competitive elements in our culture are combined with a fear of not being successful and this is what tends to augment anxiety and conflict within the individual. This sort of competitiveness breeds distrust and pits man against man. Yet we talk about cooperation and democracy, in which consideration of others and good sportsmanship are emphasized. Small wonder many adolescents feel caught.

Horney states that "the rivalry between father and son, mother and daughter, one child and another, is not a general human phenomenon but is the response to culturally conditioned stimuli" (7). However, the majority of psychologists and psychoanalysts feel such rivalry is a universal phenomenon with its specific forms manifesting themselves by cultural conditioning. In school, the child and adolescent learns that he is likely to secure more immediate rewards if he does compete openly for them. And yet, threaded through both his home and school conditionings, he is also taught the Christian ethic of the Golden Rule and brotherly love. How then is the adolescent to use rivalry in the home and competition in the school as a foundation for fair play and constructive achievement in later, maturer years?

In our society, we hold that every man and woman be judged by the kind of person he is and by his contribution, regardless of race, creed or sex. Yet we know that there are distinctions in our culture, not only in minority but also majority groupings. Every schoolboy knows you can be born in a log cabin and die in a White House, but at what emotional cost does he learn that you must have a certain skin pigmentation and belong only to certain religions before you can die in the White House? Every school girl is taught she has a right to use her abilities in business or the professions. Yet the tradition persists that women are frail, belong in the home, and their true purpose is motherhood.

Our Western technological culture has developed in us a cult of the machine. At this point in our development, we are almost victims of the machine, for we hold a mystical, unquestioning, nearly religious awe and veneration for gadgets, any gadget, if it is only complex enough and cryptic enough and costs enough. Our cultural postulate dictates the infallibility of machines, instruments and gadgets, a Power more ruthless even than the old Hebrew concept of Yahweh, since ours is not even jealous and vengeful, caring nothing about individuals. The novelist Faulkner grieves for all people beneath a culture which holds any mechanical contrivance superior to any man simply because the one, being mechanical, is infallible, while the other, being nothing but man, is not just subject to failure but doomed to it (4).

Our culture holds that only that which is scientific may be accepted as important or factual by an educated, rational individual. Yet we know, and particularly for the adolescent, that irrational beliefs and satisfactions are important. The secret handshake, Rock-'N-Roll, swallowing live goldfish, tree-sitting, hot-rod cars, the panty-raids, and the "peculiar" craze of each new generation of adolescents, are not only expressions of the need for recognition of individuality and of independence from adult authoritarian figures, but also a manifestation of the need to break away from the anxious realities of our age.

The adolescent, nurtured in such a conflicting cultural pattern, may feel he is a shuttlecock, pitched willy-nilly from one side of the badminton court of life to the other, to land, bounce or fall flat on his face. He must learn to land or bounce, to develop resiliency and flexibility, despite, on the one hand, the pressures of conformity he finds about him, and on the other, the great varieties of cultures coexisting in the United States and which help to make one child different from another.

There is no such thing as the American culture. There are many American cultures. The farm-born and -bred youth has a far different range of experience than the adolescent raised in the city. And if the boy is raised on a truck farm in New Jersey, or on cotton land in the South, cultural patternings will be considerably different from the lad who grows up on a Texas cattle ranch. Similarly, there will be differences in cultural attitudes between a slum, tenement zone dweller, and an adolescent reared in a "garden apartment" in an outlying district of a city. "If you lived on Heights Road and were not 'impossible,'" as Bunny Dedrick muses in *The Tender Age* (14), a passage of which follows at the end of this chapter, "you were in. This social dictate sometimes amused Bunny, but more often it angered him, because what the people themselves were didn't count for beans. Your grandfather could have been a henchman of Jesse James'; it didn't matter."

Economics and occupations provide different designs for living; assembly-line workers, factory hands and college teachers may have approximately the same income but, generally, their children develop along different cultural lines. In the excerpt from *Moon-Calf** which follows, Felix is intellectually able but socially out of place. His fumblings and gropings are not due to adolescence alone but primarily to the different cultural and social stratifications from which he stems and in which, in this scene, he finds himself.

He rang the bell at exactly seven o'clock, having walked around the block twice and consulted his Ingersoll watch at every moment to make sure. He was warmly greeted by Mrs. Alden, and inducted into the drawing-room, where he slipped on the smooth floor and had to walk carefully. In confusion he shook hands with what seemed a vast roomful of people. All his faculties were in eclipse; he did not hear the names of the people he was meeting, and had no idea which was which. . . . Helen hurried in just then, and he fixed his eyes on her in a sort of baffled and hopeless trust.

He would have been astonished to learn that he gave the impression of being a very self-possessed young man. He thought he was behaving like an idiot.

Presently they were all seated at the dinner-table. The service was simple, but Felix was embarrassed by unfamiliar articles of cutlery, and it was not for some time that he discovered his napkin hidden beneath his plate. There was a salad—the first salad that Felix had ever seen. He rashly refused the mayonnaise, not knowing what it was for. Mrs. Alden casually offered it to him again, but he felt obliged to

* From *Moon-Calf* by Floyd Dell. Copyright 1920 by Doubleday & Co., Inc. Reprinted by permission of the author. Pp. 182-183.

stand by his original action rather than confess a mistake. He desperately ate his lettuce plain, as if he preferred it that way; but he thought everybody saw through his ruse, and was secretly laughing at him.

He was at first silent; and it was his impression that he remained so throughout the evening. But as a matter of fact Helen managed the conversation so skillfully—she knew upon what subjects Felix would and would not talk—that he perforce took part in it almost at once. He did so unconsciously, his whole mind being occupied with a memory of that bungled salad.

After dinner they all went to a great, cool, comfortable "attic" room. Felix, sitting down at once, became aware that the other men were still standing, waiting until the women were seated. Felix turned scarlet, but remained desperately in his big chair. He looked at Helen, across the room. Mrs. Alden, at his side, said something about poetry, and he replied with a long, clear-cut sentence, which might have been written in a book rather than uttered in conversation. Socially, Felix was in a state of collapse—except for Helen, he saw nobody in the room; but his powers of speech were curiously liberated. He was in a daze, alternately shot through with red flashes of shame at his clumsiness, and cooled by the sea-blue of Helen's eyes across the room. The slippery floor, the salad, and that last piece of ineptitude here in the attic, chased each other through his mind like nightmares; and all the while, in utter unconsciousness, he talked. When he ceased, it was on a period, and suddenly.

There was a startling effect to this talk, so unlike human conversation. It was as though he were reading aloud. . . . At midnight the party broke up. The others remarked to their hostess what a nice time they had had, and bade a special and kindly goodbye to Felix, asking him to come and see them; which so confused Felix that he slipped past his hostess without a farewell greeting. He was on the steps when he realized his omission; he turned uncertainly, but he was afraid he would bungle the affair still more if he went back. So he stumbled down the steps and ran home, cursing himself for a clumsy fool.

Had Felix's social and cultural heritage been on the drawing-room level, his feelings of being a "clumsy fool" would

probably never have existed. But in addition, there are differences in culture which are not measured by geography,
job or money. There are groups in the United States which
have strongly patterned ways of life that do not follow the
usual trend of American culture but which do give these
groups satisfactions. The Amish in Pennsylvania, the High-
landers in Tennessee, the Mormons in Colorado, and many
Indian tribes in the Southwest and West, value their culture
and maintain their unique traditions to this day. Then, too,
many immigrants to the United States, although admiring
American technological advances, cling to the values and
customs of their parents, rearing their children according to
their own upbringing, instilling in them the values of their
own culture. In Bellamann's *Kings Row*,* Madame von Eln,
from "her own small fortress against the thoughtless crudity
of this Western World," had tried to instill in Parris the
"breeding" emphasized among upper-crust European families.

The fire crackled and the room was alive with the moving
light. Madame felt much better. She held up her thin brown
hands toward the flame. The glow rimmed each finger with a
line of transparent red. She felt for her glasses and put them
on. She seemed absorbed in studying her hands—like a child.
The veins stood in clear relief. Odd. The pattern was slightly
different on the two hands. She had never noticed that! She
pressed hard on one hand with the fingers of the other. Four
white spots showed on the warm olive skin. They showed
white for a long time. Very slowly the blood crept back, but
she could still see the spots, a little paler than the surrounding area. Probably a sign of something, or a symptom. Probably not a very good sign, either, she thought. All signs are
bad in the shadow of disaster.

She continued to play with her fingers, but she no longer
saw them. She was beginning to wonder about Parris. Her
own phrase—"He is a good boy—I suppose"—came back to
her mind. What did she really know about this boy who was
the central idol of her heart? Very little, really. He had good

* From *Kings Row* by Henry Bellamann. Copyright 1941 by Simon &
Schuster, Inc. Reprinted by permission of the publishers. Pp. 160-163.

manners, a quick and responsive sympathy, and a good mind. "I suppose," she spoke the words aloud. Oh, of course, of course he had a good mind! She had been reassured on that point by everyone.

But what was he like, deeper down than the surface? What did he dream of, look forward to? What did he desire?

The answers to these questions—these all-important questions—would not come from Parris or from her observation of him. Her own training had given him an exterior that communicated little, for all its seemingly expressive vivacity. Now, as she thought of it, she realized that he was far less vivacious than he used to be. Growing up, becoming a young man—adolescence. Adolescence. She didn't remember that anyone used that word when she was young. She couldn't recall just when she first knew exactly what it meant. People said it—Dr. Gordon and Dr. Tower—as though it covered a whole world of mysterious things. Now what, really, was mysterious about it? She tried to remember her own growing up. Growing up. You simply became more like older people, thought less childishly, and became interested in the opposite sex. Rather silly, too, about that time. And full of curiosity. But she had married early, and the mysteries were of short duration.

Parris was less lively. He talked a good deal but less gaily. He was—she hunted for a description—he was darker. Yes: that described him exactly. She wondered why. She must observe him a bit more closely. Maybe she had been neglecting him a little. He came and went as he pleased. She was vaguely disturbed to realize that she didn't know much about his friends, or where he went.

She would try to understand him better. Where she would find her answer—that was another matter. Not in Parris, she thought again, no; not in herself, because they were quite unlike. She tried to recall her daughter, Parris' mother. A slight shade crossed her face. She realized that it had been a long time since she had thought of Marian. The curious expression on Madame's face deepened. It seemed part reluctance—reluctance to think of her daughter at all, part pity and regret. She had never understood Marian very well. Marian had been like her erratic young father—hardheaded, rebellious, but with little of his quick changefulness and ready affection. She had never really liked Marian much.

That was doubtless unnatural. Madame moved petulantly in her chair. A child was an accident. There was no more reason for loving a child than there was for a child loving a parent. So often children did not love parents. No, she hadn't really liked Marian. As for Marian's father—wasn't it strange that she remembered his characteristics so well but couldn't recall exactly how he had looked?

Obviously, she wouldn't be able to understand Parris through his mother. Parris' father, Sumter Mitchell—what an attractive boy he had been! A simple, forthright person— pretty much what people called "typically American," whatever it was that they meant by that. Anyway, he must have given Parris good qualities—more solid ones, she had no doubt, than Parris had from her own blood.

It might have been better if Parris could have had less of her own "foreign" ways, and more of the Mitchell manner. She knew that people commented on her bearing and conduct and thought her peculiar and alien. That was silly. Her family had been in America long before the Revolution. Languages had simply been a tradition of the family. She wondered if speaking foreign languages gave one foreign ways. Maybe, to some extent. She gesticulated, and most people didn't. Parris did, too. Then, of course, Franz von Eln had really been a foreigner. She found this hard to realize now. He had been an interesting person with his extreme enthusiasms and wild schemes. Yes; she had loved Franz von Eln, but he had been pretty difficult in those last years. Drank too much and, like most Germans, was quick-tempered and belligerent when he was drunk. Life, even with all of its practical difficulties, had been better after his death. It was inconsistent, of course, the way she leaned this way and that for help, and yet had to keep a certain independence in order to be happy. Too close trammels of any kind irked her —more than irked her, she thought. They made her crazy. Parris, maybe, had something of that in him. Well, she had left a wide circle of freedom about him—mental elbowroom, just as she demanded, and had to have, for herself. He had been happier because of that, she was sure.

She had tried to keep that circle cleared of the very elements and factors which had crowded and cramped her own early years—those elements . . . . she brought herself to a mental standstill for a moment. Why . . . yes, it was true.

That crowding in on her by family and relatives, that continuous invasion of herself—it was that which had pushed her into her precipitate first marriage. She hadn't escaped, however. She had merely exchanged one kind of mental clutter for another. Then her second marriage—oh, dear, that had been a life! . . . She had had to achieve her mental elbowroom, achieve it and hold it. She hoped she had been tactful, and wise, in these matters with Parris—she who had never been really wise in anything.

. . . And she had taught him good manners. From the first she had been determined to hold her own small fortress against the thoughtless crudity of this Western World. She had determined to live here that she might be independent and escape return to stuffy relatives, but she had been equally determined not to become too close-woven a part of the kind of life she observed about her. The older men—almost pioneers, they had been—Thurston St. George, Isaac Skeffington, and the others—had been more nearly her kind. She hadn't liked the women—still didn't like them, and the women of Kings Row had not liked her. That attitude had changed for the greater part. She had been respected at last, and held the respect, but in earning respect she had lost feminine friendships. Not that she had ever cared! All she wanted was to be left alone. Men were superior to women, anyway. Men like Thurston St. George and Isaac Skeffington kept their Eastern manner much better than their wives had. They were better company. She quirked an eyebrow and smiled. She quite simply preferred men. And that was the way it should be.

But Parris . . . she brought her wandering attention back with an effort. She must look the whole question of Parris' rearing full in the face. She wanted most eagerly to reassure herself.

Perhaps we can now begin to recognize that within the culture of different societies, any individual brought up within a given society is going to come out with the personality characteristics of his society. Differing societies have different personality norms. More than one pattern of human relations can exist. For example, the life of the Comanche Indian is geared almost exclusively to war and manly acts of bravery. In noncompetitive societies like the Navaho, war is less likely to occur. In Marquesan culture, where the men greatly outnumber the women, the social position of the latter is greatly enhanced and they occupy a position of power (8). The Dobu generate not only hostility to outsiders but foster distrust of each other and take this as a matter of course (1).

Thus, while it becomes obvious that many configurations of human behavior can and do exist, the essential idea is that the typical individual in these societies is trained to develop personality characteristics which conform to the ideal embodied in that culture. In other words, the fact that human groups have developed so many ways of producing so many different types of adult personalities suggests that the possibilities of planned and manipulated personality development are very real.

Mead discovered that the storm and stress of adolescent personality in our society is not true in Samoa. But while the Samoan girls' minds were "perplexed by no conflicts, troubled by no philosophic queries, beset by no remote ambitions" (9), they "have a low level of appreciation of personality differences, and a poverty of conception of personal relations" (10).

In many primitive societies adolescents are supported by rituals in their period of doubt and indecision. Initiation rites are used to test young people before they are welcomed into a recognized position in which rights, duties and their status are clearly defined. In our society, the passage from childhood to young adulthood is not marked for all children by any one significant ritual. Rather, the milestones marking maturity fall at varying ages: the ages when a boy or girl is permitted to drive a car, to marry without parental consent, to be drafted or to vote may range all the way from sixteen years to twenty-one. This unchartered process of acquiring adult status may well breed confusion for some youngsters as to when they are, in our culture, in fact grown up.

Earmarked as our culture is by conformity, individualism, flux and change, the need for personal security, for achievement and success—which the adolescent may find capricious and illusory—what is left for him? How can the adolescent be trained for life in so fluid and seemingly conflicting and contradictory a culture?

"The answer, it seems to me," writes Gillin (6), "is that the children of today must be trained, if this is possible, to develop their own inner resources to the highest degree. They must be trained in adaptability, in the ability to analyze new situations and to respond to them successfully; they must be educated to realize the relativity of the external 'absolutes' and to recognize the underlying requirements of both personal and social integration. This is admittedly an ideal: some individuals are capable of approaching it more closely than others. But to those who can grasp it at all will fall the responsibility of caring for and protecting those who are incapable of grasping it, if the latter are to survive."

Survival will come, for all, we are optimistic enough to assume, because there is no such thing as the American culture. Because there is no one American culture, the possibility for adjustment is good. The diversity of culture in the United States is a very real and a very positive force for retaining one's identity, despite the pressures toward conformity.

We are a relatively young country, as countries and nations go. Less than 170 years have elapsed since George Washington was inaugurated first President. We emphasize our youngness. We place a premium on youth. In the early days of national growth, sturdy young people were the life blood necessary to push back the frontiers. Young people formed the backbone for settling the hinterland. Young people survived the rigors of climate, hunger, and Indian attack.

The cult of the young developed. We thrived on it, we emphasized it, perhaps unduly, so that the concept of "rugged individualism" flowered with little attention paid to the larger social welfare. We have come a long way since then, so that today our complicated culture permits the development of great individuality and offers more constructive emotional experiences without sacrificing the larger good. At the same time, we hold on to our "youngness," so much so that adolescence has become a kind of cultural arbiter in the United States. "Few men in this country can afford to abandon the gestures of the adolescent . . ." (3). Adults do not like to give this period up. Witness the American Legion annual convention hijinks, our New Year's Eve revelries, the incredible and horrendous toll of automobile fatalities. We are the "joiningest" people in creation. Europeans may choose one meaningful professional, educational or social group, but Americans join and join. We are a gregarious people; more and more hotels in more and more cities are finding it more and more difficult to be host to the more and more conventions that are being held more and more frequently. This joiningness and belongingness may be a holdover from the vast geographical distances of pre-automobile and rapid movement days, when to be neighborly and join forces meant survival on the frontier.

Thus, it becomes apparent that not only does the culture influence the youngster, but the latter can and does do something to the culture. The impact goes two ways. How healthy an interchange takes place may very well depend on how maturely and how willingly we face change, recognize the requirements of personal and cultural forces, and integrate technological advances into our cultural pattern.

The Tender Age*

Heights Road at the north end, the residential section, was the most desirable street in town. If you lived on Heights Road and were not "impossible," as his mother would say, you were in. This social dictate sometimes amused Bunny, but more often it angered him, because what the people themselves were didn't count for beans. Your grandfather could have been a henchman of Jesse James'; it didn't matter. Of course, it was better if you could refer to him as a pillar of society, but if you could afford to live on Heights Road no one gave a damn about your grandfather. As long as you dressed decently and used acceptable English, and as long as your name could be pronounced, the town was your oyster.

But, like everything else in this stupid world, it wasn't as simple as all that. Bunny grinned wryly. Take Silverman: What name could be easier to pronounce? When he was younger, he had often played with Benny and Eileen. They lived in the house just up the hill and across the street from the Dedricks, a brick house more austere, if anything, than the houses all around it. The Silvermans even went to junior dancing school at the Woman's Club with him, and their parents exchanged greetings and served on civic committees with Bunny's mother and dad; but there, at such a measly, sneaky line that Bunny was always confused, familiarity ended. The Silvermans knew that; no one had to tell Eileen and Benny. They were still friendly enough with Bunny when he saw them, but no one had to suggest that the senior dancing class was crowded; Benny and Eileen just didn't go. Eileen wouldn't date any of his crowd, either, even if they asked her; and Benny didn't go to high school with the gang, but commuted to a private school for boys in New York.

Bunny didn't know which annoyed him more: the fact that the situation existed at all, or the fact that Benny and Eileen accepted it so completely. Hell, he liked them both, and Benny and Eileen always acted as if they thought he was O.K., so why did they have to change? Because their mother and father insisted upon it? Because Howard and others like him made cracks about the kikes? Couldn't Bunny, Benny, and Eileen be friends or not, as they decided for themselves? Once he had asked Jan about it; sometimes she had pretty good sense and could straighten him out when he got mixed up. She had told him, not unkindly, that it was easy for him to talk, but that if he had been a Jew, like the Silvermans, he would see it was sometimes safer—easier, anyway—not to get involved. He couldn't go along with Jan exactly, but she did give him something to think about: there were two kinds of guts: those you had, and could prove you had, when you were just yourself; and the kind of guts you imagined you would have, but couldn't prove, if you were someone else.

The Silvermans weren't the only ones who had sneaked in on Heights Road when the city fathers were busy playing golf. The Laskis were there; they came from some place in Europe just before the war. Their children were all younger than Bunny, so he had no immediate contact with them as he did with the Silvermans. But they wore little suits and dresses that were fancy with lace and ribbons, and for a time they spoke with their parents in Polish or German or something more fluently than they spoke in English. Bunny could remember when they first moved to town. A whole bunch of kids, himself included—Benny and Eileen too, come to think of it—used to go up to their house and stand hooting and jabbering at the Laski children until their mother would call them in. They soon tired of that game; it was just smart-aleck stuff, and Bunny didn't feel very proud of himself when he thought about it. But at least he had changed and was ashamed of himself. Of course, now even Anne and Howard accepted them—or were resigned to them—but when Dick Ames, Carrie's husband, had a few too many, he would invariably start bitching about all the money the Administration poured into Europe "for a lot of God-damn' foreigners. Look at that pack up on the Road there; they have more dough than all of us put together. People like that just use us for suckers."

It was stupid talk, and what you'd expect from Dick Ames, but did Howard ever contradict him? Not on your life! But when they got discussing something real important—Babe Ruth's batting average in 1931, or whether Martinis were smoother four to one or three and a half to one—Howard would argue with him until they were both snarling with rage.

And then there was the Pigelli tribe. Gus Pigelli made his dough putting up acres of cheap houses down on the flats across the highway from Heights Road—they and their friends and relatives swarmed all over the old Whiteside house they had picked up for practically nothing because no one else wanted it. "My heavens," Anne once said, "how many grandmothers can that family possibly have?" Every time she or her friends passed the house, they remarked

what a shame it was, and how Alice Whiteside would roll
over in her grave if she could see the place now: those urns,
that trellis—and why, oh, why, did they have to paint the
house yellow and green?

You'd think it was a palace, for crying out loud, instead
of the ugliest house in town.

To be completely honest about it, Bunny couldn't stand
the three Pigellis who were in school with him, and they
didn't like Bunny. It wasn't too long ago that they used to
chase him home from school every day. When he had complained to Anne, she said that they were horrible children
who didn't have any breeding—"but Bunny, don't let them
chase you." If he didn't want to be chased, though, he had to
fight, and both the Pigelli boys and their sister were bigger
than Bunny. So he always ran, and he hated them still, and
wished they lived a million miles away, but it had nothing
to do with Heights Road. He didn't like them around because to this day every time he saw one of them he was
reminded of his cowardice.

Only a short block beyond the Adams house, at the south
end of town, near the State Highway, Heights Road began
to fall apart. Here the big Doremus place, with the rambling
porch all around it and the cupola that had been the pride
of Mae's father, was now nothing more than a rooming house.
And on the other side of it, all the big old houses had been
razed to make way for garden apartments. Each building in
the group was spaced from the others by fresh green lawns,
parking areas for the convertibles, and play yards for the
children. Bunny thought them easily as bad as Gus Pigelli's
look-alike houses that had everyone screaming.

The garden apartments occupied most of the crest of the
hill on both sides of Heights Road before it dipped down to
intersect the Highway. Directly on the Highway was an immense building that looked, as they came down on it in the
soft light of evening, like a papier-mâché tunnel Bunny used
to have for his electric trains. It housed, for the convenience
of the Heights Garden Apartments, a supermarket, a modern
furniture store, a de luxe bowling alley, a chromium bar and
grill, a bakery, a neon movie house, a cut-rate drugstore,
and a mortician's parlor. Maybe it was efficient and all that,
but Bunny thought it was about as stimulating as a prison.

REFERENCES

(1) Benedict, Ruth. *Patterns of Culture.* NY: New American Library, 1952.
(2) Davis, Alison. "Socialization and Adolescent Personality," in *43rd Yearbook,* National Society for the Study of Education, 1944.
(3) Erikson, Erik H. *Childhood and Society.* NY: Norton, 1950, p. 298.
(4) Faulkner, William. Letter to the Editor, *New York Times,* December 26, 1954.
(5) Fromm, Erich. *Escape from Freedom.* NY: Farrar & Rinehart, 1941, p. 12.
(6) Gillin, John. "Personality Formation from the Comparative Cultural Point of View," in Kluckhohn, Clyde & Murray, Henry (Eds.), *Personality in Nature, Society and Culture.* NY: Knopf, 1949, p. 172.
(7) Horney, Karen. *The Neurotic Personality of Our Time.* NY: Norton, 1937, p. 285.
(8) Linton, Ralph. "Marquesan Culture," in Kardiner, Abram, *The Individual and His Society.* NY: Columbia University Press, 1939, pp. 137-196.
(9) Mead, Margaret. *Coming of Age in Samoa.* NY: New American Library, 1954, p. 107.
(10) Mead, Margaret. *Ibid.,* p. 146.
(11) Siegel, Max. "Compulsory Education and Adolescent Personality," in Krugman, Morris (Ed.), *Orthopsychiatry and the Schools.* NY: American Orthopsychiatric Association, 1958, p. 237.
(12) Stendler, Celia B. "What Kind of Adult Will Your Child Be?" *New York Times Magazine,* December 12, 1954.
(13) Sullivan, Harry S. *The Interpersonal Theory of Psychiatry.* NY: Norton, 1953, pp. 260-262.
(14) Thacher, Russell. *The Tender Age.* NY: Macmillan, 1952, p. 57.
(15) Thompson, Clara. *Psychoanalysis: Evolution and Development.* NY: Hermitage, 1950, p. 207.
(16) West, Jessamyn. *Cress Delahanty.* NY: Harcourt, Brace, 1953. 311 pp.

CHAPTER SEVEN

On Learning

> "You must know that there is nothing higher and
> stronger and more wholesome and good for life than
> some good memory, especially a memory of child-
> hood. People talk to you a great deal about your
> education, but some good, sacred memory, preserved
> from childhood, is perhaps the best education. If a
> man carries many such memories with him into
> life, he is sage to the end of his days, and if one has
> only one good memory left in one's heart, even
> that time may some time be the means of saving us."
>
> FYODOR DOSTOEVSKY, *The Brothers Karamazov*

"When I was fourteen," said Mark Twain, "my father was
so stupid I could hardly stand to have him around. At twenty-
one, I was astonished at how much he had learned in the
past seven years." Adolescence is a time of continuously
widening horizons, even though it might be the brash broad-
ening experience Twain ironically indicates. It is a time of
academic training, of tremendous readiness to absorb, yet of
great ambivalence toward learning.

In terms of mental ability or power, the adolescent is
approaching the peak in development. By the time he is
about eighteen he has either already reached his peak or will
show only a slight increase from that point on (9). But while
he has reached the apex in intellectual ability, his judgment,
which is dependent on experience as well as on intelligence,
may be far from mature. The adolescent simply has not lived
long enough to apply his intellectual powers to life experiences.

One evidence of mental growth is the appearance of the
ability to do abstract thinking, which begins about the age of
twelve (2). This is an important development, in view of the

fact that the norms of society are abstract and the gradual understanding of them is a vital factor in the adjustment of the child to his environment. "Even when a child has the intelligence growth to comprehend abstract terms, they do not concern him until he develops a social consciousness. This occurs with the emotional growth of maturation. All his life he has heard about the concepts of truthfulness, right and wrong, and has been expected to respect them; but it is not until adolescence that he begins fully to appreciate their implications and to comprehend the standards by which he has always been supposed to live" (2). Don Bradley, in *A Wreath for the Enemy*,* is rebelling against the restrictions laid down by his parents when he attempts to explore ideas.. Don feels disloyal to them but too many doors are being opened which he cannot ignore.

Adults perplexed me. I was forever expecting them to riot in the freedom of having grown up, having got away, and they never rioted. I was not unhappy, but I awaited with impatience the exciting end of minor tasks and tyrannies. Yet when I saw grownups living the sequel, it didn't look as though it were exciting. Horses, I was convinced, had more fun than people had.

The bus was jogging the last mile into Whiteford now. Crusoe alone, I thought, possessed that quality, that flourish; though it was only his mind that could kick up its heels; I saw the comet-streak of it, dashing from one idea to another.

At home we never talked ideas; we only talked about things. Abstract argument and discussion were quenched sooner or later by an uneasy glance traveling from parent to parent; signal for the veto—"Let's change the subject, shall we?"—my least favorite way of ending a conversation, the axe coming down. Eva and I liked to argue when we were alone. We never reached conclusions; there was little common ground between us in those days. She was essentially lighthearted, a non-worrier; she sailed where I floundered. But we enjoyed a statement of the problem—any problem. And to the parents the only thing more indecent than a

* From *A Wreath for the Enemy* by Pamela Frankau. Copyright 1952, 1954 by Pamela Frankau. Reprinted by permission of Harper & Brothers. Pp. 76-79.

problem was the stating of it. We had learned to submit, to spend the evenings as they liked us to spend them, listening to the wireless and playing card games.

We believed that, if challenged, they would diagnose the art of conversation as "unhealthy," the adjective most mysteriously applicable to other arts, to introspection, to religions that showed and to extremes of all kinds.

It was difficult not to compare Crusoe's tang with the aridity of home; not to compare the freedom of his company with the cramping restrictions that were becoming yearly more recognizable, and less bearable. The disloyalty worried me. Hints of a disturbing pattern had begun to emerge. I saw it when I looked back on my earlier friends. Every parental reaction had been the same. "Rather an odd chap, isn't he?" . . . "Why do you have to pick these queer fish?" . . . "Nice fellow, but a bit nutty."

Those friends were small pointers on the way to Crusoe. My admiration for the oddity, the rebel, the clown and the eccentric, never faltered. I couldn't hope to imitate them; I simply needed them. It was natural, in the sad struggle whose importance my mind would not confess, to leap at the antithesis of Bradley-ism. But I couldn't settle for it yet.

And the issue was, for the moment, kept small. Because life at home was only "The Holidays," that series of half-true intervals between the long stretches of real life. School was real life. There was no disloyalty in this feeling; it came naturally. Eight months out of every twelve were lived here.

Real life was life in the crowd; life in a line; a line of desks in the classroom, a line of narrow beds in the dormitory. The smells of real life were floor-polish and blackboard-chalk, carbolic soap, hot tea-urns, other people's socks and hair-oil. Its sounds were the clatter of the crowd's heavy boots, the shapeless roar of the crowd-voice, the rattling of the crowd's knives and forks at table.

It was, I suppose, a life of limited adventure. I was at my most alive when I played games. Adventures in learning were spasmodic; sudden responses of affection and understanding; most often the response of my ear to words. Occasionally a sense of the past gave me mysterious pleasure (flint arrows, Roman roads, Hadrian's Wall; "the barrow and the camp abide"). Sometimes the noise of battle sounded clear through the Greek or Latin embalming it, so that you saw the walls of Troy.

But those moments had come seldom, before this term. I had perhaps owned an inquiring mind that wasn't sure where its inquiries should begin. Now they were in full cry. Crusoe's knowledge illuminated alike the classics and the crowd. Dead languages spoke with a new liveliness; music stopped being dull as he taught me how to listen; religion was widening beyond the boundaries of "O.T.," "N.T." and attendance at chapel. His wild explorations of human behavior set me to watching my masters and my fellows with keen eyes. I was conscious of doors opening in all directions; they opened and I walked through them. Was I changing as I walked?

Despite "Bradley-ism," Don's horizons are stretching as he seeks ways to push them farther and farther out. He is eager to learn and to absorb, to seek new intellectual experiences and to change. Because of his parents' conformism, his admiration and need for the rebel, the eccentric or the clown predominates. His greatest interest lies in such people and he learns the most from them. It is a well-known psychological principle that emotions and personal relevance influence learning and memory. In a very real sense, attitudes operate to make a person, as he matures, more and more a product of his own biases (11). The adolescent, with insufficient life experience, tends to be motivated by personal predilection and bias which he has learned from family, peers and teachers or protested against in them. Emotions, more than the knowledge he has acquired, prevail, distorting judgment and influencing behavior. The period of his most intensive academic schooling comes when he is experiencing the most stress, for this is the time when the adolescent must learn to accept his physical self, learn a trade or profession, learn to face up to his emotional limitations and strengths, and learn how to get along with others. The adolescent's mind is as busy as a terrier working on a soup bone, but at this point in his development, the bone is frequently several sizes too big for him to handle. These factors affect the adolescent's academic pursuits. In *The Last Puritan*, Santayana describes the adjustment of Oliver, the only son of well-to-do parents, to the strain of a new high school, its students and its teachers and how they affect his personality development.

Studies of high school and college grades have shown, generally, that the grades of leaders are superior to those of nonleaders (19). In general, gifted students tend to be superior in character traits and interests as well as in ability (4). They usually have the respect of classmates. But although a gifted student may be respected by his peers, he may lack genuine acceptance by them. This may stem from such antisocial activities as always "knowing the right answers"; displaying impatience with others; expressing boredom; becoming dictatorial; and drawing attention to himself. In order to gain prestige or self-satisfaction from classroom performance, or to be acceptable to peers, neither high nor low intelligence is important (9). But when any student is faced with the threat of failure, or where his intellectual abilities are constantly being frustrated, or where he is subjected to unpleasantnesses or scorn, he will be faced not only with loss of prestige but also other social reprisals. Many bright high school students suffer from hostile anti-intellectualism among their classmates. Others avoid the intellectually difficult; and frequently, little pressure is exerted to induce students to do their best. Zelda and her two children in *The Young People** are well aware of these factors, each for his or her own reason.

Oh well, Jim could probably fix the broken flagstone; he could fix anything, do anything with his hands. When he was eleven he had built a tool house next to the garage, and they had used it ever since, and at sixteen he had found an old jalopy in a junk yard and fixed it up so it was running still, better, she sometimes thought, than their new, eight cylinder, automatic shift job.

"You ought to be an engineer," Zelda had said to him once, while he was still in high school.

* From *The Young People* by Gertrude Schweitzer. Reprinted by permission of Thomas J. Crowell Co. Copyright 1953. Pp. 20-21.

He had just shrugged. "It's too tough—too much math."
"What if it is tough? Nothing worth while comes easy."
"I'll find something that does," he said, and grinned.

He exasperated her beyond endurance sometimes, for she felt that he was capable of so much, yet he seemed to care about nothing very deeply, to have no lasting interests. He had slid through high school with a minimum of study and made Dartmouth only because his father was an alumnus. Zelda was sure he could have been a superior student, but he would not bother. He derided Ann, who worked hard and stood near the top of her class.

"Think you'll remember any of that glup? A year from now you won't know the difference between osmosis and fried chicken, and nobody'll care."

"I'll remember it until the Regents," Ann said.

It was not pure intellectual curiosity that motivated Ann. There was considerable competition in her school for high grades, and it was a mark of prestige to be known as a "brain," as long as you were otherwise normal and not "book happy."

In her day, Zelda thought, school marks and school itself had seemed highly unimportant. Anyone who took it seriously, or who would not cut classes when there was something better to do, was considered the equivalent of a drip. But they had been moved not by an indifference to knowledge, like Jim, but by a superior scorn of formal education. They had believed you could learn much more by reading on your own, by thinking for yourself, by discussion among your contemporaries. Jim, as far as Zelda knew, rarely opened a book, and Ann's reading was all from the mimeographed list prescribed in school.

The young Marquis says to Felix, in Mann's *The Confessions of Felix Krull*, that "Learning, especially conspicuous learning, is not a gentlemen's affair" (15). Many adolescents feel that it is not a "regular guy's" affair either and, in their need to conform and to maintain friendships, willingly suffer themselves mediocrity in their pursuit of knowledge. Similarly, Tar, in Sherwood Anderson's novel of the same name, believes "books are all right, but it's better not to let other boys know you like them" (1). And Herbie Bookbinder, the young hero in Herman Wouk's *City Boy,* "had always had this mysterious blind spot toward baseball. Boys who were fools in the classrooms could juggle names and figures by the hour. Rabbitt Maranville batted .235 in '26, Wilcey Moore pitched one shutout in '27, and so forth forever more, it seemed while he knew nothing . . ." (23).

There is good reason to believe that because the basic motivations reside in human relations, the striving for external tokens of approval in the form of tangible rewards, prizes, and marks is subordinate to the striving for direct recognition and approval from a parent, a teacher or a peer (22). The teacher may try to make examinations and marks objective, and stress that a boy or girl earns his score on a test, that it is not just given to him. But the student does not hear the teacher—he still interprets a high mark to mean that the teacher approves of him and a low score as casting him out. Pearson says, "As one watches children through their years of growth, one is impressed by the fact that the motive of learning in order to be rewarded by the teacher's love is very important and powerful and continues not only through grade school but also into senior high school and college. . . . If, to the child, the teacher seems to be interested in learning, he too must become interested in learning in order to be like the teacher and so be liked by him. . . . The reward which is most gratifying to the child is that of love from the adult, whether this be the parent or the professional educator. When the child loves the teacher he will do anything to please him, even to learning the most uninteresting subject, but he anticipates a real expression of love from the teacher in return and as long as he gets it, he will continue to learn" (16). The educational history of Mr. Polly* is a tragic wasteland for him as well as for many an adolescent who is choked off because of poor motivation.

* From *The History of Mr. Polly* by H. G. Wells. Reprinted by permission of Dodd, Mead & Company and by the Executors of the Estate of H. G. Wells. Copyright © 1909 by Dodd, Mead & Company, Inc. Pp. 12-15.

Mr. Polly went into the National School at six and left the private school at fourteen, and by that time his mind was in much the same state that you would be in, dear reader, if you were operated upon for appendicitis by a well-meaning, boldly enterprising, but rather over-worked and under-paid butcher boy, who was superseded towards the climax of the operation by a left-handed clerk of high principles but intemperate habits,—that is to say, it was in a thorough mess. The nice little curiosities and willingnesses of a child were in a jumbled and thwarted condition, hacked and cut about —the operators had left, so to speak, all their sponges and ligatures in the mangled confusion—and Mr. Polly had lost much of his natural confidence, so far as figures and sciences and languages and the possibilities of learning things were concerned. He thought of the present world no longer as a wonderland of experiences, but as geography and history, as the repeating of names that were hard to pronounce, and lists of products and populations and heights and lengths, and as lists of dates—oh! and boredom indescribable. He thought of religion as the recital of more or less incomprehensible words that were hard to remember, and of the Divinity as of a limitless Being having the nature of a schoolmaster and making infinite rules, known and unknown rules, that were always ruthlessly enforced, and with an infinite capacity for punishment and, most horrible of all to think of! limitless powers of espial. (So to the best of his ability he did not think of that unrelenting eye.) He was uncertain about the spelling and pronunciation of most of the words in our beautiful but abundant and perplexing tongue,—that especially was a pity because words attracted him, and under happier conditions he might have used them well—he was always doubtful whether it was eight sevens or nine eights that was sixty-three—(he knew no method for settling the difficulty) and he thought the merit of a drawing consisted in the care with which it was "lined in." "Lining in" bored him beyond measure.

But the indigestions of mind and body that were to play so large a part in his subsequent career were still only beginning. His liver and his gastric juice, his wonder and imagination kept up a fight against the things that threatened to overwhelm soul and body together. Outside the regions devastated by the school curriculum he was still intensely curious. He had cheerful phases of enterprise, and about thirteen he suddenly discovered reading and its joys. He began to read stories voraciously, and books of travel, provided they were also adventurous. He got these chiefly from the local institute, and he also "took in," irregularly but thoroughly, one of those inspiring weeklies crammed with imagination that the cheap boys' "comics" of today have replaced. At fourteen, when he emerged from the valley of the shadow of education, there survived something, indeed it survived still, obscured and thwarted, at five and thirty, that pointed—not with a visible and prevailing finger like the finger of that beautiful woman in the picture, but pointed nevertheless—to the idea that there was interest and happiness in the world. Deep in the being of Mr. Polly, deep in that darkness, like a creature that has been beaten about the head and left for dead but still lives, crawled a persuasion that over and above the things that are jolly and "bits of all right," there was beauty, there was delight, that somewhere— magically inaccessible perhaps, but still somewhere, were pure and easy and joyous states of body and mind.

He would sneak out on moonless winter nights and stare up at the stars, and afterwards find it difficult to tell his father where he had been.

He would read tales about hunters and explorers, and imagine himself riding mustangs as fleet as the wind across the prairies of Western America, or coming as a conquering and adored white man into the swarming villages of Central Africa. He shot bears with a revolver—a cigarette in the other hand—and made a necklace of their teeth and claws for the chief's beautiful young daughter. Also he killed a lion with a pointed stake, stabbing through the beast's heart as it stood over him.

He thought it would be splendid to be a diver and go down deep into the green mysteries of the sea.

He led stormers against well-nigh impregnable forts, and died on the ramparts at the moment of victory. (His grave was watered by a nation's tears.)

He rammed and torpedoed ships, one against ten.

He was beloved by queens in barbaric lands, and reconciled whole nations to the Christian faith.

He was martyred, and took it very calmly and beautifully —but only once or twice after the Revivalist week. It did not become a habit with him.

He explored the Amazon, and found, newly exposed by the fall of a great tree, a rock of gold.

Engaged in these pursuits he would neglect the work immediately in hand, sitting somewhat slackly on the form and projecting himself in a manner tempting to a school-master with a cane. . . . And twice he had books confiscated.

Recalled to the realities of life, he would rub himself or sigh deeply as the occasion required, and resume his attempts to write as good as copperplate. He hated writing; the ink always crept up his fingers and the smell of ink offended him. And he was filled with unexpressed doubts. *Why* should writing slope down from right to left? *Why* should down-strokes be thick and upstrokes thin? *Why* should the handle of one's pen point over one's right shoulder?

Too rarely does a student ever ask why; the bored, defense-less young person succumbs to pallid, incompetent teaching and to a course of study that lacks challenge. A curriculum that is too easy or too difficult or is remote from the individual's tastes and talents may lead to a feeling of frustration because of abilities not actualized or because of unrealistic or too-high aspirations (5). Or it can lead to extensive and elaborate daydreaming, as with Mr. Polly. The purpose of education is to train the ego in skills that will enable it to deal with the realities of life (6). If the adolescent is forced to go on with schoolwork that he dislikes or sees no sense to, the resistance, resentment, and real possibility of failure is present. Not only does he himself suffer a sense of disappointment, but also has to endure the scorn of teachers, parents, and peers. "Motivation is inseparable from effective learning and from sustained interest; emotional investments are responsible for the frequent lack or indifference, for the rise or decline in learning power," Blos (3) states.

These emotional investments of the adolescent are hard to stabilize and classify. He loves and hates with equal intensity. One moment he wants to possess all the available knowledge there is in the world, so that he can be sure of everything; the next moment, he feels why bother, nothing will help. Learning will give all the answers; learning does not have the answers. He may accept a severe and unjustified reprimand with a graciousness and tolerance that embarrass his harassed teacher, Josselyn points out, and the next day show extreme rage because the same teacher asks him very patiently to try to write more legibly (10). He resents being told what to do by teachers yet insists on being given clearly structured assignments that leave no room for independent planning.

In learning there must basically be ego satisfactions. But since the adolescent himself is unsure what these satisfactions are or should be, he cannot use his acquired knowledge too creatively. The mature individual utilizes learning for the benefit of others as well as himself. Learning is an instrument given to an individual for social purposes rather than for egotistical gain and self-aggrandizement (12). Dewey looks at learning as a total experience for the individual. Liss postulates that all learning is a transmutation of libido from early id sources, and as differentiation into ego and superego takes place, diversification and elaboration of symbol also takes place (13). It is the integration and stabilization of the ego-id-superego constellation that the adolescent strives to achieve in order for effective learning to occur.

There are many factors which affect the ability to learn: physical, economic, specific disability in some learning area, degree of maturity or learning readiness, and family problems and discords. The literature suggests the last-named factor has the most significant effect on the ability to learn. However, attitudes and feelings relating to any of them can create an emotional problem. None of these factors, of course, are necessarily inhibitory in their effect on achievement; they may, on the contrary, be the cause of compensatory achievement. Given plenty of opportunity to explore new problems, to grow in freedom, to develop his own interests, abilities, and understandings, the adolescent must also be guarded from the consequences of his excesses and helped to adjust to reasonable restrictions. Students who complain that they cannot see any sense in certain subjects probably mean that these subjects make no impact on their self-concepts, and that they are not related to the real business of living as they see it (21). Since the self-concept arises primarily in the way an individual meets his psychosocial needs, the learning process for the adolescent, who is experiencing a variety of changes in many directions almost simultaneously, assumes a very personal meaning. Instability of behavior, fluctuating interests and attitudes, and irregular school attendance may be the acting out of the conflict between his own desire for active exploration which symbolizes adulthood and the demand of the school that he accept instruction (20). Often, dazed parents and teachers think the adolescent lives on the wrong side of a one-track mind. The youngster is an opinionated, positive know-it-all, they feel, when in actuality he is frightened and unsure of himself.

The cockiness of the protagonist in *I'm Owen Harrison Harding** is apparent at once in the very title of the novel. Owen's behavior in school borders on the downright insolent; it arises in some measure because teacher "was always correcting you instead of listening to what you said," and because teacher "sure didn't know how I felt or he would have kept quiet."

. . . I wasn't even too worried about seeing Mr. Harris, but when I walked back to my home room at three-thirty I stood outside for a long time before I walked in. I wasn't too crazy about seeing Mr. Harris all of a sudden. Right while I was standing at the door I remembered I'd hardly seen him since my mother died. He'd been out of school all the week before with a cold, and the week before that I'd been out of school for the funeral and everything. The longer I stood there, the more I wished I didn't have to go in and see him.

Finally I just barged in, and Mr. Harris looked up from a whole bunch of papers he was leafing through.

* From *I'm Owen Harrison Harding* by James W. Ellison. Copyright © 1955 by James Whitfield Ellison. Reprinted by permission of Doubleday & Co., Inc. Pp. 162-170.

"Be with you in a minute, Owen."

I just stood there like a dunce.

Then I asked him if he wanted the door closed and he said yes, so I closed it. I almost asked him if he wanted it locked too, but he didn't seem to be in a very happy mood.

"Have a seat," he said. I figured he meant the one beside his desk.

I sat down on that one. "Is your cold better, Mr. Harris?" That was a very stupid question. His nose was red as all hell.

"The cold's fine," he said. He spread his palms outward, like he always did when he was about to say something he thought was witty. "If the cold gets any better I'll end up in an oxygen tent." He had a big laugh over that one, and his nose started running like crazy. I managed to laugh a little myself, although it was sort of a strain. He wasn't nearly as witty as he thought he was.

"Well, Owen," he said, putting his pen down on the desk and leaning way the hell back in his seat. "Well, school's about over for the year."

"About three more weeks," I said.

"Three weeks and two days, to be exact."

"Boy, that's not long."

"You're right, Owen, it isn't." He put a pencil between his teeth and began chewing it. He rocked back and forth in the chair and it squeaked like hell.

"That's sure not long," I said. I tried to think of something else to say, but I couldn't. He was pretty quiet like he was waiting for me to say something big and important.

"Three weeks and two days'll fly by in no time," I said.

"Yes, Owen, they will." He started to say something else but his nose was too stuffed. He pulled out his snotty-looking handkerchief and blew the hell out of his nose. I kept waiting for it to bleed. After he put the handkerchief back in his pocket he pulled his chair in closer to the desk, and gave me one of these very worried looks that teachers love to use. They're very corny looks, like doctors love to use when they check your heart.

"I would like to help you, Owen," he said.

"What d'you mean, Mr. Harris?"

"You must realize that you're doing very badly. For instance in Geometry and Biology"—he looked through some stupid records that must have been mine—"if you don't pass those examinations, you could be kept back a year."

"I know that. I've meant to try har—"

"Look here, Owen—Owen, I don't believe for one minute that it's all your fault." He was beginning to look very embarrassed. "You've been having trouble at home. . . . You were out the week before last. . . . Owen, I want you to know how sorry I am about your mother. . . ." He pulled out the snotty-looking handkerchief and blew his nose again.

I didn't look at him when he looked at me. I just wished like hell he wouldn't get sad with me like everybody else. It's the worst thing somebody can do to you; it makes you feel sadder than you felt in the first place. If they'd only laugh or do something silly.

"Now in all your other classes," he said very loudly, "you're doing all right. You'll pass them, anyhow. It's only Geometry and Biology that I'm worr—"

"I'm going to study very hard for those exams," I said.

"It's a little late in the year," he said.

"I know it. I can do the work, though."

"Mr. Forman says that you seem to have a difficult time with logic. You see, Owen, Geometry isn't easy for everyone. It hasn't anything to do with your general aptitude, you know. I mean it hasn't anything to do with your general intelligence. It's just difficult for some minds to grasp. Perhaps if you'd let me help you—"

"I can do it, Mr. Harris."

"Well, I don't know, Owen. You haven't showed any aptitude for it. I mean you haven't showed any."

"I can get it," I said.

Mr. Harris drummed his fingers on the desk and looked at me in a funny way, like I was a stranger who'd just barged in on him. I wondered if he was P Od at me. He seemed very nervous the way he kept drumming his fingers. God, he made me nervous doing that!

"Look here," he said, "I could help you. I could spend the next few evenings with you, and we could do a lot of cramming." He took the pencil out of his mouth and began playing with the pen. "Your mother, Owen. She was sick for quite a while, wasn't she?"

"Yes, she was," I said.

"That's too bad. It's a shame, it really is. At one time or

another we all have to go through these crises, Owen. And no wonder your work has been affected by it."

"It hasn't," I said.

He gave me the old X-ray eye treatment—one of those I-can-see-right-through-you looks. Sometimes he talked like he wasn't a teacher, when there was something wrong and he felt he had to know you. He did that sometimes, because he was a pretty good guy. But it always made me uncomfortable, because he really was a teacher and he didn't know very much about you at all. *He* sure didn't know how I felt or he would have kept quiet.

"I don't understand," he said. "What did you say?"

"I said my work hadn't been affected by anything. I just don't like the work, that's all."

He got up from his chair.

"So you don't feel you need my help?" he said.

"I can do the work okay. I'll pass the exams."

"I hope you can, Owen. I hope so for your sake."

"I can do it all right," I said.

Mr. Harris walked over to the window and looked outside. He had his hands behind his back. All of a sudden he turned around and looked at me.

"I've gone to no little trouble to try and talk with you," he said. He looked at me with one stupid eyebrow raised. "Frankly you surprise me."

"Why, Mr. Harris?"

He was making me feel goddam uncomfortable.

"Your attitude is frankly—if you don't mind my being frank—quite hostile towards authority. Here I'm trying to help you, and you refuse to accept my help. I realize you may not be feeling—"

"I'm sorry if I said something wrong, Mr. Harris. I really am. I'll listen to anything about my work."

He was really beginning to look P Od.

"All right. We'll get down to the facts." He walked back to his desk and sat down. He fiddled around with some yellow sheets that were probably my stupid records; it looked like he had a whole pile of them on his desk. He told me that Mr. Greenbaum, the principal, had told him to check up on me because I was liable to flunk. He said that if a student's never been kept back a grade before, the homeroom teacher has to check his records and talk to him. He said that it was just his job and that he had to do it, and that if I listened closely and kept my mind on what he said we could get through with the whole deal very quickly. He really looked angry.

"In junior high school you made the honor roll five times. Your total average through junior high school was eighty-nine per cent. *Eighty-nine per cent!*" he said. The way he looked at me I thought he was going to ask me if I'd paid off the teachers. He took out his handkerchief and blew his nose again. "I hate to tell you what your average is now. It's not good—I'll tell you that. You're doing very badly."

I stared at this half-rotten apple on his desk. I wondered if one of the hundred per centers had given it to him.

"I didn't do very well in the ninth grade, though," I said. "It's not only in high school I've done bad."

"Bad*ly,* Owen. Bad*ly.*"

"*Bad*ly," I said. He was always correcting you instead of listening to what you said. "I did very badly in the ninth grade. Almost as badly as I'm doing now."

Mr. Harris looked at me for a long time and moved his lips like he was thinking of what to say next. He always took one hell of a long time to say anything, and when he did say something he said it so slowly you almost went to sleep. "Now, if you'll bear with me, we'll run quickly through your grades by years. In the seventh grade you did your best work. In the eighth grade you slipped slightly—not much, but a little. And then in the ninth grade—zooooommmm"— Mr. Harris made like a diving airplane with his hand; it looked sillier than hell—"your average dropped below eighty per cent. And since you've been in high school," he said, picking up one of the yellow sheets and squinting at it, "you've barely maintained a passing seventy-five." He laid the sheet on his desk. "That's the story, Owen."

"It's pretty bad," I said.

"Yes, it certainly is. And I'm supposed to find out why it's so bad. There must be a reason."

"The only reason is, I haven't studied."

"Yes, but why haven't you studied?" he asked me.

"I don't know. I don't like to study, I guess."

"Well, do you know why you don't like to study?"

"No," I said. "I don't know. The work doesn't seem to interest me."

He leaned way the hell back in his chair again. I thought maybe he'd fall on his head, but he didn't.

"What does interest you, Owen?"

"I don't know. A lot of things," I said. He was really making me nervous. "I like a lot of things."

He rubbed the sort of flabby skin on his cheeks and looked at me. "What kind of things do you like?"

I wanted to tell him I like people to mind their own business, but I couldn't do that. I started cracking my knuckles. He really made me jumpy. The trouble is, when somebody asks you what you like to do it's hard to think of anything. I kept trying, though.

"I like to go for long walks," I said.

He laughed like I didn't know what the hell I was talking about. "Everybody likes to walk," he said.

"No they don't. Not for miles and miles like I do."

He blinked at me with his fishy eyes. He was sort of a handsome guy, but he did have fishy eyes. After he spent about a minute trying to stare me down, he riffled through my stupid records again. I was dying for a cigarette. "On your intelligence quotient test," he said, "the one you took last semester, you did very well. One hundred thirty-one. That's really quite high, Owen. It places you definitely near the top of your class. And the interesting part is, you didn't do quite as well on your IQ tests in junior high school when you were getting better grades!"

He frowned at me like I was a goddam foreign spy.

"That's very interesting," I said.

"What d'you suppose the answer is?" he asked me.

"Well," I said, "maybe I've gotten too smart for school." Boy, that was the biggest mistake going! He stuck the chewed-up pencil in his mouth again and almost bit it in two.

"Owen—I'm not going to become personal. I don't believe that's my province. But if you'll permit me, I'd like to make a personal observation."

"I don't mind," I said. "Say anything you want."

"Well," he said, "after talking to some of your teachers, I've come to a conclusion. I think that you're unreasonable. You're very unreasonable." He folded his arms across his chest and stared at me. "You apparently never give anyone a chance to teach you. You seem to think that you're too wise to be taught. You disrupt classes whenever possible. Why, one of your teachers claims that you openly insulted her."

"Oh, I can tell you about that," I said.

"You can—"

"That's Miss Reynolds," I said. "I had her last semester for English. She talked like a fascist."

"Like a *what*?"

"A fascist. She talked like one, I mean." I told him how she seemed to be nuts about Hitler, and what a creep she thought Roosevelt was. He seemed interested so I told him about painting the mustache on my lip, and giving her the old "Heil Hitler" routine. He seemed to be kind of amused by the story, but the funny thing was, after I told it to him he didn't act like he wanted to talk to me any more.

He stood up, so I stood up.

I started walking to the door.

"By the way, Owen . . ."

I turned around.

"I talked with your father on the phone yesterday. Did he tell you?"

"No, he didn't, Mr. Harris."

"Well, we had a good long talk. He seems like a swell fellow. Do you happen to know how awfully concerned he is about you, Owen?"

"I know. I know he's very concerned."

"He wanted me to talk to you. He felt that, perhaps, through me you might take more interest in your work. I was willing to try, but frankly you're not easy to talk to."

"I know that. I'm not easy to talk to." I stood by the door with my hand on the doorknob. I wished to hell he'd let me go.

"Your father's the one who suggested I might help you with the Geometry and Biology exams."

"My dad did that?"

"That's right. It was his idea."

"I thought that was something the school made you do, Mr. Harris. I thought they made you help somebody who's flunking."

"No. All we have to do is give you a pep talk."

"Did you tell my dad you'd help me?"

"I said that I'd talk to you about it."

He put on his coat and walked over to where I was standing by the door. He put his hand on my shoulder. That made me feel sort of funny, but I couldn't do anything about it. "Look here, Owen," he said, "would you like to reconsider?"

"You mean about you helping me?"

"That's right. Only, Owen, say 'your helping me' instead of 'you helping me.' It's about time you began to learn a few of the basic rules."

"I suppose my dad'll find out if you don't help me."

"I imagine so. He might ask you."

"Well, you can help me if you want to. I don't know why you'd want to, though."

He smiled, and when he smiled you thought there was something inside that made him do it. He made you want to smile. "I don't know why, either. I'm really quite lazy."

"Teachers aren't ever lazy, are they?"

"Sure they are," he said. "At least some of us are."

"Boy—that's a new one on me."

"Who else has a job with three months off in the summer?"

"I suppose that's one way of looking at it," I said. "Except you probably need at least three months after teaching guys like me."

He opened the door and made me walk out in the hall ahead of him. That's always very embarrassing to me—who should go first and everything. We ended up almost going through at the same time and killing each other.

We walked down the hall together.

"When d'you want to start with me?" I said.

"Tomorrow night after school," he said.

"I hope I'll be able to get it," I said. "I really expected to flunk both Geometry and Biology."

"You'll get it," Mr. Harris said. "That's one reason I'm interested in helping you. I have a feeling that potentially you're excellent college material."

"Me? What makes you think that, Mr. Harris?"

He laughed. "I'm not sure. I just have a hunch. Miss Reynolds showed me some of your essays and, rough as they were, they showed a great deal of thought. And you mistrust many things about school, which I believe is the sign of a growing mind. You're pretty skeptical right now, and I don't happen to think that's bad for a young mind."

He was making me feel good. Nobody had ever talked to me that way before. As far back as I could remember people had said all kinds of things about me, but nobody ever told me I had any brains. He really made me feel very good, even though I thought he was feeling so expansive he would have given anybody he was with right then a snow job.

"Would you like to ride downtown with me? I've got the car in the parking lot."

"Sure," I said.

The teacher's task is a formidable one. It is when his own personality reaches out, as it does to Owen, that he is able to communicate with the student and respond on a meaningful level. The teacher assumes a role secondary only to parents. A teacher's success may be measured not only by his academic standards but also in respect to his understanding of the psychosexual and biosocial needs of his adolescent student. Despite the highly flexible and contradictory personality of the latter, the understanding teacher will find him responsive to educational effort. His major task is to enable the student to take part in the culture on the ego level, while preserving the original energy on the drive level (17). In considering any educational influence, Fenichel states it is necessary to distinguish three factors: "that which is being influenced, i.e., the mental structure of the child; the influencing stimuli, which converge upon this structure; and the influencing process, i.e., the alterations that occur in the child's mind in response to these stimuli" (7).

The teacher's task is further complicated by the revolutionary changes taking place in the body of the adolescent. The glands of internal secretion relate not only to physical development and functioning but also directly to the psychological responses of the individual and thus to his learning ability. The learning process involves both physiological and emotional factors. "When we find two-thirds of the girls in the junior high school to be matured in sexual functions while two-thirds of the boys associated with them are immature in this respect, we know that we are putting together two groups which show, in the mass, basically different orientations towards life. The problem is complicated still further by differential rates of maturing within each sex . . . For . . . two groups of boys (one group having achieved puberty, the other not) to be given identical educative experiences, identical responsibilities, and identical social and extra-curricular opportunities is manifestly inappropriate even though they exhibit the same ability to learn at the moment. Certain basic personality pre-occupations are bound to be quite different and the traditional school organization and curriculum is bound to handicap one or the other group with severe tensions" (18).

Thus, the adolescent frequently seems to be jittery and restless, bidding for the approval and attention of the teacher, impertinent, unable to concentrate, confused and illogical in his thinking, and at the same time earnest, voluble and apparently sincere. The student reacts not only with his intellect in the learning process but also through personal meaning and urgencies related to it. The unsettled and untidy world of the adolescent, which frequently is the taproot of teachers' and parents' despair, makes it difficult for the adolescent to learn the tidy rules of mathematics, of chemical formulae, of grammar. But gradually, and usually by late adolescence, he mobilizes his resources and is able to integrate his intellectual and emotional needs.

While knowledge and skills are the proper aims of education, they are not exclusive goals. The full development of the adolescent requires that his inner life of feelings should keep apace with his attainments (8). Education is concerned with the socialization of the individual whose development is progressing normally. To achieve this socialization, the adolescent's intellectual needs must be met and modified, not so much by direct teaching, perhaps, but by the general spirit that surrounds him in the classroom. It is here that the adolescent spends more time than any place except the home. The kinds of experiences he has in the school can either challenge him to work up to his capacities and help him greatly to solve his problems of growing up, or his experiences can serve to develop only a fraction of his capacities for growth and for social contribution and may actually complicate and deepen his problems (14). The adolescent must find meaning for himself while learning to adjust to societal expectations and the schools must guide him into socially useful forms of self-realization and assist him in the discovery of means for rich and satisfying experiences.

REFERENCES

(1) Anderson, Sherwood. *Tar*. NY: Boni & Liveright, 1926, p. 141.
(2) Beverly, Bert I. *A Psychology of Growth*. NY: Whittlesey, 1947, p. 164; p. 165.
(3) Blos, Peter. *The Adolescent Personality*. NY: Appleton-Century-Crofts, 1941, p. 496.
(4) Cole, Luella. *Psychology of Adolescence*. NY: Rinehart, 1954, p. 574.
(5) Coleman, James C. *Abnormal Psychology and Modern Life*. Chicago: Scott, Foresman, 1956, pp. 565-6.
(6) English, O. Spurgeon & Pearson, Gerald H. J. *Emotional Problems of Living*. NY: Norton, 1955, p. 300.
(7) Fenichel, Otto. "The Means of Education," in Eissler, Ruth S., et al. (Eds.), *The Psychoanalytic Study of the Child*, Vol. I. NY: International Universities Press, 1945, p. 281.
(8) Gesell, Arnold, et al. *Youth: The Years from Ten to Sixteen*. NY: Harper, 1956, p. 455.
(9) Horrocks, John E. *The Psychology of Adolescence*. Boston: Houghton Mifflin, 1951, p. 225; p. 241.
(10) Josselyn, Irene M. *The Happy Child*. NY: Random House, 1955, p. 126.
(11) Kuhlen, Raymond G. *The Psychology of Adolescent Development*. NY: Harper, 1952, p. 406.
(12) Liss, Edward. "Motivation in Learning," in Eissler, Ruth S., et al. (Eds.), *The Psychoanalytic Study of the Child*, Vol. X. NY: International Universities Press, 1955, p. 101.
(13) Liss, Edward. "The Ego Ideal Role in Learning," in *Orthopsychiatry and the School*. NY: American Orthopsychiatric Association, 1958, p. 103.
(14) Low, Camilla M. "The Adolescent and Education." *Amer. J. Orthopsychiatry*, 26:485, 1956.
(15) Mann, Thomas. *The Confessions of Felix Krull, Confidence Man*. NY: Knopf, 1955, p. 236.
(16) Pearson, Gerald H. J. *Psychoanalysis and the Education of the Child*. NY: Norton, 1954, pp. 148-9.
(17) Peller, Lili E. "The School's Role in Promoting Sublimation," in Eissler, Ruth S., et al. (Eds.), *The Psychoanalytic Study of the Child*, Vol. XI. NY: International Universities Press, 1956, p. 448.
(18) Prescott, Daniel A. *Emotion and the Educative Process*. Washington, DC: American Council on Education, 1938. Pp. 248-9.

(19) Regents Council on the Readjustment of High School Education. *Bright Kids, We Need Them.* Albany, NY: University of the State of New York, 1956.
(20) Segel, David. *Frustration in Adolescent Youth.* Washington, DC: Federal Security Agency, 1951, p. 38.
(21) Small, John J. "Why a Core Based on Adolescent Needs?" *Educational Administration & Supervision,* 43:112, 1957.
(22) Symonds, Percival M. "What Education Has to Learn from Psychology," *Teachers College Record,* 56:285, 1954.
(23) Wouk, Herman. *City Boy.* NY: Simon & Schuster, 1948, p. 105.

CHAPTER EIGHT

On Choosing a Career

> "The youth gets together his materials to build a bridge to the moon, or, perchance, a palace or temple on the earth, and, at length, the middle-aged man concludes to build a woodshed with them."
>
> HENRY THOREAU

The choice of a right vocation has much to do with man's happiness. The greatest portion of his life is spent in working hours. How he spends them and the satisfactions he derives from them may very well reflect his feelings of self-esteem, his relations with his family, his attitude toward his friends. Because success on the job is so paramount in adulthood, it is a terrible blow to fail, either actually or in relation to one's expectations.

In order to prevent such failures and to insure proper choice of their children's vocations, parents more likely than not attempt to direct the kind of education they shall have, the college they will attend, the job to prepare for. In high school, the youngster is enrolled either in a college preparatory, secretarial or trade course. Much depends on the economic position of the family. Nearly thirty years ago, the Lynds reported in *Middletown* that whereas every business class family among the group of forty interviewed planned to send their children through high school and college, in almost every case of the 124 working class families interviewed, plans were contingent on ability to afford it (16). These findings were validated in a more recent study (7), with this one difference: that lower income group boys and girls are today attending high school, if not always finishing it (8).

An example of the influence of economic status in the

family and how it exerts a powerful influence on the youngsters in it is seen in Carl Jonas's novel, *Jefferson Selleck.**
Selleck is writing his memoirs. He recalls that when his son
Tom was fourteen years old, he and his wife, Gertrude, sent
him to Exeter Academy, a high-toned preparatory academy
because they thought that "if he were to go to an Eastern
college, as we desired, it would be a great advantage (to Tom)
to go to an Eastern prep school." On a football week end, in
which Tom is starred for his team and of which Jefferson
Selleck is very proud, the following scene is recorded by Mr.
Selleck. The "footnotes" in this passage are part of the novel
proper.

   And curiously enough it was on this afternoon, or the
Sunday afternoon the day after the game rather, at the very
high water mark of Tom's career, that he and I had our first
really serious conflict with each other, although already there
had been small ones, I must admit, over trivial things like
using our car or money.
   Tom lived in Peabody Hall and he and I were up in his
room talking over his prospects for the future. As we talked,
he threw in a bombshell which was an announcement that
he did not intend to go to college.
   Now this was quite a shock, for Gertrude and I, while not
completely agreed, were fairly well agreed upon Tom's
future. Gertrude wanted him to go to Princeton, and I
wanted him to go to Yale, for I have always felt that it is a
fine thing for a man to be able to say he is a "Yale man." But
I did not entirely object to Princeton except that for a boy
who will do business in the Middle West the connotations
of Princeton are not always quite to his advantage. But either
school, in that respect, is preferable to Harvard, although
Bert Bernstein did send his son to Harvard. However, the
point is that both Gertrude and I very definitely intended
that Tom go on to college in the East and make a creditable
record.
   "But, Dad," Tom said, in a rather arrogant way which he

* From *Jefferson Selleck* by Carl Jonas. Copyright 1951, by Carl Jonas.
Reprinted by permission of Little, Brown & Co. Pp. 186-194.

was affecting at the moment, "I said that I just don't intend
to go to college."

Now had Tom been a dull boy, this would have been
different. He had a very fine scholastic record. He was a
member of the Lantern Club, which is the Academy literary
society, the Golden Branch, which is the debating society,
and won the Glidden Latin Prize.

"Look here, son," I said. "If I get you right, I think you
must have jumped your trolley."

"Dad," Tom said, with a little dark groove appearing between his eyebrows, "you don't seem to understand that I'm
grown-up now."

He was seventeen then and would be eighteen the following summer.

"I'm grown-up now and I've had enough of formal schooling," he said.

"And what do you plan to do instead of going on to college?" I asked him, a little sarcastically, I imagine.

He said: "I want to get a job on a tramp steamer and go
round the world and find out what life is."

I suppose if I had handled things differently, his whole
reaction would have been different.[6] But, fortunately sometimes and unfortunately on other occasions, I have always
dealt with things quite directly.

As it was, I said, "Son, your mother and I have not spent
two to three thousand dollars a year on your education just
for you to go out and see what life is. If we had wanted that,
we could have given it to you for nothing."

Tom said, in that same lofty manner he had then, "I'm
afraid that the automobile accessory business may perhaps
qualify you in some things, but not concerning my life or
how to run it."

And that, I'm ashamed to say, made me angry for I'm a
little bit hotheaded. I said, "You're going to go to Yale,
young man, or Princeton, and you're going to get into one of
those clubs they have there and play football and graduate
with flying colors and be a credit to your family."

6 Tom Selleck's comment was: "It might have been very different. It was
what I needed and I never got it until several years later when I was in the
service, and I had made my bad mistakes by that time. If he had let me go
then, I might even have been willing to go home afterward and work in his
business."

"Can't you understand," he said, "that I just don't want to go to college? I want to get out and start living."

I said, "When I was your age I had to get out and start in living, and it isn't all it's cracked up to be, I can tell you. I worked on your great-uncle's farm in Illinois. I pitched hay and I followed the horses. Why, I would have given my right eye for the advantages you've had and are having."

Tom became so angry that he was almost on the point of tears, and I was almost as angry also.

"Don't you see that's what I want?" he said. "I want to pitch hay and follow horses or do almost anything where there are living and breathing people. What do you know about life, you fat old bastard?"

Now I think that you must admit that when a son speaks that way to a father it's reason enough for the father to get angry, and I did get angry.

"You're just a seventeen-year-old punk," I said, "and you're not dry behind the ears yet. You don't know anything, and you might as well know that. You aren't going to tell me what you're going to do. I'm going to tell you, and you're going to like it. You're going to buckle down now and pass your college boards. Then you're going on to college and make a good record, and then you're coming home and go to work in the business, and then you may be able to talk a little about what life is."

What I said must have cowed him to some extent, for he did not answer, and until his Christmas vacation we left it at that point.

As I look back on this from the perspective of this moment, I can see I was probably wrong to have shouted at him in that manner. Perhaps I should have reasoned with him, but there is such a gap between generations frequently that reasoning is sometimes very close to an impossible thing to do. An adult has a wisdom which is beyond the grasp of the boy, and sometimes there is no way to make the boy understand this. Why, the adult wishes to say to the boy, should God have made you more capable of running the world at seventeen years old than your elders in their fifties? One admits freely that reasoning and persuasion are the right ways for producing action, but there are times when reasoning and persuasion seem to miss the point. And then you have a choice between the use of force and the allowing of the child to go ahead with mistakes of the most serious nature. Life for me has rarely presented clear-cut choices between right and wrong, but choices rather between mistakes of a larger or a smaller degree in which I have tried always to choose the smaller. And especially has this been true in my dealings with my son. Even where reasoning might have been possible he was a difficult boy to reason with, for, as with all the McCulloughs (and he was at least half McCullough) he had a kind of reserve, a kind of secretiveness which would suddenly appear just at the moment when you had thought you were closest to him. And this is true even to this day, even now when we have finally reached a friendly, satisfying affectionate, and even mutually confiding relationship. As an example, I can mention an occasion on which I congratulated him on one of his *Saturday Evening Post* covers. "Just some more of the old crap," he answered, which left me completely at a loss, for considering what they pay him, if that is not real art I must not know what real art is then.

But to return to the question which came up so unexpectedly that afternoon in the autumn of 1939 in Peabody Hall on the Exeter campus—we left the matter at the point at which I have just described until he came home for his vacation the following Christmas. We talked it all over again along with Gertrude, who felt as I did, that he must go to college. Whether a boy learns anything in college or not is not the point. The point is that a college degree is just one of those credentials a boy must have today if he is going to take any place in the world of business. Or even if he does not have a degree, it is a distinct advantage for him to be able to say that he has attended college and is a "college man," a member of a good fraternity, and so forth and so on.

That Christmas we argued this out through several sessions and finally came to an agreement which, although not a perfect one, was one from which all of us gained something.

He agreed that he would try college for one year provided it was the college of his choice, and that if at the end of that year he wished to drop out and get his job on a tramp steamer, I would freely allow him to do so. He further agreed to make a good scholastic record during that year at college.

Gertrude and I had expected that the college of his choice would be Yale or Princeton. However, he chose Cornell, which was a sensible choice, for if a man is going to do business in the Middle West it is in some ways better for him to be able to say he is a "Cornell man" even than a "Yale man," inasmuch as the implications are more democratic. There is quite a strong Cornell alumni association in Gateway. Herb Johnson of the *Times Examiner*, in fact, is a Cornell man, and so is Charley Mason. What Tom's reasons for that choice were, I don't know. Possibly it was because Cornell is a coeducational institution.[7]

Be that as it may, both Gertrude and I heaved a sigh of relief when all of us had arrived at this decision. And I was quite sure, as more or less became the case, that once he was in college he would not want to leave it.

However, I never anticipated the rebellion which would come over him during his college years, for I can only interpret his college behavior as rebellion. I never felt it in growing up and, as I look back on it, I had much more to rebel against than he did. While my upbringing was stern almost to the point of austereness, his was quite lenient, and almost all of his desires were respected. During my growing up I had had almost no spending money except what I earned, while Tom, although chronically broke, always had a very liberal allowance. I was the youngest of five children, which meant that most of my possessions were inherited after use by three or four others, while he, being the oldest, always had things new and without having to wait in turn for them to come down to him. I really am unable still to see what he rebelled at, but all the children of his generation seemed to have to go through this period of rebellion. And what can one call his queer behavior at Cornell which culminated in a runaway marriage in his senior year but rebellion of the most extreme nature?

But I must say that during that first year at Cornell, his behavior was all that we could have wished. He played freshman football, which was to be expected after his Exeter record. He was pledged to the Chi Psi fraternity which is a very good one, and was to be expected also after his Exeter record, joined with the fact that Charley Mason, my very good friend, was an active Chi Psi alumnus. His scholastic

[7] Tom Selleck says: "My reasons were not very creditable when I think them over. I wanted to go East but to assert myself I wanted to go to a college which neither Dad nor Mother had thought of. However, had I followed the logic of my convictions at that time it would have been the University of Chicago."

record was as good as could be expected. There was really only one thing I could have complained about, which was the amount of money which he was spending, but, as Gertrude said, you can't send a boy to a good college and then expect him to act and dress as though he were a pauper. And then I myself have always believed in spending money. It gives a boy a kind of prestige which he cannot quite get in any other manner.

It was not until his second year at Cornell that the strangeness began to show up in his behavior, and what set it off I cannot imagine, unless it was the fact that he worked in a summer theater on Cape Cod the summer of 1940 which, although I considered it a waste of time, seemed harmless enough at the moment. Our first hint of his strangeness came when we learned that he would not go out for football in the autumn.

"Football is childish," he wrote me, "and I have decided that I am here primarily to get an education."

I was perplexed, and I wrote to him telling him that football for those who were fortunate enough to be talented at it was not only an important part of college but for some even the whole of it also. I wrote trying to explain to him what an advantage it was to a man in business to have a fine athletic record behind him, and perhaps a gold football to hang from his watch chain. I told him that *mens sana in corpore sano* was a very sound idea, and he wrote back: "I am trying to get a sound mind. I already have a sound body, and I can keep it sound playing tennis."

And that would not have disturbed me so much if he had gone out for tennis, for I think he could have made the team. But he would not go out for the team. He insisted on playing it for fun only. I wrote to him that he must realize that his career in college was not just that but the beginning of his career in life also, and that he must meet, rather than shun, the challenges which it presented. You cannot imagine how bewildered I was when he wrote in answer: "The challenge of the world today is reactionary fascism, not the goalpost nor even the diploma."

Well what can a father do about that kind of business? What could he do even if he understood it, and I certainly could not understand at all what had gotten into Tom to so warp his whole viewpoint. It is true that in my college days we talked about politics on a world scale, but we certainly did not let it interfere with athletics, and what we did talk about was certainly more American and healthy. We talked about people like J. P. Morgan and Andrew Carnegie, and Teddy Roosevelt, and about things like Christianity and success, and then, of course, later when things were making up toward the war, the Huns and freedom of the seas and so forth.

What was it, I asked myself over and over again, that had gotten into him? Was it the erratic streak which went through the McCulloughs,[8] or was it something about the times he lived in which, I will admit, were trying times for us all, what with the corrupting influences of the New Deal and the fact that England was in the war already. Neither of these things seemed to entirely answer my questions. The sons and daughters of my friends seemed to be carrying on revolts of their own, but very understandable ones compared to Tom's, for they seemed to run only toward staying up late at night and cracking up automobiles. But Tom . . . If I did not know and trust him I would say that he was almost Communistic in his behavior. And it was not Cornell, either, for I looked closely at Cornell, talked to my friends and their sons about it, and found it to be the very soundest kind of American institution. It would have been understandable had he been attending the University of Chicago. The only conclusion I could come to was that he was revolting against something somewhere of which we had no knowledge, and the only answer was to let it run its course, which fortunately it seemed to do after we were in the war and he was in the service.

Instead of playing football and being a big man on the campus as he could have, he wrote essays and short stories for the campus literary magazine, and now and then made illustrations for it, and where he picked up drawing I have no idea, for there was certainly nothing of this in either Gertrude's or my family. He spent his time reading and listening to phonograph records. He drank more than he should have, although that did not worry me particularly. It

---

[8] Mrs. Selleck had a brother, Maxwell McCullough, rarely mentioned by any of the family, who went to Paris to live after the First War, and became the organist in the American Church there. This is the erratic quality to which Mr. Selleck refers here.

was not that he drank, it was who he drank with that concerned me. The only thing he did which we could be proud of was to keep up an extremely high scholastic average, but what compensation is a Phi Beta Kappa average to a father whose son might have been an all-American halfback?

This strange behavior began, as I have said, in his second year and it progressed in violence from that time onward. During his third year he began going on week ends to New York as often as he was able, which is not alarming in itself, for when we are young all of us like to enjoy the pleasures of the city. The alarming thing was what he did when he went down there. He did not go to places like the Stork Club or Twenty One as so many of the other boys did, but to plays, the Metropolitan Museum and the Museum of Modern Art, which is a queer place if there ever was one. And when he did go to night clubs he went to queer little places in Greenwich Village. It is all very well for a boy on a fling to go down to Greenwich Village or up to Harlem, but to practically live in the Village or to make friends of the Negroes up in Harlem is a completely different matter. Of course, one can say that all is well that ends well, but I could not say it at that moment. I am sure that Cornell did not approve of this, and I know for a fact that his brothers in Chi Psi disapproved of it completely. By senior year he was hardly on speaking terms with any of them in the lodge there.

In recent years, since Tom and I have become friends at last, he has tried to explain all this to me. "It was a normal enough way for me to go," he says. "Every son somehow has to kill his father, and father for me was not only you but business and Gateway, and everything I grew up with." This, I presume, is in the field of psychiatry, about which I know nothing, and the explanation is just as bewildering as the fact, and it sounds a little bloodthirsty into the bargain. The only thing I knew for sure was that underneath, Tom was a good boy and would be straightened out somehow when he grew older.

This excerpt from *Jefferson Selleck* illustrates the wide gap in understanding that frequently exists between parents and children. Without question, Jefferson Selleck thought what he was doing for his son's future was for Tom's own good and was done with every good intention. But what Mr. Selleck wanted for his son's future was not what Tom wanted. Mr. Selleck was looking for prestige, for status of position and for economic security. These could be secured by attending the "best" college, by joining the "best" fraternity, by being a Big Man On Campus. What he overlooked were Tom's interests, personality, and emotional satisfactions. The result was Tom's rebellion which Mr. Selleck could not understand, and the eventual "agreement" for Tom to go to Cornell. In actuality, this was not so much an agreement as it was a compromise, satisfying no one and dissatisfying everyone.

Parents who try to influence the choice of school or career for their children unduly and without insight into their children's feelings are often "killed," as Tom puts it. The adolescent has to retain his own identity, not live the father's or mother's life. So often, the well-meaning parent brings pressure to bear on son or daughter to enter this or that school, or this or that profession for selfish motivational reasons, all the time honestly believing they are doing it for "Tom's sake." In reality, of course, such a parent is doing it for his own sake. He may be compensating for his own deficiencies. Prevented in his own youth from entering a career of his choice—perhaps by a well-intentioned father, or prevented because of inability, or financial limitations— the parent now wishes to see his unfulfilled dreams realized through his seed. The parent projects his hopes for glory onto his child, with the fond hope the fulfillment of these projections will redound to his credit.

Too many sons and daughters, as adults, harbor deep resentments because they are unhappy in the vocational work that was forced upon them by their parents or relatives. Parents who believe that their authority is definitely above the desires of a child may insist that the latter follow the parents' dictates in matters of such grave importance as choosing a career. What the youngster wants is "foolish," or

a "passing fancy," or "impractical." However, the parent
may be motivated by selfish reasons rather than the "foolish-
ness" or "impracticability" of the adolescent. Although the
action in *The Old Wives' Tale** is laid in an earlier time
than ours, what transpires in the following selection has an
eternal ring of truth to it. Sophia, the adolescent daughter,
wants to teach, but mother and father have other ideas.

Mrs. Baines scrutinized the child's eyes, which met hers
with a sort of diffident boldness. She knew everything that a
mother can know of a daughter, and she was sure that Sophia
had no cause to be indisposed. Therefore she scrutinized
those eyes with a faint apprehension.

"If you can't find anything better to do," said she, "butter
me the inside of this dish. Are your hands clean? No, better
not touch it."

Mrs. Baines was now at the stage of depositing little pats of
butter in rows on a large plain of paste. The best fresh
butter! Cooking butter, to say naught of lard, was unknown
in that kitchen on Friday mornings. She doubled the expanse
of paste on itself and rolled the butter in—supreme operation!

"Constance has told you about leaving school?" said Mrs.
Baines, in the vein of small-talk, as she trimmed the paste
to the shape of a pie-dish.

"Yes," Sophia replied shortly. Then she moved away from
the table to the range. There was a toasting-fork on the rack,
and she began to play with it.

"Well, are you glad? Your Aunt Harriet thinks you are
quite old enough to leave. And as we'd decided in any case
that Constance was to leave, it's really much simpler that
you should both leave together."

"Mother," said Sophia, rattling the toasting-fork, "what am
I going to do after I've left school?"

"I hope," Mrs. Baines answered with that sententiousness
which even the cleverest of parents are not always clever
enough to deny themselves, "I hope that both of you will do
what you can to help your mother—and father," she added.

* From *The Old Wives' Tale* by Arnold Bennett. Doubleday & Co. Pp.
34-38; 45-47.

"Yes," said Sophia, irritated. "But what am I going to *do*?"

"That must be considered. As Constance is to learn the millinery, I've been thinking that you might begin to make yourself useful in the underwear, gloves, silks, and so on. Then between you, you would one day be able to manage quite nicely all that side of the shop, and I should be——"

"I don't want to go into the shop, mother."

This interruption was made in a voice apparently cold and inimical. But Sophia trembled with nervous excitement as she uttered the words. Mrs. Baines gave a brief glance at her, unobserved by the child, whose face was towards the fire. She deemed herself a finished expert in the reading of Sophia's moods; nevertheless, as she looked at that straight back and proud head, she had no suspicion that the whole essence and being of Sophia was silently but intensely imploring sympathy.

"I wish you would be quiet with that fork," said Mrs. Baines, with the curious, grim politeness which often characterized her relations with her daughters.

The toasting-fork fell on the brick floor, after having rebounded from the ash-tin. Sophia hurriedly replaced it on the rack.

"Then what *shall* you do?" Mrs. Baines proceeded, conquering the annoyance caused by the toasting-fork. "I think it's me that should ask you instead of you asking me. What shall you do? Your father and I were both hoping you would take kindly to the shop and try to repay us for all the——"

Mrs. Baines was unfortunate in her phrasing that morning. She happened to be, in truth, rather an exceptional parent, but that morning she seemed unable to avoid the absurd pretensions which parents of those days assumed quite sincerely and which every good child with meekness accepted.

Sophia was not a good child, and she obstinately denied in her heart the cardinal principle of family life, namely, that the parent has conferred on the offspring a supreme favour by bringing it into the world. She interrupted her mother again, rudely.

"I don't want to leave school at all," she said passionately.

"But you will have to leave school sooner or later," argued Mrs. Baines, with an air of quiet reasoning, of putting herself on a level with Sophia. "You can't stay at school forever, my pet, can you? Out of my way!"

She hurried across the kitchen with a pie, which she whipped into the oven, shutting the iron door with a careful gesture.

"Yes," said Sophia. "I should like to be a teacher. That's what I want to be."

The tap in the coal cellar, out of repair, could be heard distinctly and systematically dropping water into a jar on the slopstone.

"A school-teacher?" inquired Mrs. Baines.

"Of course. What other kind is there?" said Sophia, sharply. "With Miss Chetwynd."

"I don't think your father would like that," Mrs. Baines replied. "I'm sure he wouldn't like it."

"Why not?"

"It wouldn't be quite suitable."

"Why not, mother?" the girl demanded with a sort of ferocity. She had now quitted the range. A man's feet twinkled past the window.

Mrs. Baines was startled and surprised. Sophia's attitude was really very trying; her manners deserved correction. But it was not these phenomena which seriously affected Mrs. Baines; she was used to them and had come to regard them as somehow the inevitable accompaniment of Sophia's beauty, as the penalty of that surpassing charm which occasionally emanated from the girl like a radiance. What startled and surprised Mrs. Baines was the perfect and unthinkable madness of Sophia's infantile scheme. It was a revelation to Mrs. Baines. Why in the name of heaven had the girl taken such a notion into her head? Orphans, widows, and spinsters of a certain age suddenly thrown on the world—these were the women who, naturally, became teachers, because they had to become something. But that the daughter of comfortable parents, surrounded by love and the pleasures of an excellent home, should wish to teach in a school was beyond the horizons of Mrs. Baines's common sense. Comfortable parents of to-day, who have a difficulty in sympathizing with Mrs. Baines, should picture what their feelings would be if their Sophias showed a rude desire to adopt the vocation of chauffeur.

"It would take you too much away from home," said Mrs. Baines, achieving a second pie.

She spoke softly. The experience of being Sophia's mother for nearly sixteen years had not been lost on Mrs. Baines,

and though she was now discovering undreamt-of dangers in
Sophia's erratic temperament, she kept her presence of mind
sufficiently well to behave with diplomatic smoothness. It
was undoubtedly humiliating to a mother to be forced to use
diplomacy in dealing with a girl in short sleeves. In *her* day
mothers had been autocrats. But Sophia was Sophia.

"What if it did?" Sophia curtly demanded.

"And there's no opening in Bursley," said Mrs. Baines.

"Miss Chetwynd would have me, and then after a time I
could go to her sister."

"Her sister? What sister?"

"Her sister that has a big school in London somewhere."

Mrs. Baines covered her unprecedented emotions by gazing into the oven at the first pie. The pie was doing well,
under all the circumstances. In those few seconds she reflected rapidly and decided that to a desperate disease a
desperate remedy must be applied.

London! She herself had never been further than Manchester. London, 'after a time'! No, diplomacy would be
misplaced in this crisis of Sophia's development!

"Sophia," she said, in a changed and solemn voice, front-
ing her daughter, and holding away from her apron those
floured, ringed hands, "I don't know what has come over
you. Truly I don't! Your father and I are prepared to put
up with a certain amount, but the line must be drawn. The
fact is, we've spoilt you, and instead of getting better as you
grow up, you're getting worse. Now let me hear no more of
this, please. I wish you would imitate your sister a little
more. Of course if you won't do your share in the shop, no
one can make you. If you choose to be an idler about the
house, we shall have to endure it. We can only advise you
for your own good. But as for this . . ." She stopped, and let
silence speak, and then finished: "Let me hear no more of
it."

It was a powerful and impressive speech, enunciated
clearly in such a tone as Mrs. Baines had not employed since
dismissing a young lady assistant five years ago for light
conduct.

"But, mother. . . ."

A commotion of pails resounded at the top of the stone
steps. It was Maggie in descent from the bedrooms. Now, the
Baines family passed its life in doing its best to keep its

affairs to itself, the assumption being that Maggie and all the shop-staff (Mr. Povey possibly excepted) were obsessed by a ravening appetite for that which did not concern them. Therefore the voices of the Baineses always died away, or fell to a hushed, mysterious whisper, whenever the foot of the eavesdropper was heard.

Mrs. Baines put a floured finger to her double chin. "That will do," she said, with finality.

Maggie appeared, and Sophia, with a brusque precipitation of herself, vanished upstairs.

* * * * * *

When Sophia entered the room, the paralytic followed her with his nervous gaze until she had sat down on the end of the sofa at the foot of the bed. He seemed to study her for a long time, and then he murmured in his slow, enfeebled, irregular voice:

"Is that Sophia?"

"Yes, father," she answered cheerfully.

And after another pause, the old man said: "Ay! It's Sophia."

And later: "Your mother said she should send ye."

Sophia saw that this was one of his bad, dull days. He had, occasionally, days of comparative nimbleness, when his wits seized almost easily the meanings of external phenomena.

Presently his sallow face and long white beard began to slip down the steep slant of the pillows, and a troubled look came into his left eye. Sophia rose and, putting her hands under his armpits, lifted him higher in the bed. He was not heavy, but only a strong girl of her years could have done it.

"Ay!" he muttered. "That's it. That's it."

And, with his controllable right hand, he took her hand as she stood by the bed. She was so young and fresh, such an incarnation of the spirit of health, and he was so far gone in decay and corruption, that there seemed in this contact of body with body something unnatural and repulsive. But Sophia did not so feel it.

"Sophia," he addressed her, and made preparatory noises in his throat while she waited.

He continued after an interval, now clutching her arm, "Your mother's been telling me you don't want to go in the shop."

She turned her eyes on him, and his anxious, dim gaze met hers. She nodded.

"Nay, Sophia," he mumbled, with the extreme of slowness. "I'm surprised at ye . . . Trade's bad, bad! Ye know trade's bad?" He was still clutching her arm.

She nodded. She was, in fact, aware of the badness of trade, caused by a vague war in the United States. The words "North" and "South" had a habit of recurring in the conversation of adult persons. That was all she knew, though people were starving in the Five Towns as they were starving in Manchester.

"There's your mother," his thought struggled on, like an aged horse over a hilly road. "There's your mother!" he repeated, as if wishful to direct Sophia's attention to the spectacle of her mother. "Working hard! Con—Constance and you must help her . . . Trade's bad! What can I do . . . lying here?"

The heat from his dry fingers was warming her arm. She wanted to move, but she could not have withdrawn her arm without appearing impatient. For a similar reason she would not avert her glance. A deepening flush increased the lustre of her immature loveliness as she bent over him. But though it was so close he did not feel that radiance. He had long outlived a susceptibility to the strange influences of youth and beauty.

"Teaching!" he muttered. "Nay, nay! I canna' allow that."

Then his white beard rose at the tip as he looked up at the ceiling above his head, reflectively.

"You understand me?" he questioned finally.

She nodded again; he loosed her arm, and she turned away. She could not have spoken. Glittering tears enriched her eyes. She was saddened into a profound and sudden grief by the ridiculousness of the scene. She had youth, physical perfection; she brimmed with energy, with the sense of vital power; all existence lay before her, when she put her lips together she felt capable of outvying no matter whom in fortitude of resolution. She had always hated the shop. She did not understand how her mother and Constance could bring themselves to be deferential and flattering to every customer that entered. No, she did not understand it; but her mother (though a proud woman) and Constance seemed to practise such behavior so naturally, so unquestioningly, that she had never imparted to either of them her feelings; she guessed that she would not be comprehended. But long ago she had decided that she would never "go into the shop." She knew that she would be expected to do something, and she had fixed on teaching as the one possibility. These decisions had formed part of her inner life for years past. She had not mentioned them, being secretive and scarcely anxious for unpleasantness. But she had been slowly preparing herself to mention them. The extraordinary announcement that she was to leave school at the same time as Constance had taken her unawares, before the preparations ripening in her mind were complete—before, as it were, she had girded up her loins for the fray. She had been caught unready, and the opposing forces had obtained the advantage of her. But did they suppose she was beaten?

No argument from her mother! No hearing, even! Just a curt and haughty 'Let me hear no more of this'! And so the great desire of her life, nourished year after year in her inmost bosom, was to be flouted and sacrificed with a word! Her mother did not appear ridiculous in the affair, for her mother was a genuine power, commanding by turns genuine love and genuine hate, and always, till then, obedience and the respect of reason. It was her father who appeared tragically ridiculous; and, in turn, the whole movement against her grew grotesque in its absurdity. Here was this antique wreck, helpless, useless, powerless—merely pathetic—actually thinking that he had only to mumble in order to make her 'understand'! He knew nothing; he perceived nothing; he was a ferocious egoist, like most bedridden invalids, out of touch with life,—and he thought himself justified in making destinies, and capable of making them! Sophia could not, perhaps, define the feelings which overwhelmed her; but she was conscious of their tendency. They aged her, by years. They aged her so that, in a kind of momentary ecstasy of insight, she felt older than her father himself.

"You will be a good girl," he said. "I'm sure o' that."

It was too painful. The grotesqueness of her father's complacency humiliated her past bearing. She was humiliated, not for herself, but for him. Singular creature! She ran out of the room.

Fortunately Constance was passing in the corridor, otherwise Sophia had been found guilty of a great breach of duty.

"Go to father," she whispered hysterically to Constance, and fled upwards to the second floor.

And so Sophia's dreams of a teaching career are broken. Her bitter frustration is both immediate and long-lasting, producing a rebellion which climactically results in leaving home and country. On the other hand, the passive acquiescence of Theobald, in Samuel Butler's *The Way of All Flesh*,* to his father's double-edged persuasiveness for him to enter the clergy, is indicative of this adolescent's personality, as well as the enormous parental pressure put on him.

Before he [Theobald] was well out of his frocks it was settled that he was to be a clergyman. It was seemly that Mr. Pontifex, the well-known publisher of religious books, should devote at least one of his sons to the Church; this might tend to bring business, or at any rate to keep it in the firm; besides, Mr. Pontifex had more or less interest with bishops and Church dignitaries and might hope that some preferment would be offered to his son through his influence. The boy's future destiny was kept well before his eyes from his earliest childhood and was treated as a matter which he had already virtually settled by his acquiescence. Nevertheless a certain show of freedom was allowed him. Mr. Pontifex would say it was only right to give a boy his option, and was much too equitable to grudge his son whatever benefit he could derive from this. He had the greatest horror, he would exclaim, of driving any young man into a profession which he did not like. Far be it from him to put pressure upon a son of his as regards any profession and much less when so sacred a calling as the ministry was concerned. He would talk in this way when there were visitors in the house and when his son was in the room. He spoke so wisely and so well that his listening guests considered him a paragon of rightmindedness. He spoke, too, with such emphasis and his rosy gills and bald head looked so benevolent that it was difficult not to be carried away by his discourse. I believe two or three heads of families in the neighborhood gave their sons absolute liberty of choice in the matter of their professions—and am not sure

* From *The Way of All Flesh* by Samuel Butler. Reprinted by permission of E. P. Dutton & Co., Inc., 1949. Pp. 35-37.

that they had not afterwards considerable cause to regret having done so. The visitors, seeing Theobald look shy and wholly unmoved by the exhibition of so much consideration for his wishes, would remark to themselves that the boy seemed hardly likely to be equal to his father and would set him down as an unenthusiastic youth, who ought to have more life in him and be more sensible to his advantages than he appeared to be.

No one believed in the righteousness of the whole transaction more firmly than the boy himself; a sense of being ill at ease kept him silent, but it was too profound and too much without break for him to become fully alive to it, and come to an understanding with himself. He feared the dark scowl which would come over his father's face upon the slightest opposition. His father's violent threats, or coarse sneers, would not have been taken *au sérieux* by a stronger boy, but Theobald was not a strong boy, and rightly or wrongly, gave his father credit for being quite ready to carry his threats into execution. Opposition had never got him anything he wanted yet, nor indeed had yielding, for the matter of that, unless he happened to want exactly what his father wanted for him. If he had ever entertained thoughts of resistance, he had none now, and the power to oppose was so completely lost for want of exercise that hardly did the wish remain; there was nothing left save dull acquiescence as of an ass crouched between two burdens. He may have had an ill-defined sense of ideals that were not his actuals; he might occasionally dream of himself as a soldier or a sailor far away in foreign lands, or even as a farmer's boy upon the wolds, but there was not enough in him for there to be any chance of his turning his dreams into realities, and he drifted on with his stream, which was a slow, and, I am afraid, a muddy one.

Family attitudes play a big role in vocational choice. The family may place a hierarchy on the vocational scale: some are better than others. In different parts of the United States, teaching for a man is low on the scale; for a girl, it is an unexcelled opportunity. The hours are "short"; vacations long; maternity leaves provided; it is "secure." For a man, the scale runs first, medicine; then dentistry, law, accounting, engineering, and last, business.

In truth, it is not only the values the family places on certain professions that makes it a vexing problem for the adolescent to determine his goals. The advancement of science, and economic and social changes, make it difficult for the individual to be familiar with the diversity and degree of occupations. The young person today, his parents or even vocational guidance experts, cannot be expected to know all the jobs that are available. The latest *Dictionary of Occupational Titles* lists more than 40,000 occupations (5). The complexity and increasing specialization of jobs make it impossible for the individual to know more than just a very few of them.

Thus, the adolescent in contemporary American society, faced with the need of making a vocational choice and preparing for it, is almost inevitably powerfully influenced by the adults in his immediate environment. Many studies have shown the influence of the father's job on the occupational choice of American youth (17). This influence is so vast because the occupation of the father is associated with an individual's outlook on life and his educational, recreational, and vocational opportunities (18). Most individuals confront the problem of choosing an occupation at least twice: once for themselves, and again, as parents, for their children (9).

Adolescents are not only aware of the differential prestige attached to vocations, but they also know the position of their own families in the prestige system, and they understand the connection which exists between the father's occupation and the family's economic and prestige positions. Adolescents in each social class, in Hollingshead's study, tended to name the types of occupations with which they were most familiar. Thus, the children of business and professional people knew most about, and chose, careers in business and the professions; "they also realized that these vocations would insure them at least as much prestige as their parents enjoyed" (13). In similar fashion, children whose parents owned small businesses or pursued clerical trades knew most about these occupations; and children in the lowest social and economic scale were oriented toward the service trades and indecision (14). Within a psychological frame of reference, the fundamental process by which the ego acquires efficiency is identification with the parents, their values, attitudes, and feelings. The ego, according to Alexander, can learn not only from its own trials and errors but also from the experience of others. "Identification leads ultimately, however, to increased independence. In assuming the attitudes of the parents the child dispenses gradually with their actual support and becomes self-sufficient" (1).

Hollingshead points up the fact that in the American tradition, it has heretofore been unquestioned that youngsters would go into an occupation at least as good as their fathers, and that many would "better" themselves. America, the tradition went, was the land of unlimited horizons; America was rich in opportunities and provided these opportunities equally for all; America was the place where vaulting ambition and hard work would suffice to make a man's dreams come true. But wars and peace, foreign markets and economic policies, depressions and inflation, restrictive immigration laws and the drying up of labor supplies, the disappearance of the geographic frontier and the opening up of new technological worlds have all brought about changes in the American dream which have not yet been fully understood. The old tradition still survives: "The world is mine oyster, and I with sword will open it." While it survives, it is beginning to wear thin, for America's youth, it becomes apparent, is either being forced to accept or is willing to accept, the vocational patterns the class system holds out to it.

This problem has been described as a social, not a personal, one. Our open-class society, which permits occupational movement, is becoming more restrictive because of operative economic and social forces. "This movement from one occupation to another is called occupational mobility; it may be

vertical or horizontal mobility, depending on whether the
movement is to an occupation of higher or lower status, or
to one of the same prestige, income, and ability level. The
American tradition notwithstanding, vertical mobility has
generally been less common" (19).

There is less occupational mobility than formerly because
society has become more stabilized. Social stratification becomes more stringent for each succeeding generation because
of the limitations imposed on the child by virtue of his
father's occupational level and by narrowing opportunities.
If the United States, as it becomes older, becomes static as
well, vocational opportunities for youth will become more
delimited. If emphasis is placed on prestige and security
values and on getting ahead, the traditional American dream
"seems destined to be shattered even more rudely than it has
in the past. More people . . . will find themselves, and their
children, working at tasks to which relatively little prestige
has been attached in the past. Gaps between aspiration and
achievement, which result in dissatisfaction and maladjust-
ment, will presumably become greater and more numerous.
. . . Fortunately that is not likely to be the end of the story,
and it need not be if education and public opinion are so
modified as to develop more enlightened attitudes. For in its
essence the American dream consists not of aspiration and
prestige, but rather of a desire for a high standard of living
in a mobile society, one which allows talent its special outlets
and mediocrity a chance to develop to the fullest its ordinary
potentialities. In the scramble to 'get ahead' we have lost
sight of the fact that what we sought was opportunity, com-
fort, and security" (20).

To fulfill the American dream, Super asserts, our warped
tradition must be reshaped. It can be done by providing the
necessary variety of educational opportunities requisite in a
democracy; by building up attitudes making any worthy
occupation acceptable; by respecting individuality strongly
enough to make it possible for physician's sons to become

semiskilled workers, without pressure or loss of social and self-respect (21).

In the world of high school, where the adolescent spends many of his hours, teachers play a large role in the occupational determination process of the young person. Their influence does not necessarily have to be direct, as it is with parents. It can be accomplished by indirection, by the presentation of materials, and by their biases of different careers. In *Father and Son,** young Danny's teacher suggests to him he has "a calling." This interview provides a profound emotional experience for Danny.

Danny waited while Sister straightened up some papers. He was alone with her in the classroom. He wondered what she wanted. He was apprehensive. He had an idea of what she might have on her mind.

"All right, Danny, we can talk now," she said.

Danny went up to her. He stood on the dais facing her, and she sat at her desk.

"You didn't get along very well last year with Sister Bertha, did you?" she asked.

"Well, Sister—" he began, but he halted, not knowing what to say.

"Such things happen, and often it is neither the fault of the pupil nor of the teacher. But I didn't ask you to stay here to talk to you about bygones. I always say, let bygones be bygones. You know, Danny, in the short time I have been teaching you, I have grown to think a lot of you."

He smiled sheepishly.

"I'm telling you this because I don't think that it will go to your head. I don't think you can be spoiled. I have observed that you possess some fine qualities."

He grinned, ill at ease.

"Yes, you are a very loyal boy. And you have stick-to-itiveness. Without these virtues, a boy is not going to amount to anything in this world. But you have some qualities and you are a very smart boy."

"Well, Sister, I try to learn my lessons and do my home-

* From *Father and Son* by James T. Farrell. Reprinted by permission of The Vanguard Press. Pp. 32-36.

work," he began, and then he paused; he waited for her to go on.

"But also, there are some other things about you. You have the germ of destruction in you. I have never seen a boy with more of the germ of destruction in him than you have. I watch you closely. You are always destroying something. You mark up your books. You chew pencils. You get in fights. Last summer when Sister Bertha learned that I was coming here in her place, she spoke to me about all you boys. She told me how you like to fight. It's because you have this germ of destruction in you. But she evidently didn't see the other qualities you have. If you didn't have them, you would be destroying something every minute of the day."

He didn't know what to say. He didn't know how true it was. Of course, he did like to break windows, and last summer he and Dick Buckford used to go around and throw rotten tomatoes at people on back porches, break windows, and throw things in houses, but he didn't know.

"Your grandmother is a wonderful woman. I can see that your home life with her has been very wholesome. Its good influence must have helped save you."

He didn't know where she got all these ideas, but it was swell to know she didn't even suspect how things had been at home, and about Aunt Margaret. She didn't know how a few years ago on Indiana Avenue some kids wouldn't play with him because their mothers said there was too much cursing in his house.

She paused a moment and then went on:

"Danny, this morning, when I talked of vocations, you were one of the boys to whom I was really talking."

That was what he had been suspecting. He had been thinking about what she had said all day. Going home at noon with the gang, he had deliberately cursed to make it look as if he wasn't one of the kids she meant.

"Danny, look me in the eye!"

She held him in a piercing but sympathetic gaze. He looked at her, struggling with himself, to make his expression as honest a one as he could. He told himself that he would tell the truth and he would be honest and answer her questions. This was too important for him to lie about.

"Danny, have you ever thought that you might have a vocation?"

He didn't want to have a vocation. All day a voice inside him kept telling him he had a vocation. He hesitated answering her.

"Yes, Sister," he blurted out.

Immediately he wished he hadn't said it. He wished he had taken time really to think it over.

"I was certain I was right about you," she said, suddenly smiling with gratification.

He had never spoken with any person who could look you in the eye as steadily and for as long a time as Sister could.

"How long have you had thoughts about it?"

"Well, Sister, today, when you talked to us in catechism," he answered haltingly.

"Before that?"

He tried to think.

"Now and then the idea came to me. It would sometimes come and go, just like sometimes I would think that the most wonderful way to die would be as a martyr. But I can't say for how long."

"Danny, I knew it. That explains why the germ of destruction is so strong in you. It's your temptation. God has given you that kind of tendency, and He has given you the character to have loyalty and stick-to-itiveness to counteract it. The reason is because He has singled you out as a boy to receive the call."

She was sure a smart nun. She knew more about him than he knew himself.

"Have you made up your mind, Danny?"

"Well . . . No, not exactly."

He lowered his head and scraped his feet on the dais.

"Danny, I want you to know I'm your friend. You don't have to look at me just as the teacher who makes you do homework and sometimes has to punish you. You must feel that I am a real friend of yours."

No nun had ever talked to him like this. But then no teacher had ever been as wonderful as Sister Magdalen.

"Danny, I am certain you have a vocation."

Outside, the sun had gone down. From the street faint echoes of children at play could be heard.

"Your grandmother has money and she can put you through the schooling to be a priest. That won't be a handicap to you as it would be to some boys."

What gave her that idea? But then he couldn't say it really wasn't so, because he'd like it thought that his folks had a lot of money.

"You have all the qualities needed for a priest. As a priest a boy like you should have a wonderful career open to him. Danny, keep this in mind. God needs boys like you. The Church needs boys like you."

He hated to think of all the dreams he'd have to give up if he became a priest.

"And you were right by instinct in not making up your mind too soon. But I do want you to think this over. We will talk about it again, and we'll talk like two friends, not merely as teacher and pupil."

It was rapidly growing dark. The light seeping through the window was getting faint. Danny glanced off. The sky seemed sad. Life suddenly seemed sad to him.

"But, goodness, it's getting late. I have to go over to the convent. I have this stack of papers to correct," she said, pointing to a large, neatly arranged pile of papers on her desk.

She picked up her papers and books and got to her feet. She towered over him. Her beads rattled as she crossed the room.

"Are you playing football these days, Danny?" she asked, walking down the back stairs with him.

"Sometimes, Sister, but not a lot."

"You like baseball better, don't you?"

"Yes, Sister."

He walked with her across a short stretch of sidewalk from the high stairs of the school building to the back door of the yellow brick convent which faced Indiana Avenue. It stood at the end of the large schoolyard.

"Now, Danny, you think over what I said—carefully. And you better run along."

"Yes, Sister. And goodbye, Sister."

She smiled at him. The convent door closed. He suddenly felt very much alone. His feelings were so mixed up and confused that he was hardly able to have any thoughts. He walked by the side of the convent and out the gate of the iron picket fence.

Danny was a bit too young to make a realistic choice of life work and the Sister's insights were too frightening for him to accept. Ginzberg et al. divide the process of occupational decision-making into three distinct periods: the ages between six and eleven, when the youngster makes a fantasy choice; the eleven to eighteen age bracket, when the preadolescent and adolescent make a tentative choice; and the young adult period when a realistic choice is made (10). It was found in interviews with 20,000 youths that most of them had some kind of plan for themselves, a few had no idea whatever of their vocational future, while the plans of many were in the realm of wishful thinking and daydreams rather than tied closely to reality (2). The youth may say he would like to be an engineer, not because of any personal fitness for the profession, but because his uncle is an engineer and he likes his uncle! The chauffeur-driven Cadillac of a successful local business man, the glamorous, travel-full life of the peripatetic sailor, or the excitement of the trial lawyer's work are the stuff of which adolescents may weave their tentative choices of future careers.

An example of a realistic choice is formed in Sinclair Lewis's novel, *Bethel Merriday*.* Her choice originated in fantasy but Bethel experiences a revelation which opens up glorious vistas in her occupational thinking. She is profoundly moved by her first theater performance and is inspired to become an actress.

Once upon a time Sladesbury, with its population of more than a hundred thousand, had known a dozen touring companies a year: Sothern and Marlowe, Maude Adams in *Peter Pan*, Arnold Daly in *Candida;* and had supported a permanent stock company, presenting fifty plays, from *As You Like It* to *Charley's Aunt,* in fifty weeks of the year.

Now in 1931 not one professional play had been presented in Sladesbury for more than five years. The block of old-fashioned spacious buildings which had contained the Twitchell Theater—opened by Edwin Booth—the Latin Academy, and the Armory of the Honorable Company of

* From *Bethel Merriday* by Sinclair Lewis. Copyright 1940 by Sinclair Lewis. Reprinted by permission of Doubleday & Co., Inc. Pp. 14-17.

Foot had been replaced by a gold-and-scarlet filling station, a Serv-Ur-Self food market, and a Bar-B-Q Lunch which lent refinement to hamburger sandwiches by cooking them with electricity.

The former stock-company theater, the Crystal, had long been a motion-picture establishment. But by Bethel's fifteenth birthday, June 1, 1931, it was certain that the Crystal would gamble again with living actors. The Sladesbury that manufactured aeroplane motors was going to become as modern as Athens in 500 B.C. The *Daily Advocate* announced that the "Caryl McDermid Stock Company of Broadway Actors" would take over the Crystal, on June 15th, and play through the summer.

For Bethel, heaven had come to Charter Oak Avenue.

She cut out the daily notices and pictures of the company. She pondered over the photographs of McDermid, the actor-manager, with his handsome square face, his lively eyes, his thick hair low on his forehead, his wide mouth. Proudly, as though he belonged to her—was she not the greatest local patroness of the drama?—Bethel noted that sometimes he looked like a factory executive, sometimes like a soldier-explorer, once, in rags, like a poet vagabond; proudly she learned that he had been a star in the silent motion pictures and had toured with Otis Skinner and Frank Craven.

She had always considered it shameless to be seen loitering on Charter Oak Avenue, whistled at by the interested knots of young loafers who at this period were called "drugstore cowboys," but now she went out of her way to stop in front of the Crystal and study the pictures of the cast: McDermid bejeweled in *Richelieu* and terrifying as the Emperor Jones; Miss Maggie Sample comic as Mrs. Wiggs; and the pale glory of Irma Wheat as St. Joan.

Dearest to Bethel of all these pictured gods was Elsie Krall, a fragile girl who seemed, for all the stiffness of Shakespearean ruff and brocade, not much older than herself. If she had one friend like Elsie, she would attack Broadway in another year, and a year after that she would be a famous actress!

When the large red-and-black show bills were plastered about town, and the names of Mr. McDermid and Miss Wheat stared at her, she felt as though it were her own name that was thus startingly discovered.

The first play of the McDermid season was *The Silver*

Cord, by Sidney Howard, of whom Bethel had never heard—as she had never heard of Pinero or Somerset Maugham or Clyde Fitch. The press notes said that the play was "a story of mother love fighting for itself." Bethel pictured the mother as a pioneer in a log cabin, doing exciting things with an axe.

She wanted so feverishly to go to the opening night that she did not let herself go till Wednesday. But it was a youthful self-discipline in her (the kind that might someday take her through all-night rehearsals), rather than a Connecticut Puritanism whereby anything she wanted to do was wicked. By no discipline, however, could she keep away longer than Wednesday.

It was a part of the era and the country that it did not occur to her parents, since it was known that she had no taste for glossy young drunks, to prohibit her going out by herself in the evening, provided she was back by eleven-thirty. And even in these depression days, when the family were putting off buying a new car and Mr. Merriday was worrying about having to cut the staff in his store, it was sacred to them that Bethel should have "her own income"—two dollars a week, theoretically her salary for working in the store on Saturdays.

She could get no one to go with her to the theater.

She knew that her father and mother and brother would no more go to a play than to a chess tournament, and that neither Charley Hatch nor Alva Prindle would pay a dollar to hear six actors, when for half of that they could see six hundred. Bethel felt as lone and venturesome as a young-lady Christian martyr in a den of Roman lions. She longed to wear her party dress of yellow taffeta, but even as a Christian martyr she could not endure the comments of her brother, and it was in the humility of skirt and sweater that she went off to her first play.

"Give you a lift?" yelled Charley, as she passed the Hatch cottage.

"No! I—I got to meet a friend," said Bethel.

The crowd that was wavering into the Crystal Theater was none too large, but Bethel was a little frightened by it. She felt herself the only greenhorn and hoped that she would not betray herself. By the most acute figuring she had arrived at the theater exactly five minutes before the announced curtain time, so she was a quarter of an hour early. She was in awe of the veteran-looking doorman, who snatched her ticket and irreverently tore it, of the young gentleman who was demanding hats to check, of the supercilious girl ushers.

She climbed, panting, to the balcony, and came out under a noble ceiling with frescoes of pink goddesses sitting on gilt clouds and leering. She was shamed by having to crawl past the rigid knees of four early-comers, and wanted to apologize to them, and was afraid to. But when she had sunk down on the stony leatherette seat in the front row of the balcony, she felt secure, she felt at home.

She looked beatifically at the curtain, which appropriately depicted the Bay of Naples. The orchestra members, handsomest and most artistic of men, crawled from under the stage and scratched themselves a little and whispered and looked up—not at her, Bethel hoped—and then relented and sat down to play a Wienerwalz.

Bethel's soul skipped with ecstasy. She read every word in the slim program, even the advertisement of The Mount Vernon Funeral Home, Where Sympathy Is Our Watchword, Phone Night or Day. She noted that Elsie Krall, the girl actress whose picture she had loved, was playing a character called Hester. She primly folded the program, then bent over the rail and prayed for a larger house. But the place was only half filled when her heart turned over as the orchestra shivered and stopped. The house lights were dimmed, and for the first time during the fifteen years she had waited for it, Bethel knew the magic pause, the endless second of anticipation, with just a fringe of light at the bottom of the curtain, before it went up.

She had never been so happy.

Bethel subsequently chooses acting as her vocational goal and this choice helps to stabilize the picture she has of herself currently and for the future. It concretizes her thinking and planning and enables her to concentrate on one area and look forward, with real anticipation, to the satisfactions she will derive from working in the world of the theater. She has a basis for action, now that she has a star by which to steer her life.

The image that Bethel had of herself played a large, determinant role in her choice of occupation, as it does with all adolescents. The choice of a vocation often expresses the adjustment of the individual; the psychologically well-adjusted person is likely to be a vocationally happy person (12). It is a well-established fact that poor personality adjustment is the major cause of dismissal from jobs in normal times, the major factor in friction on the job, and a fundamental factor in job dissatisfaction (3). It has also been well-established that adolescence is a period of emotional conflicts, of tensions and stresses, of struggle for emotional weaning away from the family, of the need for independence while at the same time needing to be dependent on parents. Coping simultaneously with emotional pressures and with the pressures brought to bear on him to make a vocational choice, the adolescent is compelled to choose at a time when he is ill-equipped to do so and when parents are frequently at a loss as to how they can help.

The adolescent is not only confused about the present, writes Josselyn, but his dreams of the future are equally unstable. "Although he spends hours chatting with his parents about his ambition to be a lawyer, his grades suggest that he won't be able to enter college. Yet the high school psychologist indicates that he could easily qualify if he would study. He dreams of being an experimental chemist and cuts chemistry laboratory at the slightest excuse. He outlines his future as a concert pianist and refuses to practice. He plans a successful business career and then wishes to leave high school and work as an unskilled laborer" (15). To achieve equilibrium in adolescence, the ego indiscriminately uses all the defense mechanisms that it used in early childhood and latency (6). But, says Erikson, the integration taking place in the form of ego identity is more than the sum of the childhood identifications. "It is the accrued experience of the ego's ability to integrate these identifications with the vicissitudes of the libido, with the aptitudes developed out of endowment, and with the opportunities offered in social roles. The sense of ego identity, then, is the accrued confidence that the inner sameness and continuity are matched by the sameness and continuity of one's meaning for others, as evidenced in the tangible promise of a 'career' . . . It is primarily the inability to settle on an occupational identity which disturbs young people" (4).

What is not always realized is that vocational decisions are made continuously; an individual cannot make a single decision that will settle his vocational future. Ginzberg et al. found three basic postulates in their approach to a general theory of occupational choice: (a) choosing a career is a process which takes place over ten or more years; (b) this process is irreversible, since each decision during adolescence is related to one's experience up to that point, which in turn has an influence on the future; and (c) that the ultimate choice of occupation has the quality of compromise, inasmuch as choosing a career involves balancing subjective feelings with the opportunities and limitations of reality (8).

In their study, Ginzberg et al. designated the period from eleven through seventeen as the period of tentative choices and they divide this period into four stages. First, the "interest stage," in which the preadolescent of eleven and twelve makes a choice primarily in terms of his likes, dislikes, and interests. Secondly, the "capacity stage," in which the thirteen- and fourteen-year-old begins to consider his capacities objectively and for the first time becomes aware of external factors—different occupations, returns, preparation, and training. Third, the "value stage," which characterizes the fifteen- and sixteen-year-old's attempt to find a place for himself in society. He recognizes that he must determine occupational choice not only on the basis of what he is interested in and able to do, but also what the reality situation will permit him to do and the satisfactions he will derive from a particular career. He must formulate and clarify the whole range of factors that are significant for his choice and evaluate them in the light of his own goals. And fourth, the "transition stage" usually finds the seventeen-year-old approaching the end of high school and pointing either to work or to college.

The period of realistic choices on the part of the late adolescent and young adult of middle and upper income families is divided into three distinct stages. The first is the "exploration" period, in which the entering year or two of college are spent in the acquisition of experience by which the student will resolve his occupational choice. Second is the "crystallization" period, wherein the individual commits himself to a career, based on his evaluation of all pertinent factors. And third the "specification" stage, which is marked by the young adult's firm choice of an area of specialization within the field he has chosen in the crystallization period.*

If we have hitherto felt that the adolescent's approach to selecting a career is largely haphazard, perhaps now it can be seen that this is more apparent than real. There is a definite sequence—although they may be unaware of it—by which most young people go about the business of making vocational choices. The way the adolescent faces up to the problem depends on his physical, emotional, educational, and intellectual development which are, in turn, related to key people in his environment, the influence of his parents, and their social and economic status in the community. Based on these factors, he will experiment and explore and choose. In Thomas Mann's novel, *The Confessions of Felix Krull, Confidence Man,* the youthful protagonist acts out his fantasy wish to be a band conductor, poses as an artist's model, is costumed by his godfather in the garb of a Roman flute-player, an English page, a Spanish bullfighter, a youthful abbé, an Austrian officer, a German mountaineer. With the bankruptcy and suicide of his father and the need to fend for himself, Felix turns pimp, jewel thief, and mixes with the *haute monde* while working as an elevator operator and waiter in a fashionable hotel in Paris. When the time comes

* The above is almost entirely a paraphrase of *Occupational Choice,* pages 75 and 95.

for him to impersonate a marquis, his previous experiences well equip him for this and other more spurious occupational roles. Thus, all through his life, Felix has been discovering his abilities. While this is putting abilities to negative use, the more common expectancy would be for a positive application of the adolescent's talents.

Since choosing an occupation, preparing for, and entering into it is only one of the problems that the adolescent must face, and since this choice is dependent on the factors cited above, attention on the part of the responsible adults as well as the youngsters must be given them. There is no crystal ball—or "aptitude test"—which can tell an individual what he "is best suited for." The resolution of the problem of goals comes about through an ongoing process over a number of years, based on the totality of experience provided through the environment and the opportunities available to the youngster.

REFERENCES

(1) Alexander, Franz. *Fundamentals of Psychoanalysis*. NY: Norton, 1948, p. 92.
(2) Bell, Howard M. *Matching Youth and Jobs*. Washington, DC: American Council on Education, 1940, pp. 5-8.
(3) Brewer, J. M. "Causes for Discharge," *Personnel J.*, 1927, 6:171-172.
(4) Erikson, Erik H. *Childhood and Society*. NY: Norton, 1950, p. 228.
(5) Federal Security Agency. *Dictionary of Occupational Titles*. (2nd Ed.). Washington, DC: U.S. Government Printing Office, 1949. Volume I, p. XI.
(6) Freud, Anna. *The Ego and the Mechanisms of Defense*. NY: International Universities Press, 1946.
(7) Ginzberg, Eli, Ginsburg, Sol. W., Axelrad, Sidney, & Herma, John L. *Occupational Choice: An Approach to a General Theory*. NY: Columbia University Press, 1951, p. 134.
(8) Ginzberg, Eli, et al. *Ibid.*, p. 151.
(9) Ginzberg, Eli, et al. *Ibid.*, p. 4.
(10) Ginzberg, Eli, et al. *Ibid.*, p. 60.
(11) Ginzberg, Eli, et al. *Ibid.*, p. 198.
(12) Hepner, H. W. *Psychology Applied to Life and Work*. NY: Prentice-Hall, 1950, p. 216.
(13) Hollingshead, August B. *Elmtown's Youth. The Impact of Social Classes on Adolescents*. NY: Wiley, 1949, p. 285.
(14) Hollingshead, August B. *Ibid.*, p. 285.
(15) Josselyn, Irene. *The Happy Child*. NY: Random House, 1955, p. 130.

(16) Lynd, Robert S. & Lynd, Helen M. *Middletown.* NY: Harcourt, Brace, 1929, p. 186.

(17) Samson, Ruth & Stefflre, Buford. "Like Father . . . Like Son," *Personnel & Guidance J.,* 31:35-39, 1952.

(18) Strang, Ruth. *Behavior and Background of Students in College and Secondary School.* NY: Harper, 1937.

(19) Super, Donald E. *The Dynamics of Vocational Adjustment.* NY: Harper, 1942, p. 16.

(20) Super, Donald, E. *Ibid.,* p. 37.

(21) Super, Donald, E. *Ibid.,* p. 38.

CHAPTER NINE

On Becoming an Adult

> "When one is young and on the threshold
> of life's long deception, rashness is all."
>
> FRANÇOISE SAGAN, *A Certain Smile*, p. 128

The word adolescence comes from the Latin *adolescere*, meaning to "approach maturity." The past participle of *adolescere* is *adultus* and this means "full grown" or "mature." Reaching maturity or attaining adulthood has been defined in many ways and has come to mean innumerable things to different people. However, a common core of acceptable meaning can be sensed from the following definitions.

Williams asserts an adult is one who is able to see reality without investing it with infantile symbolism, who is able to act in accordance with reality and who can adjust to a situation with a minimum of conflict (13). To be truly adult, says Josselyn, means to have the ability to cope with all the anxieties of life without the protection and security extended to the child (8). A time arrives in the growth of the individual, when, ideally speaking, according to Binger, his emotional development is in step with his physical (1). And Flugel declares that normal psychic development involves a gradual emergence from a dependency condition on parental authority and care to one in which the individual is largely dependent upon his own efforts in regard to his livelihood, judgment and conduct (4).

When, in the American culture, does the adolescent become an adult? There is no clear-cut pattern such as exists in many primitive cultures. Rather, in our society, adult status is assumed gradually and with great variations which are dependent on physical achievement, emotional development, social relations and parental roles. Parallel to the physical changes which take place in the body from birth through adulthood is the development of the psychic process in which recognition of the concept of self takes place on the basis of life experience. For Ellen, in *Winter in April*,* the initial glimmer of maturing involves her first sleeveless dancing gown. This simple matter brings with it her first womanly joy and sorrow and the realization that she must grow up.

So Ellen has had her dance; she has entered the world of society through the little wicket reserved for the friends of Mrs. Billingsley. She went off on Eric's arm like a young lady, so happy and lovely that a lump came into my throat. No more the child, the little girl I watched grow up with her dolls, her first long dress, her little sail boat . . . but with Eric's flowers pinned to her shoulder, her eyes shining, and her dress making a rustle as she moved. I found Katy weeping in the kitchen. Dear Ellen . . . soon you will be leaving us in earnest. And what shall we do then, Katy and I?

I did not go to the dance; for one thing, Eric was wearing my dress suit. But I heard all about it afterwards, from Matilda: how pretty Ellen looked, what a good time she had had, and how pleased everyone had been with her. I have reason to believe that certain people gathered the impression that Eric was a nobleman; and that Matilda did not say anything to deny it. I do not blame her; and I do not grudge Ellen that little extra pleasure. In a democracy such as ours, one cannot afford to throw away one's advantages.

All the next day she moved about in a haze of joy, in a cloud of glory. It seemed as though she had put forever behind her the doubts and anxieties of childhood; she seemed a woman grown, in her bearing, and in the tender glance of her eyes, brimming with secrets, and with a certain mischief. All this magic has been done overnight, and by a dress without any sleeves.

And it is as a woman that she faces, finally, her first real

* From *Winter in April* by Robert Nathan. Copyright 1938. Reprinted by permission of Alfred A. Knopf, Inc. Pp. 223-228.

sorrow. For Eric is leaving us. The call of what he feels to be
his duty is too loud for him to ignore any longer. He is going
to Spain to join his friends in the loyalist army.

It is not a surprise, after all; even Ellen knew that it was
coming. But that does not make us feel any less unhappy.
Alma goes about with her mouth open in a continual O, and
her eyes started as a child who has seen something in the
dark. And Katy has aged all over again.

I shall miss him more than any of them, for now I shall not
have anyone to help me with my work. But I know that he
must do what he thinks is right.

I have given him a warm sweater as a going-away present,
because it is cold in Spain, in the mountains; and a copy of
John Brown's Body by my friend, Stephen Benét. He will not
find anywhere more beauty or a nobler spirit in our language.

> "American muse, whose strong and diverse heart
> So many men have tried to understand . . ."

Katy cooked him a cake for the boat; and Matilda gave
him a box of medicines. I do not know what Ellen gave him;
she did not tell me. But I think it must have been a locket
which belonged to her mother, for I cannot find it anywhere.

I left them alone together when he came to say goodbye;
and went out for a walk by myself. The first light snow had
fallen, and the city was bright and still with winter. I thought
of Stephen's lines:

> "I know this girl . . .
> I know her heart touched with the wilderness-stone
> That turns good money into heaps of leaves
> And builds an outcast house of apple-twigs
> Beside a stream that never had a name.
> She will forget what I cannot forget,
> And she may learn what I shall never learn.
> But, while the wilderness-stone is strong in her,
> I'd have her use it for a touchstone yet
> And see the double face called good and bad
> With her own eyes."

When I came back, she met me at the door. She held her
head high; and there was a look on her face such as I had seen
in 'seventeen, when the mothers were sending their sons to

France. "Never mind, grandfather," she said. "He'll come back to us again some day.

"We should be proud," she said; and her lips trembled. "We ought to be very proud," she said.

She stood beside me, looking out at the wintry street. "He kissed me goodbye," she told me simply. "He said I was like his sister."

I put my arm around her; and she leaned her head on my shoulder, and wept. "Oh grandfather," she cried.

"Isn't there any place for young people any more in the world?

"Because we won't be young forever; and if there's no place left . . ."

But in a little while she lifted her head again, and stood up straight and tall.

"I guess maybe I don't want to grow up so hard," she said. "But I guess maybe I'd better."

Ellen's ambivalence is characteristic of adolescents. Their mixed feelings about becoming adult are based on the conflict between wanting to continue to enjoy the protection of childhood (the while resenting it) and yet to be accorded the privileges and powers of adult status. Frequent swings between these two feelings predominate, invariably to parental distress, before a more mature pattern is established. The parental anguish intensifies the situation, more likely than not because the parents themselves are ambivalent about their youngster growing up. Unfortunately, the adolescent and his parents seldom have their moments together; when the adolescent is asserting himself, mother or father may be pulling him back to childhood status; and when his feeling is infantile, they are wishing for a young adult upon whom they may lean (14). In *The Young People*,* the ambivalence of both mother and son is apparent; each understands the situation but is helpless to better it, the one to refrain from asking questions, the other to volunteer more information.

* From *The Young People* by Gertrude Schweitzer. Copyright 1953. Reprinted by permission of Thomas B. Crowell, Inc. Pp. 97-99,

"You're quiet, Jim," his mother said. "Is anything wrong?"

He shook his head. She was always asking him if anything was wrong. Sometimes he thought she was hoping there was something he would have to tell her about so she could console him. She would have liked him to tell her everything, the way he had when he was a little boy, and she knew he wouldn't, but she kept trying.

"He's probably tired," Lex said. "Work always makes me tired. How did it go anyhow, Jim?"

"Okay."

"Oh, you mustn't ask him," Zelda said. "You mustn't pry. This is a very personal matter."

Jim grinned at her. "Now, mom."

"Don't 'now, mom' me." She sounded mad, but he knew she'd get over it in a minute. "It's so childish to think there's some virtue in keeping everything to yourself. Isn't it normal for us to be interested in what happened your first day in your father's office? Do you think you'll lose caste, or something, if you tell us?"

"But I did tell you. I pasted ads in a scrapbook and I had lunch at Whitney's and I sat in on a meeting about a radio commercial for Culverton's whiskey. What more do you want me to say?"

He knew, of course. He knew she would love it if he told her what he had been thinking while he pasted the ads, and what he felt while he was at the meeting. She'd have loved to hear about the martini at Whitney's and why he ordered it and why he had wished he were at a hamburger stand instead and about how he had made his father think he got a kick out of the man with the sling and about Hallie Breed. She'd have eaten it all up if he could have told her, but you couldn't tell your mother any of that.

You couldn't let anybody know you that well, when it came down to it. If he hadn't told Libby so much, it would have been better too. She'd have thought his father's office was the dream of his life, and there wouldn't have been any argument. As soon as people knew what you were really thinking and feeling, they tried to make you think and feel something else.

"Leave him alone, Zel," Lex said. "Let's all have a drink. I'll take the orders."

Jim stood up. "I'll get them. I just want a coke myself. How about you two?"

Lex wanted a scotch highball. Jim's mother said she'd have a coke too. She took his hand and pulled him down to her. "All right, have it your own way," she said, and kissed his cheek. "Pretend you're an atomic secret, if you want to, and see if I care. I'll never ask you another question."

He kissed her too. "Sure you will, mom," he said. "You'll try not to, but you will. It's all right. I know you can't help it."

As he went inside, he heard her say to Lex, "Don't ever be a mother. You can't win."

He chuckled to himself. She was all right.

The process of maturing involves the freeing of the adolescent from parental control. Jim wants to shake himself free but, like many adolescents, he is frightened. Although he may protest his ability to take care of himself, the adolescent is actually more frightened and thus more clinging than he has been since infancy (9). This explains why, no matter how wise a parent may be, he can never be right for any length of time.

The adolescent wants to be recognized for himself, to be independent, to be grown up. But it is hard to tell the adolescent's conformity from his dissent since he hits them both so hard. The adolescent will try to appear indifferent to anyone's opinion or advice. To accept it would be to acknowledge his status as a child; to disagree is to show his strength as an adult. Psychological weaning from parental authority almost inevitably leads to stress and conflict, for there is a very real need for the adolescent to free himself from the parental figure and to rely on himself and his peers. The essence of the adolescent struggle for selfhood is the struggle for independence from the opinion of grownups; it is rooted in large part in the need to shake off adult controls. Adults are likely to assist unwittingly in this process, for they have neither the closeness, the authority, nor the know-how to maintain the earlier parent-child relations (12). In D. H.

Lawrence's *The Rainbow,** a callous, immature mother and a harsh, bitter father try to prevent their daughter Ursula from becoming free.

He looked round as if at an apparition. Ursula stood shadowily within the candle-light.

"What now?" he said, not coming to earth.

It was difficult to speak to him.

"I've got a situation," she said, forcing herself to speak.

"You've got what?" he answered, unwilling to come out of his mood of organ-playing. He closed the music before him.

"I've got a situation to go to."

Then he turned to her, still abstracted, unwilling.

"Oh, where's that?" he said.

"At Kingston-on-Thames. I must go on Thursday for an interview with the Committee."

"You must go on Thursday?"

"Yes."

And she handed him the letter. He read it by the light of the candles.

"Ursula Brangwen, Yew Tree Cottage, Cossethay, Derbyshire.

"Dear Madam, You are requested to call at the above offices on Thursday next, the 10th, at 11:30 a.m., for an interview with the committee, referring to your application for the post of assistant mistress at the Wellingborough Green Schools."

It was very difficult for Brangwen to take in this remote and official information, glowing as he was within the quiet of his church and his anthem music.

"Well, you needn't bother me with it now, need you?" he said impatiently, giving her back the letter.

"I've got to go on Thursday," she said.

He sat motionless. Then he reached more music, and there was a rushing sound of air, then a long, emphatic trumpet-note of the organ, as he laid his hands on the keys. Ursula turned and went away.

He tried to give himself again to the organ. But he could

* From *The Rainbow* by D. H. Lawrence. Copyright 1915 by D. H. Lawrence, 1943 by Frieda Lawrence. Reprinted by permission of The Viking Press, Inc., N.Y. Pp. 343-346.

not. He could not get back. All the time a sort of string was tugging, tugging him elsewhere, miserably.

So that when he came into the house after choir-practice his face was dark and his heart black. He said nothing, however, until all the younger children were in bed. Ursula, however, knew what was brewing.

At length he asked:

"Where's that letter?"

She gave it to him. He sat looking at it. "You are requested to call at the above offices on Thursday next—" It was a cold, official notice to Ursula herself and had nothing to do with him. So! She existed now as a separate social individual. It was for her to answer this note, without regard to him. He had even no right to interfere. His heart was hard and angry.

"You had to do it behind our backs, had you?" he said, with a sneer. And her heart leapt with hot pain. She knew she was free—she had broken away from him. He was beaten.

"You said, 'let her try,' " she retorted, almost apologizing to him.

He did not hear. He sat looking at the letter.

"Education Office, Kingston-on-Thames"—and then the type-written "Miss Ursula Brangwen, Yew Tree Cottage, Cossethay." It was all so complete and so final. He could not but feel the new position Ursula held, as recipient of that letter. It was an iron in his soul.

"Well," he said at length, "you're not going."

Ursula started and could find no words to clamour her revolt.

"If you think you're going dancing off to th' other side of London, you're mistaken."

"Why not?" she cried, at once hard fixed in her will to go.

"That's why not," he said.

And there was silence till Mrs. Brangwen came downstairs.

"Look here, Anna," he said, handing her the letter.

She put back her head, seeing a type-written letter, anticipating trouble from the outside world. There was the curious, sliding motion of her eyes, as if she shut off her sentient, maternal self, and a kind of hard trance, meaningless, took its place. Thus, meaningless, she glanced over the letter, careful not to take it in. She apprehended the contents with her callous, superficial mind. Her feeling self was shut down.

"What post is it?" she asked.

"She wants to go and be a teacher in Kingston-on-Thames, at fifty pounds a year."

"Oh, indeed."

The mother spoke as if it were a hostile fact concerning some stranger. She would have let her go, out of callousness. Mrs. Brangwen would begin to grow up again only with her youngest child. Her eldest girl was in the way now.

"She's not going all that distance," said the father.

"I have to go where they want me," cried Ursula. "And it's a good place to go to."

"What do *you* know about the place?" said her father harshly.

"And it doesn't matter whether they want you or not, if your father says you are not to go," said the mother calmly.

How Ursula hated her!

"You said I was to try," the girl cried. "Now I've got a place and I'm going to go."

"You're not going all that distance," said her father.

"Why don't you get a place at Ilkeston, where you can live at home?" asked Gudrun, who hated conflicts, who could not understand Ursula's uneasy way, yet who must stand by her sister.

"There aren't any places in Ilkeston," cried Ursula. "And I'd rather go right away."

"If you'd asked about it, a place could have been got for you in Ilkeston. But you had to play Miss High-an'-mighty, and go your own way," said her father.

"I've no doubt you'd rather go right away," said her mother, very caustic. "And I've no doubt you'd find other people didn't put up with you for very long either. You've too much opinion of yourself for your good."

Between the girl and her mother was a feeling of pure hatred. There came a stubborn silence. Ursula knew she must break it.

"Well, they've written to me, and I s'll have to go," she said.

"Where will you get the money from?" asked her father.

"Uncle Tom will give it me," she said.

Again there was silence. This time she was triumphant.

Then at length her father lifted his head. His face was

abstracted, he seemed to be abstracting himself, to make a pure statement.

"Well, you're not going all that distance away," he said. "I'll ask Mr. Burt about a place here. I'm not going to have you by yourself at the other side of London."

"But I've *got* to go to Kingston," said Ursula. "They've sent for me."

"They'll do without you," he said.

There was a trembling silence when she was on the point of tears.

"Well," she said, low and tense, "you can put me off this, but I'm *going* to have a place. I'm *not* going to stop at home."

"Nobody wants you to stop at home," he suddenly shouted, going livid with rage.

She said no more. Her nature had gone hard and smiling in its own arrogance, in its own antagonistic indifference to the rest of them. This was the state in which he wanted to kill her. She went singing into the parlour.

"C'est la mère Michel qui a perdu son chat,
  Qui crie par la fenêtre qu'est-ce qui le lui rendra—"

In this passage, the almost universal struggle between adolescents and parents can be observed. It is not a question of breaking away completely from parental control. Rather, what the adolescent wants and needs are parents who accept him as the individual he is, and not in terms of the infantile images they have of him. By the same token, the adolescent has to learn to accept his parents for what they are, human beings with problems of their own, as illustrated by Mr. and Mrs. Brangwen.

Some parents literally demand that their adolescent children suddenly "grow up and be a man." Others would like to see their adolescent children forever remain adolescents, or even children. Adult reactions are often really infantile reactions which the adult has never outgrown and thereby become adult, capable of dealing with adult problems on an adult basis. As a pawn in an all-out fight between two strong people to vindicate themselves by making their son conform to their own disparate images, Richard, in Anthony West's *Heritage*,* becomes enviably aware of and prepared for the perils of adulthood. "I was flattered and excited, I recognized that I was being invited by one adult to make a party against another on level terms and took my first step forward into that world of lies, treachery, deceit, and fierce emotions that lay beyond childhood. The pretenses that fathers and mothers love each other and their children as a matter of course could now be abandoned, the fathers loved the fathers, the mothers the mothers, the children looked after themselves, and occasionally their interests coincided, the important thing was not to be caught up in one's own lies, or to be fooled by anyone else's."

Neither Max Town, Richard's celebrated journalist father, nor Naomi Savage, his equally famous actress mother, are ever quite sure where the illusion of their creative vehicles ends and the self-deception of their own lives begins. Richard's realization of this develops in the following scene, where his mother tells him of her plans to marry a Colonel.

"I'm sorry, Mother, it just rubbed me up the wrong way the idea of you two whispering about my clothes and making plans for me as if I was a baby or an idiot."

"If you don't want to be treated like a baby don't behave like one. You're too old to sulk."

"I'll try not to . . ." I felt a swift return of confidence. She was using the old way of making me feel small and it wouldn't do any longer. I was, after all, a man who had a mistress in France, and she just didn't know the first thing about the new being she had to deal with. It was fun holding out on her, and it made me feel pleasantly superior. I thought I'd show her how far from sulking I was. "When are you and the angel getting married?"

She surveyed me with surprise.

"I didn't think you'd take it like this—I was going to lead up to it, and break it to you gently when you'd seen a

little more of Jack. He really is an angel. He's kindness itself. I'm sure you'll like him when you know him."

"I'm sure I will, and I hope you're very happy together."

"You really don't mind, Dickie lamb? Because I do love
him most terribly, and I just can't do anything else." She
said it in her nice bright party voice, the one belonging to
the nice girl having a wonderful time and ready to be grateful to all the world for it. The word love made me look into
her eyes, and I saw Naomi was sizing me up from within
the loving ingenue. It was a moment of recognition, and
when she turned away to stare into the bright coal fire in
the grate, she spoke to me without pretense of any kind. "My
contract with Kenning and Archer runs out at the end of the
month and I'm not going to renew it. I'm not going to act
any more. We're going to live down on Jack's place in
Wil'shire."

A coal slid on the fire, which flared up in a wavering red
flame. She stared through it, wrapt in a new dream, and the
firelight danced on her remote, entranced face. I was
stunned. Castlereagh Gardens was the one fixed point in my
life, and I suddenly saw it vanishing. And the stage was the
one place where Naomi seemed to have a solid existence.
Now even that was about to disappear. Everything was breaking up and dissolving under my feet, soon there would be
nothing left but some fancy in her head. To cover my des-
peration I fixed on the one unimportant point in it all, the
cadence of the word Wil'shire.

"You always used to say Wiltshire," I said, hardly thinking what I was saying.

"I'm sure I never did, everyone says Wil'shire," she said.

"Wil'shire," I said, "Wil'shire. I'll try to remember. I'm
sure it will please Jack."

She looked at me with undisguised anger, and I suddenly
realized both what the implication of the remark was, and
that for the first time I had been cruel to an adult in the
way that adults are cruel to each other.

"Oh, you're impossible," she said, and left the room.

I felt partly triumphant at having won one of our scenes
for a change, and partly ashamed of myself. And because I
was more ashamed than triumphant I became angry to cover
it. How could she want to marry such a dull man, a man
with a sort of Midas touch of boredom, who could kill any-

thing he touched? How could she, after having loved Max? I recalled the exact way he had butted in to spoil the pleasure of buying the muffins. My eyes fell on the tea tray, there they were under a rounded porcelain cover with a little green and gold handle resembling an acorn on the top. None of us had touched them. I lifted the cover and found that they were still passably warm. I ate one, and then another. They were greasy and leathery as usual, but somehow delicious. It is difficult to go on being elaborately unhappy or very angry when you are sitting by an open fire eating well-buttered muffins in a curtained room, and I soon managed to come to terms with the new situation.

Richard ultimately achieves his freedom and a healthy sense of mature wisdom in a final scene where he ruminates on the relationship he has had with the adults in his world. He faces up to reality and luxuriates in the happiness and fulfillment it brings him. He is willing to see the role he has played and no longer externalizes his difficulties. His emancipation from the adults gives him autonomy of thought and action. In the passage which follows,* Richard has unaccountably been called back home from school by his stepfather, the Colonel.

"Hallo, Hilary," I said. "I'm very glad to see you. How did you know I was coming by this train?"
"I didn't, sir. The Colonel said I was to meet all incoming trains from one o'clock on."
"I'm afraid you've had a long wait."
"It's of no importance, sir. May I take your bag?"
His back was rigid as he walked off towards the car, and when we sat side by side bowling off through Teffont towards Marshwood he was stiffer than ever and sternly silent.
"You don't happen to know what the trouble is," I asked after five silent minutes.
"I'm sure I don't know, sir."
It was clear that whatever it was was very bad.
The downs lay like dark waves frozen into immobility under the sky which was indigo except for a faintly green

* From *Heritage* by Anthony West. Copyright 1955 by Anthony West. Reprinted by permission of Random House, Inc. Pp. 300-309.

radiance in the west and the air that blew in through the open windows of the car was rich with the harvest smell of ripe straw. Though I couldn't see them I knew that behind every hedge the crisp fresh stubbles dotted with shocked-up wheat and oats stretched away into the semi-darkness. In a few more weeks shooting would begin. It was very good to be home, even if I had come back to trouble of some kind.

The Colonel was in his study and I was shocked to find him as I did. He was sitting in front of his green leather-topped desk with his hands in his lap staring at the pigeon-holes in front of him. When I came in he swiveled his head round towards me with an expression that had momentarily something hopeful in it but which then drained away leaving a woebegone blank in the place of his usual warm and hearty look. It is a case of illness, I thought, he has had a stroke, but I instantly realized that if it were so he would be in bed and under medical care.

"It's you," he said flatly. "I'm glad you've come . . . though I see, now that you're here, I was wrong to send for you. There's nothing you can do. I'm sorry, my boy. . . ." He slumped back in his chair. "I don't know what to say. . . ."

"Is there anything wrong, sir?"

"Yes, yes, there is. Everything's as wrong as it can possibly be." He raised his eyebrows and passed a hand across his forehead. "I can hardly believe that things are as wrong as they are. . . . It's your mother. She's gone . . . left me. . . . She doesn't mean to come back."

"You mean she's run away."

"Yes." He rubbed his forehead again with the same look of utter bewilderment. "It's very hard for me to credit . . . she seemed happy enough and she never complained . . . did she never say anything to you?"

"Not a word, sir."

"No hint of any kind? Nothing?" He faced me. "You had no idea of this American project?"

"American project, no . . ." A great light began to dawn upon me, I saw Larry shaking with laughter, and heard him saying, "It's got a wonderful part in it for an older woman."

"Well, I'll tell you what's happened." He stood up and began to pace the far end of the room. "About a month ago Naomi told me she was worried about one or two little symptoms, not of anything serious, but of something that

ought to be looked into. Some woman's thing that she should
consult a specialist about. So we made appointments in London. I was to have gone with her, but then the appointments
were changed to days when I happened to have pressing
things to attend to down here, quarter sessions, that sort of
thing . . . so she went alone. She went up to town for a
second examination three days ago. She telephoned me to
say that Sir Charles Wykes, that's the doctor fella, wanted to
give her a more thorough going-over than the first day's
appointment allowed, night before last, and that she'd be
home, last night it would have been . . . well, she didn't
come. I telephoned her hotel. She wasn't there. I supposed
she'd gone to stay with a friend. I called all the friends I
could think of but she wasn't with any of them. I got a letter
this morning . . . posted in Southampton. She sailed on the
Queen Mary the night she was supposed to come back here.
She's out at sea now on her way to New York . . . you're sure
you know nothing about all this?"

"No, nothing . . . at least . . ." I tried to tell him about
Larry Brook.

"I can't make head or tail of that rigmarole . . . the thing
that I can't endure is what she says here . . ." he pulled a
letter out of his pocket with the immediately recognizable
scrawl on it. ". . . She says she's been very happy here, begs
me to forgive her, says she'll always be grateful to me, says
she's not the sort of woman to make me happy, says she
doesn't fit into my life, says that in all fairness she can't go
on with a deception, says she's going to Reno, means divorce . . ." He flapped the letter at me. "Can you understand
all that? Do you know what she's thinking about? What she
can mean? Say if you know." He stopped, staring at me. "Do
you know?"

"Yes, sir. She's an actress. She's going back to the stage.
She doesn't exist anywhere else. Larry Brook came to her
with a perfect part, written for her. She couldn't bear not to
take it. She will open in the play, I should say, towards the
beginning of November in New York."

"I'll go after her. I'll contest the divorce. I'll make her
see reason . . . she must be having some kind of break-
down. . . ." He stared again. "This Larry Brook . . . do you
think she cares for him?"

"Not in that way. Don't torment yourself with thinking

you've been left for anyone, a man. She's gone to the theatre, to be what she is."

There was a long silence.

"She told me she was sick of it . . . that the whole life had become horrible to her. Was she lying to me?"

"No, she believed it, absolutely, then."

"Have I been the damnedest of fools?"

"No."

"You couldn't very well have said yes. . . ."

"I would have if it had been true."

He grinned like a dog that has had poison.

"Then what in God's name has happened?"

"You offered her the perfect part, written for her, and she couldn't bear not to take it. It was a part she'd dreamed of playing all her life . . ."

"Then I have been a damned fool."

"If you want to put it like that you can. But there's something else to be said. She was happier in the role you gave her, for longer, than anyone else ever made her."

"But in the end it wasn't a good enough part."

"She exhausted the possibilities that were in it for her."

"And now she's off to something else. . . ." He twisted his face into a grimace. "Upon my soul, you don't make her out very attractive. I can hardly bear to hear you talk this way about her."

"Tigers may not seem very attractive to goats, to see how splendid they are you have to take into account that they're tigers. She's Cleopatra to me, Shakespeare's not Shaw's, she's Nora, all kinds of people, quite different—irreconcilable. She's been a loving mother, and an absolutely indifferent one who had a child by mistake, she's been a cold-hearted bully, and a wonderful friend. I wouldn't, now I'm not demanding that she always appear in a particular role, have her any different. The price would be to destroy her. It's too high."

"You have at least a claim on her that she can't very well shake off when it suits her."

"It's the sort of claim that I have on the wind to bring me air to breathe. I count myself lucky to get it."

He considered it, and then spoke quietly in an extremely gentle voice.

"But I love her, you see, Richard."

"Then you can't want to tie her down—she has to be all the different women she has to be."

"It's very hard to see that."

"It's painful, but we have to face it."

We faced each other again for a space and then I saw that his face cleared. He touched the bell and after a minute Manson appeared, grave-faced, and electrified with an over-mastering curiosity that made his eyes flicker nervously between us.

"Oh, Manson, young Richard here has been traveling all day. I can see that he's famished. What have we got for him?"

"There is the cold lamb, sir," said Manson in a sepulchral voice. "I think Cook has a cherry tart, and there would be cream—unless of course Master Richard would prefer something in the way of cheese?"

"I think the tart would be the thing."

"I expect you'd like to eat and tumble into bed," said the Colonel, "you look quite tuckered out. How about a try in your room?"

I saw that it was his way of asking to be left alone, and said that I would like that very much.

When Manson brought up my supper he was a man clearly torn between a variety of emotions. His feelings towards me were complex; he was loyal to the house and to the Colonel, he knew that some affront had been put on it and some hurt done to the Colonel, but he was not sure of its precise nature. He did not know how far, as Naomi's son, and an interloper, I was involved, but had expected that I would be in some way against the Colonel. Having seen us together in an ambiguous situation that suggested friendliness rather than hostility he had revised his assumptions, which had been like Hilary's—had indeed been worked out with Hilary in a series of below-stairs conferences which had engaged Cook, the three housemaids, Driver, Naomi's maid, and Manson himself—and was now off balance, hesitant between the poker-face treatment that would imply that I had become an outsider, and the old friendliness. All he knew was that Naomi had vanished, and that her vanishing had left the Colonel in greater distress than he had ever seen him in before, even after his father's death. He concluded that there had been a final break, but he could not be sure. He hovered over me and the tray as if he could not bring himself to go away without extracting some clue, some clinching remark, that would enable him to go downstairs as the bearer of news.

While he fiddled with the tray, unpacked my bag, and sorted the clothes I had taken off before slipping into pyjamas and a dressing gown, taking some things for the wash, the shoes for cleaning, and the jacket and trousers to be pressed, he gave me one skillfully contrived opportunity after another to be communicative. At last, throwing all discretion aside, and discarding all the ruling conventions governing relations between master and man in which he had been encasing himself for some thirty years, he took the bull by the horns.

"Do you notice anything missing from the room, Master Richard?"

I looked vaguely round taking in the Admirals, the shelf where *Jorrock's* and *The Tactical Use of the Heavy Machine Gun*—a more interesting book than I had first thought— still held their places, at the Kodiak bear, the solid desk and bed, the big comfortable armchair.

"No, nothing, I think. . . ." I wondered if he had been counting the silver.

"Might I draw your attention to the mantelpiece?"

The trophies I had collected since I had come to Marshwood, a small jar of Roman glass, a flint axe head, a few framed photographs, were all there. But the green bowls had gone.

"I've searched everywhere for your bowls, sir, but I haven't been able to find them."

"Well, don't worry. They're not in the least important. I just liked the color of them."

"I was afraid you might think that there had been some carelessness when the room was being cleaned. I made sure that the maids were not responsible. It seems, sir," he emphasized his words, "that they've gone."

"Very well, it can't be helped. I shall have to look about and see what I can find to take their place." I couldn't endure the probing any longer. "Well, thank you, Manson, I have everything I want. Good night."

When he had gone I went over to the fireplace and stood looking at the empty spaces where the two bowls had been. Their absence was startling because it undermined everything that I thought I knew about Naomi, the whole basis of our relationship. I went and sat over on the window seat. The enormous night offered all its mysteries, a chained dog

down at the home farm barked furiously and I guessed that
a fox was about. What new role had Naomi embarked upon?
I tried to assemble what I knew like the pieces of a jigsaw
puzzle. I saw her as she had played to Max, the New Woman
proud of herself and her freedom going out to choose herself an equal as a partner; I saw her again, as she had
created herself for me, as the innocent victim of a Byron-like
seducer; I saw her again in those middle years as a woman
of the theatre existing only in her roles, a woman whose
personal life was a mere diversion; and then I saw her once
more as the natural aristocrat who, trapped by necessity into
the humiliations of the life of the theatre, had been rescued and had returned to her true level as the Lady of
Marshwood House . . . and what then? I knew that, as certainly as the sun would rise in the morning, there lay ahead
a scene which I would have to play with the Colonel. He
would tell me that what had happened had changed nothing
between us, that I was still his heir and that I was to think
of Marshwood as my home. He would mean what he said
and we would both in our hearts know that everything was
changed at the roots, that Naomi's departure had made my
position at Marshwood altogether false and that we would
inevitably as the years went by drift apart. The true link
between us was broken, and if he still made me his heir he
would be handing his beloved house across a gulf, to one
who would be as much a stranger as any other future owner
that chance might bring along. Had she gone simply to bring
that breach about? Could it be simply that she found that
her place at center stage had been usurped by the juvenile
as the result of the Colonel's action in handing me the
future of his house and its properties? Had she, as the implications of this came home to her, thrown up the part and
left the stage? I wondered too what had taken her so pre-
cipitately back to it. The magnitude of the challenge presented by Larry's play—it was in Larry's mind Frank Jowett's
opportunity, it was a machine to lift this youth with all his
natural gifts out of obscurity into a position to take the
theatrical chieftainship which his great actor-manager grandfather had enjoyed—provided a motive. It was a second
chance, an opportunity to re-enact the Marshwood situation.
She would act Frank off the stage and make his dazzling opening a mere background sparkle in the blaze of her splendid

return. Could she be as simple in her motives as all that? I turned back to look at the blank spaces where the bowls had stood. She could only have taken them because I had given them to her, because she knew that they had meant something to me, because I had given them to her in the first place as a token of love, because in the end she loved me. . . .

But then if love was in her heart why had she been so wantonly cruel to the Colonel, tearing, plucking herself out of his life, as in the old days the public hangman had torn the heart out of a quartered traitor? I caught sight of myself across the room in a looking glass, and without thinking lifted my chin a little, improved my posture, and spoke aloud: "Yes, why? . . ." And it struck me poignantly that I was acting The Colonel's Heir. I recalled my other roles. The Wronged Child, The Unrecognized Genius, The Fool for Love, the low comedy part Max's Boy. . . . It occurred to me that I had always taken the Colonel as all of one piece, a man made as one saw him. It had never occurred to me to wonder what roles he had played before I knew him, what role he had played to Naomi. I saw what had been involved in his marriage in a new light, what presented itself as at first blush a disinterested desire to love, protect and cherish an unhappy woman could also be interpreted as a grandiose project of the Svengali kind in reverse. He had taken up a spectacular public figure, dynamically engaged in exhibitionist displays of her personality, and had transformed her into his private treasure, an accessory to the life of his house. The irony of her words in the peony garden revealed themselves—"It's nice to think I've given the place something." The whole measure of her distance from the Colonel lay in the remoteness of that gift to the place from the true nature of her unique creative and interpretive genius. What a lust for power lay behind the desire to pull her down from the summit where she belonged to become a performer in the Colonel's private play in his private theatre. It was in line with the rest of him, power was the motive that would make a man wish to shape a crowd of odd lots into a regiment of troops, and having done that to keep them at the level of a first-class formation. And as I saw his desire to pull her down plainly for the first time I saw myself beside him mewling and protesting that she was not a cozy Mummy figure. What could she do but leave us . . . she was not one of those like

Alice, one of the dressers of life, standing ready in the wings with the costume for the quick change, or waiting in the dressing room with all the apparatus for a new role. She was one of the leads round whom the plays of life turned. The curtain had come down on the Marshwood comedy and we, the supers, had to look for other parts. We might grumble that she had prematurely ended a long run by walking out and setting us "at liberty," as they say in the theatrical employment advertisements, but that was only because we shrank from recognizing her right to a larger theatre than we could or would provide.

The quiet dark outside the room presented itself not as a void now but as a darkened stage on which anything and everything might happen. A huge tragedy called war was in preparation, a piece with parts of every kind in it, the Colonel as a soldier already probably had his chosen for him in some file in the War Office in London. I would be able to choose my own. And when that piece was played out the whole of life would open out again before us. It was not at all a bad thing to be "at liberty" and free.

Normal development implies a change from dependency upon others to dependence upon the self. Richard had grown up as a shuttlecock in a fierce competition between famous, estranged, egocentric, unmarried parents. He, like all children, was at first almost entirely dependent on the judgment of others. But as capabilities mature and experience widens, the adolescent, in order to develop mind and character successfully, has to demand a gradually increasing degree of autonomy in so far as thought and conduct are concerned. Success in adult life requires the capacity for determining for oneself the nature and course of the principal activities. "As development proceeds, the ideas concerning right conduct . . . become more and more dissociated from their original authoritarian sanctions, new 'inner' sanctions being substituted for the old 'external' ones which are abandoned" (5).

The "right" values may often prove perplexing to the adolescent. He feels caught; the dilemma may seem unsolvable to him. At such times, he may turn to an adult for two reasons: first, hoping against hope that help lies there, and secondly, to test the adult. Such a situation arises between Francie and her mother Katie in *A Tree Grows in Brooklyn*.*

Katie heard the story. "It's come at last," she thought, "the time when you can no longer stand between your children and heartache. When there wasn't enough food in the house you pretended that you weren't hungry so they could have more. In the cold of a winter's night you got up and put your blanket on their bed so they wouldn't be so cold. You'd kill anyone who tried to harm them—I tried my best to kill that man in the hallway. Then one sunny day, they walk out in all innocence and they walk right into the grief that you'd give your life to spare them."

Francie gave her the letter. She read it slowly and as she read, she thought she knew how it was. Here was a man of twenty-two who evidently (to use one of Sissy's phrases) had been around. Here was a girl sixteen years old; six years younger than he. A girl—in spite of bright-red lipstick and grown-up clothes and a lot of knowledge picked up here and there—who was yet tremulously innocent; a girl who had come face to face with some of the evil of the world and most of its hardships, and yet had remained curiously untouched by the world. Yes, she could understand her appeal for him.

Well, what could she say? That he was no good or at best just a weak man who was easily susceptible to whoever he was with? No, she couldn't be so cruel as to say that. Besides the girl wouldn't believe her anyhow.

"Say something," demanded Francie. "Why don't you say something?"

"What can I say?"

"Say that I'm young—that I'll get over it. Go ahead and say it. Go ahead and lie."

"I know that's what people say—you'll get over it. I'd say it too. But I know it's not true. Oh, you'll be happy again, never fear. But you won't forget. Everytime you fall in love it will be because something in the man reminds you of *him*."

* From *A Tree Grows in Brooklyn* by Betty Smith. Copyright 1943 by Betty Smith. Reprinted by permission of Harper & Brothers. Pp. 397-398.

"Mother. . . ."

Mother! Katie remembered. She had called her own mother "mama" until the day she had told her that she was going to marry Johnny. She had said, "Mother, I'm going to marry . . ." She had never said "mama" after that. She had finished growing up when she stopped calling her mother "mama." Now Francie . . .

"Mother, he asked me to be with him for the night. Should I have gone?"

Katie's mind darted around looking for words.

"Don't make up a lie, Mother. Tell me the truth."

Katie couldn't find the right words.

"I promise you that I'll never go with a man without being married first—if I ever marry. And if I feel I must—without being married, I'll tell you first. That's a solemn promise. So you can tell me the truth without worrying that I'll go wrong if I know it."

"There are two truths," said Katie finally.

"As a mother, I say it would have been a terrible thing for a girl to sleep with a stranger—a man she had known less than forty-eight hours. Horrible things might have happened to you. Your whole life might have been ruined. As your mother, I tell you the truth.

"But as a woman . . ." she hesitated. "I will tell you the truth as a woman. It would have been a very beautiful thing. Because there is only once that you love that way."

Francie thought, "I should have gone with him then. I'll never love anyone as much again. I wanted to go and I didn't go and now I don't want him that way any more because *she* owns him now. But I wanted to and I didn't and now it's too late." She put her head down on the table and wept.

It is necessary for young people to solve courageously and with some success the various problems that confront them if they are to move into their more mature years with some assurance of being able to meet successfully the problems typical of later years (10). Nearly all parents say they want their children to have an easier time of life than they themselves have experienced. But in trying to protect them from some of the trials of life, parental supervision more likely than not subverts the adolescent's self-supervision. Over-protection leads to underachieving; in this instance, to an inability to achieve maturity. Parental intentions are well-meaning and "for the best interests" of the youngster. In *The Yearling*,* Jody's father has had to kill his yearling deer, his only real companion. It is Jody's first bitter taste of deprivation, his first hard wrenching from the joys of his early boyhood. At first, Jody responds by refusing to face the situation: he runs away, gets lost, almost starves, but in the process realizes that he must go home.

Darkness overtook him half a mile from home. Even in the dusk, landmarks were familiar. The tall pines of the clearing were recognizable, blacker than the creeping night. He came to the slat fence. He felt his way along it. He opened the gate and went into the yard. He passed around the side of the house to the kitchen stoop and stepped up on it. He crept to the window on bare silent feet and peered in.

A fire burned low on the hearth. Penny sat hunched beside it, wrapped in quilts. One hand covered his eyes. Jody went to the door and unlatched it and stepped inside. Penny lifted his head.

"Ory?"

"Hit's me."

He thought his father had not heard him.

"Hit's Jody."

Penny turned his head and looked at him wonderingly, as though the gaunt ragged boy with sweat and tear-streaks down the grime, with hollow eyes under matted hair, were some stranger of whom he expected that he state his business.

He said, "Jody."

Jody dropped his eyes.

"Come close."

He went to his father and stood beside him. Penny reached out for his hand and took it and turned it over and rubbed it slowly between his own. Jody felt drops on his hand like a warm rain.

* Reprinted from *The Yearling* by Marjorie Kinnan Rawlings (copyright 1938 by Marjorie Kinnan Rawlings) with permission of Charles Scribner's Sons. Pp. 424-428.

"Boy—I near about give you out."

Penny felt along his arm. He looked up at him.

"You all right?"

He nodded.

"You all right—You ain't dead nor gone. You all right."
A light filled his face. "Glory be."

It was unbelievable, Jody thought. He was wanted.

He said, "I had to come home."

"Why, shore you did."

"I ain't meant what I said. Hatin' you—"

The light broke into the familiar smile.

"Why, shore you ain't. 'When I was a child, I spake as a
child.' "

Penny stirred in his chair.

"They's rations in the safe. In the kittle there. You
hongry?"

"I ain't et but oncet. Last night."

"Not but oncet? Then now you know. Ol' Starvation—"
His eyes shone in the firelight as Jody had pictured them.
"Ol' Starvation—he's got a face meaner'n ol' Slewfoot, ain't
he?"

"Hit's fearful."

"There's biscuits there. Open the honey. There's due to be
milk in the gourd."

Jody fumbled among the dishes. He ate standing, wolfing
down the food. He dipped into a dish of cooked cow-peas
with his fingers, scooping them into his mouth. Penny stared
at him.

He said, "I'm sorry you had to learn it that-a-way."

"Where's Ma?"

"She's drove the wagon to the Forresters to trade for seed-
corn. She figgered she'd try to plant a part of a crop agin.
She carried the chickens, to trade. It hurted her pride tur-
rible, but she was obliged to go."

Jody closed the door of the cabinet.

He said, "I should of washed. I'm awful dirty."

"There's warm water on the hearth."

Jody poured water in the basin and scrubbed his face
and arms and hands. The water was too dark even for his
feet. He threw it out of the door and poured more, and sat
on the floor and washed his feet.

Penny said, "I'd be proud to know where you been."

"I been on the river. I aimed to go to Boston."

"I see."

He looked small and shrunken inside the quilts. Jody said, "How you makin' it, Pa? You better?"

Penny looked a long time into the embers on the hearth.

He said, "You jest as good to know the truth. I ain't scarcely wuth shootin.'"

Jody said, "When I git the work done, you got to leave me go fetch ol' Doc to you."

Penny studied him.

He said, "You've done come back different. You've takened a punishment. You ain't a yearlin' no longer. Jody—"

"Yes, sir."

"I'm goin' to talk to you, man to man. You figgered I went back on you. Now there's a thing ever' man has got to know. Mebbe you know it a'ready. 'Twa'n't only me. 'Twa'n't only your yearlin' deer havin' to be destroyed. Boy, life goes back on you."

Jody looked at his father. He nodded.

Penny said, "You've seed how things goes in the world o' men. You've knowed men to be low-down and mean. You've seed ol' Death at his tricks. You've messed around with ol' Starvation. Ever' man wants life to be a fine thing, and a easy. 'Tis fine, boy, powerful fine, but 'tain't easy. Life knocks a man down and he gits up and it knocks him down agin. I've been uneasy all my life."

His hands worked at the folds of the quilt.

"I've wanted life to be easy for you. Easier'n 'twas for me. A man's heart aches, seein' his young uns face the world. Knowin' they got to git their guts tore out, the way his was tore. I wanted to spare you, long as I could. I wanted you to frolic with your yearlin'. I knowed the lonesomeness he eased for you. But ever' man's lonesome. What's he to do then? What's he to do when he gits knocked down? Why, take it for his share and go on."

Jody said, "I'm 'shamed I runned off."

Penny sat upright.

He said, "You're near enough growed to do your choosin'. Could be you'd crave to go to sea, like Oliver. There's men seems made for the land, and men seems made for the sea. But I'd be proud did you choose to live here and farm the clearin'. I'd be proud to see the day when you got a well dug, so's no woman here'd be obliged to do her washin' on a seepage hillside. You willin'?"

"I'm willin'."

"Shake hands."

He closed his eyes. The fire on the hearth had burned to embers. Jody banked them with the ashes, to assure live coals in the morning.

Penny said, "Now I'll need some he'p, gittin' to the bed. Looks like your Ma's spendin' the night."

Jody put his shoulder under him and Penny leaned heavily on it. He hobbled to his bed. Jody drew the quilt over him.

"Hit's food and drink to have you home, boy. Git to bed and git your rest. 'Night."

The words warmed him through.

" 'Night, Pa."

He went to his room and closed the door. He took off his tattered shirt and breeches and climbed in under the warm quilts. His bed was soft and yielding. He lay luxuriously, stretching his legs. He must be up early in the morning, to milk the cow and bring in wood and work the crops. When he worked them, Flag would not be there to play about with him. His father would no longer take the heavy part of the burden. It did not matter. He could manage alone.

He found himself listening for something. It was the sound of the yearling for which he listened, running around the house or stirring on his moss pallet in the corner of the bedroom. He would never hear him again. He wondered if his mother had thrown dirt over Flag's carcass, or if the buzzards had cleaned it. Flag—He did not believe he should ever again love anything, man or woman or his own child, as he had loved the yearling. He would be lonely all his life. But a man took it for his share and went on.

In the beginning of his sleep, he cried out, "Flag!"

It was not his own voice that called. It was a boy's voice. Somewhere beyond the sink-hole, past the magnolia, under the live oaks, a boy and a yearling ran side by side, and were gone forever.

In the talk with his father, Jody recognizes his experience as his coming of age. He is willing to make the effort which adult life demands, passing from the self-centered isolation of infancy to fuller communion with his fellow creatures. Individuals attain this maturity at different ages and reach it earlier for some aspects of life than for others. Jody's experience came early. It is generally agreed that achievement of physical and psychological maturity occurs, on the average, during the late teens or early twenties (11). Because of the physical changes which the adolescent experiences his behavior frequently follows these characteristics: a "desire for isolation, which leads to withdrawal from the group to which he formerly belonged; hypercritical attitude toward his former friends and their activities, which leads to quarrels and may lead to the breaking up of friendships of long standing; boredom; disinclination to work; restlessness; instability; antagonism toward family, friends, and society in general; sex antagonism; heightened emotionality; lack of self-confidence and feelings of personal inadequacy; preoccupation with sex; excessive modesty; daydreaming, mainly of the 'martyr' type; irritability; obstinacy; and heightened sensitivity, resulting in hurt feelings" (7). Such negativism, when it persists beyond adolescence as it does in the case of *A Raw Youth* in Dostoevsky's novel of the same name,* arrests maturity and leads to difficult social and emotional adjustments for the individual.

No, it was not being illegitimate, with which I was so taunted at Touchard's, not my sorrowful childhood, it was not revenge, nor the desire to protest, that was at the bottom of my idea; my character alone was responsible for everything. At twelve years old, I believe, that is almost at the dawn of real consciousness, I began to dislike my fellow-creatures. It was not that I disliked them exactly, but that their presence weighed upon me. I was sometimes in my moments of purest sincerity quite sad that I never could express everything even to my nearest and dearest, that is, I could but will not; for some reason I restrain myself, so that I'm mistrustful, sullen and reserved. Again, I have

* From *A Raw Youth* by Fyodor Dostoevsky. Copyright 1923. Reprinted by permission of The Macmillan Co. P. 82.

noticed one characteristic in myself almost from childhood, that I am too ready to find fault, and given to blame others. But this impulse was often followed at once by another which was very irksome to me: I would ask myself whether it were not my fault rather than theirs. And how often I blamed myself for nothing! To avoid such doubts I naturally sought solitude. Besides, I found nothing in the company of others, however much I tried, and I did try. All the boys of my own age anyway, and all my schoolfellows, all, every one of them, turned out to be inferior to me in their ideas. I don't recall one single exception.

Yes, I am a gloomy person; I'm always shutting myself up. I often love to walk out of a room full of people. I may perhaps do people a kindness, but often I cannot see the slightest reason for doing them a kindness. People are not such splendid creatures that they are worth taking much trouble about. Why can't they approach me openly and directly, why must I always be forced to make the first overtures?

That is the question I asked myself. I am a grateful creature, and I have shown it by a hundred imbecilities. If some were frank with me, I should instantly respond with frankness and begin to love them at once. And so I have done, but they have all deceived me promptly, and have withdrawn from me with a sneer. The most candid of all was Lambert, who beat me so much as a child, but he was only an open brute and scoundrel. And even his openness was only stupidity. Such was my state of mind when I came to St. Petersburg.

The isolation this callow young man feels, his contempt for and inability to relate to people, his egocentricity, his fixation at the adolescent level, minimize his chances to achieve a healthy, mature, adult way of life. In facing the world, the adolescent has to acquire a realistic self-concept which will enable him to learn from the past, not only to suffer from it. According to Freud, the basis of neurosis lies in the conflict between the child and his parents and the failure of the child to solve this conflict satisfactorily. In terms of maturing, it might mean the inability or prevention of the child from growing up emotionally. To mature implies a gradual emancipation from the jurisdiction of parents and their substitutes in later life, as teachers or employers. Anne Frank, at one point in her *Diary*, writes, "I can't really love Mummy in a dependent childlike way—I just don't have that feeling" (6).

The impetus toward psychological maturity furnished by the intensified emotional and instinctive drives at puberty normally is powerful enough to so modify and enrich the personality that an individual often seems like a different person after adolescence than he was ever before (3). To grow to accept and respect his own uniqueness and that of others; to develop the capacity to tolerate frustration and disappointments; to find pleasure and satisfaction in living and working and in their association with other people: these are the important earmarks in maturity (2). Upon these qualities will depend the individual's choice of profession, success of marriage, excellence as a parent, contribution as a citizen, general efficiency, and emotional and physical health.

REFERENCES

(1) Binger, Carl. "The Concept of Maturity," in Gruenberg, Sidonie M. (Ed.), *Our Children Today*. NY: Viking, 1952, p. 197.
(2) Binger, Carl. *Ibid.*, pp. 208-209.
(3) Blanchard, Phyllis. "Adolescent Experiences in Relation to Personality and Behavior," in Hunt, J.McV. (Ed.), *Personality and the Behavior Disorders*, Vol. II. NY: Ronald, 1944, p. 711.
(4) Flugel, J. C. *The Psycho-Analytic Study of the Family*. London: Hogarth, 1931, p. 41.
(5) Flugel, J. C. *Ibid.*, p. 45.
(6) Frank, Anne. *The Diary of a Young Girl*. NY: Doubleday, 1952, 258 pp.
(7) Hurlock, Elizabeth. *Adolescent Development*. NY: McGraw-Hill, 1955, p. 63.
(8) Josselyn, Irene M. "Growing to Adulthood," in Gruenberg, Sidonie M. (Ed.), *Our Children Today*. NY: Viking, 1952, p. 182.
(9) Josselyn, Irene M. *Ibid.*, p. 182.
(10) Lloyd-Jones, Esther & Fedder, Ruth. *Coming of Age*. NY: Whittlesey, 1941, pp. v-vi.
(11) Munn, Norman L. *The Evolution and Growth of Human Behavior*. Boston: Houghton Mifflin, 1955, p. 494.

(12) Murphy, Gardner. *Personality: A Biosocial Approach to Origins and Structure.* NY: Harper, 1947, p. 512.
(13) Williams, Frankwood E. *Adolescence. Studies in Mental Hygiene.* NY: Farrar & Rinehart, 1930, p. 15.
(14) Zachry, Carolyn B. "Problems of Adolescents," *Bull. Menninger Clinic,* 4:68, 1940.

Appendices: Bibliography

The Novel of Adolescence

The bibliography of novels of adolescence which follows is not intended to be exhaustive but rather selective. The literary quality is varied, as might be expected, but there is merit in all of the selections. The basis for selection rested on the reading of the author, reliance on book reviews in periodicals and newspapers, and finally on the annotated reports in the Book Review Index. Some of the 480 novels in the list deal exclusively with an adolescent personality; others in part. They cover the years 1900-1958. There are no geographic boundaries to the novel of adolescence. Represented in this list will be found fictional adolescents from India, China, Russia (there seems to be nothing translated on the subject from contemporary U.S.S.R.), Western Europe, New Zealand, and, of course, Great Britain and the United States. Some of the novels are amusing and even hilarious, others are poignant, and still others quite serious. But they all have something to tell us about the adolescent in the world today.

Abaunza, Virginia. *Sundays from Two to Six*. Indianapolis: Bobbs-Merrill, 1957. 222 p.

Abel, Hilde. *The Guests of Summer*. Indianapolis: Bobbs-Merrill, 1951. 271 p.

Ader, Paul. *Leaf Against the Sky*. NY: Crown, 1948. 311 p.

Agee, James. *The Morning Watch*. Boston: Houghton, Mifflin, 1951. 120 p.

Alain-Fournier. *The Wanderer*. NY: Doubleday, 1953. 254 p.

Albee, George. *The Boys*. NY: Ballantine, 1957. 310 p.

Aldington, Richard. *Death of a Hero*. NY: Covici-Friede, 1929. 389 p.

Aldis, Dorothy. *All the Year Round*. Boston: Houghton, Mifflin, 1938. 245 p.

Aldis, Dorothy. *Poor Susan*. NY: Putnam, 1942. 204 p.
Aleichem, Shalom. *Adventures of Mottel*. NY: Schuman, 1953. 342 p.
Allen, James L. *Kentucky Warbler*. NY: Doubleday, 1918. n. p.
Amrine, Michael. *All Sons Must Say Goodbye*. NY: Harper, 1942. 309 p.
Anderson, Sherwood. *Tar*. NY: Boni & Liveright, 1926. 346 p.
Armstrong, Charlotte. *Mischief*. NY: Coward-McCann, 1950. 182 p.
Athas, Daphne. *The Fourth World*. NY: Putnam, 1956. 318 p.
Austin, Mary. *Starry Adventure*. Boston: Houghton, Mifflin, 1931. 420 p.

Baker, Danys Val. *The White Rock*. NY: Appleton-Century, 1947. 216 p.
Baker, Dorothy D. *Young Man with a Horn*. Boston: Houghton, Mifflin, 1938. 243 p.
Bakker, Piet. *Ciske the Rat*. NY: Doubleday, 1958. 211 p.
Balchin, Nigel. *The Fall of a Sparrow*. NY: Rinehart, 1956. 309 p.
Baldwin, James. *Go Tell It on the Mountain*. NY: Knopf, 1953. 303 p.
Bartlett, Vernon. *Calf-Love*. Phila: Lippincott, 1929. 277 p.
Barton, Betsey Alice. *The Shadow of the Bridge*. NY: Duell, Sloan & Pierce, 1950. 279 p.
Basso, Hamilton. *The View from Pompey's Head*. NY: Doubleday, 1954. 409 p.
Beechwood, Mary. *Memphis Jackson's Son*. Boston: Houghton, Mifflin, 1956. 267 p.
Beheler, Laura. *The Paper Dolls*. Boston: Houghton, Mifflin, 1956. 218 p.
Bellamann, Henry. *King's Row*. NY: Simon & Schuster, 1941. 674 p.
Bellow, Saul. *The Adventures of Augie March*. NY: Viking, 1953. 536 p.
Bennett, Arnold. *Clayhanger*. London: Methuen, 1910. 574 p.
Bennett, Arnold. *The Old Wives' Tale*. London: Hodder & Stoughton, 1930. 612 p.
Benson, Sally. *Junior Miss*. NY: Random, 1941. 214 p.
Benson, Theodora. *Salad Days*. NY: Harper, 1929. 287 p.
Beresford, John Davys. *The Early History of Jacob Stahl*. NY: Doran, 1911. 513 p.
Beresford, John Davys. *An Imperfect Mother*. NY: Macmillan, 1920. 311 p.
Beresford-Howe, Constance. *The Unreasoning Heart*. NY: Dodd, Mead, 1946. 236 p.
Berto, Guiseppe. *The Sky Is Red*. Norfolk, Conn: New Directions, 1948. 397 p.
Best, Herbert. *Young 'un*. NY: Macmillan, 1944. 271 p.
Bishop, John Peale. *Act of Darkness*. NY: Scribner, 1935. 368 p.
Bjarnhof, Karl. *The Stars Grow Pale*. NY: Knopf, 1958. 311 p.
Björkman, Edwin A. *Gates of Life*. NY: Knopf, 1923. 384 p.
Björkman, Edwin A. *The Soul of a Child*. NY: Knopf, 1922. 322 p.

Boles, Paul D. *Parton's Island*. NY: Macmillan, 1958. 191 p.
Böll, Heinrich. *Tomorrow and Yesterday*. NY: Criterion, 1957. 250 p.
Bond, Ruskin. *The Room on the Roof*. NY: Coward-McCann, 1957. 160 p.
Bottome, Phyllis. *Jane*. NY: Vanguard, 1957. 304 p.
Bowen, Elizabeth. *Death of the Heart*. NY: Knopf, 1939. 418 p.
Bowen, Robert O. *Sidestreet*. NY: Knopf, 1954. 212 p.
Boylen, Margaret. *The Marble Orchard*. NY: Random, 1956. 238 p.
Brecht, Harold. *Downfall*. NY: Harper, 1929. 342 p.
Brincourt, André. *Paradise Below the Stairs*. NY: Duell, Sloan & Pierce, 1952. 292 p.
Brinig, Myron. *Singermann*. NY: Farrar, 1929. 446 p.
Britton, Lionel. *Hunger and Love*. NY: Harper, 1931. 623 p.
Bromfield, Louis. *The Wild Country*. NY: Harper, 1948. 274 p.
Buckley, David. *Pride of Innocence*. NY: Holt, 1957. 346 p.
Bunin, Ivan A. *Mitya's Love*. NY: Holt, 1926. 212 p.
Bunin, Ivan A. *The Well of Days*. NY: Knopf, 1934. 306 p.
Burress, John. *Apple on a Pear Tree*. NY: Vanguard, 1953. 312 p.
Burt, Nathaniel. *Scotland's Burning*. Boston: Little, Brown, 1954. 300 p.
Butler, Samuel. *The Way of All Flesh*. NY: Dutton, 1949. 360 p.

Calitri, Charles J. *Rickey*. NY: Scribner, 1952. 216 p.
Capote, Truman. *The Grass Harp*. NY: Random, 1951. 181 p.
Capote, Truman. *Other Voices, Other Rooms*. NY: Random, 1948. 231 p.
Carson, Josephine. *Drives My Green Age*. NY: Harper, 1957. 224 p.
Cary, Joyce. *A House of Children*. NY: Harper, 1956. 276 p.
Castillo, Michel del. *Child of Our Time*. NY: Knopf, 1958. 281 p.
Chamberlain, Anne. *The Tall Dark Man*. NY: Bobbs-Merrill, 1955. 215 p.
Chase, Mary Ellen. *Mary Peters*. NY: Macmillan, 1935. 377 p.
Childs, Marquis W. *The Cabin*. NY: Harper, 1944. 243 p.
Cicellis, Kay. *No Name in the Street*. NY: Grove, 1953. 245 p.
Clark, William Van Tilburg. *The City of Trembling Leaves*. NY: Random, 1945. 690 p.
Clayton, John Bell. *Six Angels at My Back*. NY: Macmillan, 1952. 200 p.
Cleary, Jon. *The Sundowners*. NY: Scribner, 1952. 290 p.
Clewes, Winston. *Sweet River in the Morning*. NY: Appleton-Century, 1946. 227 p.
Cocteau, Jean. *The Holy Terrors*. Norfolk, Conn: New Directions, 1957. 193 p.
Cocteau, Jean. *The Imposter*. NY: Noonday, 1957. 132 p.
Coffin, Robert, P. T. *Lost Paradise*. NY: Macmillan, 1933. 284 p.
Coffin, Robert, P. T. *Red Sky in the Morning*. NY: Macmillan, 1935. 288 p.

Colette. *Claudine at School*. NY: Boni & Liveright, 1930. 297 p.

Colette. *Claudine in Paris*. NY: Farrar, Straus & Cudahy, 1958. 204 p.

Colette. *The Ripening Seed*. NY: Farrar, Straus & Cudahy, 1956. 186 p.

Compton-Burnett, Ivy. *Mother and Son*. NY: Messner, 1955. 256 p.

Cotterell, Geoffrey. *The Strange Enchantment*. Phila: Lippincott, 1957. 512 p.

Craig, Margaret. *Julie*. NY: Crowell, 1952. 247 p.

Creal, Margaret. *A Lesson in Love*. NY: Simon & Schuster, 1957. 281 p.

Cronin, A. J. *Hatters Castle*. Boston: Little, Brown, 1931. 605 p.

Cronin, A. J. *The Green Years*. Boston: Little, Brown, 1944. 347 p.

Cross, Ian. *The God Boy*. NY: Harcourt Brace, 1957. 184 p.

Dahl, Borghild M. *Homecoming*. NY: Dutton, 1953. 251 p.

Daly, Edwin. *Some Must Watch*. NY: Scribner, 1957. 306 p.

Daly Maureen. *Seventeenth Summer*. NY: Dodd, Mead, 1942. 255 p.

Davenport, Marcia. *My Brother's Keeper*. NY: Scribner, 1954. 457 p.

Davis, Clyde Brion. *The Age of Indiscretion*. Phila: Lippincott, 1950. 284 p.

Davis, Clyde Brion. *Eyes of Boyhood*. Phila: Lippincott, 1953. 323 p.

Davis, Clyde Brion. *The Newcomer*. Phila: Lippincott, 1954. 216 p.

Davis, Clyde Brion. *Playtime Is Over*. Phila: Lippincott, 1949. 432 p.

Davis, Reuben. *Shim*. Indianapolis: Bobbs-Merrill, 1953. 283 p.

Davis, Wesley F. *The Time of the Panther*. NY: Harper, 1958. 282 p.

De Jong, David C. *Two Sofas in the Parlor*. NY: Doubleday, 1952. 253 p.

Delafield, E. M. *Nothing Is Safe*. NY: Harper, 1937. 284 p.

De la Roche, Mazo. *Growth of a Man*. Boston: Little, Brown, 1938. 380 p.

Dell, Floyd. *Moon-Calf*. NY: Doubleday, 1920. 394 p.

Dennis, Patrick. *Auntie Mame*. NY: Vanguard, 1955. 254 p.

Denzer, Peter W. *Find the Dreamer Guilty*. NY: Dutton, 1955. 247 p.

Dhôtel, André. *Faraway*. NY: Simon & Schuster, 1957. 245 p.

Doan, Daniel. *The Crystal Years*. NY: Abelard-Schuman, 1953. 254 p.

Dorsey, George A. *Young Low*. NY: Doran, 1917. n.p.

Dreiser, Theodore. *An American Tragedy*. NY: Boni & Liveright, 1925. 409 p.

Dubin, Harry E. *Hail, Alma Pater*. NY: Hermitage, 1954. 287 p.

Du Bois, William. *A Season to Beware*. NY: Putnam, 1956. 320 p.

Echard, Margaret. *Born in Wedlock*. NY: Doubleday, 1956. 256 p.

Eddy, Roger. *The Bulls and the Bees*. NY: Crowell, 1956. 178 p.

Ellison, James Whitfield. *I'm Owen Harrison Harding*. NY: Doubleday, 1955. 250 p.

Ellson, Hal. *Summer Street*. NY: Ballantine, 1954. 132 p.

Erno, Richard B. *My Old Man*. NY: Crown, 1955. 224 p.

Eustis, Helen. *The Fool Killer*. NY: Doubleday, 1954. 219 p.

Faralla, Dana. *The Madstone*. Phila: Lippincott, 1958. 253 p.
Farrell, James T. *Father and Son*. NY: Vanguard, 1940. 616 p.
Farrell, James T. *No Star Is Lost*. NY: Vanguard, 1938. 637 p.
Farrell, James T. *Young Lonigan*. NY: Vanguard, 1932. 308 p.
Farrell, James T. *The Young Manhood of Studs Lonigan*. NY: Vanguard, 1934. 412 p.
Faviell, Frances. *Thalia*. NY: Farrar, Straus & Cudahy, 1957. 289 p.
Fenwick, Elizabeth. *Days of Plenty*. NY: Harcourt, Brace, 1956. 252 p.
Ferber, Edna. *The Girls*. NY: Doubleday, Page, 1921. 374 p.
Ferber, Edna. *Mother Knows Best*. NY: Grosset & Dunlap, 1928. 267 p.
Ferber, Edna. *So Big*. NY: Doubleday, Page, 1924. 360 p.
Feuchtwanger, Lion. *Simone*. NY: Viking, 1944. 238 p.
Fielding, Gabriel. *In the Time of Greenbloom*. NY: Morrow, 1957. 407 p.
Fineman, Irving. *This Pure Young Man*. NY: Longmans, 1930. 368 p.
• Fisher, Dorothy Canfield. *The Bent Twig*. NY: Holt, 1915. 480 p.
Fisher, Dorothy Canfield. *The Deepening Stream*. NY: Harcourt, Brace, 1930. 393 p.
Fisher, Stephen. *Giveaway*. NY: Random, 1954. 276 p.
Fisher, Vardis. *In Tragic Life*. Caldwell, Idaho: Caxton, 1932. 464 p.
Fitzgerald, F. Scott. *Tender Is the Night*. NY: Bantam, 1951. 345 p.
Foldes, Jolan. *Prelude to Love*. NY: Farrar, 1938. 271 p.
Foote, John T. *A Change of Idols*. NY: Appleton-Century, 1935. 52 p.
Forbes, Esther. *Johnny Tremain*. Boston: Houghton, Mifflin, 1943. 256 p.
Foster, Michael. *To Remember at Midnight*. NY: Morrow, 1938. 281 p.
Fournier, Alain. *The Wanderer*. Boston: Houghton, Mifflin, 1928. 306 p.
France, Anatole. *The Bloom of Life*. NY: Dodd, Mead, 1923. 296 p.
France, Anatole. *Little Pierre*. NY: Dodd, Mead, 1924. 276 p.
France, Anatole. *Pierre Nozière*. NY: Dodd, Mead, 1924. 276 p.
Frankau, Pamela. *A Wreath for the Enemy*. NY: Harper, 1952. 310 p.
Frost, Frances M. *Yoke of Stars*. NY: Rinehart, 1939. 368 p.

Galsworthy, John. *The Dark Flower*. NY: Scribner, 1914. 316 p.
Galsworthy, John. *The Forsythe Saga*. NY: Scribner, 1933. 921 p.
Gardner, Mac. *Mom Counted Six*. NY: Harper, 1944. 267 p.
Gary, Romain. *The Company of Men*. NY: Simon & Schuster, 1950. 248 p.
Gaskell, Jane. *Strange Evil*. London: Hutchinson, 1957. 256 p.
Gide, André. *The Counterfeiters*. NY: Knopf, 1952. 432 p.
Gide, André. *Strait Is the Gate*. NY: Vintage, 1957. 148 p.
Gipson, Fred. *Old Yeller*. NY: Harper, 1956. 158 p.
Glaeser, Ernst. *Class of 1902*. NY: Viking, 1929. 397 p.
Glasgow, Ellen. *They Stooped to Folly*. NY: Doubleday, 1929. 351 p.
Glaspell, Susan. *Brook Evans*. NY: Stokes, 1928. 312 p.
Godden, Rumer. *An Episode of Sparrows*. NY: Viking, 1955. 247 p.

Godden, Rumer. *The Greengage Summer.* NY: Viking, 1958. 218 p.
Godden, Rumer. *The River.* Boston: Little, Brown, 1946. 176 p.
Gollomb, Joseph. *Unquiet.* NY: Dodd, Mead, 1935. 529 p.
Goodin, Peggy. *Clementine.* NY: Dutton, 1946. 246 p.
Goodin, Peggy. *Take Care of My Little Girl.* NY: Dutton, 1950. 189 p.
Gorham, Charles. *Trial by Darkness.* NY: Dial, 1952. 410 p.
Grace, Carol. *The Secret in the Daisy.* NY: Random, 1955. 121 p.
Granberry, Edwin. *The Erl King.* NY: Macaulay, 1930. 285 p.
Green, Julien. *The Closed Garden.* NY: Harper, 1928. 398 p.
Grubb, Davis. *A Dream of Kings.* NY: Scribner, 1955. 357 p.
Guido, Beatriz. *The House of the Angel.* NY: McGraw-Hill, 1957. 172 p.
Gulbranssen, Trygve. *Beyond Sing the Woods.* NY: Putnam, 1936. 313 p.
Gunnarsson, Gunnar. *The Night and the Dream.* Indianapolis: Bobbs-Merrill, 1938. 333 p.

Hackett, Francis. *The Green Lion.* NY: Doubleday, 1936. 337 p.
Halevy, Julian. *The Young Lovers.* NY: Simon & Schuster, 1955. 313 p.
Hallinan, Nancy. *The Rough Winds of May.* NY: Harper, 1955. 425 p.
Halper, Albert. *The Golden Watch.* NY: Holt, 1953. 246 p.
Hardy, Thomas. *Jude The Obscure.* NY: Modern Library, 1927. 488 p.
Harnden, Ruth. *I, a Stranger.* NY: McGraw-Hill, 1950. 195 p.
Harriman, John. *Winter Term.* NY: Howell, Soskin, 1940. 373 p.
Harris, Mark. *Something about a Soldier.* NY: Macmillan, 1957. 175 p.
Harris, Mary K. *I Am Julie.* NY: Crowell, 1956. 278 p.
Harris, Sara. *The Wayward Ones.* NY: Crown, 1952. 220 p.
Hartley, L. P. *The Go-Between.* NY: Knopf, 1954. 311 p.
Hastings, Michael. *The Game.* NY: McGraw-Hill, 1958. 169 p.
Hatvany, Lajos. *Bondy, Jr.* NY: Knopf, 1931. 372 p.
Head, Ann. *Fair with Rain.* NY: McGraw-Hill, 1957. 181 p.
Henning, William E. *The Haycott Album.* Phila: Lippincott, 1956. 222 p.
Henning, William E. *Heller.* NY: Scribner, 1947. 294 p.
Henry, B. A. *The Gutenheim Way.* NY: Yoseloff, 1957. 189 p.
Herbert, A. P. *The Water Gipsies.* NY: Doubleday, 1930. 414 p.
Herbert, Frederick Hugh. *I'd Rather Be Kissed.* NY: Random, 1954. 241 p.
Herbert, Frederick Hugh. *Meet Corliss Archer.* NY: Random, 1944. 275 p.
Hériat, Philippe. *The Spoiled Children.* NY: Putnam, 1956. 367 p.
Hesse, Hermann. *Demian.* NY: Holt, 1948. 207 p.
Hillyer, Laurie. *Time Remembered.* NY: Macmillan, 1945. 175 p.
Hooke, Nina W. *Close of Play.* NY: Dutton, 1936. 304 p.
Hooke, Nina W. *Striplings.* NY: Dutton, 1933. 320 p.
Howard, Elizabeth. *The Beautiful Visit.* NY: Random, 1950. 343 p.

Hughes, Richard. *A High Wind in Jamaica (The Innocent Voyage)*.
NY: Harper, 1929. 399 p.

Humphrey, William. *Home from the Hill*. NY: Knopf, 1958. 312 p.

Hunter, Evan. *The Blackboard Jungle*. NY: Simon & Schuster, 1954.
309 p.

Huxley, Aldous. *Eyeless in Gaza*. NY: Harper, 1936. 473 p.

Huxley, Aldous. *The Genius and the Goddess*. NY: Harper, 1955.
168 p.

Huxley, Aldous. *Time Must Have a Stop*. NY: Harper, 1944. 311 p.

Jackson, Charles. *The Buffalo Wallow*. Indianapolis: Bobbs-Merrill,
1953. 253 p.

Jackson, Charles. *The Sunnier Side*. NY: Farrar, Straus, 1950. 311 p.

Jackson, Shirley. *Hangsaman*. NY: Farrar, Straus, & Young, 1951. 280 p.

Jarrell, Randall. *Picture From an Institution*. NY: Knopf, 1954. 277 p.

Johnson, Alvin S. *Spring Storm*. NY: Knopf, 1936. 351 p.

Johnson, Josephine. *Wildwood*. NY: Harper, 1946. 162 p.

Johnson, Nora. *The World of Henry Orient*. Boston: Atlantic-Little,
Brown, 1958. 214 p.

Jonas, Carl. *Jefferson Selleck*. Boston: Little, Brown, 1951. 303 p.

Joseph, Donald. *October's Child*. NY: Stokes, 1929. 344 p.

Joyce, James. *A Portrait of the Artist As a Young Man*. NY: Modern
Library, 1916. 299 p.

Karig, Walter. *Lower Than Angels*. NY: Farrar & Rinehart, 1945. 370 p.

Kauffman, Lane. *Six Weeks in March*. Phila: Lippincott, 1956. 250 p.

Kennedy, Mark. *The Pecking Order*. NY: Appleton-Century-Crofts,
1953. 278 p.

Keogh, Theodora. *Meg*. NY: Creative Age, 1950. 242 p.

Keogh, Theodora. *The Tatooed Heart*. NY: Farrar, Straus, 1953. 261 p.

Keun, Irmgard. *The Bad Example*. NY: Harcourt, Brace, 1955. 182 p.

Kirstein, Lincoln. *Flesh Is Heir*. NY: Harcourt, Brace, 1932. 311 p..

Kohner, Frederick. *Gidget*. NY: Putnam, 1957. 156 p.

Kroll, Harry H. *Waters Over the Dam*. Indianapolis: Bobbs-Merrill,
1944. 299 p.

La Capria, Raffaele. *Day of Impatience*. NY: Farrar, Straus, 1954. 207 p.

Lacretelle, Jacques de. *Silbermann*. NY: Boni & Liveright, 1924. 191 p.

Lapsley, Mary. *Parable of the Virgins*. NY: Smith, 1931. 359 p.

Laverty, Maura. *Never No More*. NY: Longmans, Green, 1942. 284 p.

Lawrence, D. H. *The Rainbow*. NY: Modern Library, 1915. 467 p.

Lawrence, D. H. *Sons and Lovers*. NY: Viking, 1933. 491 p.

Laxness, Halldor. *Independent People*. NY: Knopf, 1946. 470 p.

Lee, Harry. *Fox in the Cloak*. NY: Macmillan, 1938. 557 p.

Lehman, Rosamund. *The Ballad and the Source*. NY: Reynal & Hitchcock, 1945. 250 p.

Lehman, Rosamund. *Dusty Answer*. NY: Holt, 1927. 348 p.

Lehman, Rosamund. *Invitation to the Waltz*. NY: Holt, 1932, 309 p.

L'Engle, Madeleine. *Camilla Dickinson*. NY: Simon & Schuster, 1951. 245 p.

L'Engle, Madeleine. *Small Rain*. NY: Vanguard, 1945. 371 p.

Leslie, Shane. *The Oppidan*. NY: Scribner, 1922. n.p.

Levin, Meyer. *Compulsion*. NY: Simon & Schuster, 1956. 495 p.

Levin, Meyer. *The Old Bunch*. NY: Viking, 1937. 964 p.

Levy, Melvin P. *Lafayette Carter*. Phila: Lippincott, 1956. 224 p.

Lewis, Flannery. *Abel Dayton*. NY: Macmillan, 1940. 304 p.

Lewis, Sinclair. *Bethel Merriday*. NY: Doubleday, Doran, 1940. 390 p.

Liepmann, Heinz. *Nights of an Old Child*. Phila: Lippincott, 1937. 260 p.

Lincoln, Victoria. *Celia Amberley*. NY: Rinehart, 1949. 370 p.

Lincoln, Victoria. *February Hill*. NY: Farrar, 1934. 337 p.

Lincoln, Victoria. *Out from Eden*. NY: Rinehart, 1951. 311 p.

Llewellyn, Richard. *How Green Was My Valley*. NY: Macmillan, 1940. 495 p.

Lofts, Norah. *White Hell of Pity*. NY: Knopf, 1937. 273 p.

Lothar, Ernst. *The Prisoner*. NY: Doubleday, 1945. 308 p.

Lumbard, C. G. *Senior Spring*. NY: Simon & Schuster, 1954. 243 p.

Lundberg, Daniel. *River Rat*. NY: Reynal & Hitchcock, 1941. 281 p.

Macaulay, Rose. *The World My Wilderness*. Boston: Little, Brown, 1950. 244 p.

Machen, Arthur. *The Secret Glory*. NY: Knopf, 1922. n.p.

MacKenzie, Compton. *Youth's Encounter*. NY: Appleton, 1913. 502 p.

Mallet, Françoise. *The Illusionist*. NY: Farrar, Straus, 1952. 250 p.

Mallet-Joris, Françoise. *The Red Room*. NY: Farrar, Straus & Cudahy, 1956. 247 p.

Mann, Thomas. *Buddenbrooks*. NY: Knopf, 1924. 2 Vols., 389 p.; 359 p.

Mann, Thomas. *Confessions of Felix Krull, Confidence Man*. NY: Knopf, 1955. 384 p.

Mann, Thomas. *Royal Highness*. NY: Knopf, 1926. 338 p.

Mann, Thomas. *Tonio Kröger*. In *Stories of Three Decades*. NY: Knopf, 1936. Pp. 85-132.

Mann, Thomas. *Young Joseph*. NY: Knopf, 1935. 311 p.

Mannin, Ethel. *The Living Lotus*. NY: Putnam, 1956. 320 p.

Mannin, Ethel, *Pity the Innocent*. NY: Putnam, 1957. 256 p.

Manning, Olive. *The Doves of Venus*. NY: Abelard-Schuman, 1956. 313 p.

Manning-Sanders, Ruth. *Growing Trees*. London: Morrow, 1931. 370 p.

Marks, Percy. *A Tree Grown Straight*. NY: Stokes, 1936. 339 p.

Marquand, John P. *The Late George Apley*. Boston: Little, Brown, 1937. 354 p.

Marquand, John P. *The Second Happiest Day*. NY: Harper, 1953. 409 p.

Marquand, John P. *So Little Time*. Boston: Little, Brown, 1943. 595 p.

Marsh, Ellen. *Drink to the Hunted*. NY: Dutton, 1945. 413 p.

Marshall, Joyce. *Presently Tomorrow*. Boston: Little, Brown, 1946. 309 p.

Martin du Gard, Roger. *The Thibaults*. NY: Viking, 1939. 871 p.

Masters, Kelly R. *Piney*. Boston: Little, Brown, 1950. 273 p.

Mathilda. *My Lovely Mama!* Indianapolis: Bobbs-Merrill, 1956. 179 p.

Maugham, W. Somerset. *Of Human Bondage*. NY: Doubleday, 1929. 648 p.

Mauriac, François. *The Desert of Love*. NY: Bantam, 1952. 183 p.

Mauriac, François. *Destinies*. NY: Covici, 1929. 215 p.

Mauriac, François. *Flesh and Blood*. NY: Farrar, Straus, 1955. 190 p.

Maurois, André. *The Family Circle*. NY: Appleton, 1932. 330 p.

Maxwell, William. *The Folded Leaf*. NY: Harper, 1945. 310 p.

McCullers, Carson. *Member of the Wedding*. Boston: Houghton, Mifflin, 1946. 195 p.

McLean, Kathryn. *Transfer Point*. NY: Harcourt, Brace, 1947. 195 p.

McNichols, Charles. *Crazy Weather*. NY: Macmillan, 1944. 195 p.

Meller, Sidney. *Roots in the Sky*. NY: Macmillan, 1938. 579 p.

Metalious, Grace. *Peyton Place*. NY: Messner, 1956. 372 p.

Michaelson, John N. *Morning, Winter, and Night*. NY: Sloane, 1952. 188 p.

Miller, Nolan. *Why I Am So Beat*. NY: Putnam, 1954. 213 p.

Mishima, Yukio. *The Sound of Waves*. NY: Knopf, 1956. 183 p.

Mitchell, William. *Who Has Seen the Wind*. Boston: Little, Brown, 1947. 300 p.

Mittelhölzer, Edgar. *Shadows Move among Them*. Phila: Lippincott, 1951. 334 p.

Moberg, Vilhelm. *When I Was a Child*. NY: Knopf, 1956. 280 p.

Montagu, Elizabeth. *This Side of the Truth*. NY: Coward-McCann, 1958. 193 p.

Moody, Ralph. *Man of the Family*. NY: Norton, 1951. 272 p.

Moore, Pamela. *Chocolates for Breakfast*. NY: Rinehart, 1956. 252 p.

Moore, Ruth. *The Fire Balloon*. NY: Morrow, 1948. 347 p.

Moravia, Alberto. *The Time of Indifference*. NY: Farrar, Straus, & Young, 1953. 303 p.

Moravia, Alberto. *Two Adolescents*. NY: Farrar, Straus, 1950. 268 p.

Morgan, Charles. *A Breeze of Morning*. NY: Macmillan, 1951. 211 p.

Morley, Blythe. *The Intemperate Season*. NY: Farrar, Straus, 1948. 204 p.

Morris, Wright. *The Huge Season*. NY: Viking, 1954. 306 p.

Morton, Frederic. *Asphalt and Desire*. NY: Harcourt, Brace, 1952. 282 p.

Motley, Willard. *Knock on Any Door*. NY: Appleton-Century, 1947. 504 p.

Musil, Robert. *Young Torless*. NY: Pantheon, 1955. 217 p.

Narayan, R. K. *Swami and Friends*; and *Bachelor of Arts*. Lansing, Michigan: Michigan State College Press, 1954. 179 p. 166 p.
Nathan, Robert. *Long after Summer*. NY: Knopf, 1948. 146 p.
Nathan, Robert. *Winter in April*. NY: Knopf, 1938. 228 p.
Neff, Wanda F. *We Sing Diana*. Boston: Houghton, Mifflin, 1928. 339 p.
Newby, Percy H. *The Young May Moon*. NY: Knopf, 1951. 320 p.
Nexø, Martin A. *Ditte: Daughter of Man*. NY: Holt, 1921. n.p.
Noble, Barbara. *The Years That Take the Best Away*. NY: Doubleday, Doran, 1930. 325 p.

Oakey, Virginia. *Thirteenth Summer*. NY: Wyn, 1955. 250 p.
Orme, Alexandra. *Natalie*. NY: Simon & Schuster, 1957. 337 p.

Packer, Peter. *White Crocus*. NY: McGraw-Hill, 1947. 275 p.
Parrish, Anne. *The Methodist Faun*. NY: Harper, 1929. 334 p.
Patchett, Mary E. *Cry of the Heart*. NY: Abelard-Schuman, 1957. 255 p.
Pease, Howard. *Dark Adventure*. NY: Doubleday, 1950. 229 p.
Peters, Fritz. *Finistère*. NY: Farrar, Straus, 1951. 307 p.
Peyrefitte, Roger. *Special Friendships*. NY: Vanguard, 1950. 392 p.
Phillips, Thomas H. *The Golden Lie*. NY: Rinehart, 1951. 279 p.
Plagemann, Bentz. *This Is Goggle*. NY: McGraw-Hill, 1955. 243 p.
Portobello, Petronella. *Mother of the Deb*. Boston: Houghton Mifflin, 1957. 192 p.
Portune, Robert. *The Old Man and the Sky*. NY: Putnam, 1958. 316 p.
Postani, Bettina. *Before the Cock Crows*. Boston: Little, Brown, 1957. 198 p.
Powell, Anthony. *A Question of Upbringing*. NY: Scribner, 1951. 230 p.
Powell, Dawn. *A Cage for Lovers*. Boston: Houghton Mifflin, 1957. 178 p.
Pratt, Theodore. *Valley Boy*. NY: Duell, Sloan & Pearce, 1946. 331 p.
Price, Emerson. *Inn of That Journey*. Caldwell, Idaho: Caxton, 1939. 266 p.
Proffitt, Josephine. *And Never Been Kissed*. NY: Macmillan, 1949. 247 p.
Proffitt, Josephine. *Dear Guest and Ghost*. NY: Macmillan, 1950. 259 p.
Proust, Marcel. *Within a Budding Grove*. NY: Random, 1934. 356 p.

Radiguet, Raymond. *The Devil in the Flesh*. NY: New American, 1949. 144 p.
Raphaelson, Dorshka. *Morning Song*. NY: Random, 1948. 280 p.
Ratel, Simonne. *The Green Grape*. NY: Macmillan, 1937. 307 p.
Rawlings, Marjorie. *The Yearling*. NY: Scribner, 1938, 428 p.
Rehder, Jessie. *Remembrance Way*. NY: Putnam, 1956. 255 p.
Reid, Ann A. *Love Lies Bleeding*. NY: Smith, 1930. 310 p.
Richardson, Dorothy M. *Pilgrimage*. NY: Knopf, 1917. n.p.
Richardson, Dorothy M. *Pointed Roofs*. Knopf, 1915. n.p.

Richardson, Henry H. *The Getting of Wisdom*. NY: Norton, 1931. 275 p.
Ritner, Ann. *The Green Bough*. Phila: Lippincott, 1950. 255 p.
Roark, Garland. *The Cruel Cocks*. NY: Doubleday, 1957. 284 p.
Robertson, Eileen A. *Summer's Lease*. Boston: Houghton, Mifflin, 1940. 408 p.
Rollins, William. *The Obelisk*. NY: Brewer, 1930. 419 p.
Rolvaag, O. E. *Peder Victorious*. NY: Harper, 1928. 350 p.
Rolland, Romain. *Jean-Christophe*. NY: Modern Library, 1910. 504 p.
Ronald, J. *Man Born of Woman*. Phila: Lippincott, 1951. 318 p.
Rooney, Frank. *The Courts of Memory*. NY: Vanguard, 1954. 507 p.
Rooney, Frank. *The Heel of Spring*. NY: Vanguard, 1956. 314 p.
Rosaire, Forrest. *East of Midnight*. NY: Knopf, 1945. 372 p.
Rosaire, Forrest. *White Night*. Phila: Lippincott, 1956. 224 p.
Rosenfeld, Isaac. *Passage from Home*. NY: Dial, 1946. 280 p.
Ross, Walter. *The Immortal*. NY: Simon & Schuster, 1958. 245 p.
Rossi, Jean-Baptiste. *Awakening*. NY: Harper, 1952. 244 p.
Roth, Joseph. *Radetzky March*. NY: Viking, 1933. 430 p.
Runbeck, Margaret. *Pink Magic*. Boston: Houghton, Mifflin, 1949. 231 p.
Ryerson, Florence & Clements, Colin C. *This Awful Age*. NY: Appleton, 1930. 267 p.

Sabatier, Robert. *Boulevard*. NY: McKay, 1958. 249 p.
Sagan, Françoise. *Bonjour Tristesse*. NY: Dutton, 1955. 128 p.
Sagan, Françoise. *A Certain Smile*. NY: Dutton, 1956. 128 p.
Sale, Elizabeth. *Recitation from Memory*. NY: Dodd, Mead, 1943. 298 p.
Salinger, J. D. *The Catcher in the Rye*. Boston: Little, Brown, 1945. 159 p.
Sandburg, Helga. *The Wheel of Earth*. NY: McDowell, Obolensky, 1958. 396 p.
Santayana, George. *The Last Puritan*. NY: Scribner, 1936. 602 p.
Sassoon, Siegfried. *Memoirs of a Fox-Hunting Man*. NY: Coward, 1929. 376 p.
Schmitt, Gladys. *Alexandra*. NY: Dial, 1947. 316 p.
Schweitzer, Gertrude. *The Young People*. NY: Crowell, 1953. 311 p.
Scott, Jessie. *Charity Ball*. NY: Macmillan, 1946. 309 p.
Scott, Virgil. *The Hickory Stick*. NY: Swallow & Morrow, 1948. 750 p.
Seager, Allan. *Amos Berry*. NY: Simon & Schuster, 1953. 376 p.
Sedgewick, Anne D. *The Little French Girl*. Boston: Houghton, Mifflin, 1924. 508 p.
Sélincourt, Hugh de. *One Little Boy*. NY: Boni & Liveright, 1924. 266 p.
Sender, Ramon J. *Before Noon*. Albuquerque, NM: University of New Mexico Press, 1958. 416 p.
Seymour, Beatrice K. *Frost at Morning*. Boston: Little, Brown, 1935. 324 p.

Shaw, Irwin. *Lucy Crown.* NY: Random, 1956. 339 p.

Shaw, Jane. *The Weir.* NY: Coward-McCann, 1954. 180 p.

Sheean, Vincent. *Bird of the Wilderness.* NY: Random, 1941. 322 p.

Shulman, Irving. *The Amboy Dukes.* NY: Doubleday, 1947. 273 p.

Shulman, Irving. *Children of the Dark.* NY: Holt, 1956. 270 p.

Simmons, Herbert A. *Corner Boy.* Boston: Houghton, Mifflin, 1957. 266 p.

Sinclair, Jo. *The Changelings.* NY: McGraw-Hill, 1955. 323 p.

Sinclair, Jo. *Wasteland.* NY: Harper, 1946. 321 p.

Sinclair, May. *Mary Olivier.* NY: Macmillan, 1919. 380 p.

Sklar, George. *The Two Worlds of Johnny Truro.* Boston: Little, Brown, 1947. 372 p.

Skelton, Peter. *The Charm of Hours.* NY: Morrow, 1954. 248 p.

Skouen, Arne. *Stoker's Mess.* NY: Knopf, 1948. 237 p.

Smith, Betty. *A Tree Grows in Brooklyn.* NY: Harper, 1943. 420 p.

Smith, Dorothy. *He Went for a Walk.* NY: Dutton, 1954. 256 p.

Smith, Emma. *The Far Cry.* NY: Random, 1950. 248 p.

Soldati, Mario. *The Confession.* NY: Knopf, 1958. 180 p.

Sourian, Peter. *Miri.* NY: Pantheon, 1957. 219 p.

Spring, Howard. *My Son, My Son!* NY: Viking, 1938. 649 p.

Stafford, Jean. *The Catherine Wheel.* NY: Harcourt, Brace, 1952. 281 p.

Stafford, Jean. *The Mountain Lion.* NY: Harcourt, Brace, 1947. 231 p.

Steen, Marguerite. *The Wise and the Foolish Virgins.* Boston: Little, Brown, 1932. 287 p.

Steinbeck, John. *East of Eden.* NY: Viking, 1952. 602 p.

Stern, G. B. *The Rueful Mating.* NY: Knopf, 1932. 566 p.

Steuer, Arthur. *The Terrible Swift Sword.* NY: Coward-McCann, 1956. 254 p.

Stewart, John Craig. *Through the First Gate.* NY: Dodd, Mead, 1950. 280 p.

Stolz, Mary S. *Pray Love, Remember.* NY: Harper, 1954. 345 p.

Stolz, Mary S. *Ready or Not.* NY: Harper, 1953. 243 p.

Stolz, Mary S. *Two by Two.* Boston: Houghton, Mifflin, 1954. 310 p.

Stong, Philip. *The Long Lane.* NY: Farrar, 1939. 308 p.

Street, James H. *In My Father's House.* NY: Dial, 1941. 348 p.

Strong, Leonard. *The Sea Wall.* NY: Knopf, 1933. 395 p.

Stuart, Jesse. *Hie to the Hunters.* NY: McGraw-Hill, 1950. 265 p.

Styron, William. *Lie Down in Darkness.* Indianapolis: Bobbs-Merrill, 1951. 400 p.

Suckow, Ruth. *The Bonney Family.* NY: Knopf, 1928. 296 p.

Suckow, Ruth. *The Folks.* NY: Farrar & Rinehart, 1934. 727 p.

Suckow, Ruth. *The Odyssey of a Nice Girl.* NY: Knopf, 1925. 363 p.

Summers, Hollis. *City Limit.* Boston: Houghton, Mifflin, 1948. 275 p.

Summers, James L. *Prom Trouble.* Phila: Westminster, 1955. 222 p.

Swados, Harvey. *Out Went the Candle.* NY: Viking, 1955. 374 p.

Tamas, Istvan. *Students of Spalato.* NY: Dutton, 1944. 283 p.

Tarkington, Booth. *Alice Adams.* NY: Doubleday, Page, 1922. 434 p.

Tarkington, Booth. *The Fighting Littles.* NY: Doubleday, 1941. 304 p.

Tarkington, Booth. *Penrod.* NY: Grosset & Dunlap, 1914. 345 p.

Tarkington, Booth. *Seventeen.* NY: Harper, 1916. 328 p.

Taylor, Elizabeth. *A Game of Hide-and-Seek.* NY: Knopf, 1951. 312 p.

Tesch, Gerald. *Never the Same Again.* NY: Putnam, 1956. 318 p.

Thacher, Russell. *The Tender Age.* NY: Macmillan, 1952. 277 p.

Thiess, Frank. *Farewell to Paradise.* NY: Knopf, 1929. 183 p.

Thiess, Frank. *The Gateway to Life.* NY: Knopf, 1927. 325 p.

Thirkell, Angela. *The Duke's Daughter.* NY: Knopf, 1951. 322 p.

Thirkell, Angela. *High Rising.* NY: Knopf, 1951. 282 p.

Thompson, Charles. *Halfway Down the Stairs.* NY: Harper, 1957. 288 p.

Toohey, John P. *Growing Pains.* NY: Dial, 1929. 312 p.

Torres, Tereska. *Not Yet.* NY: Crown, 1957. 190 p.

Townsend, Leo. *The Young Life.* NY: Day, 1958. 288 p.

Trist, Margaret. *Morning in Queensland.* Phila: Lippincott, 1958. 254 p.

Troyat, Henri. *Amelie in Love.* NY: Simon & Schuster, 1956. 370 p.

Undset, Sigrid. *The Wild Orchid.* NY: Knopf, 1931. 411 p.

Vail, Amanda. *Love Me Little.* NY: McGraw-Hill, 1957. 128 p.

Van Druten, John. *The Vicarious Years.* NY: Scribner, 1956. 187 p.

Van Druten, John. *Young Woodley.* NY: Day, 1929. 301 p.

Vaughan, Auriel R. M. *Jemima.* Boston: Little, Brown, 1952. 279 p.

Viertel, Peter. *The Canyon.* NY: Harcourt, Brace, 1940. 288 p.

Vilmorin, Louise de. *Julietta.* NY: Messner, 1954. 147 p.

Vittorini, Elio. *The Red Carnation.* Norfolk, Conn: New Directions, 1954. 244 p.

Vorse, Mary Heaton. *The Prestons.* NY: Boni & Liveright, 1918. n.p.

Wadelton, Thomas. *Silver Buckles on His Knee.* NY: Coward-McCann, 1945. 167 p.

Wagner, Eliot. *Grand Concourse.* Indianapolis: Bobbs-Merrill, 1954. 352 p.

Wagoner, David. *Rock.* NY: Viking, 1958. 253 p.

Walker, Mildred. *Winter Wheat.* NY: Harcourt, Brace, 1944. 306 p.

Wallop, Douglass. *Night Light.* NY: Norton, 1953. 378 p.

Walpole, Hugh. *Fortitude.* NY: Doran, 1913. 484 p.

Ware, Edmund. *Rider in the Sun.* London: Lothrop, 1936. 197 p.

Warrick, Lasnar. *Yesterday's Children.* NY: Crowell, 1943. 202 p.

Webb, Mary. *The House in Dormer Forest.* NY: Dutton, 1929. 288 p.

Webb, Mary. *Precious Bane.* NY: Dutton, 1926. 356 p.

Webber, G. *Years of Eden.* Boston: Little, Brown, 1951. 238 p.

Weeks, Joseph. *All Our Yesterdays.* NY: Rinehart, 1955. 374 p.

Weidman, Jerome. *The Lights Around the Shore.* NY: Simon & Schuster, 1943. 279 p.

Weldon, John Lee. *The Naked Heart.* NY: Farrar, Straus, 1953. 213 p.
Wells, H. G. *The Bulpington of Blup.* NY: Macmillan, 1933. 414 p.
Wells, H. G. *Joan and Peter.* NY: Macmillan, 1918. 594 p.
Werfel, Franz. *Class Reunion.* NY: Simon & Schuster, 1929. 204 p.
Wertenbaker, Charles. *To My Father.* NY: Farrar, 1936. 499 p.
Wescott, Glenway. *The Apple of the Eye.* NY: Dial, 1924. 292 p.
West, Anthony. *Heritage.* NY: Random, 1955. 309 p.
West, Jessamyn. *Cress Delahanty.* NY: Harcourt, Brace, 1953. 311 p.
Westheimer, David. *The Magic Fallacy.* NY: Macmillan, 1950. 96 p.
Wetzel, Donald. *The Rain and the Fire and the Will of God.* NY: Random, 1957. 184 p.
Wharton, Edith. *The Children.* NY: Appleton, 1928. 347 p.
White, Victor. *Peter Domanig.* Indianapolis: Bobbs-Merrill, 1944. 704 p.
Wickenden, Dan. *The Running of the Deer.* NY: Morrow, 1937. 343 p.
Wickenden, Dan. *Walk Like a Mortal.* NY: Morrow, 1940. 530 p.
Williamson, Henry. *Dandelion Days.* NY: Dutton, 1930. 318 p.
Willingham, Calder. *End As a Man.* NY: Vanguard, 1947. 350 p.
Windham, Donald. *The Dog Star.* NY: Doubleday, 1950. 221 p.
Winsloe, Christa. *The Child Manuela (Mädchen in Uniform).* NY: Farrar, 1931. 310 p.
Winslow, Anne G. *The Springs.* NY: Knopf, 1949. 227 p.
Winsor, Kathleen. *America, with Love.* NY: Putnam, 1957. 320 p.
Wolfe, Thomas. *Look Homeward, Angel.* NY: Scribner, 1929. 626 p.
Wolfe, Thomas. *Of Time and the River.* NY: Scribner, 1935. 912 p.
Wolff, Renate C. *Johannes.* NY: Simon & Schuster, 1958. 313 p.
Woolf, Virginia. *Orlando.* NY: Harcourt, 1928. 333 p.
Woolf, Virginia. *To the Lighthouse.* NY: Harcourt, Brace, 1927. 310 p.
Woolf, Virginia. *The Waves.* NY: Harcourt, Brace, 1931. 297 p.
Wouk, Herman. *Marjorie Morningstar.* NY: Doubleday, 1955. 565 p.
Wylie, Max. *Go Home and Tell Your Mother.* NY: Rinehart, 1950. 306 p.

Yaffe, James. *Nothing But the Night.* Boston: Atlantic-Little, Brown, 1957. 336 p.
Yaray, Hans. *One Page Missing.* NY: Holt, 1948. 248 p.
Yoseloff, Martin. *The Family Members.* NY: Dutton, 1948. 221 p.

Zur Muhlen, Herminia. *The Wheel of Life.* NY: Stokes, 1933. 301 p.

Psychology and Literature

The 416 items in this bibliography on psychology and literature have a broad base. Included are orthodox, Freudian psychoanalytic interpretations of literature, neo-Freudian analyses, interpretations from the Sullivanian, Jungian and other analytic schools, as well as still other books and articles by literary critics, writers, and professors of English, philosophy and psychology. These references, then, represent a wide selection, but with no attempt to be exhaustive. Most of the work done in foreign languages has been omitted, for instance. Literary criticism as such has not been included, nor have most of the articles appearing in the popular literary journals. The criterion used was the relevancy of psychological and psychoanalytic theory as applied to literature.

Abell, Walter H. *The Collective Dream in Art: A Psycho-historical Theory of Culture Based on Relations between the Arts, Psychology, and Social Sciences.* Cambridge, Mass: Harvard University Press, 1957. 378 p.

Abrams, Meyer H. "Unconscious Expectations in the Reading of Poetry." *J. English Literary History,* 9:235-244, 1942.

Adams, Robert M. "Literature and Psychology: A Question of Significant Form." *Lit. & Psychol.,* 5:67-72, 1955.

Albrecht, Milton C. "Psychological Motives in the Fiction of Julien Green." *J. Personality,* 16:278-303, 1948.

Albrecht, Milton C. "The Relationship of Literature and Society." *Amer. J. Sociology,* 59: 425-436, 1954.

Alexander, Doris. "Psychological Fate in Mourning Becomes Electra." *Publication of the Modern Lang. Assoc.,* 68:923-934, 1953.

Aldridge, John W. *In Search of Heresy: American Literature in an Age of Conformity.* NY: McGraw-Hill, 1956. 208 p.

Allen, Charles A. "Katherine Anne Porter: Psychology as Art." *Southwest Review,* 41: 223-230, 1956.

Allen, Clifford, "Homosexuality and Oscar Wilde: A Psychological Study." *Int. J. Sexol.*, 2:205-215, 1949.

Allen, Clifford. "The Problem of John Ruskin: A Psycho-sexological Analysis." *Int. J. Sexol.*, 4:7-14, 1950.

Allport, Gordon. *The Use of Personal Documents in Psychological Science.* Soc. Sci. Research Coun. Bull., No. 49, 1942.

Alm, Richard S. *A Study of the Assumptions Concerning Human Experience Underlying Certain Works of Fiction Written For and About Adolescents.* Minneapolis, Minn: University of Minnesota, 1954. Doctoral dissertation. 1044 p.

Ames, Van Metes. "The Novel: Between Art and Science." *Kenyon Review,* 5:34-48, 1942.

Anthony, Katherine S. *Margaret Fuller: A Psychological Biography.* NY: Harcourt, 1920. n.p.

Arnheim, Rudolf. "Agenda for the Psychology of Art." *J. Aesthetics & Art Criticism,* 10:310-314, 1952.

Arnheim, Rudolf. "Artistic Symbols—Freudian and Otherwise." *J. Aesthetics & Art Criticism,* 12:93-97, 1953.

Astrov, Vladimir. "Hawthorne and Dostoievski as Explorers of the Human Conscience." *New England Quart.,* 15:296-319, 1942.

Aswell, Mary Louise (Ed). *The World Within.* NY: McGraw-Hill, 1947. 376 p.

Atkin, I. "The Experiment of Dr. Moreau." *J. Clin. Psychopath.,* 8:667-671, 1947.

Atkins, Lois. "Psychological Symbolism of Guilt and Isolation in Hawthorne." *Amer. Imago,* 11:417-425, 1954.

Aulagne, Louis. "Les Fées d' 'A la Recherche du Temps Perdu'." *Psyche,* 7:357-362; 410-434, 1952.

Bachler, Karl. "Männer, Mächte und Dämonen." *Psychol. Berater Gesunde Prakt. Lebensgestalt.,* 4:290-294, 1952.

Bacon, Deborah. *The Meaning of Nonsense: A Psychoanalytic Approach to Lewis Carroll.* NY: Columbia University Ph.D. Thesis, 1950. 276 p.

Baker, Sidney J. "Shakespeare and Sex." *Int. J. Sexol.,* 4:35-39, 1950.

Balcom, Lois. *The Value of a Comparative Analysis of an Author's Autobiographical and Fictional Writings for Interpretation of Aspects of His Personality: A Study Based on Selected Works of William Dean Howells.* Dissertation Abstr., 16:373, 1956.

Baldridge, Marie. "Some Psychological Patterns in the Poetry of T. S. Eliot." *Psychoanalysis,* 3:19-47, 1954.

Barker, Warren J. "The Stereotyped Western Story." *Psychoanalytic Quart.,* 24:270-280, 1955.

Barr, Donald. "Freud and Fiction." *Saturday Review,* May 5, 1956, p. 36.

Barrett, William G. "Writers and Madness." *Partisan Review,* 14:5-22, 1947.

Barrett, William G. "Mark Twain's Osteopathic Cure." *Psychoanalytic Quart.*, 22:539-547, 1953.

Barrett, William G. "On the Naming of Tom Sawyer," *Psychoanalytic Quart.*, 24:424-436, 1955.

Basler, Roy P. "Psychological Pattern in the 'Love Song of J. Alfred Prufrock'." *Twentieth Century English,* pp. 384-400, 1946.

Basler, Roy P. *Sex, Symbolism, and Psychology in Literature.* New Brunswick: Rutgers University Press, 1948. 226 p.

Beauvoir, Simone de. *The Second Sex.* NY: Knopf, 1953. 732 p.

Bellak, Leopold. "Psychology of Detective Stories and Related Problems." *Psychoanalytic Review,* 32:403-407, 1945.

Beres, David. "Communication in Psychoanalysis and in the Creative Process: a Parallel." *J. Amer. Psychoanalytic Assoc.,* 5:408-423, 1957.

Beres, David. "A Dream, A Vision, and A Poem." *Int. J. Psycho-Analysis,* 32:97-116, 1951.

Bergler, Edmund. "Can the Writer 'Resign' from his Calling?" *Int. J. Psycho-Analysis,* 34:40-42, 1953.

Bergler, Edmund. "The Dislike for Satire at Length." *Psychiat. Quart., Suppl.,* 26:190-201, 1952.

Bergler, Edmund. "Further Contributions to the Psychoanalysis of Writers." *Psychoanalytic Review,* 34:449-469, 1947; 35:33-50, 1948.

Bergler, Edmund. "Psychoanalysis of Writers and of Literary Production," in Róheim, Géza (Ed.), *Psychoanalysis and the Social Sciences.* NY: International Universities Press, 1947. Pp. 247-296.

Bergler, Edmund. "True Feelings and 'Tear Jerkers' in Literary Work." *Amer. Imago,* 10:83-86, 1953.

Bergler, Edmund. *The Writer and Psychoanalysis.* NY: Brunner, 1954. 295 p.

Berne, Eric. "The Psychological Structure of Space With Some Remarks on Robinson Crusoe." *Psychoanalytic Quart.,* 25:549-567, 1956.

Bewley, Marius. "Hawthorne and 'The Deeper Psychology'." *Mandrake,* 2:366-373, 1956.

Blake, J. "Insight Through Fiction." *High School J.,* 33:199-201, 1950.

Bodenheim, Maxwell. "Psychoanalysis and American Fiction." *Nation,* 114:683-84, 1922.

Bodkin, Maud. *Archetypal Patterns in Poetry: Psychological Studies of Imagination.* NY: Vintage, 1958. 324 p.

Bonaparte, Marie. *Life and Works of Edgar Allen Poe: A Psychoanalytic Interpretation.* NY: Anglobooks, 1951. 749 p.

Bonaparte, Marie. "The Murders in the Rue Morgue." *Psychoanalytic Quart.,* 4:259-293, 1935.

Bottome, Phyllis. "Is Neurosis a Handicap to Genius?" *Lit. & Psychol.,* 5:20-25, 1955.

Boussoulas, Nicholas I. *La Peur et l'Universe dans l'Oeuvre d'Edgar Poe.* Paris: Presses Universitaires de France, 1952. 126 p.

Bowling, L. E. "What Is the Stream of Consciousness Technique?" *Publications of the Modern Lang. Assoc.,* 65:333-345, 1950.

Bragman, L. J. "The Case of Algernon Charles Swinburne: A Study in Sadism." *Psychoanalytic Review,* 21:51-74, 1934.

Bree, Germaine & Guiton, Margaret. *An Age of Fiction: The French Novel from Gide to Camus.* New Brunswick, NJ: Rutgers University Press, 1958.

Breitbart, Sara. " 'Hedda Gabler'—A Critical Analysis." *Amer. J. Psychoanalysis,* 8:55-58, 1948.

Brenner, Arthur B. "The Fantasies of W. S. Gilbert." *Psychoanalytic Quart.,* 21: 373-401, 1952.

Brody, Benjamin. "Psychoanalytic Psychologists Evaluate Their Academic Training." *Amer. Psychologist,* 10:29-30, 1955.

Brooks, Cleanth & Warren, Robert Penn. *Understanding Fiction.* NY: Crofts, 1943. 608 p.

Brumbaugh, Thomas B. "Concerning Nathaniel Hawthorne and Art as Magic." *Amer. Imago,* 11:399-405, 1954.

Bruner, Jerome S. "Freud and the Image of Man." *Partisan Review,* 23:340-347, 1956.

Bunker, Henry A. "A Dream of an Inhibited Writer." *Psychoanalytic Quart.,* 22:519-524, 1953.

Burgum, Edwin Berry. *The Novel and the World's Dilemma.* NY: Oxford University Press, 1947. 352 p.

Burke, Kenneth. *The Philosophy of Literary Form.* Baton Rouge: Louisiana State University Press, 1944. n.p.

Burke, Kenneth. *A Rhetoric of Motives.* NY: Prentice-Hall, 1950. 355 p.

Burns, Wayne. "His Mother's Son: The Emotional Development of Charles Reade." *Lit. & Psychol.,* 4:31-47, 1954.

Buxbaum, Edith. "The Role of Detective Stories in a Child Analysis." *Psychoanalytic Quart.,* 10:373-381, 1941.

Buytendijk, F. F. J. *De Psychologie van de Roman, Studies Over Dostojevsky.* Utrecht: Spectrum, 1950. 111 p.

Bychowski, Gustav. "From Catharsis to Work of Art: The Making of an Artist," in Wilbur, George B., and Muensterberger, Warner (Eds.), *Psychoanalysis and Culture.* NY: International Universities Press, 1951. Pp. 390-409.

Bychowski, Gustav. "Struggle against the Introjects." *Int. J. Psycho-Analysis,* 39:182-187, 1958.

Bychowski, Gustav. "Walt Whitman: A Study in Sublimation," in Róheim, Géza, (Ed.), *Psychoanalysis and the Social Sciences,* Vol. 3. NY: International Universities Press, 1951. Pp. 223-261.

Calverton, V. F. *Sex Expression in Literature.* NY: Boni & Liveright, 1926. 337 p.

Campbell, Oscar J., Van Gundy, Justine, & Shrodes, Caroline (Eds.). *Patterns for Living.* NY: Macmillan, 1947. 878 p.

Camus, Albert. "Philosophy and Fiction," in *The Myth of Sisyphus.* NY: Knopf, 1955. Pp. 93-103.

Carpenter, Frederic I. *American Literature and the Dream*. NY: Philosophical, 1955. 220 p.

Carpenter, Thomas P. "The Material of Abnormal Psychology in Some Contemporary English and American Novels." *Abstracts of Dissertations*, Stanford University, 22:27-30, 1947.

Carroll, John B. (Ed.). *Language, Thought, and Reality. Selected Writings of Benjamin Lee Whorf*. NY: Wiley, 1956. 294 p.

Charcot, J. M. & Richter, Paul. *Les Démoniaques dans l'Art*. Paris: Delahaye, 1887.

Chase, Richard V. "*Finnigans Wake:* An Anthropological Study." *Amer. Scholar*, 8:418-426, 1944.

Choisy, Maryse. "Le Problème de la Création." *Psyche*, 7:705-729, 1952.

Cleckley, Hervey. *The Caricature of Love*. NY: Ronald, 1957. 319 p.

Coggins, K. "Introversion and the Appreciation of Literature." *Amer. J. Psychol.*, 55:560-561, 1943.

Collins, Carvel. "A Conscious Literary Use of Freud?" *Lit. & Psychol.*, 3:2-4, 1953.

Collins, Carvel. "The Interior Monologues of *The Sound and the Fury*." *English Institute Essays*, 1952. Pp. 29-56.

Coriat, Isador H. "Anal-Erotic Character Traits in Shylock." *Int. J. Psycho-Analysis*, 2:354-360, 1921.

Coriat, Isador H. "Psychoanalyse der Lady Macbeth." *Imago* (Vienna), 4:384, 1914.

Cornford, F. M. "The Unconscious Element in Literature and Philosophy." *Int. J. Psycho-Analysis*. Vol. 4, 1922.

Cowley, Malcolm. "Psychoanalysis and Writers." *Harpers*, 209:87-93, 1954.

Cowley, Malcolm (Ed.). *Writers at Work: The Paris Review Interviews*. NY: Viking, 1958. 309 p.

Crane, A. R. "Psychology and Poetry." *Australian Psychol. Phil.*, 29:21-35, 1951.

"Creativity and Creative Consciousness," A Symposium. *Psychotherapy*, 1:359-375, 1956.

Daly, C. D. "The Menstruation Complex in Literature." *Psychoanalytic Quart.*, 4:307-340, 1935.

Daly, C. D. "The Mother Complex in Literature," in Lorand, Sandor (Ed.), *Yearbook of Psychoanalysis*, Vol. 4. NY: International Universities Press, 1948. Pp. 172-210.

Das, J. P., Rath, R., & Das, Rhea S. "Understanding Versus Suggestion in the Judgment of Literary Passages." *J. Abn. & Soc. Psychol.*, 51:624-628, 1955.

Davis, David B. *Homicide in American Fiction, 1798-1860: A Study in Social Values*. Ithaca, NY: Cornell University Press, 1957. 346 p.

Deegan, Dorothy V. *The Stereotype of the Single Woman in American Novels*. NY: King's Crown, 1951. 252 p.

Desmonde, William H. "The Ritual Origin of Shakespeare's 'Titus Andronicus'." *Int. J. Psycho-Analysis*, 36:61-65, 1955.

Devereux, George. "Why Oedipus Killed Laius." *Int. J. Psycho-Analysis*, 34:131-141, 1953.

DeVoto, Bernard. "Freud in American Literature." *Psychoanalytic Quart.*, 9: 236-245, 1940.

DeVoto, Bernard, "Freud's Influence on Literature." *Saturday Review Lit.*, 20:10-11, 1939.

Donnelly, John. "Incest, Ingratitude, and Insanity." *Psychoanalytic Review*, 40: 149-155, 1953.

Donnelly, Mable C. "Freud and Literary Criticism." *College Engl.*, 15:155-158, 1953.

Doolittle, Hilda. *Tribute to Freud*. NY: Pantheon, 1956. 180 p.

Dostoevsky, Fyodor. "A Simple Affair? October, 1876 (From 'Diary of a Writer')." *Psychoanalytic Review*, 37:164-171, 1950.

Doyle, L. F. "Hounds of Freud." *America*, 75:501-502, 1946.

Duncan, Hugh D. *Annotated Bibliography on the Sociology of Literature, with an Introductory Essay on Methodological Problems in the Field*. Chicago: University of Chicago Press, 1947. Mimeographed.

Duncan, Hugh D. *Language and Literature in Society*. Chicago: University of Chicago Press, 1953. 262 p.

Edel, Leon. *The Psychological Novel, 1900-1950*. Phila: Lippincott, 1955. 221 p.

Edel, Leon. "Willa Cather's *The Professor's House:* An Inquiry into the Use of Psychology in Literary Criticism." *Lit. & Psychol.*, 4:69-79, 1954.

Eissler, K. R. "On Hamlet." *Samiksa*, 7:85-132, 1953.

Elton, William (Ed.). *Aesthetics and Language*. NY: Philosophical, 1954. 186 p.

Ephron, Beulah K. "The Reader and the Writer," in Lindner, Robert (Ed.), *Explorations in Psychoanalysis*. NY: Julian, 1953. Pp. 116-127.

Evans, Jean. *Three Men; an Experiment in the Biography of Emotion*. NY: Knopf, 1954. 297 p.

Farnell, Frederic J. "Eroticism as Portrayed in Literature." *Int. J. Psycho-Analysis*, 1:396-413, 1920.

Farrell, James T. *The League of Frightened Philistines*. NY: Vanguard, 1945. 210 p.

Farrar, John. "Sex Psychology in Modern Fiction." *Independent*, 117: 669-70, 1926.

Feldman, A. Bronson. "Fifty Years of the Psychoanalysis of Literature: 1900-1950." *Lit. & Psychol.*, 5:40-42, 54-64, 1955.

Feldman, A. Bronson. "Imaginary Incest: a Study of Shakespeare's Pericles." *Amer. Imago*, 12:155-177, 1955.

Feldman, A. Bronson. "James Joyce's 'A Painful Case' (1905)." *Psychoanalysis*, 5:3-12, 1957.

Feldman, A. Bronson. "Othello in Reality." *Amer. Imago*, 11:147-179, 1954.

Feldman, A. Bronson. "Othello's Obsessions." *Amer. Imago*, 9:147-164, 1952.

Feldman, A. Bronson. "Reik and the Interpretation of Literature," in Lindner, Robert (Ed.), *Explorations in Psychoanalysis*. NY: Julian, 1953. Pp. 97-115.

Feldman, A. Bronson. "Shakespeare's Early Errors." *Int. J. Psycho-Analysis*, 36:114-133, 1955.

Feldman, A. Bronson. "Shakespeare Worship." *Psychoanalysis*, 2:57-72, 1953.

Feldman, A. Bronson. "The Yellow Malady; Short Studies of 5 Tragedies of Jealousy." *Lit. & Psychol.*, 6:38-52, 1956.

Feldman, Eugene S. "Sherwood Anderson's Search." *Psychoanalysis*, 3:44-51, 1955.

Feldman, Harold. "Unconscious Envy in Brutus." *Amer. Imago*, 9:307-335, 1952.

Fiedler, Leslie A. "Boys Will Be Boys!" *New Leader*, 41:23-26, 1958.

Fiedler, Leslie A. "From Redemption to Initiation." *New Leader*, 41:20-23, 1958.

Fiedler, Leslie A. "Good Good Girl and Good Bad Boy." *New Leader*, 41:22-25, 1958.

Fiedler, Leslie A. "The Invention of the Child." *New Leader*, 41:22-24, 1958.

Flanagan, John C. "The Critical Incident Technique." *Psychol. Bull.*, 51:327-358, 1954.

Florance, Edna C. "The Neurosis of Raskolnikov: a Study in Incest and Murder." *Arch. Crim. Psychodynamics*, 1:344-396, 1955.

Flugel, J. C. "Maurice Bedel's 'Jerome'—a Study of Contrasting Types." *Psychoanalytic Quart.*, 1:653-682, 1932.

Forster, E. M. *Aspects of the Novel*. NY: Harcourt, Brace, 1927. 250 p.

Foster, Jeannette H. "An Approach to Fiction Through the Characteristics of Its Readers." *Library Quart.*, 6:129-174, 1936.

Foster, Jeannette H. *Sex Variant Women in Literature*. NY: Vantage, 1956. 412 p.

Fraiberg, Louis. "Freud's Writings on Art." *Int. J. Psycho-Analysis*, 37:82-96, 1956.

Fraiberg, Louis. "Psychology and the Writer: The Creative Process." *Lit. & Psychol.*, 5:72-77, 1955.

Fraiberg, Selma. "Tales of the Discovery of the Secret Treasure." *The Psychoanalytic Study of the Child*, 9:218-241. NY: International Universities Press, 1954.

Frank, Anne. *The Diary of a Young Girl*. NY: Doubleday, 1952. 285 p.

Freud, Sigmund. "Creative Writers and Daydreaming," in Strachey,

John (Ed.), *The Standard Edition of the Complete Works of Sigmund Freud*, Vol. 9. London: Hogarth & The Institute of Psycho-Analysis, 1953.

Freud, Sigmund. *Delusion and Dream*. Boston: Beacon, 1956. 238 p.

Freud, Sigmund. "Dostoevsky and Parricide," in Strachey, John (Ed.), *Standard Edition of the Complete Works of Sigmund Freud*, Vol. 21. London: Hogarth & The Institute of Psycho-Analysis, 1953.

Freud, Sigmund. "Formulations on the Two Principles of Mental Functioning," in Strachey, John (Ed.), *The Standard Edition of the Complete Works of Sigmund Freud*, Vol. 12. London: Hogarth & The Institute of Psycho-Analysis, 1953.

Freud, Sigmund. *The Origins of Psycho-Analysis*. Bonaparte, Marie, Freud, Anna, & Kris, Ernst (Eds.). NY: Basic Books, 1954. Pp. 256-7.

Freud, Sigmund. "Some Character-Types Met with in Psycho-Analytic Work." *Collected Papers*, 4:318-344. London: Hogarth, 1925.

Freud, Sigmund. "The Theme of the Three Caskets," in Strachey, James (Ed.), *Standard Edition of the Complete Psychological Works of Sigmund Freud*, Vol. 12. London: Hogarth & The Institute of Psycho-Analysis, 1953.

Freud, Sigmund. "Wit and Its Relation to the Unconscious," in *Basic Writings of Sigmund Freud*. NY: Modern Library, 1938.

Friedman, Joel & Gassel, Sylvia. "The Chorus in Sophocles' Oedipus Tyrannus. A Psychoanalytic Approach to Dramatic Criticism, I." *Psychoanalytic Quart.*, 19:213-226, 1950.

Friedman, Joel & Gassel, Sylvia. "Orestes. A Psychoanalytic Approach to Dramatic Criticism, II." *Psychoanalytic Quart.*, 20:423-433, 1951.

Friedman, Melvin J. *Stream of Consciousness: A Study in Literary Method*. New Haven: Yale University Press, 1955. 279 p.

Fromm, Erich. *The Forgotten Language. An Introduction to the Understanding of Dreams, Fairy Tales and Myths*. NY: Rinehart, 1951, 263 p.

Fruhock, W. M. "Thomas Wolfe: of Time and Neurosis." *Southwest Review*, 33:349-360, 1948.

Gale, Robert L. "Freudian Imagery in James' Fiction." *Amer. Imago*, 11:181-190, 1954.

Geismar, Maxwell. *American Moderns. From Rebellion to Conformity*. NY: Hill & Wang, 1958.

Geismar, Maxwell. *Rebels and Ancestors: The American Novel*. Boston: Houghton Mifflin, 1953. 435 p.

Gelfant, Blanche H. *The American City Novel*. Norman, Okla: University of Oklahoma Press, 1954. 289 p.

Gerber, Helmut E. "J. D. Beresford: The Freudian Element." *Lit. & Psychol.*, 6:78-86, 1956.

Ghiselin, Brewster (Ed.). *The Creative Process*. NY: New American Library, 1955. 251 p.

Glickberg, Charles I. "Literature and Science: A Study in Conflict." *Scientific Monthly*, 59:467-472, 1944.

Glicksberg, Charles I. "Marxism, Freudianism, and Modern Writings." *Queen's Quart.*, 54:297-310, 1947.

Glicksberg, Charles I. "Poetry and the Freudian Aesthetic." *Univ. of Toronto Quart.*, 17:121-129, 1948.

Glicksberg, Charles I. "Psychoanalytic Aesthetics." *Prairie Schooner*, 39:13-23, 1955.

Goodman, Paul. "On a Writer's Block." *Complex*, 7:42-50, 1952.

Gordon, Caroline. *How to Read a Novel*. NY: Viking, 1957. 247 p.

Grant Duff, I. F. "A One-Sided Sketch of Jonathan Swift." *Psychoanalytic Quart.*, 6:238-259, 1937.

Grant, Vernon W. *The Psychology of Sexual Emotion*. NY: Longmans, Green, 1957. 270 p.

Greenacre, Phyllis. "The Mutual Adventures of Jonathan Swift and Lemuel Gulliver." *Psychoanalytic Quart.*, 24:20-62, 1955.

Greenacre, Phyllis. *Swift and Carroll, A Psychoanalytic Study of Two Lives*. NY: International Universities Press, 1955. 306 p.

Greenacre, Phyllis. "Experiences of Awe in Childhood," in Eissler, Ruth S., et al. (Eds.), *The Psychoanalytic Study of the Child*, 11:9-30. NY: International Universities Press, 1956.

Greenacre, Phyllis. "The Childhood of the Artist," in Eissler, Ruth S., et al. (Eds.), *The Psychoanalytic Study of the Child*, 12:47-72. NY: International Universities Press, 1957.

Gregory, Hoosag K. *The Prisoner and His Crimes: A Psychological Approach to William Cowper's Life and Writings*. Unpublished Ph.D. Thesis, Harvard University, 1951.

Griffiths, D. E. & Hobday, A. F. "The Novel as a Case Study." *Ed. Res. Bull.*, 31:19-21, 1952.

Grinstein, Alexander. "The Dramatic Device: A Play Within a Play." *J. Amer. Psychoanalytic Assoc.*, 4:49-52, 1956.

Grotjahn, Martin. "A Letter by Sigmund Freud with Recollections of His Adolescence." *J. Amer. Psychoanalytic Assoc.*, 4:644-652, 1956.

Gui, Weston A. "Bottom's Dream." *Amer. Imago*, 9:251-305, 1952.

Gunn, Douglas G. "Factors in the Appreciation of Poetry." *Brit. J. Educ. Psychol.*, 21:96-104, 1951.

Hacker, Frederick J. "On Artistic Production," in Lindner, Robert (Ed.), *Explorations in Psychoanalysis*. NY: Julian, 1953. Pp. 128-138.

Hagopian, John V. "Chaucer as Psychologist in Troilus and Criseyde." *Lit. & Psychol.*, 5:5-11, 1955.

Hagopian, John V. "A Psychological Approach to Shelley's Poetry." *Amer. Imago*, 12:25-45, 1955.

Halliday, James L. *Mr. Carlyle, My Patient: A Psychosomatic Biography*. NY: Grune & Stratton, 1950, 227 p.

Hamilton, Robert V. "Psycholinguistic Analysis." *J. Soc. Psychol.*, 41: 271-286, 1955.

Harding, M. Esther. *Journey Into Self*. NY: Longmans, Green, 1956. 301 p.

Harding, M. Esther. *Woman's Mysteries: Ancient and Modern. A Psychological Interpretation of the Feminine Principle as Portrayed in Myth, Story and Dreams*. NY: Pantheon, 1955. 256 p.

Harrison, Charles T. "Santayana's 'Literary Psychology'." *Sewanee Review*, 61:206-220, 1953.

Hatcher, Harlan H. "The Novel as an Educative Force." *College English*, 2:37-46, 1940.

Hazard, Paul. *Books, Children and Men*. Boston: Horn, 1948. 176 p.

Hecht, M. Bernard. "Uncanniness, Yearning, and Franz Kafka's Works." *Amer. Imago*, 9:45-55, 1952.

Heiserman, Arthur & Miller, James E. "J. D. Salinger: Some Crazy Cliff." *Western Humanities Review*, 10:129-137, 1956.

Hertzman, Max. "Psychology, Literature, and the Life Situation." *Psychoanalysis*, 3:2, 1955.

Hitschmann, Edward. "Boswell: The Biographer's Character," in Lorand, Sandor (Ed.), *Yearbook of Psychoanalysis*. Vol. 5. NY: International Universities Press, 1949. Pp. 294-305.

Hitschmann, Edward. *Great Men. Psychoanalytic Studies*. NY: International Universities Press, 1956. 278 p.

Hitschmann, Edward. "Samuel Johnson's Character, A Psychoanalytic Interpretation." *Psychoanalytic Review*, 32:207-218, 1945.

Hodgart, M. "Psychology and Literary Criticism." *The Listener*, Sept. 11, 1952. P. 420.

Hoffman, Frederick J. *Freudianism and the Literary Mind*. Baton Rouge: Lousiana State University Press, 1945. 364 p.

Hoffman, Frederick J. "Freudianism: A Study of Influences and Reactions, Especially as Revealed in the Fiction of James Joyce, D. H. Lawrence, Sherwood Anderson, and Waldo Frank." *Ohio State Univ. Abstracts of Doctoral Dissertations*. No. 41, 1943. Pp. 81-88.

Hoffman, Frederick J. *The Modern Novel in America, 1900-1950*. Chicago: Regnery, 1951. 216 p.

Hoffman, Frederick J. "Psychoanalysis and Literary Criticism." *Amer. Quart.*, 2:144-154, 1950.

Hoffman, Frederick J. "Psychology and Literature." *Lit. & Psychol.*, 6:111-115, 1956.

Hollander, Edwin P. "Popular Literature in the Undergraduate Social Psychology Course." *Amer. Psychologist*, 11:95-96, 1956.

Hollingsworth, Alan M. "Freud, Conrad and The Future of an Illusion." *Lit. & Psychol.*, 5:78-83, 1955.

Hopwood, V. G. "Dream, Magic and Poetry." *J. Aesthetics & Art Criticism*, 10:152-159, 1951.

Hulbeck, Charles R. "The Creative Personality." *Amer. J. Psychoanalysis*, 5:49-58, 1945.

Humboldt, Charles. "The Human Essence in Soviet Fiction." *Mainstream*, 11:3-32, 1958.

Humphrey, Robert. "Form and Function of Stream of Consciousness in William Faulkner's *The Sound and the Fury*." *University of Kansas City Review*, 19:24-40, 1952.

Humphrey, Robert. *Stream of Consciousness in the Modern Novel*. Berkeley: University of California Press, 1954. 127 p.

Hungerford, Edward A. "Mrs. Woolf, Freud, and J. D. Beresford." *Lit. & Psychol.*, 5:49-51, 1955.

Hunt, Everett L. "The Social Interpretation of Literature." *English J.*, 24:214-219, 1935.

Hyman, Stanley E. "Psychoanalysis and the Climate of Tragedy," in Nelson, Benjamin (Ed.), *Freud and the Twentieth Century*. NY: Meridian, 1957. Pp. 167-185.

Hyman, Stanley E. "The Psychoanalytic Criticism of Literature." *Western Review*, 12:106-115, 1948.

Jeffrey, L. N. "Browning as Psychologist: Three Notes." *Coll. Engl.*, 17:345-348, 1956.

Jekels, L. "The Riddle of Shakespeare's Macbeth," in *Selected Papers*. NY: International Universities Press, 1952.

Jones, Alexander E. "Mark Twain and Sexuality." *Publications of the Modern Lang. Assoc.*, 51:595-616, 1956.

Jones, Ernest. "The Death of Hamlet's Father." *Int. J. Psycho-Analysis*, 29:174-176, 1948.

Jones, Ernest. *Hamlet and Oedipus. A Classic Study in the Psychoanalysis of Literature*. NY: Doubleday Anchor, 1954. 194 p.

Jones, Ernest. "Literature," in *The Life and Work of Sigmund Freud*, Vol. 3. NY: Basic Books, 1957. Pp. 417-431.

Jung, Carl G. "Psychology and Literature," in *Modern Man in Search of a Soul*. NY: Harcourt, Brace, 1933. 244 p.

Kahn, S. J. "Psychology in Coleridge's Poetry." *J. Aesthet.*, 9:208-226, 1951.

Kanzer, Mark. "Applied Psychoanalysis. Arts and Aesthetics." *The Annual Survey of Psychoanalysis*, 2:438-493, 1954; 3:511-546, 1956; 4:355-389, 1957. NY: International Universities Press.

Kanzer, Mark. "Dostoyevsky's Matricidal Impulses." *Psychoanalytic Review*, 35:115-125, 1948.

Kanzer, Mark. "The Central Theme in Shakespeare's Works." *Psychoanalytic Review*, 38:1-16, 1951.

Kanzer, Mark. "Contemporary Psychoanalytic Views of Aesthetics." *J. Amer. Psychoanalytic Assoc.*, 5:515-524, 1957.

Kanzer, Mark. "Gogol: A Study of Wit and Paranoia." *J. Amer. Psychoanalytic Assoc.*, 3:110-125, 1955.

Kanzer, Mark. "The Oedipus Trilogy." *Psychoanalytic Quart.*, 9:561-572, 1950.

Kanzer, Mark. "The 'Passing of the Oedipus Complex' in Greek Drama." *Int. J. Psycho-Analysis*, 29:1-4, 1948.
Kanzer, Mark & Tarachow, Sidney. "Applied Psychoanalysis. Arts and Aesthetics." *The Annual Survey of Psychoanalysis* 1:363-389, 1952. NY: International Universities Press.
Kaplan, Charles. "Holden and Huck: the Odysseys of Youth." *College English*, 18:76-80, 1956.
Karpe, Marietta. "The Origins of Peter Pan." *Psychoanalytic Review*, 43:104-110, 1956.
Karpe, Marietta, & Karpe, Richard. "The Meaning of Barrie's 'Mary Rose'." *Int. J. Psycho-Analysis*, 38:408-411, 1957.
Kaufman, F. W., & Taylor, W. S. "Literature as Adjustment." *J. Abn. & Soc. Psychol.*, 31:229-234, 1936.
Kligerman, Charles. "A Psychoanalytic Study of the Confessions of St. Augustine." *J. Amer. Psychoanalytic Assoc.*, 5:469-484, 1957.
Kligerman, Charles. "Psychology of Herman Melville." *Psychoanalytic Review*, 40:125-143, 1953.
Knight, Everett W. *Literature Considered as Philosophy*. NY: Macmillan, 1958. 240 p.
Krapf, E. Edward. "Shylock and Antonio: A Psychoanalytic Study of Shakespeare and Antisemitism." *Psychoanalytic Review*, 42:113-130, 1955.
Kris, Ernst. "Psychoanalysis and the Study of Creative Imagination." *Bull. N.Y. Academy Medicine*, 29:334, 1953.
Kris, Ernst. *Psychoanalytic Explorations in Art*. NY: International Universities Press, 1952. 358 p.
Kris, Ernst & Kurz, O. *Die Legende vom Künstler*. Vienna: Krystall Verlag, 1934.

Laforgue, René. *The Defeat of Beaudelaire*. London: Hogarth, 1932.
Landis, Paul N. *The Psychological Treatment of the Historical Novel*. Urbana: University of Illinois Ph. D. dissertation, 1926.
Langer, Marie. "Viaje al Centro de al Tierra (Julio Verne); Une Fantasia de Adolescente." *Rev. Psicoanal.*, B. Aires, 7:3-9, 1949.
Lee, Harry B. "The Creative Imagination." *Psychoanalytic Quart.*, 18:351-360, 1949.
Lee, Irving J. "A Study of Emotional Appeal in Rhetorical Theory, with Special Reference to Invention, Arrangement, and Style." *Summaries of Doctoral Dissertations*, Northwestern Univ., 7:36-40, 1939.
Lesser, Simon O. "The Attitude of Fiction." *Modern Fiction Studies*, 2:47-55, 1956.
Lesser, Simon O. *Fiction and the Unconscious*. Boston: Beacon, 1957. 322 p.
Lesser, Simon O. "Freud and Hamlet Again." *Amer. Imago*, 12:207-220, 1955.

Lesser, Simon O. "The Functions of Form in Narrative Art." *Psychiatry*, 18:51-63, 1955.

Lesser, Simon O. "Some Unconscious Elements in the Responses to Fiction." *Lit. & Psychol.*, 4:2-5, 1953.

Lesser, Simon O. "Tragedy, Comedy and the Esthetic Experience." *Lit. & Psychol.*, 6:131-139, 1956.

Levey, Harry B. "Poetry Production as a Supplemental Emergency Defense Against Anxiety." *Psychoanalytic Quart.*, 7:232-242, 1938.

Levi, Joseph. "Hawthorne's *The Scarlet Letter:* A Psychoanalytic Interpretation." *Amer. Imago*, 10:291-306, 1953.

Levin, Meyer. "A New Fear in Writers." *Psychoanalysis*, 2:34-38, 1953.

Lewandowski, Herbert. *Das Sexualproblem in der modernen Literatur und Kunst. . . . Seit 1800.* Dresden: Aretz, 1927.

Lind, Sidney E. "Poe and Mesmerism." *Publications of the Modern Lang. Assoc.*, 57:1077-1094, 1947.

Loeli, Giorgio. "Alcoholism and Homosexuality in Tennessee Williams' 'Cat on a Hot Tin Roof'." *Quart. J. Stud. Alcohol.*, 17:543-553, 1956.

Lowenthal, Leo. *Literature and the Image of Man. Sociological Studies of the European Drama and Novel, 1600-1900.* Boston: Beacon, 1957. 242 p.

Lowenthal, Leo. "The Sociology of Literature," in Schramm, Wilbur (Ed.), *Communications in Modern Society.* Urbana: University of Illinois Press, 1948. Pp. 83-100.

Lucas, Frank L. *Literature and Psychology.* Ann Arbor, Mich: Ann Arbor Books, 1957. 339 p.

McCarthy, Harold T. *Henry James: The Creative Process.* NY: Yoseloff, 1958. 172 p.

McCole, Camille J. "Sherwood Anderson, Congenital Freudian." *Catholic World*, 130:129-133, 1929.

McColley, Grant (Ed.) *Literature and Science: An Anthology from English and American Literature, 1600-1900.* Chicago: Packard, 1940. 528 p.

McCurdy, Harold G. "Aesthetic Choice as a Personality Function." *J. Aesthet. & Art Criticism*, 12:373-377, 1954.

McCurdy, Harold G. "Literature and Personality." *Character & Personality*, 7:300-308, 1939.

McCurdy, Harold G. "Literature and Personality: Analysis of the Novels of D. H. Lawrence." *Character & Personality*, 8:181-203; 311-322, 1940.

McCurdy, Harold G. "Literature as a Resource in Personality Study: Theory and Methods." *J. Aesthetics & Art Criticism*, 8:42-46, 1949.

McCurdy, Harold G. *The Personality of Shakespeare; a Venture in Psychological Method.* New Haven: Yale University Press, 1953. 243 p.

McCurdy, Harold G. *Psychological Analysis of Literary Productions as a Revelation of Personality.* Doctoral dissertation, Duke University, 1938.

McCurdy, Harold G. "A Study of the Novels of Charlotte and Emily Bronte As an Expression of Their Personalities." *J. Personality,* 16:109-152, 1947.

McCusker, L. G. "Creative Teaching Through Fiction." *Education,* 77:276-280, 1957.

Maier, Norman R. F. & Reninger, H. Willard. *A Psychological Approach to Literary Criticism.* NY: Appleton, 1933. 154 p.

M. Aloyse, Sister. "The Novelist as Popularizer: Joyce and 'Psychological' Fiction," in Feehan, Joseph (Ed.), *Dedalus on Crete: Essays on the Implications of Joyce's Portrait.* Los Angeles: St. Thomas More Guild, 1956. Pp. 29-42.

Manheim, Leonard F. *The Dickens Pattern—A Study in Psychoanalytic Criticism.* Microfilm Abstracts, 10:218-219, 1950.

Manheim, Leonard F. "The Law as Father." *Amer. Imago,* 12:17-23, 1955.

Manheim, Leonard F. "The Personal History of David Copperfield: A Study in Psychoanalytic Criticism." *Amer. Imago,* 9:21-43, 1952.

Mann, Thomas. "Freud and the Future." *Int. J. Psycho-Analysis,* 37: 106-115, 1956.

Mann, Thomas. *Freud, Goethe, Wagner.* NY: Knopf, 1937. 211 p.

Marcuse, Ludwig. "Freud's Aesthetik." *Publications of the Modern Lang. Assoc.,* 72:446-463, 1957.

Martin, A. R., Trilling. L., & Vivas, E. "The Legacy of Sigmund Freud: An Appraisal." *Kenyon Review,* 2:135-185, 1940.

Menninger, C. F. "The Insanity of Hamlet." *Bull. Menninger Clinic,* 6:1-8, 1952.

Miller, Milton L. "Balzac's Père Goriot." *Psychoanalytic Quart.,* 6:78-85, 1937.

Miller, Milton L. *Nostalgia: A Psychoanalytic Study of Marcel Proust.* Boston: Houghton, Mifflin, 1956. 306 p.

Moloney, James M., & Rockelein, Laurence. "A New Interpretation of Hamlet." *Int. J. Psycho-Analysis,* 30:92-107, 1949.

Monroe, Nellie E. *The Novel and Society.* Chapel Hill, NC: University of North Carolina Press, 1941. 282 p.

Moore, Merrill. "Notes on a Limerick." *Amer. Imago,* 13:147-148, 1956.

Moore, Merrill. "Some Psychiatric Considerations Concerning Creative Writings and Criticism." *Amer. J. Psychiatry,* 112:423-429, 1955.

Morgan, Douglas N. "Creativity Today: A Constructive Analytic Review of Certain Philosophical and Psychological Work." *J. Aesthetics & Art Criticism,* 12:1-24, 1953.

Morgan, Douglas N. "Psychology and Art Today." *J. Aesthetics & Art Criticism,* 9:81-96, 1950.

Morley, Helena. *The Diary of "Helena Morley."* NY: Farrar, Straus & Cudahy, 1957. 281 p.

Morrell, Roy. "The Psychology of Tragic Pleasure." *Essays in Criticism* (Oxford), 6:22-37, 1956.

Morris, Ruth. "The Novel As Catharsis." *Psychoanalytic Review,* 31:88-104, 1944.

Mullahy, Patrick. *Oedipus: Myth and Complex.* NY: Hermitage, 1948. 538 p.

Muller, Armand. "L'art et la psychoanalyse." *Rev. Franç. Psychanal.,* 17:297-319, 1953.

Murray, Henry A. "Personality and Creative Imagination." *English Institute Annual,* 1942. Pp. 139-162.

Myers, Henry A. *Tragedy—A View of Life.* Ithaca: Cornell University Press, 1956. 224 p.

Nelson, Benjamin (Ed.). *Freud: On Creativity and the Unconscious.* NY: Harper Torchbooks, 1958. 310 p.

Neumann, Erich. *Amor and Psyche: The Psychic Development of the Feminine, a Commentary on the Tale of Apuleius.* NY: Pantheon, 1956. 181 p.

O'Brien, Justin. *The Novel of Adolescence in France.* NY: Columbia University Press, 1937. 240 p.

Oberndorf, Clarence P. *Oliver Wendell Holmes: Psychiatric Novels.* NY: Columbia University Press, 1946. 274 p.

Oberndorf, Clarence P. "Psychoanalysis in Literature and Its Therapeutic Value," in Róheim, Géza (Ed.), *Psychoanalysis and the Social Sciences.* NY: International Universities Press, 1947. Pp. 297-310.

Odier, Charles. "A Literary Portrayal of Ambivalence." *Int. J. Psycho-Analysis,* 4:321-322, 1923.

Offenbacher, E. "Contributions to the Origin of Strindberg's Miss Julia." *Psychoanalytic Review,* 31:81-87, 1944.

Ortega y Gasset, José. *The Dehumanization of Art and Notes on the Novel.* Princeton: Princeton University Press, 1948. 103 p.

Parker, Clifford S. *The Defense of the Child by French Novelists.* Menasha, Wisconsin: Banta, 1925. 140 p.

Paul, Sherman. *The Shores of America: Thoreau's Inward Exploration.* Urbana: U. of Illinois Press, 1958. 432 p.

Pauncz, Arpad. "The Lear Complex in World Literature." *Amer. Imago,* 11:51-83, 1954.

Pauncz, Arpad. "Psychopathology of Shakespeare's King Lear." *Amer. Imago,* 9:57-78, 1952.

Pederson-Krag, Geraldine. "Detective Stories and the Primal Scene." *Psychoanalytic Quart.,* 18:207-214, 1949.

Petrullo, Helen B. "The Neurotic Hero of Typee." *Amer. Imago,* 12:317-323, 1955.

Phillips, William (Ed.). *Art and Psychoanalysis.* NY: Criterion, 1957. 552 p.

Plank, Robert. "Portraits of Fictitious Psychiatrists." *Amer. Imago,* 13: 259-267, 1956.

Plottke, Paul. "Individual Psychology in the Analysis of Literature: Dr. Jekyll and Mr. Hyde." *Indiv. Psychol. Bull.,* 9:9-17, 1951.

Poggioli, Renato. *The Phoenix and the Spider: A Book of Essays about Some Russian Writers and Their View of the Self.* Cambridge, Mass: Harvard University Press, 1957. 238 p.

Pollock, Thomas C. *The Nature of Literature: Its Relations to Science, Language, and Human Experience.* Princeton: Princeton University Press, 1942. 318 p.

Portnoy, I. "The Magic Skin: A Psychoanalytic Interpretation." *Amer. J. Psychoanalysis,* 9:67-74, 1949.

Preger, J. W. "A Note on William Blake's Lyrics." *Int. J. Psycho-Analysis,* 1:196-199, 1920.

Proctor-Gregg, Nancy. "Variation on a Theme," in Lorand, Sandor (Ed.), *Yearbook of Psychoanalysis,* 10:251-257. NY: International Universities Press, 1955.

Rahv, Philip. *Image and Idea.* Norfolk, Conn: New Directions, 1957. 241 p.

Ramsay, A. W. "Psychology and Literary Criticism." *Criterion,* 15:627-643, 1936.

Rank, Otto. *The Myth of the Birth of the Hero.* NY: Brunner, 1952. 100 p.

Ransom, John Crowe. "Freud and Literature." *Saturday Review Lit.,* 1:161-162, 1924.

Raushenbush, Esther. *Literature for Individual Education.* NY: Columbia University Press, 1942. 262 p.

Read, Herbert. *The Nature of Literature.* NY: Grove, 1958. 381 p.

Read, Herbert. "Psychoanalysis and the Problem of Aesthetic Value," in Lorand, Sandor (Ed.), *Yearbook of Psychoanalysis,* 8:344-360. NY: International Universities Press, 1952.

Reed, Raoul. "Psychoanalysis in Literature." *Freeman,* 5:490-491, 1922.

Reik, Theodor. "In My Mind's Eye, Horatio." *Complex,* 7:15-31, 1952.

Reik, Theodor. "Jessica, My Child!" *Amer. Imago,* 8:3-27, 1951.

Reik, Theodor. "The Psychology of Irony: A Study Based on Anatole France." *Complex,* 1:14-26, 1950.

Reik, Theodor. *The Secret Self: Psychoanalytic Experiences in Life and Literature.* NY: Farrar, Straus & Young, 1952. 329 p.

Rein, David M. "Conrad Aiken and Psychoanalysis." *Psychoanalytic Review,* 42:402-411, 1955.

Riesman, David. *The Oral Tradition, the Written Word, and the Screen Image.* Yellow Springs, Ohio: Antioch Press, 1956. 40 p.

Rinaker, Clarissa. "A Psychoanalytic Note on Jane Austen." *Psychoanalytic Quart.,* 5:108-115, 1936.

Riviere, Joan. "The Inner World in Ibsen's *Master Builder.*" *Int. J. Psycho-Analysis,* 33:173-180, 1952.

Riviere, Joan. "The Unconscious Phantasy of an Inner World Reflected in Examples from English Literature." *Int. J. Psycho-Analysis,* 33: 160-172, 1952.

Roback, A. A. "The Psychology of Literature," in Roback, A. A. (Ed.), *Present-Day Psychology.* NY: Philosophical, 1954. Pp. 867-896.

Robbe-Grillet, Alain. "A Fresh Start for Fiction." *Evergreen Review,* 1:97-104, 1958.

Roberts, Donald R. "A Freudian View of Jonathan Swift." *Lit. & Psychol.,* 6:8-17, 1956.

Rose, William. "The Psychological Approach To Literature," in *German Studies.* Oxford, England: Blackwell, 1952.

Rosenblatt, Louise M. *Literature As Exploration.* NY: Appleton-Century, 1938. 340 p.

Rosenzweig, Saul. "The Ghost of Henry James: A Study of Thematic Apperception." *Character & Personality,* 12:79-100, 1943.

Rosenzweig, Saul. "The James' Stream of Consciousness." *Contemporary Psych.,* 3:250-257, 1958.

Ross, T. A. "A Note on the Merchant of Venice." *Brit. Med. Psychol.,* 14:303-311, 1934.

Sachs, Hanns. *The Creative Unconscious; Studies in the Psychoanalysis of Art* (2nd Ed.). Cambridge, Mass.: Sci-Art, 1951. 358 p.

Sachs, Hanns. "Edgar Allen Poe." *Psychoanalytic Quart.,* 4:294-306, 1935.

Sachs, Wulf. *Black Anger.* NY: Grove, 1957. 324 p.

Sachs, Wulf. *Psychoanalysis: Its Meaning and Practical Applications.* London: Cassell, 1934. 246 p.

Sartre, Jean-Paul. *The Psychology of Imagination.* NY: Philosophical Library, 1948. 285 p.

Schilder, Paul. "Psychoanalytic Remarks on Alice in Wonderland and Lewis Carroll." *J. Nervous & Mental Disease,* 1938.

Schneider, Daniel E. *The Psychoanalyst and the Artist.* NY: International Universities Press, 1954. 306 p.

Schoen, M. "Aesthetic Experience in the Light of Current Psychology." *J. Aesthetics & Art Criticism,* 1:23-33, 1941.

Schorer, Mark (Ed.). *Society and Self in the Novel.* NY: Columbia University Press, 1956. 155 p.

Schreck, Alfred. "Analyse des Entstehens eines lyrischen Gedichtes." *Z. Psychother. med. Psychol.,* 2:149-152, 1952.

Schücking, Levin. *The Sociology of Literary Taste.* NY: Oxford University Press, 1944. 78 p.

Schwartz, Emanuel K. "A Psychoanalytic Study of the Fairy Tale." *Amer. J. Psychotherapy,* 10:740-762, 1956.

Segal, Hanna. "A Psycho-Analytical Approach to Aesthetics." *Int. J. Psycho-Analysis,* 33:196-207, 1952.

Selander, S. "The Influence of Psycho-Analysis in Modern Literature." *Dagens Nyheter,* December 5-6, 1931.

Seyppel, Joachim H. "The Animal Theme and Totemism in Franz Kafka." *Lit. & Psychol.,* 4:49-65, 1954.

Sharpe, Ella F. "From King Lear to the Tempest." *Int. J. Psycho-Analysis,* 27:19-30, 1946.

Sharpe, Ella F. "Psycho-Analytic View of Shakespeare," in Brierly, Marjorie (Ed.), *Collected Papers on Psycho-Analysis.* NY: Anglobooks, 1952. 280 p.

Sharpe, Ella F. "Psychophysical Problems Revealed in Language: An Examination of Metaphor," in *Collected Papers on Psycho-Analysis.* London: Hogarth, 1950.

Sharpe, Ella F. "An Unfinished Paper on Hamlet." *Int. J. Psycho-Analysis,* 39:98-109, 1948.

Shrodes, Caroline, Van Gundy, Justine, & Husband, Richard (Eds.). *Psychology Through Literature.* NY: Oxford University Press, 1943. 389 p.

Sievers, W. David. *Freud on Broadway: A History of Psychoanalysis and the American Drama.* NY: Hermitage, 1955. 479 p.

Singer, Irving (Ed.). "Literary Psychology," in *Essays in Literary Criticism of George Santayana.* NY: Scribners, 1956. Pp. 394-401.

Siyavusgil, Sabri E. "Les problèmes psychologiques de la personnalité littraire," in Baumgarten, Franziska (Ed.), *La Psychotechnique dans le Monde Moderne.* Paris: Presses Universitaires de France, 1952. Pp. 111-117.

Skinner, John. "Lewis Carroll's Adventures in Wonderland." *Amer. Imago,* 4:3-31, 1947.

Slochower, Harry. "Freud and Marx in Contemporary Literature." *Sewanee Review,* 49:315-324, 1941.

Slochower, Harry. "Freudian Motifs in 'Moby Dick'." *Complex,* 16-25, 1950.

Slochower, Harry. "Shakespeare's Hamlet: The Myth of Modern Sensibility." *Amer. Imago,* 7:197-238, 1950.

Spiegel, Leo A. "The New Jargon: Psychology in Literature." *Sewanee Review,* 40:476-491, 1932.

Splaver, Sarah. "The Career Novel." *Personnel & Guidance J.,* 31:371-372, 1953.

Steinberg, A. H. "Fitzgerald's Portrait of a Psychiatrist." *University of Kansas City Review,* 21:219-222, 1955.

Steinberg, A. H. "Hardness, Light, and Psychiatry in *Tender is the Night.*" *Lit. & Psychol.,* 3:3-8, 1953.

Steinberg, Erwin. "Freudian Symbolism and Communication." *Lit. & Psychol.,* 3:2-5, 1953.

Stekel, Wilhelm. "Poetry and Neurosis." *Psychoanalytic Review,* 10:73-96, 190-208, 316-328, 457-466, 1922; 11:48-60, 1923.

Sterba, Editha. "The School Boy Suicide in André Gide's Novel *The Counterfeiters.*" *Amer. Imago,* 8:307-320, 1951.

Sterba, Richard. "The Problem of Art in Freud's Writings." *Psychoanalytic Quart.,* 9:256-268, 1940.

Svendsen, Kester, & Mentz, Samuel I. "Relations of Literature and Science, Selected Bibliography for 1953." *Symposium*, 8:208-213, 1954.

Symons, Norman. "The Graveyard Scene in 'Hamlet'." *Int. J. Psycho-Analysis*, 9:96-119, 1928.

Taylor, Velma L. *An Analysis of Fictional Short Stories Found in Current Magazines Read Most Often by Indiana High School Students with Reference to Treatment of American Social Classes*. Bloomington, Indiana: University of Indiana. Unpublished Ph. D. Thesis, 1953. 191 p.

Trilling, Lionel. *Freud and the Crisis of our Culture*. Boston: Beacon, 1955, 59 p.

Trilling, Lionel. "Freud and Literature," in Schorer, Mark (Ed.), *Criticism, The Foundation of Modern Literary Judgment*. NY: Harcourt, Brace, 1948. 553 p.

Trilling, Lionel. *A Gathering of Fugitives*. Boston: Beacon, 1956. 167 p.

Trilling, Lionel. "The Legacy of Sigmund Freud; II: Literary and Aesthetic." *Kenyon Review*, 2:162-168, 1940.

Trilling, Lionel. *The Liberal Imagination*. NY: Viking, 1950. 303 p.

Trollope, L. "Freud and Literature." *Horizons*, 1947.

Tymms, Ralph. *Doubles in Literary Psychology*. Cambridge, England: Bowes and Bowes, 1949. 126 p.

Van Bark, Bella S. " 'The Sudden Guest'—A Critical Analysis." *Amer. J. Psychoanalysis*, 8:59-62, 1948.

Vandenberg, Steven G. "Great Expectations or The Future of Psychology (As Seen in Science Fiction)." *Amer. Psychologist*, 11:339-342, 1956.

Vander Sterren, H. A. "*The King Oedipus* of Sophocles," in Lorand, Sandor (Ed.), *The Yearbook of Psychoanalysis*, 9:314-327. NY: International Universities Press, 1953.

Vollmerhausen, Joseph W. "Pavilion of Women: A Psychoanalytic Interpretation." *Amer. J. Psychoanalysis*, 10:53-60, 1950.

Wangh, Martin. "Othello: The Tragedy of Iago." *Psychoanalytic Quart.*, 9:202-212, 1950.

Wangh, Martin. "The Scope of the Contribution of Psychoanalysis to the Biography of the Artist." *J. Amer. Psychoanalytic Assoc.*, 5:564-575, 1957.

Webster, Peter D. "A Critical Examination of Franz Kafka's 'The Castle'." *Amer. Imago*, 8:35-60, 1951.

Weissman, Philip. "Conscious and Unconscious Autobiographical Dramas of Eugene O'Neill." *J. Amer. Psychoanalytic Assoc.*, 5:432-441, 1957.

Wellek, Rene & Warren, Austin. "Literature and Psychology," in *Theory of Literature*. NY: Harvest, 1956. Ch. 8.

White, R. K. "Black Boy: A Value Analysis." *J. Abn. & Soc. Psychol.*, 42:440-461, 1947.

White, Robert W. *Lives in Progress.* NY: Dryden, 1952. 376 p.

White, William. "Father and Son: Some Comments on Hemingway's Psychology." *Dalhousie Review,* 31:276-284, 1952.

Wilbur, George B. & Muensterberger, Warner (Eds.) *Psychoanalysis and Culture.* NY: International Universities Press, 1951. 462 p.

Wile, Ira S. "The Personality of King Lear As A Young Man." *Amer. J. Orthopsychiatry,* 5:325-336, 1935.

Wilmer, Harry A. "Saturday's Psychiatrist." *Amer. Imago,* 12:179-186, 1955.

Wilson, Robert N. "Literary Experience and Personality." *J. Aesthetics & Art Criticism,* 15:47-57, 1956.

Wilson, Robert N. "Literature, Society, and Personality." *J. Aesthet. & Art Criticism,* 10:297-309, 1952.

Wise, Carroll A. *Psychiatry and the Bible.* NY: Harper, 1956. 169 p.

Wolfenstein, Martha. "Analysis of a Juvenile Poem," in Eissler, Ruth S., et al. (Eds.), *The Psychoanalytic Study of the Child,* 11:450-472. NY: International Universities Press, 1956.

Wolfenstein, Martha. *Children's Humor; A Psychological Analysis.* Glencoe, Ill: Free Press, 1954. 224 p.

Wood, Austin B. "Psychodynamics Through Literature." *Amer. Psychologist,* 10:32-33, 1955.

Wood, Margaret M. *Paths of Loneliness.* NY: Columbia University Press, 1954. 250 p.

Wormhoudt, Arthur. "Cold Pastoral." *Amer. Imago,* 8:275-285, 1951.

Wormhoudt, Arthur. *The Demon Lover: A Psychoanalytic Approach to Literature.* NY: Exposition, 1949. 150 p.

Wormhoudt, Arthur. "The Five Layer Structure of Sublimation and Literary Analysis." *Amer. Imago,* 13:205-219, 1956.

Wormhoudt, Arthur. "Freud and Literary Theory." *Amer. Imago,* 6:217-25, 1949.

Wormhoudt, Arthur. *Hamlet's Mouse Trap; A Psychoanalytic Study of the Drama.* NY: Philosophical, 1956, 221 p.

Wormhoudt, Arthur. "A Psychoanalytic Interpretation of 'The Love Song of J. Alfred Prufrock'." *Perspective,* 2:109-117, 1949.

Wright, Celeste T. "Katherine Mansfield and the 'Secret Smile'." *Lit. & Psychol.,* 5:44-48, 1955.

Wyatt, Frederick. "Some Comments on the Use of Symbols in the Novel." *Lit. & Psychol.,* 4:15-23, 1954.

Textbooks on Adolescence

Inasmuch as extensive bibliographies on the psychology and development of the adolescent are easily accessible to the student, the citations that follow are merely representative of the literature. The list consists primarily of textbooks, with just a sprinkling of articles from professional journals. In addition, the reader will find herein some books which do not deal with adolescents exclusively, but which are directly related in one way or another to their growth.

Abel, Theodora M. & Kinder, E. F. *The Subnormal Adolescent Girl.* NY: Columbia University Press, 1942, 215 p.

Adler, Alfred. *The Education of Children.* NY: Greenberg, 1930, 309 p.

Adolescence. Forty-Third Yearbook of the National Society for the Study of Education, Part I. Chicago: University of Chicago Press, 1944.

Aichhorn, August. *Wayward Youth.* NY: Viking, 1935, 249 p.

Alexander, Franz. *Fundamentals of Psychoanalysis.* NY: Norton, 1948, 312 p.

Allport, Gordon W. *Becoming.* New Haven: Yale University Press, 1955, 106 p.

Almy, Millie. *Child Development.* NY: Holt, 1955, 490 p.

Anderson, John E. *The Psychology of Development and Personality Adjustment.* NY: Holt, 1949, 720 p.

Ashley-Montagu, M. F. *Adolescent Sterility.* Springfield, Ill: Thomas, 1946, 148 p.

Ausubel, David P. *Theory and Problems of Adolescent Development.* NY: Grune & Stratton, 1954, 580 p.

Baldwin, Alfred L., Kalhorn J., & Breese, F. H. *Patterns of Parent Behavior.* Washington, DC: American Psychological Association, 1945. Psychological Monograph 58, No. 268.

Balser, Benjamin H. (Ed.). *Psychotherapy of the Adolescent.* NY: International Universities Press, 1957, 270 p.

Barker, Roger G. & Wright, Herbert F. *The Midwest and Its Children: The Psychological Ecology of an American Town.* Evanston, Ill: Row, Peterson, 1955, 532 p.

Barron, Milton L. *The Juvenile in Delinquent Society.* NY: Knopf, 1954, 347 p.

Baruch, Dorothy. *How To Live with Your Teen-ager.* NY: McGraw-Hill, 1953, 261 p.

Baruch, Dorothy. *New Ways in Discipline.* NY: Whittlesey, 1949, 280 p.

Beauvoir, Simone de. *The Second Sex.* NY: Knopf, 1953, 732 p.

Benedict, Ruth. *Patterns of Culture.* NY: New American Library, 1952, 272 p.

Bernard, Harold W. *Adolescent Development in American Culture.* Yonkers, NY: World, 1957, 644 p.

Bernfeld, Siegfried. "Types of Adolescence." *Psychoanalytic Quart.,* VII, 1938.

Bettelheim, Bruno. *Symbolic Wounds: Puberty Rites and the Envious Male.* Glencoe, Ill: Free Press, 1954, 286 p.

Black, John W. & Ausherman, Marian. *The Vocabulary of College Students in Classroom Speeches.* Columbus, Ohio: Bureau of Educational Research, The Ohio State University, 1955, 68 p.

Bloch, Herbert A. & Flynn, Frank T. *Delinquency: The Juvenile Offender in America Today.* NY: Random, 1956, 612 p.

Bloch, Herbert A. & Niederhoffer, Arthur. *The Gang: A Study in Adolescent Behavior.* NY: Philosophical, 1958, 231 p.

Blood, Robert O. *Anticipating Your Marriage.* Glencoe, Ill: Free Press, 1955, 482 p.

Blos, Peter. *The Adolescent Personality. A Study of Individual Behavior.* NY: Appleton-Century-Crofts, 1941, 517 p.

Bornstein, Berta. "On Latency," in Eissler, R. S. et al. (Eds.). *The Psychoanalytic Study of the Child,* 6:279-285. NY: International Universities Press, 1951.

Bromley, Dorothy D. & Britten, F. H. *Youth and Sex. A Study of 1300 College Students.* NY: Harper, 1938, 303 p.

Brown, Fred & Kempton, Rudolf T. *Sex Questions and Answers.* NY: McGraw-Hill, 1950, 264 p.

Butterfield, Oliver McK. *Love Problems of Adolescence.* NY: Emerson, 1939, 212 p.

Carmichael, Leonard (Ed.). *Manual of Child Psychology.* NY: Wiley, 1954, 1295 p.

Cohen, Albert K. *Delinquent Boys: The Culture of the Gang.* Glencoe, Ill: Free Press, 1955, 202 p.

Cole, Luella. *Attaining Maturity.* NY: Farrar & Rinehart, 1944, 212 p.

Cole, Luella. *Psychology of Adolescence.* NY: Rinehart, 1954, 712 p.

Cole, Luella & Morgan, John J. B. *Psychology of Childhood and Adolescence.* NY: Rinehart, 1947, 416 p.

Crow, Lester D. & Crow, Alice. *Adolescent Development and Adjustment.* NY: McGraw-Hill, 1956, 555 p.

Cruickshank, William M. (Ed.). *Psychology of Exceptional Children and Youth.* NY: Prentice-Hall, 1955, 594 p.

Cruze, Wendell W. *Adolescent Psychology and Development.* NY: Ronald, 1953, 278 p.

Cutts, Norma E. & Moseley, Nicholas. *The Only Child.* NY: Putnam, 1954, 245 p.

Davis, Allison & Dollard, John. *Children of Bondage: The Personality Development of Negro Youth in the Urban South.* Washington, DC: American Council on Education, 1940, 299 p.

Davis, Allison & Havighurst, Robert J. *Father of the Man.* Boston: Houghton, Mifflin, 1947, 245 p.

Deutsch, Helene. *The Psychology of Women.* NY: Grune & Stratton, 1944-45, 2 Vols.

Devereux, George. *Therapeutic Education.* NY: Harper, 1956, 424 p.

Dollard, John, et al. *Frustration and Aggression.* New Haven: Yale University Press, 1939, 209 p.

Dreikurs, Rudolf. *Psychology in the Classroom.* NY: Harper, 1957, 237 p.

Eckert, Ralph G. *Sex Attitudes in the Home.* NY: Association, 1956, 242 p.

Edelston, H. *Problems of Adolescence.* NY: Philosophical Library, 1957, 174 p.

Education. "Helping Adolescents Meet Their Problems" (Complete issue). December 1955.

Eissler, K. R. (Ed.). *Searchlights on Delinquency.* NY: International Universities Press, 1949, 474 p.

Eissler, Ruth S., Freud, Anna, Hartmann, Heinz, & Kris, Ernst (Eds.). *The Psychoanalytic Study of the Child,* Vols. I-XIII. NY: International Universities Press, 1946-1958.

Elias, L. I. *High School Youths Look at Their Problems.* Agric. Experim. Station, State College of Washington, 1947, 101 p.

Elliott, Grace. *Understanding the Adolescent Girl.* NY: Womans Press, 1949, 134 p.

Eng, Helga K. *Psychology of Child and Youth Drawing from the Ninth to the Twenty-Fourth Year.* London: Routledge, 1957, 205 p.

English, O. Spurgeon & Pearson, Gerald H. J. *Emotional Problems of Living.* NY: Norton, 1955, 592 p.

Erikson, Erik H. *Childhood and Society.* NY: Norton, 1950, 397 p.

Escalona, Sibylle. *Understanding Hostility in Children.* New Haven, Conn: Yale University Press, 1954, 48 p.

Espenshade, Anna. *Motor Performance in Adolescence.* Monographs of the Society for Research in Child Development, Vol. 5, No. 2, 1940, 126 p.

Faegre, Marion L. *The Adolescent in Your Family*. Washington, DC: Children's Bureau of Publications, 1954, 106 p.

Farnham, Marynia L. *The Adolescent*. NY: Harper, 1951, 243 p.

Fenichel, Otto. *The Psychoanalytic Theory of Neurosis*. NY: Norton, 1945, 703 p.

Fleming, Charlotte M. *Adolescence, Its Social Psychology*. NY: International Universities Press, 1949, 262 p.

Flugel, J. C. *The Psycho-Analytic Study of the Family*. London: Hogarth, 1931, 259 p.

Ford, C. S. & Beach, F. A. *Patterns of Sexual Behavior*. NY: Harper, 1951, 307 p.

Fraiberg, Selma. "Some Considerations in the Introduction to Therapy in Puberty," in Eissler, Ruth S., et al. (Eds.), *The Psychoanalytic Study of the Child*, 10:264-286. NY: International Universities Press, 1955.

Frank, Lawrence K. & Frank, Mary. *Your Adolescent at Home and in School*. NY: Viking, 1956, 336 p.

Frank, Lawrence K., et al. *Personality Development in Adolescent Girls*. New Orleans: Child Development Publications, Society for Research in Child Development, Inc., 1953 (Volume XVI, Serial No. 53), 316 p.

Friedlander, Kate. *The Psycho-Analytic Approach to Juvenile Delinquency*. NY: International Universities Press, 1947, 296 p.

Freud, Anna. *The Ego and the Mechanisms of Defense*. NY: International Universities Press, 1946, 196 p.

Freud, Anna. "Adolescence," in Eissler, Ruth S., et al. (Eds.). *The Psychoanalytic Study of the Child*, 13:254-278. NY: International Universities Press, 1958.

Freud, Sigmund. *The Ego and the Id*. London: Hogarth, 1927, 88 p.

Freud, Sigmund. "Three Essays on the Theory of Sexuality," in Strachey, James (Ed.), *Standard Edition of the Complete Psychological Works of Sigmund Freud*, Vol. 7. London: Hogarth & The Institute of Psycho-Analysis, 1953.

Fromm, Erich. *Man for Himself*. NY: Rinehart, 1947, 254 p.

Gaitskell, Charles D. & Gaitskell, M. R. *Art Education During Adolescence*. NY: Ryerson, 1954, 116 p.

Gallagher, J. Roswell & Harris, Herbert I. *Emotional Problems of Adolescents*. NY: Oxford University Press, 1958, 122 p.

Garrison, Karl C. "Adolescence," In Roback, A. A., *Present-day Psychology*. NY: Philosophical Library, 1955, 995 p.

Garrison, Karl C. *Psychology of Adolescence*. (5th Ed.) Englewood Cliffs, NJ: Prentice-Hall, 1956, 602 p.

Gerty, Ursula M. *The Adaptive Behavior of Adolescent Children Whose Mothers Were Hospitalized at Saint Elizabeths Hospital With a Diagnosis of Schizophrenia*. Washington, DC: Catholic University Press, 1955, 210 p.

Gesell, Arnold, Ilg, Frances L., & Ames, Louise Bates. *Youth: The Years From Ten To Sixteen*. NY: Harper, 1956, 542 p.

Gillespie, James M. & Allport, Gordon W. *Youth's Outlook on the Future*. Garden City, NY: Doubleday, 1955, 61 p.

Ginzberg, Eli, Ginsburg, Sol W., Axelrad, Sidney & Herma, John L. *Occupational Choice: An Approach To A General Theory*. NY: Columbia University Press, 1951, 271 p.

Glueck, Sheldon & Glueck, Eleanor. *Unravelling Juvenile Delinquency*. Cambridge, Mass: Harvard University Press, 1950, 399 p.

Gordon, C. W. *The Social System of the High School: A Study in the Sociology of Adolescence*. Glencoe, Ill: Free Press, 1957, 184 p.

Green, Sidney L. & Rothenberg, Alan B. *A Manual of First Aid for Mental Health in Childhood and Adolescence*. NY: Julian, 1953, 278 p.

Gruenberg, Sidonie M. (Ed.) *Our Children Today*. NY: Viking, 1952, 366 p.

Hall, G. S. *Adolescence: Its Psychology and its Relations to Physiology, Anthropology, Sociology, Sex, Crime, Religion and Education*. NY: Appleton-Century-Crofts, 1904, 2 Vols.

Harsh, Charles M. & Schrickel, H. G. *Personality: Development and Assessment*. NY: Ronald, 1950, 518 p.

Havighurst, Robert J. *Human Development and Education*. NY: Longmans, Green, 1953, 338 p.

Havighurst, Robert J., et al. *A Survey of the Education of Gifted Children*. Chicago: University of Chicago Press, 1955, 114 p.

Havighurst, Robert J. & Taba, Hilda. *Adolescent Character and Personality*. NY: Wiley, 1949, 315 p.

Hendrickson, Robert C. & Cook, Fred J. *Youth in Danger*. NY: Harcourt Brace, 1956, 300 p.

Hilgard, Ernest R. *Introduction to Psychology*. NY: Harcourt Brace, 1953, 659 p.

Hollingshead, August B. *Elmtown's Youth. The Impact of Social Classes on Adolescents*. NY: Wiley, 1949, 480 p.

Hopkins, L. Thomas. *The Emerging Self in Home and School*. NY: Harper, 1954, 366 p.

Horney, Karen. *The Neurotic Personality of Our Time*. NY: Norton, 1937, 299 p.

Horney, Karen. *Our Inner Conflicts*. NY: Norton, 1945, 250 p.

Horney, Karen. "Personality Changes in Female Adolescents." *Am. J. Orthopsychiatry*, 5:19-26, 1935.

Horrocks, John E. *The Psychology of Adolescence*. Boston: Houghton, Mifflin, 1951, 614 p.

Hunt, J. McV. (Ed.). *Personality and the Behavior Disorders*. NY: Ronald, 1944, 2 Vols.

Hurlock, Elizabeth B. *Adolescent Development*. NY: McGraw-Hill, 1955, 590 p.

Hurlock, Elizabeth B. *Developmental Psychology.* NY: McGraw-Hill, 1953, 556 p.

Inhelder, Bärbel & Piaget, Jean. *The Growth of Logical Thinking: From Childhood to Adolescence.* NY: Basic Books, 1958, 356 p.
Iovetz-Tereshchenko, Nicholai M. *Friendship-Love in Adolescence.* London: Allen & Unwin, 1936, 367 p.
Isaacs, Susan. *Childhood and After.* NY: International Universities Press, 1949, 245 p.

Jennings, Helen H. *Leadership and Isolation: A Study of Personality in Interpersonal Relationships.* NY: Longmans, 1950, 240 p.
Jersild, Arthur T. *In Search of Self.* NY: Teachers College, 1952, 147 p.
Jersild, Arthur T. *The Psychology of Adolescence.* NY: Macmillan, 1957, 439 p.
Jones, Ernest. "Some Problems of Adolescence." *Papers on Psycho-Analysis.* London: Baillière, Tindall, 5th Ed., 1948.
Jones, Harold E. *Development in Adolescence: Approaches to the Study of the Individual.* NY: Appleton-Century-Crofts, 1943, 166 p.
Jones, Harold E. *Motor Performance and Growth.* Berkeley, Calif: University of California Press, 1949, 181 p.
Josselyn, Irene M. *The Adolescent and His World.* NY: Family Service Association of America, 1954, 124 p.
Josselyn, Irene M. *The Happy Child. A Psychoanalytic Guide to Emotional and Social Growth.* NY: Random, 1955, 410 p.

Kardiner, Abram. *The Individual and His Society.* NY: Columbia University Press, 1939, 503 p.
Katz, Elihu & Lazarsfeld, Paul F. *Personal Influence.* Glencoe, Ill: Free Press, 1955, 400 p.
Katz, Irwin. *Conflict and Harmony in an Adolescent Interracial Group.* NY: New York University Press, 1955, 47 p.
Kinsey, Alfred C., et al. *Sexual Behavior in the Human Female.* Phila: Saunders, 1953, 842 p.
Kinsey, Alfred C., et al. *Sexual Behavior in the Human Male.* Phila: Saunders, 1948, 804 p.
Kluckhohn, Clyde & Kelly, William H. "The Concept of Culture," in Linton, Ralph (Ed.), *The Science of Man in the World Crisis.* NY: Columbia University Press, 1945, pp. 78-106.
Kluckhohn, Clyde & Murray, Henry (Eds.). *Personality in Nature, Society and Culture.* NY: Knopf, 1949, 561 p.
Krugman, Morris (Ed.). *Orthopsychiatry and the Schools.* NY: American Orthopsychiatric Association, 1958, 265 p.
Kuhlen, Raymond G. *The Psychology of Adolescent Development.* NY: Harper, 1952, 675 p.

Lawton, Shailer. *The Sexual Conduct of the Teen-Ager.* NY: Greenberg, 1951, 180 p.

Lee, Alfred McClung. *Fraternities without Brotherhood, A Study of Prejudice on the American Campus.* Boston: Beacon, 1955, 159 p.

Lehner, George F. J. & Kube, Ella. *The Dynamics of Personal Adjustment.* NY: Prentice-Hall, 1955, 498 p.

Lerrigo, Marion O. & Southard, Helen. *Learning about Love.* NY: Dutton, 1956, 62 p.

Levy, John & Munroe, Ruth L. *The Happy Family.* NY: Knopf, 1938, 319 p.

Liss, Edward. "Motivations in Learning," in Eissler, Ruth S., et al. (Eds.), *The Psychoanalytic Study of the Child,* 10:100-118. NY: International Universities Press, 1955.

Lloyd-Jones, Esther & Fedder, Ruth. *Coming of Age.* NY: Whittlesey, 1941, 280 p.

Lott, George M. *The Story of Human Emotions from a Teenage Viewpoint.* NY: Philosophical, 1958, 228 p.

Macfarlane, J. W., Allen, L., & Honzik, M. P. *A Developmental Study of the Behavior Problems of Normal Children between Twenty-One Months and Fourteen Years.* Berkeley: University of California Press, 1954, 22 p.

Mallinson, Vernon (Ed.). *The Adolescent at School: Experiments in Education.* London: Heinemann, 1949, 165 p.

Malm, M. & Jamison, O. G. *Adolescence.* NY: McGraw-Hill, 1952, 512 p.

Martin, W. E. & Stendler, C. B. *Child Development.* NY: Harcourt Brace, 1953, 519 p.

Mead, Margaret. *From the South Seas: Studies of Adolescence and Sex in Primitive Societies.* NY: Morrow, 1939.

Mead, Margaret. *Male and Female.* NY: Morrow, 1949, 477 p.

Merry, Frieda K. & Merry, Ralph V. *The First Two Decades of Life.* NY: Harper, 1950, 600 p.

Mohr, George J. & Despres, Marian A. *The Stormy Decade: Adolescence.* NY: Random, 1958, 272 p.

Munn, Norman L. *The Evolution and Growth of Human Behavior.* Boston: Houghton, Mifflin, 1955, 525 p.

Murdock, George P. "The Common Denominator of Cultures," in Linton, Ralph (Ed.), *The Science of Man in the World Crisis.* NY: Columbia University Press, 1945, pp. 123-142.

Murphy, Gardner. *Personality.* NY: Harper, 1947, 999 p.

Neisser, Edith G. *The Eldest Child.* NY: Harper, 1957, 174 p.

Nervous Child. "Difficulties of Adolescence in the Boy" (entire issue), Vol. 4, No. 2, 1944-45.

Nervous Child. "Difficulties of the Adolescent Girl" (entire issue), Vol. 4, No. 1, 1944-45.

Newman, F. B. *The Adolescent in Social Groups: Studies in the Observation of Personality.* Applied Psychology Monographs, No. 9, 1946.

Opler, Marvin K. *Culture, Psychiatry and Human Values*. Springfield, Ill: Thomas, 1956, 242 p.

Pearson, Gerald H. J. *Adolescence and the Conflict of Generations*. NY: Norton, 1958, 186 p.

Pearson, Gerald H. J. *Psychoanalysis and the Education of the Child*. NY: Norton, 1954, 357 p.

Pearson, Gerald H. J. "A Survey of Learning Difficulties in Children," in Eissler, Ruth S. et al. (Eds.), *The Psychoanalytic Study of the Child*, 7:322-386. NY: International Universities Press, 1952.

Peck, Harris B. & Bellsmith, Virginia. *Treatment of the Delinquent Adolescent*. NY: Family Service Association, 1955, 147 p.

Prescott, Daniel A. *The Child in the Educative Process*. NY: McGraw-Hill, 1957, 502 p.

Prescott, Daniel A. *Emotion and the Educative Process*. Washington, DC: American Council on Education, 1938, 323 p.

Pressey, Sidney L. & Kuhlen, Raymond G. *Psychological Development Through the Life Span*. NY: Harper, 1957, 654 p.

Pressey, Sidney L. & Robinson, Francis P. *Psychology and the New Education*. NY: Harper, 1944, 654 p.

Radke, M. J. *The Relation of Parental Authority to Children's Behavior and Attitudes*. Minneapolis: University of Minnesota Press, 1946.

Reich, Annie. "The Discussion of 1912 on Masturbation and Our Present-Day View," in Eissler, Ruth S., et al. (Eds.), *The Psychoanalytic Study of the Child*, 6:80-94. NY: International Universities Press, 1951.

Remmers, H. H. & Radler, D. H. *The American Teenager*. Indianapolis-NY: Bobbs-Merrill, 1957, 267 p.

Rockwood, L. T. & Ford, M. E. N. *Youth, Marriage and Parenthood*. NY: Wiley, 1945, 298 p.

Rondell, Florence & Michaels, Ruth. *The Adopted Family*, Book I. NY: Crown, 1951, 64 p.

Rothney, John W. *The High School Student: A Book of Cases*. NY: Dryden, 1953, 271 p.

Saul, Leon J. *Emotional Maturity*. Phila: Lippincott, 1947, 338 p.

Schilder, Paul. *The Image of the Appearance of the Human Body*. NY: International Universities Press, 1950, 353 p.

Schneiders, A. A. *The Psychology of Adolescence*. Milwaukee: Bruce, 1951, 550 p.

Segel, David. *Frustration in Adolescent Youth*. Washington, DC: Federal Security Agency, Bulletin, 1951, No. 1, 1951, 65 p.

Segel, David. *Intellectual Abilities in the Adolescent Period*. Washington, DC: Office of Education, 1948. Bulletin No. 6.

Seidman, Jerome M. *The Adolescent: A Book of Readings*. NY: Dryden, 1953, 798 p.

Shaffer, Laurance F. & Shoben, Edward J., Jr., *The Psychology of Adjustment*, 2nd Ed. Boston: Houghton, Mifflin, 1956, 672 p.

Shaw, Clifford R. *The Jack Roller*. Chicago: University of Chicago Press, 1930, 205 p.

Shaw, Franklin J. & Orb, Robert S. *Personal Adjustment in the American Culture*. NY: Harper, 1953, 388 p.

Sheldon, William H. *Varieties of Delinquent Youth*. NY: Harper, 1949, 899 p.

Sheldon, William H. *The Varieties of Human Physique*. NY: Harper, 1940, 347 p.

Sherif, Musafer & Cantril, Hadley. *The Psychology of Ego-Involvements; Social Attitudes and Identifications*. NY: Wiley, 1947, 525 p.

Shuttleworth, Frank K. *The Adolescent Period: A Graphic Atlas and a Pictorial Atlas*. Monographs of the Society for Research in Child Development, 1949, 14, Ser. No. 49, 1 & 2. Evanston: Child Development Publ., 1951. (Pages unnumbered.)

Shuttleworth, Frank K. *The Physical and Mental Growth of Girls and Boys Ages Six to Nineteen in Relation to Age and Maximum Growth*. Washington, DC: National Research Council, 1939. Vol. 4, No. 3.

Spiegel, Leo A. "A Review of Contributions to a Psychoanalytic Theory of Adolescence," in Eissler, Ruth S., et al. (Eds.), *The Psychoanalytic Study of the Child*, 6:375-393. NY: International Universities Press, 1951.

Stewart, Robert S. & Workman, Arthur D. *Children and Other People*. NY: Dryden, 1956, 276 p.

Stolz, Herbert R. & Stolz, L. H. *Somatic Development of Adolescent Boys*. NY: Macmillan, 1951, 557 p.

Stone, L. Joseph & Church, Joseph. *Childhood and Adolescence: A Psychology of the Growing Person*. NY: Random, 1957, 456 p.

Strang, Ruth. *The Adolescent Views Himself: A Psychology of Adolescence*. NY: McGraw-Hill, 1957, 581 p.

Straus, Robert & Bacon, S. D. *Drinking in College*. New Haven, Conn: Yale University Press, 1953, 221 p.

Sullivan, Harry S. *Conceptions of Modern Psychiatry*. Washington, DC: William Alanson White Psychiatric Foundation, 1947, 147 p.

Sullivan, Harry S. *The Interpersonal Theory of Psychiatry*. NY: Norton, 1953, 393 p.

Super, Donald E. *The Dynamics of Vocational Adjustment*. NY: Harper, 1942, 286 p.

Symonds, Percival M. *Adolescent Fantasy*. NY: Columbia University Press, 1949, 397 p.

Symonds, Percival M. *The Dynamics of Human Adjustment*. NY: Appleton-Century-Crofts, 1946, 666 p.

Symonds, Percival M. *The Psychology of Parent-Child Relationships*. NY: Teachers College, 1949, 413 p.

Tausk, Victor. "On Masturbation," in Eissler, Ruth S., et al. (Eds.), *The Psychoanalytic Study of the Child*, 6:61-79. NY: International Universities Press, 1951.

Taylor, K. W. *Do Adolescents Need Parents?* NY: Appleton-Century-Crofts, 1938, 380 p.

Thompson, Clara. *Psychoanalysis: Its Evolution and Development.* NY: Hermitage, 1950, 250 p.

Thorpe, Louis P. & Cruze, Wendell W. *Developmental Psychology.* NY: Ronald, 1956, 670 p.

Tryon, Caroline M. "Evaluations of Adolescent Personality by Adolescents," in Barker, R., et al. (Eds.), *Child Behavior and Development.* NY: McGraw-Hill, 1942, pp. 545-566.

Vedder, Clyde B. *The Juvenile Offender; Perspective and Readings.* Garden City, NY: Doubleday, 1954, 510 p.

Viitamäki, R. O. *Personality Traits between Puberty and Adolescence: Their Relationships, Development and Constancy with Reference to their Relation to School Achievement.* Helsinki, Finland: Suomalainen Tiedenkatemia, 1956, 183 p.

Wallman, Vernon. *The Adolescent at School.* London: Heinemann, 1949, 165 p.

Warters, Jane. *Achieving Maturity.* NY: McGraw-Hill, 1949, 349 p.

Wattenberg, William W. *The Adolescent Years.* NY: Harcourt Brace, 1955, 510 p.

Whiting, John W. M. & Child, Irvin L. *Child Training and Personality: A Cross-Cultural Study.* New Haven: Yale University Press, 1953, 353 p.

Whyte, William P. *Street Corner Society.* Chicago: University of Chicago Press, 1943, 284 p.

Williams, Frankwood E. *Adolescence.* NY: Farrar, Rinehart, 1930, 279 p.

Winnicott, D. W. *The Child and the Outside World: Studies in Developing Relationships.* NY: Basic Books, 1957, 190 p.

Witmer, Helen & Kotinsky, Ruth. *Personality in the Making.* NY: Harper, 1952, 454 p.

Wittels, F. "The Ego of the Adolescent," in Eissler, K. R. (Ed.), *Searchlights on Delinquency.* NY: International Universities Press, 1949, 456 p.

Zachry, Caroline B. *Emotion and Conduct in Adolescence.* NY: Appleton-Century, 1940, 563 p.

Zapoleon, Marguerite. *The College Girl Looks Ahead to her Career Opportunities.* NY: Harper, 1956, 272 p.

List of Fictional Excerpts

1. Aldington, Richard. *Death of a Hero,* pp. 135-137; 185
2. Baldwin, James. *Go Tell It on the Mountain,* pp. 63-66
3. Bellamann, Henry. *Kings Row,* pp. 191-194
4. Bennett, Arnold. *The Old Wives' Tale,* pp. 235-242
5. Bunin, Ivan. *The Well of Days,* pp. 159-162
6. Butler, Samuel. *The Way of All Flesh,* pp. 242-243
7. Clark, Walter Van Tilburg. *The City of Trembling Leaves,* pp. 47; 106-113
8. Davis, Clyde Brion. *The Newcomer,* pp. 121-124
9. Dell, Floyd. *Moon-Calf,* pp. 189-190
10. Dostoevsky, Fyodor. *A Raw Youth,* pp. 287-288
11. Ellison, James W. *I'm Owen Harrison Harding,* pp. 213-221
12. Eustis, Helen. *The Fool Killer,* pp. 67-73
13. Farrell, James T. *Father and Son,* pp. 247-250
14. Farrell, James T. *Young Lonigan,* pp. 177-179
15. Fisher, Dorothy Canfield. *The Bent Twig,* pp. 126-132; 154-157
16. Frankau, Pamela. *A Wreath for the Enemy,* pp. 203-205
17. Gide, André. *The Counterfeiters,* pp. 74-76
18. Hughes, Richard. *High Wind in Jamaica,* pp. 22-24
19. Jackson, Shirley. *Hangsaman,* pp. 81-86
20. Jonas, Carl. *Jefferson Selleck,* pp. 226-233
21. Joyce, James. *A Portrait of the Artist As a Young Man,* pp. 52-57
22. Kennedy, Jay R. *Prince Bart,* pp. 41-46
23. Lawrence, D. H. *The Rainbow,* pp. 266-269
24. Lewis, Sinclair. *Bethel Merriday,* pp. 251-254
25. Mann, Thomas, *Tonio Kröger,* pp. 142-145
26. Marquand, John P. *So Little Time,* pp. 89-102
27. Maugham, W. Somerset. *Of Human Bondage,* pp. 26-27
28. Maxwell, William. *The Folded Leaf,* pp. 24-25; 38
29. Morton, Frederic. *Asphalt and Desire,* pp. 167-170
30. Nathan, Robert. *Winter in April,* pp. 261-263
31. Rawlings, Marjorie. *The Yearling,* pp. 283-286
32. Rolland, Romain. *Jean-Christophe,* pp. 56-59
33. Schweitzer, Gertrude. *The Young People,* pp. 206-207

337

338LIST OF FICTIONAL EXCERPTS

Index